THE BEST KINGS OF THE MIDDLE AGES

For

Owain Bell

with gratitude

THE BEST KINGS OF THE MIDDLE AGES

SUCCESS STORIES OF ENGLISH KINGSHIP IN HISTORY AND THEIR LEGACY

PHIL BRADFORD

PEN & SWORD HISTORY
AN IMPRINT OF PEN & SWORD BOOKS LTD.
YORKSHIRE – PHILADELPHIA

First published in Great Britain in 2025 by
PEN AND SWORD HISTORY
An imprint of
Pen & Sword Books Ltd
Yorkshire – Philadelphia

ISBN 978 1 39908 727 8

A CIP catalogue record for this book is available from the British Library.

Typeset in Times New Roman 10/12 by
SJmagic DESIGN SERVICES, India.
Printed and bound in the UK by CPI Group (UK) Ltd.

The Publisher's authorised representative in the EU for product safety is Authorised Rep Compliance Ltd., Ground Floor, 71 Lower Baggot Street, Dublin D02 P593, Ireland.
www.arccompliance.com

For a complete list of Pen & Sword titles please contact
PEN & SWORD BOOKS LIMITED
George House, Units 12 & 13, Beevor Street, Off Pontefract Road,
Barnsley, South Yorkshire, S71 1HN, England
E-mail: enquiries@pen-and-sword.co.uk
Website: www.pen-and-sword.co.uk

or

PEN AND SWORD BOOKS
1950 Lawrence Rd, Havertown, PA 19083, USA
E-mail: uspen-and-sword@casematepublishers.com
Website: www.penandswordbooks.com

FSC www.fsc.org
MIX
Paper | Supporting responsible forestry
FSC® C013604

Contents

Acknowledgements

This volume was a natural complement to my one on the worst medieval kings, and it has been a pleasure to approach the subject from the opposite angle through the perceived success stories. I am once again grateful to Gwilym Dodd for his encouragement, and for being constantly willing to help with references and queries. Catherine Delano-Smith, while cheerfully admitting that she cannot remember quite what order the kings come in, has been endlessly encouraging and kept me busy with work on the Gough Map to ensure I do not become too obsessed with the reputations of medieval monarchs. Richard Gill and Luise Horrocks kindly read all the chapters in draft. My mum Elaine, my sister Helen, Kim Bell, Dan Critchley and Liz Forman all found themselves at some time or another driving with me to various ruins of castles or abbeys without fully understanding why we needed to visit them, but were all remarkably relaxed about doing so, especially when they involved tea rooms. Doug Chaplin kindly took the photo of Richard I's statue outside the Houses of Parliament, while Colin Nash generously used his skills with photography software to create composite images from my photos of Richard I's tombs and Eleanor crosses.

I would like to offer particular thanks to Owain Bell not just for his support for writing this volume and reading it in draft (although he has reserved his right to object to my casual dismissal of Blondel from the Richard the Lionheart story), but for his friendship and support for as long as I have known. Since my sister was nearly born in the back of his car on Stourbridge ring road almost four decades ago, he has been a firm family friend, and I have lost count of the places we have visited together across the years in our shared love of history. In that time, he has brought metros in Munich, Paris and Toulouse to a standstill, proved that electronic systems at airports and train stations across Europe should really have had more vigorous testing, left his diary on the wrong side of the Continent, lost admission tickets within seconds, and caused all manner of chaos. It has never been dull, and he has enthusiastically embarked upon more historical visits than can be counted, as he has always both indulged and supported my passion for history. Above all, he has been endlessly encouraging and kind to me across those years, and it is a great pleasure to be able to dedicate this book to him, with gratitude for everything.

Preface

On Friday, 16 September 2022, I entered a zig-zagging line of barriers in Southwark Park a little before 8 am. For the next thirteen hours, I became part of one of the greatest and most bizarre moments in modern British history, the queue for the lying in state of Queen Elizabeth II. It is hard to know exactly what compelled me to do so. I had never met Elizabeth II or even seen her in person, yet when a friend suggested we go, I unquestioningly agreed. It was an unforgettable experience. A country whose trains barely seem to run, never mind on time, whose National Health Service apparently teeters on the brink, and which basically seems incapable of functioning, nevertheless managed to turn its folkloric national pastime into an epic event which achieved its own weather forecasts, Twitter feeds, social media pages, wristband, official document of government guidelines, and even definite article and capital letters: The Queue.

Those thirteen hours in The Queue were among the most strange and memorable of my life. As it wound its way from Southwark Park, past Southwark Cathedral and The Globe and along the Thames to Tower Bridge (where we were issued with our wristbands, giving an uncanny sense of being in a 1990s theme park), it was like taking a very slow, sociable walking tour of London. The mood was exuberant, the behaviour impeccable, everyone respecting and holding one another's places when the latest caffeine shot was required from a route-side coffee shop or the toilets of The National Theatre suddenly became essential. We ate our way through our snacks and then helped bolster the suddenly soaring profits of all the cafés and shops along the route. In very un-British fashion, strangers talked merrily to one another. I chatted to people from across the country, and even to a couple from the United States who had flown in specially from Atlanta for the occasion. I would soon discover they were not the only Americans or international visitors to have made the journey. Such was the sense of history evoked by the Queen's death that this became a global phenomenon, one in which a surprising number of people did not allow the minor barriers of the Atlantic Ocean and the War of Independence to prevent them from taking part. For seventy years Elizabeth II had been a constant in a rapidly changing world, and my journey from Worcester, involving a 4 am start, began to look like a quick trip down the road compared to the journeys undertaken by some to witness this occasion and pay their respects.

The day wore on, the legs grew more weary, and as we reached the London Eye, so close to the Palace of Westminster and yet still some three hours of queuing distant, the spirits began to flag. Some genius had posted officers from Northumbria Police to oversee this part of the route, and the rousing encouragement of some insanely cheerful Geordies revived those flagging spirits. It was down the riverside path to Westminster Bridge, and finally into the Victoria Tower Gardens and the parliamentary estate. The better part of two hours elapsed even here, in what would normally be a two-minute walk at most. As darkness fell, we watched the royal standard rise and fall over the Victoria Tower to mark the King's arrival and departure. Once through a security screening that was both terrifyingly efficient and unexpectedly friendly, it was into the building and up the steps to turn onto the staircase which led down into Westminster Hall itself. The mood changed abruptly from excited, almost carnivalesque to sombre, respectful. Around halfway down those stairs, the sound with which we had all become familiar over the previous day of television coverage rang out. The staff was pounded onto the stone floor three times, the noise echoing around the cavernous hall to indicate the changing of the guard. Everything stopped. We stood still and I was able to take in the scene before me.

I had been in Westminster Hall several times before, but always as a visitor or researcher when this glorious remnant of the medieval palace was a bustling place of activity and business. Tonight was very different. It was a place of silence. At that moment, the only movement and noise came from the resplendently uniformed guards who were changing shift. The eye was automatically drawn to the centre of the hall, where atop a high purple catafalque was the coffin of Queen Elizabeth II, concealed beneath the royal standard carefully draped over it. The Imperial State Crown, something I had only ever seen behind glass in a strongroom at the Tower of London, sat on a purple cushion atop the coffin, glittering in the bright lights. The new guard took up their positions. The scene unfroze. We shuffled towards the coffin. Technically, we were meant to keep moving past, but for a brief moment, like so many others, we paused to the side of the catafalque and turned to face it. I bowed my head, a gesture of acknowledgement and respect for the mortal remains of the woman who had been my Queen for the whole four decades of my life. Then we turned and walked out into the chilly London night, glancing at the scene over our shoulders one last time as we did so.

This was the last remnant of a bygone era, a final island of medieval pageantry and spectacle surrounded by a modern city of suits and skyscrapers. Yet it showed the fascination that the monarchy could still command in that modern world. After Elizabeth II died, we were only two of hundreds of thousands who queued for hours, many through the chilly London nights, to see her lying in state. With those who earlier filed past her coffin in St Giles' in Edinburgh, or who lined the routes of a sequence of final journeys which began at Balmoral Castle and ended at Windsor Castle, the number who turned out to pay their respects in some form easily passed a million.

It was testament to a woman who had had an enormous impact and an extraordinarily long reign. She was the only monarch a large majority of people in the United Kingdom had ever known, and very probably the most recognisable woman in the world. Millions in more than 100 countries met or saw her during her seventy years on the throne, while billions knew her image from photographs and screen. Perhaps it was summed up best in one of the most eloquent and dignified tributes in the days following her death, addressed to the United Kingdom by the president of an avowedly Republican country, Emmanuel Macron of France: 'to you, she was your Queen. To us, she was *the* Queen'. For large parts of the world, Elizabeth II did indeed embody what a queen was in the twenty-first century. Yet while there was sadness and poignancy, there was no great element of shock at the death of someone of 96 who had been visibly frail for some time. A reign which had drawn to a close in the first Platinum Jubilee could be honoured solemnly by the nation.

The death of her father, George VI, in February 1952 had also brought hundreds of thousands of mourners out into the bitter London winter. On that occasion, however, there was shock. It had not been widely known just how ill the king was. He was only 56, and 'the widespread and genuine grief [...] reflected his people's perception of him as a monarch who cared, and who had apparently worked himself sacrificially to death on the nation's behalf'.[1] He had rescued and stabilised the monarchy after the abdication crisis, and been a figurehead of strength through the Second World War. Only later would it become apparent how hard he had battled against his innate shyness and debilitating stammer. Once again, one of the most perceptive comments came from a Frenchman, this time the ambassador to London, who noted that 'if the measure of a King lies in the manner in which his character and qualities correspond to the needs of a nation at a given moment in its history, then "George VI was a great King, and perhaps a very great King"'.[2] After the turbulence of Edward VIII, during the dark days of war, and in constitutional government, George VI was the right man at the right time.

It is only in more recent times that the death of a monarch has been marked by such widespread public mourning. These displays are easier in a constitutional monarchy, where the monarch does not hold power, and photography and television can give everyone a sense of knowing the sovereign. There was a time when the death of a king would often result in his body being abandoned and a rather lonely burial, as thoughts turned immediately to the new ruler. In sharp contrast to Charles III, at pains in his first days to emphasise continuity with the previous reign, the new king in the Middle Ages would often seek to present himself as a fresh start, highlighting the differences with his predecessor. Especially when the previous reign had been a long one, or ended badly, the emphasis tended to be on the negative. However, sometimes it did not take very long under the rule of the new king for that of the old to be reassessed, and nostalgia for the 'good old days' to emerge.

Reputations change over time, as societies themselves change and assess historical figures with different values. This book examines the shifting reputations of five men who have in various ways been held up as the 'best' kings of the Middle Ages: Henry II, Richard I, Edward I, Edward III and Henry V. It is a companion to my *The Worst Medieval Monarchs*, and the preface and introduction for that volume give a full outline of the premise behind this volume.[3] Once more, it might be argued that others could have merited inclusion. Alfred the Great, the only king in English history to be awarded that epithet, is excluded because he was king only of Wessex, not of England. Recent scholarship, as the title of his most recent biography indicates, has promoted the achievements of Cnut, but this is tempered by the fact that 'his use of violence was ugly, brutal and created long-lasting pain'.[4] William the Conqueror successfully imposed his rule on England and secured the realm for his dynasty, but at a similarly bloody cost, in a life which 'exemplifies forms of state-sponsored violence deployed in what was proclaimed to be a legitimate cause'.[5] As foreign conquerors, neither have ever been viewed with any fondness in English historiography and their success lay more in a violent subdual of the country. The other contender, Henry I, has never really excited the imagination, and is disqualified by his failure to secure the succession, which led to the civil war between Stephen and Matilda. That leaves the five considered in this book, those who have generally been considered the outstanding successes in either academic thought, popular reputation or both. How did this come to be?

Introduction

On 6 May 2023, eight months after his accession to the throne, King Charles III was crowned. Despite protests, objections and indifference from certain quarters, it was a spectacle which transfixed the world. Ignoring the London drizzle which anyone in Britain knew was almost inevitable for a celebratory weekend, thousands turned out to pack The Mall and millions watched around the world. A country sinking into global insignificance in the political sphere showed, as it had at the state funeral of the king's mother the previous year, that it still excelled at the theatre and ceremony of pageantry.

For a moment, a cynical twenty-first century obsessed with the slippery concepts of progress and relevance caught a glimpse of another world, one in which the mystique of monarchy gave the briefest window into the past. The ceremony took place in Westminster Abbey, for the fortieth time since William the Conqueror had been crowned there 967 years earlier. It was presided over by the 105th Archbishop of Canterbury, whose office dates back fourteen centuries, to a time long before there was an England, never mind a United Kingdom, of which to be king. Charles was the twenty-sixth monarch to sit in the coronation chair, first used for the coronation of Edward II in 1308. When the archbishop anointed the king, he poured the holy oil into a spoon which is first recorded in 1349 and appears to date from the twelfth century. The crown placed upon the king's head, the St Edward's Crown, was made for his namesake, Charles II, in 1661. To a casual observer, this was an ancient and timeless ritual stretching back through the centuries.

In reality, of course, it was not. Since William the Conqueror was crowned in 1066, the service has been repeatedly changed and adapted. In the Middle Ages, the rite was performed in Latin and Anglo-Norman French, rather than the English (albeit intentionally and gratingly archaic English) of 2023. What was once a Roman Catholic ceremony has, since late Tudor times, been a Church of England one, the declarations to uphold the Protestant succession dating from the early eighteenth century. Where a whole succession of people would once have sworn homage to the new sovereign, in 2023 this was reduced to symbolic homage by just two, the Archbishop of Canterbury and the Prince of Wales. Only a tiny fraction of the elite could once see a king be crowned, but the coronation of Charles III could be watched in all fifteen of his realms spread across thousands of miles, from Vancouver to Auckland, Belmopan to Port Moresby. Eleventh and twenty-first centuries were temporarily united in a service which intentionally transcended the ages.

Those who objected that it was an archaic ritual rather missed the point. The very success of the coronation service is its blending of ancient and modern, of seeming historic while adapting to meet changing needs. Across the millennium since William the Conqueror was crowned, what the English (and more recently the British) have required of their king has never been constant. The repeated amendments to the coronation service reflect those shifting expectations, yet in its very essence the theory of monarchy, while differently understood, remains the same. As in 1066 and at every coronation since, that of 2023 was fundamentally and obviously a Christian ceremony. Even in a secular world where such language is increasingly incomprehensible and other European monarchies have switched to swearing in ceremonies, the Westminster coronation upholds an ancient, vocational notion of monarchy. The sovereign is called, set apart and anointed by God to serve as the earthly ruler of God's people, a conscious echo of Old Testament models of priesthood for 'the Vicar of God on earth'.[1] This sacred element is emphasised by the fact that St Edward's Crown is used only for the coronation, then never worn again by the monarch, and only three people (sovereign, archbishop and crown jeweller) may set hands upon it. Yet the sense of majesty is maintained through the wearing of the Imperial State Crown at the state opening of parliament; in doing this, Charles III is in a modern way re-enacting the ceremonial crown wearings that probably began in Anglo-Saxon times, being publicly visible as crowned king. In a constitutional monarchy, it can be hard to grasp how a medieval king was not just an administrator, figurehead or embodied rubber stamp, but rather someone exercising genuine power whose office cloaked him in mystique. It is how five of those medieval kings exercised that power and how they have been viewed for doing so that is the subject of this book.

One fundamental change from past ages is that coronation no longer makes the king. Today, monarchy transfers seamlessly and immediately, the new monarch drawing their first breath as sovereign the second their predecessor has taken their last breath. For the first two kings in this volume, Henry II and Richard I, it was their coronations that gave them their legitimacy, their reigns beginning on that day. In a time before primogeniture, being the oldest son, was accepted as conferring the right to succeed, it was necessary for a candidate for the throne to persuade an archbishop to put a crown on his head to secure that throne. Not until Edward I was the idea of primogeniture so firmly accepted that he faced no challenge despite being in Sicily, and the result was that the coronation no longer conferred the kingship, but rather cemented the pact between God, king and people in visible form. It was in the coronation oaths that the theoretical expectations of a king were made manifest, although we should always remember that these represent an elite, ecclesiastical view of kingship. If some of the broad themes of the oaths met the expectations of the vast majority of the king's ordinary, illiterate subjects, it would not be too speculative to suggest that their hopes of their king might have been rather different to those of great churchmen. Many were probably not very bothered about the identity of a king they would never see, as long as he kept order and didn't tax them too heavily.

I dealt in *The Worst Medieval Monarchs* with the expectations of medieval kingship and the changing way in which kings have been judged, and that discussion underpins this volume as well.[2] However, it is worth reiterating some of the main points in relation to those kings on whom posterity has passed a positive verdict and deemed a success. All five kings considered here faced challenges to their style of rule, although they were fewer under Richard I and Henry V for the simple reason that their reigns were brief. Henry II, Edward I and Edward III, in longer reigns, all faced notable opposition and setbacks, in Henry's case one which reverberated through Europe and might have toppled a lesser man. Despite this, the five were able to successfully navigate the expectations of their subjects and their role, even if it is questionable how Richard I and Henry V would be viewed had they reigned longer and faced the longer-term consequences of some of their actions.

At the core of medieval kingship was the requirement for the monarch to be an overtly Christian ruler and defend the rights of the Church. That is an aspect with which modern, secular writers often struggle, which can sometimes lead them to downplay this element or even to try to secularise kings by reading anachronistic, post-Enlightenment ideas into their lives. Kingship was Christian and in different ways, the five kings considered here embodied that religious part of their role. All clashed with the Church, or at least individual prelates, and in the cases of Henry II and Edward I the clashes were dramatic, but none were ever viewed as impious or failing in general to be a Christian ruler. Of course, that can create problems for us. The antisemitism found in the reigns of Richard I and Edward I, on which the latter played especially strongly, is deeply troubling in a post-Holocaust world of religious pluralism. The same is true of those kings' crusading, notably Richard's, in a post-9/11 world of religious antagonism, or of Henry V's persecution of Lollards in an age of tolerance. We cannot condemn these kings for acting according to the standards of their time, nor can we evade the uncomfortable fact that such intolerance was popular, but we must avoid building heroism out of actions and attitudes we would find abhorrent. To understand the Christian nature of medieval kingship is not to condone all the ways in which it expressed itself.

Also important for a medieval king was the maintenance of law and order and the defence of the realm. It is no accident that all five kings in this volume were, to a considerable degree, warriors, and were largely successful militarily. Maintaining domestic peace did not preclude wars of conquest or retaliation elsewhere; three of these kings strongly asserted their claims over Scotland, while all ruled over lands in France and fought wars against the French, which was almost part of the job description for a medieval English king. The balancing act was to keep the peace in England during overseas absences, for the personal presence of the monarch was important and lengthy periods overseas often led to trouble at home. In part, this was because justice was ultimately the king's, so his subjects required access to him to seek that justice and his grace.

Finally, seeking counsel and establishing a wide base of consent was critical to medieval kingship. How this was done changed across the period under consideration here. Henry II and Richard I, who ruled over widespread territories on both sides of the Channel, were advised in different ways by the leading subjects of the various jurisdictions. For Edward I, Edward III and Henry V, parliament was a necessary consideration. Overall, what distinguishes these five kings from others who are remembered negatively, notably John, Edward II and Richard II, is their recognition of the need to work with their leading subjects, not in opposition to them (although Edward I occasionally forgot this key point). Unlike failures, who tended to either trust nobody or fixate on favourites, successful kings understood the importance of working with the nobility as a whole. An ability to forge a common purpose with the lords, as several of the kings considered here did through their military campaigns, underpinned success as a monarch.

It is harder to judge kings successful than it is to label them failures. In the case of the worst monarchs, their failure is normally self-evident, the reign ending in civil war or deposition. Given that keeping the crown and not finding half your country under enemy occupation were fairly critical responsibilities for any monarch, the failure standards are obvious. Verdicts on King John from the very beginning have generally been variations on how bad he was. Over the centuries, however, standards of what makes a king 'good' or admirable have changed significantly. Nowhere is this more so than in the case of Christianity, a core part of any medieval assessment which today is often played down or written out altogether. The antisemitic acts which horrify us were lauded by contemporaries. Wars of conquest which thrilled contemporaries trouble us. Our moral standards and points of reference are very different. Thus, here we must look even more closely at how contexts and cultural shifts have affected the reputations of these five kings. Can we indeed call them the 'best' kings of medieval England?

Chapter 1

Henry II: A Just King?

> Richard [I] rides in state outside Parliament, Becket was for long Christendom's most popular saint; Henry is remembered only as their opponent.[1]

> The king of England is now in Ireland, now in England, now in Normandy, he appears to fly rather than travel by horse or ship.[2]

Most people have heard of Henry II because he was responsible for the death of Thomas Becket. The story of an enraged king uttering the immortal words, 'will no one rid me of this turbulent priest?', causing four knights to charge off to Canterbury and hack down the archbishop in his cathedral, is legendary. It transformed an equally irascible, proud and often infuriatingly self-righteous cleric into a saint, casting Henry forevermore in the role of his adversary.

The conflict with Becket lasted less than a quarter of Henry II's thirty-five year reign, and was not at the forefront of the king's mind even for much of that period. As Louis VII's half-admiring, half-exasperated speculation that Henry could secretly fly demonstrates, here was a king who at times seemed superhuman. He ruled from the Cheviots to the Pyrenees, a vast stretch of a thousand miles which he managed to hold together for almost his entire reign. He was indefatigable, endlessly on the move around his patchwork of territories, his itinerary breathless. He has been held in high esteem for his legal reforms and contribution to the development of the common law. His wife, Eleanor of Aquitaine, was one of the most formidable consorts of the Middle Ages, while his four sons who lived to adulthood were so troublesome that they have been nicknamed 'the devil's brood'. The reign of Henry II was colourful and turbulent, the king the most redoubtable figure in a memorable cast of characters. He may have faded from popular memory, but Henry is certainly worthy to be remembered as far more than Becket's opponent.

Henry's Life and Reign

Henry was born on 5 March 1133 in Le Mans, the eldest son of the Empress Matilda and Geoffrey of Anjou. Matilda was the only legitimate daughter and surviving child of King Henry I, after whom her first son was named. She had previously been married to the Holy Roman Emperor, Henry V, but widowed at a young age. Geoffrey, her second husband, was Count of Anjou and Maine in central France. Henry would be Henry of Anjou before taking the throne, while the dynasty would be known as the Angevins. Father and son were also called Geoffrey and Henry Plantagenet, giving the name to the Plantagenet kings who would occupy the English throne from Henry's accession until the arrival of the Tudor dynasty more than three centuries later. The origins of the word 'Plantagenet' are obscure, although the most popular theory is that it derived from a plant (yellow broom) which the Counts of Anjou wore as an emblem. Additionally, Henry would be known variously as Fitzempress ('son of the empress') and Curtmantle (after the short cloak he was in the habit of wearing).

Henry's parents were a study in dysfunction. The hot-headed couple were ill-matched, the 25-year-old former empress unenamoured with a 14-year-old mere count. They rapidly became estranged. Enough of a reconciliation was later effected for them to conceive Henry and two further sons, securing the succession, but they were never close. Henry I died in December 1135, when his grandson was only 2. His death plunged England and Normandy into crisis. During his lifetime, the king had compelled his lords to swear an oath to support Matilda's succession. Dead, Henry had no way to make his wishes reality. There was resentment at Henry's domineering style and concerns about Matilda herself. A queen regnant was not viewed favourably in the twelfth century. Meanwhile, the quick-thinking Count of Boulogne dashed across the Channel and had himself crowned. Stephen of Blois, now King Stephen, was Henry I's nephew and Matilda's cousin. Normandy fell into line, accepting Stephen as duke; Matilda had been outplayed.

Henry grew up with his mother vainly trying to remove Stephen in England, while his father successfully displaced Stephen in Normandy. Geoffrey conquered Normandy and became duke in 1144, but Matilda never won her crown. She came tantalisingly close in 1141, only to seize defeat from the jaws of victory through her arrogant behaviour. Thereafter, she never again came remotely near success. In 1148, she withdrew from the English theatre of war, investing her hopes in her eldest son, who had already taken up the fight. After an initial education at the court in Anjou, he first travelled to England in around 1142, based mainly in Bristol, at the court of his uncle, Robert of Gloucester. The most prominent of Henry I's numerous illegitimate children, Robert was Matilda's leading lieutenant until his death in 1147. Henry had returned to Anjou in 1144 to learn about government and leadership from his father. Somewhat recklessly, aged only 14, he sailed to England with a mercenary army in early 1147 but made no headway, largely because he lacked the funds to pay his troops. His mother and uncle refused to bail him out, and he was only able to return to France when Stephen magnanimously paid off his young opponent's soldiers for him. It was a generosity typical of the king, which had an effect on the recipient; as king himself, Henry II would be noted for his own generosity in almsgiving and for some notable acts of kindness. In 1149, he returned to England to try again, heading to Carlisle. There, he was knighted by his great-uncle, King David I of Scotland. King Stephen reacted by knighting his own eldest son, Eustace, and beginning an unsuccessful campaign to have Eustace crowned to secure the succession. Henry made little progress before crossing the Channel again in early 1150. Geoffrey now surrendered the title of Duke of Normandy to Henry.

The King of France was unhappy and tried to make trouble for Geoffrey and Henry. However, his military efforts were unsuccessful and the Angevin transfer of power went ahead. One of the complexities of Henry II's reign, which would cause kings of England problems for as long as they also had French lands, was the issue of homage. In England, the king answered to no one, but as ruler of territories in France he was a vassal of the King of France and had to swear homage accordingly. Given that Henry would end up ruling far more territory in France than the French king, that led to a tense and problematic relationship in later years, but for now matters were more straightforward. Once the French had abandoned efforts to obstruct Henry's succession, the need to swear homage for the first of his French titles, Duke of Normandy, took him and Geoffrey to Paris in 1151.

The French king was Louis VII (1137–80). His wife was Eleanor of Aquitaine, a redoubtable character who complained that she had married a monk rather than a king. The vivacious Eleanor found the conservative atmosphere at the Parisian court stifling and tedious compared to her native Aquitaine. The marriage was troubled, with only daughters rather than the son needed to secure the succession. After the couple had been on a disastrous crusade together in 1147, they returned from the Holy Land in separate ships and barely on speaking terms. Ten years Henry's senior, Eleanor as Queen of France was in a different league to the 18-year-old duke. Yet the following months transformed Henry into a much more significant figure. Geoffrey died, aged only 38, in September 1151, leaving Henry as Count of Anjou and Maine. Geoffrey made Henry swear to hand these to his younger brother, another Geoffrey, when he became King of England, an oath Henry conveniently forgot.

On 21 March 1152, Louis and Eleanor's marriage was annulled, thanks to broad medieval kinship rules which made it possible to argue that pretty much anyone was too closely related for a valid marriage. Eleanor was now a highly desirable figure on the marriage market. Evading new suitors, including Henry's brother Geoffrey, she made her way to Aquitaine's capital, Poitiers. There, she and Henry were married in the cathedral on 18 May 1152. In addition to his other titles, Henry was now (by virtue of Eleanor) Duke of Aquitaine, ruling an uninterrupted swathe of land stretching from the English Channel to the Pyrenees. It made him the greatest landholder in France, and infuriated Louis VII, who just months earlier had counted Aquitaine among his own dominions. The French king invaded Normandy but was beaten back by Henry. It meant that Henry was now free to focus on the most glittering prize – the English crown.

Henry landed in Dorset in early January 1153. The following months of campaigning were desultory. After years of fighting, many were weary of the conflict and had little inclination to continue the struggle. Stephen was too securely entrenched across much of the country. Yet Henry was in a very different position to when he had last been in England. Now, as a duke and count seeking a crown, he showed 'the confidence that was to be his trademark henceforth'; from this time onwards he 'summoned people to his presence and expected them to jump'.[3] In the end, fate gave Henry the crucial break. In August, Stephen's eldest son Eustace died. His younger son, William, neither expected nor wanted the crown. Stephen had no reason to keep fighting. Negotiations at Winchester in November thrashed out a deal. Stephen was to remain king for the remainder of his life, then be succeeded by Henry. The two made some ceremonial appearances together in early 1154, but Henry returned to Normandy amid rumours of plots on his life.

His and Eleanor's first child, William, had been born there the previous summer; although William would only live until 1156, Henry and Eleanor had no problems reproducing. Between 1155 and 1166 they would have three daughters and, crucially, four more sons to secure the succession: Henry (born 1155), Richard (1157), Geoffrey (1158) and John (1166). Such reproductive success would not prove entirely unproblematic in a temperamental and often violent family. One story of the family past was seen as an explanation for the internecine strife in which Henry and his children would become embroiled. Once upon a time, a Count of Anjou had married a beautiful woman, but he noticed she never stayed in church for Mass. When he forced her to do so, she was unable to stand the holy rite and flew screaming out of the window, revealing herself to be a demon. Legend thus held that the Angevins descended from the Devil, something Richard I apparently embraced: 'from the Devil we came, to the Devil we shall return'. It is easy to see why the events of Henry's reign, in which just about every possible combination of family members fighting with each other occurred, made chroniclers turn to the idea of diabolical origins for this turbulent family.

This was all in the future. For now, Henry had to bide his time. During the summer of 1154, he agreed peace with Louis VII and worked to secure his French lands. It was in Normandy that he learned that Stephen had died at Dover on 25 October. With no risk of anyone stealing his crown, Henry did not rush to England, partly because his sailing from Barfleur was delayed by adverse weather. He landed on 8 December, his reign beginning with his coronation at Westminster Abbey on 19 December 1154. At 21, Henry II was now King of England, Duke of Normandy and Aquitaine, and Count of Anjou and Maine, arguably the most powerful ruler in Western Europe.

A stocky man of average height, freckled with red hair and beard, who largely shunned expensive clothing, Henry was not physically imposing. Yet he was a formidable and complex personality, a man who had the aura and mystique of kingship. Although the Becket affair sometimes obscures this, Henry was conventionally pious and arguably very religious, attending Mass and confession regularly. His mood was famously changeable: he could go from affable to furious and back again almost instantly. He had a hot temper, yet at times could be deeply introspective and seek seclusion. Plenty were intimidated in his presence and the king was a master of the intimidatory silence. The rages were terrible, but Henry was also capable of great amiability and of laughing at himself. As his modern biographer notes, Henry was a king who would 'rise to anger when his authority was flouted, yet be rocked with laughter when his dignity was gently mocked'.[4] He was also a man totally unable to sit still. Afraid of getting fat, he would eat his meals standing and be constantly on the move, dispatching business anywhere and everywhere, even at Mass. His endless movement drove his followers to distraction, especially on occasions when, oblivious to both geography and weather, he led them through mountains in torrential rain. Hunting and hawking were his favourite pastimes, which involved being in the saddle and riding long distances. Even sitting still, Henry demanded concentration, chess and dice apparently being among his more sedate hobbies. In one sense, Henry II was successful because he exhausted everyone into obedience.

He needed to establish his authority. As had become customary, he issued a coronation charter. With typical audacity, Henry II pretended that King Stephen's reign had never happened, looking back to the reign of his grandfather, Henry I, as the golden age he was seeking to restore. The charter turned the clock back to 1135, challenging all those who had profited from grants (or dubious acquisition) of lands in the subsequent nineteen years. At the start of 1155, Henry began to dismantle his predecessor's legacy. Years of civil war had seen the authority of the Crown diminished, its power no longer uniform throughout the country, a situation Henry was determined to change. The earls Stephen had created were stripped of their titles and their lands resumed by the Crown. They usually received their lands back as new grants from Henry. Those who resisted were met with swift reprisals; Henry marched north to deal with the defiance of William le Gros, Earl of York, and rapidly brought him into line. This set an example to others who may have been considering opposing the new king. Unlicensed castles were targeted for destruction, although some believe that the chroniclers overstated the number demolished.[5] Henry certainly worked towards more royal castles and fewer baronial ones. This applied equally to the castles of his mother's supporters, the king showing no favouritism in his desire to establish his authority.

Rebuilding the machinery of government was vital. In the autumn of 1155 many sheriffs were replaced, although where they were competent, the new king was quite happy to use men already in place. The same applied at a national level. Henry was not vindictive, using Stephen's men in his administration if their talent merited it, such as the new co-justiciar, Richard de Lucy, who would vindicate the king's trust. Mindful of the resentment of non-noble officials in Henry I's reign, the king gave de Lucy a baronial colleague, Earl Robert de Beaumont of Leicester (another former supporter of King Stephen), and they worked together until the earl's death in 1168. Other appointees, such as the new treasurer, Bishop Nigel of Ely, returned to posts they had held under Henry I. Still others were new faces, including the chancellor. On the advice of Archbishop Theobald of Canterbury, Henry appointed to this role the Archdeacon of Canterbury, Thomas Becket. Henry was determined to reform central government and demonstrate who was in control.

The appointment of a competent treasurer and justiciars was especially important as they had a key role in overseeing the exchequer. Henry inherited the royal finances in a desperate state. He worked to reassert authority over the royal demesne (the lands and estates under direct royal control), reclaiming land granted away by Stephen and determining to make it all more profitable. Traditionally, the largest source of revenue for the king was known as the county farm, a fixed amount accounted for by each sheriff annually at the exchequer and recorded in documents known as pipe rolls. The new sheriffs were appointed because they were trusted to help Henry restore this vital source of income, and most repaid the king's confidence. Additionally, in 1155 Henry launched an inquiry into the royal forests. Covering a quarter of England, royal forest was subject to a special forest law, harsh and arbitrary and often the cause of complaint. It was in Henry's interests to maximise his profits from this source, which he set about zealously. A tax, the Danegeld, was revived in 1155–56 to supplement royal revenue, although it was by this stage archaic and problematic, levied for the final time in 1161–62. Various other taxes were imposed on counties and towns. Through energetic reform, pushed by his well-chosen and hardworking officials, Henry managed to turn the royal finances around and by the 1160s they were in remarkably good shape. While hardly the stuff of heroic legends, Henry's later success depended upon the way he set his financial house in order. His achievement in establishing a system which could work regardless of his frequent absences from England, along with his ability to find and trust the right people to deliver that system, was considerable.

The assured way he had begun his kingship was widely welcomed. While benefitting from widespread war-weariness, Henry had faced major challenges to establishing his rule. He had nevertheless quickly asserted himself and by the end of 1155 commanded considerable respect for the way he had re-established the authority of the Crown. There was none of the bafflement the chroniclers had shown at Stephen's excess of tolerance. Nor was Henry blind to the importance of demonstrating his majesty and authority to his new subjects. At a council at Wallingford in April 1155, the barons swore to uphold the succession of Henry's sons, William and Henry. In the early years of his reign, he held a series of crown wearings when in England, the last a joint ceremony with Eleanor at Worcester in 1158, after which king and queen laid up their crowns on the cathedral's high altar. Despite his youth, Henry was a convincing king after years of civil war.

The security of Henry's position was shown by the fact that he was able to return to France in 1156. Stephen had been unusual, for a post-Conquest king, in the amount of time he had spent in England. After a Norman visit in 1137, he spent the remaining seventeen years of his reign in his kingdom. There was no chance of Henry II making such prolonged English stays. As King of England, he spent just over a third of his reign (around thirteen years) in the country. With extensive territories in France, he was frequently across the Channel, often for years at a time. Henry was born in France and was a French speaker. (While he also spoke Latin, he did not speak English, although he probably understood it.) Henry's position in England in the mid-1150s was basically secure, with no real internal threats to his crown. England was atypical in twelfth-century Europe for its degree of centralisation, which dated back to Anglo-Saxon times. Henry's French domains, in contrast, were a patchwork of territories with different governance systems, bordered by places with potentially hostile rulers, requiring considerably greater effort to keep together and defend. Since the nineteenth century, historians have typically referred to the lands over which Henry ruled as the 'Angevin empire'. (French historians usually refer to an *espace Plantagenêt*, a Plantagenet 'space' or 'area'.) While technically inaccurate, 'empire' is a convenient shorthand for the autonomous territories Henry ruled, requiring him to be endlessly on the move between them to maintain peace, law and order. Henry's restless personality was ideally suited to his need to be ceaselessly itinerant.

Henry was confronting greater threats to his authority across the Channel than in England. Louis VII had refused to recognise him as Duke of Aquitaine, while Henry's brother, Geoffrey, was resentful that Henry had not handed over Anjou when he became king. In February 1156, Henry and Louis met on the border between Normandy and France, with Henry swearing homage for Anjou, Aquitaine and Normandy. Discussions with Geoffrey, however, broke down, and in the summer Henry besieged his brother's castles to force him to submit. The autumn saw him and Eleanor on a royal progress through Aquitaine, as well as bringing a solution to the problem of Geoffrey. With a new, powerful ruler in the region, the people of Nantes were emboldened to depose their unpopular count. They appealed to Henry, who offered them Geoffrey as a replacement. At no cost, Henry appeased Geoffrey and secured Anjou's western border by installing a member of his family as Count of Nantes. This city, Brittany's main port controlling the mouth of the River Loire, was a valuable acquisition for the Angevins.

His year on the Continent was therefore very successful. However, Henry's absence from England allowed problems to fester there. When he crossed back in 1157, the most pressing issue he had to address was the feud between King Stephen's son, William, and Hugh Bigod, major landholders in East Anglia who both claimed the earldom of Norfolk. Back in 1155, Henry had recognised Hugh as earl while also confirming William's earlier grants. However, they continued to fight when Henry was overseas. In May 1157, at a meeting of the great council at Bury St Edmunds, the king removed both men's castles. William acquiesced gracefully, albeit not entirely happily, whereas Hugh let resentment eat away at him for twenty years, with serious consequences for Henry in the 1170s. For now, however, the king was master of East Anglia and had once more asserted his authority.

Other kings might have concentrated on consolidating an already vast collection of territories, but like a hyperactive child, Henry wanted more. In May 1157, King Malcolm IV of Scotland (1153–65) journeyed south to meet his English counterpart. Henry wanted the return of the northern areas lost to the Scots under Stephen, and Malcolm (aged only 16) judged it very unwise to resist. This was an early example of behaviour which gave Henry a reputation as a promise-breaker, since in 1149 he had promised Malcolm's father that he would confirm the Scottish gains when he became king. The Scottish border question resolved with ease and entirely in his favour, Henry's mind then turned towards a possible conquest of Ireland (in 1155 the Pope had granted him the title Lord of Ireland). Facing doubts from his barons and his mother, he settled for Wales. The Normans had established a foothold in the south of the country, although the control Henry I had established over these Norman settlers had largely vanished under Stephen. At a council at Northampton in July 1157, Henry persuaded the barons to agree to a Welsh campaign. While South Wales might have been an easier target, the king focussed his attention on Owain of Gwynedd in the north. However, for all his military success elsewhere and his careful planning of this expedition, Henry was one of several English kings who would fail in the challenging conditions of North Wales. He was lucky to survive an ambush near Flint and was forced to make peace with Owain, although he did receive homage from the Welsh prince. Henry salvaged some pride by recovering other lands lost to the Welsh under Stephen and securing the homage of Rhys of Deheubarth. While not the absolute success he wanted, Henry had asserted his rights on yet another front.

Amidst his martial concerns, the king did not neglect administrative matters. In 1158, Henry reformed England's mints and coinage. With his territorial position in the British Isles improved, albeit not as much as he had hoped, later that year Henry returned to the Continent with the aim of extending his reach there as well. On this occasion, he would be away from England for four years, a measure of the security of his kingship. When Louis VII had recognised Henry's father as Duke of Normandy, he had been given a border area known as the Norman Vexin (between Paris and Rouen) as the price of doing so. Henry wanted it back. He sent his English chancellor, Thomas Becket, at the head of an ostentatious embassy to negotiate. The idea was that Henry's eldest surviving son, Henry, should be engaged to Louis' daughter Margaret, with the Norman Vexin forming her dowry. Becket's embassy was successful, with the Knights Templar being given custody of the area and its castles until the actual wedding took place. Meanwhile, Henry's brother, Geoffrey, died unexpectedly in July 1158 and Duke Conan of Brittany took the opportunity to seize Nantes. Henry claimed overlordship of Brittany and Louis VII was not going to intervene, which quickly made Conan realise his move had not been very clever. He dashed to Normandy and met Henry at Avranches, where he ceded Nantes to him. In return, Henry confirmed Conan in his dukedom.

In 1159, Henry assembled a large army at Poitiers and headed south. It was the largest force he raised in his reign, whose troops included the likes of the King of Scotland and King Stephen's son, William. That he was able to undertake such a campaign was testament to Henry's successful efforts to reform his finances; by now he was able to exploit the wealth of his kingdom for a continental venture. His aim was to assert what he considered to be the Duke of Aquitaine's right to overlordship of the strategically significant county of Toulouse. Count Raymond V of Toulouse disputed this right. Having failed to intimidate Raymond, Henry opted for military action. Raymond had been friends with the French king since they had been together in the Holy Land on the Second Crusade, and was married to Louis' sister. Henry's venture was thus risky and provocative, although Louis himself had made exactly the same claim of overlordship when married to Eleanor. Encouraged by a belligerent Thomas Becket, a zealous fundraiser for the campaign, Henry captured Cahors and went to besiege Toulouse itself. He overstretched his supply lines and then discovered Louis himself was in the city. To attack his French overlord would have been an extremely risky gambit even for Henry. With an outbreak of disease in his camp, Henry withdrew to focus on conquering other castles. A truce was agreed at the end of 1159, which expired in the middle of 1160. Rather than resume fighting, peace was made, in which Henry yielded most of his gains. He had been overconfident, even arrogant, offending and alarming the French king.

Henry compensated by making gains through diplomatic shenanigans. Louis VII's second wife, Constance, died in October 1160. Still lacking a male heir, just two weeks later Louis announced he was going to remarry, his new bride being Adela of Champagne. Alarmed that any heir of this union might leave Louis reluctant to give his daughter Margaret her dowry, Henry took action. He persuaded the Archbishop of Rouen, in the presence of two papal legates, to marry Margaret and the younger Henry on 2 November. Henry was 5 and Margaret 2, but that they were mere 'infants wailing in the cradle' did not concern King Henry in the slightest.[6] The Knights Templar duly handed over the castles in the Norman Vexin. Louis was furious, but his attempts at a show of strength failed when Henry appeared in one of those lightning moves that had Louis wondering if his English counterpart could fly. By the spring of 1161, war was looming, but the two kings pulled back and agreed a peace treaty at Fréteval. It was an end to hostilities for now, but Henry and Louis would never be on especially good terms again.

Henry returned to England in January 1163 to find himself faced with a major problem – his new Archbishop of Canterbury. Back in April 1161, Archbishop Theobald, an elderly man in post for twenty-two years, had died. He had been loyal to Henry II, although there were tensions between England and the papacy which led to Adrian IV (Nicholas Breakspear), the only Englishman ever to be Pope (1154–59), rebuking Theobald. From the very start, Henry wanted to bring as much as possible within the remit of royal justice, with plans to deal with the shortcomings of the ecclesiastical courts when it came to dealing with criminal clergy. His ideas were given encouragement by a crisis in the papacy. At the conclave after Adrian's death, in October 1159, a majority of cardinals elected Alexander III. A minority, however, installed the losing candidate as Victor IV, who became the antipope supported by the Holy Roman Emperor. Despite strong support from the English bishops for Alexander, Henry refused to allow them to declare England's allegiance until months later, well into 1160. He sensed the advantages of a Pope who needed his support. For Henry, Theobald's death was a perfect opportunity to appoint his own man to the archbishopric of Canterbury and, taking advantage of this and a weak papacy, address what he saw as the major points of contention between Church and state. He turned to his great friend, Chancellor Thomas Becket.

Twelve years Henry's senior, Becket was the son of a London merchant of Norman descent. The friendship between the two men was famously close, although a certain edge could perhaps be read into the stories of their playful tussles. They complemented one another, the king generally indifferent to finery and appearance, the chancellor very much enjoying and indulging in the trappings of office. Crucially, Becket was a loyal chancellor who served Henry zealously, although his judgement was not always sound. Henry believed that he would continue to act in the same way inside the Church, becoming the man who could help the king achieve the reforms he wanted. Although Becket apparently warned Henry that things would change if he went ahead with the appointment, the king paid no heed, and could certainly have had little indication that Becket would morph into possibly the most insufferably self-righteous archbishop ever to sit upon the throne of St Augustine. Perhaps the only person who saw that potential in Becket was a man whose view was distinctly prejudiced, given he was the most obvious alternative candidate for Canterbury: Gilbert Foliot, Bishop of Hereford.

Becket was not even a priest, so had to be ordained the day before his consecration on 3 June 1162. To the king's surprise and anger, Becket resigned the chancellorship and suddenly became his own opposite: 'In that rapid transformation from the gay, splendidly dressed courtier who romped with the king to the proud and austere priest who mortified his flesh by abstinence and flagellation and excelled in ostentatious acts of charity and humility, one can see a great actor superbly living the parts he was called upon to play. [...] This is true of Becket's whole career; there was an element of artificiality in it all'.[7] Thomas Becket wanted to be the star of the show, and in that melodramatic determination he dragged half of Western Christendom onto his stage. His murder, and the centuries of hagiography built upon it, has tended to disguise how narcissistic and proud he was. Henry was certainly not blameless, and both men were at fault for the subsequent breakdown in Church-state relations. Someone more imbued with the Christian virtues of charity and forgiveness, however, would probably have found a way to reach accommodation with the king.

Arriving at Southampton in January 1163, Henry was met by Prince Henry and Becket, who had been appointed the prince's tutor the previous year. It was a cordial meeting which gave no hint of what was to occur at the council Henry summoned to Westminster in March. At this council, inquiries were established to investigate the country's finances and feudal estates. Becket, in the high-handed and tactless manner which would soon become all too familiar, had been carrying out his own inquiry into Canterbury estates and excommunicated one of Henry's tenants-in-chief, which breached a longstanding custom that this should never be done without the king's permission. Becket would develop a habit of hurling excommunications around like grenades into the middle of the royal camp, often as a response to his injured pride or some perceived slight. At a further council at Woodstock in July, Henry proposed a revision of the system for payments to sheriffs, but Becket called this an innovation and refused to pay from the Canterbury estates. As it was the kind of change he would have enthusiastically supported as chancellor, and it made no difference to what Canterbury paid, it came across as an unnecessarily antagonistic move. His fellow bishops were not all behind him. Gilbert Foliot had been translated from Hereford to London, and steadfastly refused to take a new oath of allegiance to the archbishop.

Leaving troublesome archbishops aside, Henry had marched to Carmarthen to deal with Rhys of Deheubarth. He duly captured the Welsh prince and returned with him as a prisoner to England. Triumphant, Henry rather arrogantly summoned all the Welsh leaders, along with Malcolm IV of Scotland, to the council at Woodstock to swear homage to him. Naturally enough, they were humiliated by the experience. While this simply led to frosty relations with Malcolm during the final months of the Scottish king's life, in Wales it provoked an uprising the following year.

When another council met at Westminster in October 1163, Becket found a new cause to fight. This time, he was on much firmer ground. At issue was the problem of criminal clergymen. Clerks, or those in holy orders, were tried by the ecclesiastical courts rather than the secular ones, but the definition of a clerk could be ludicrously broad. Simply being able to mumble a few words of Latin was often enough to secure trial as a clerk. This was desirable for any criminal, since the maximum penalty a Church court could impose was defrocking, even for a serious offence. There is evidence that there was indeed a problem with the likes of murderers and rapists claiming 'benefit of clergy' and evading secular justice, a cause of considerable resentment to lay society. Naturally enough, that even *bona fide* clergymen could escape the consequences of their crimes was seen as deeply unjust. Henry had hoped that by installing a sympathetic archbishop, he could finally deal with this affront to justice, along with other matters causing friction between Church and state. At this council, he wanted to address the matter, but Becket had other ideas.

The issue of criminal clergy and the role of the Church courts never became an issue elsewhere in Europe. In England, it pitted two immensely stubborn protagonists against one another. At the 1163 council, Becket argued that clergy had full immunity from secular jurisdiction, supported by the canon law principal that God did not judge the same offence twice. Henry was careful; rather than taking the case entirely from the Church courts, he wanted the judgement to be in the ecclesiastical courts, but for a guilty cleric to be handed over to the secular authorities for punishment after defrocking. Becket refused to give any ground. Not entirely enthusiastically, the rest of the bishops supported their primate. This provoked a furious king to demand that the bishops swear an oath to observe royal customs, effectively giving them a choice between agreeing to the new proposals or facing accusations of treason. Becket was every bit as good at legal manoeuvres as the king, so agreed that they would swear the oath with the rider, 'saving our order'. In other words, where royal and ecclesiastical law were in conflict, the bishops would obey Church rather than king. It was to become Becket's catchphrase, while this escalating unreasonableness by both men set the pattern for pretty much every meeting involving king and archbishop for the rest of the decade. Henry was livid. In retaliation, he removed his son and heir, Henry, from Becket's household.

For all their official unanimity, there were those among the bishops who were alarmed by Becket's stubbornness and the conflict it was provoking. Gilbert Foliot of London was the most obvious and implacable of these. Roger de Pont L'Evêque, Archbishop of York since 1154, seems to have conceived a dislike of Becket when they were together in Archbishop Theobald's household, and was also concerned about promoting the claims of York against Canterbury. Hilary of Chichester now visited the archbishop to plead reason with him, only to be rebuffed. Pope Alexander, however, in exile in Sens while Rome was still under the control of the antipope, was a rather harder man to ignore. Concerned at the disruption to the English Church, the Pope sent envoys to Becket telling him to show restraint. The archbishop allowed himself to be taken to the king at Woodstock, where he promised Henry that he would be obedient and observe the realm's customs. The king should have accepted this gracefully and moved on, but Becket had irritated him too much and he demanded that as Becket had made the initial statement in public, so his retraction should be public. As would happen repeatedly with Becket, the generally sensible Henry lost his sense of proportion and acted high-handedly in response to provocation.

The resulting council meeting took place in January 1164, at Clarendon. Here, far from simply receiving Becket's agreement to observe the customs of the realm, Henry presented the bishops with a document setting out these customs, sixteen articles which would become known as the Constitutions of Clarendon. While the bishops conceded, albeit not without qualification, that the document did indeed represent traditional practice, they baulked at the request to swear an oath to uphold them. Tempers flared as king and bishops argued over this demand, until Becket suddenly and unexpectedly gave in and told the others to comply. Then he changed his mind again, to the consternation of his fellow bishops. An incandescent Henry resolved to get rid of his troublesome archbishop, either by resignation or papal dismissal, but his arrogant behaviour at Clarendon had turned a Church-state affair into a potential clash between the English Crown and the papacy. Becket brought out the worst in Henry and led him to an intemperance that a more sensitive archbishop might have headed off. Neither man emerges well from the events of January 1164, but on this occasion Henry was to blame for initiating the clash.

In September, Henry had his chance for revenge when Becket sent a message in response to a summons to a royal court. Ordinarily, a failure to obey a first summons would hardly lead to a charge of contempt of court, but Henry had lost all sense of proportion as far as Becket was concerned and duly summoned the archbishop to a council at Northampton in October to answer just such a charge. While he was obviously found guilty and sentenced to forfeiture of his goods, there was a squabble over passing sentence, the barons arguing the bishops should do it as Becket was a bishop, the bishops arguing the barons should do it as it was a secular judgement. Henry had to end this buck passing by ordering the Bishop of Winchester to do the unpleasant duty, which he did with great reluctance.

Next, sensing the opportunity to humiliate Becket further, Henry began to press charges of embezzlement and malpractice from the archbishop's time as chancellor. Negotiations and arguments followed. On 12 October, Becket had to be convinced not to go to the council meeting in full Mass vestments. When he arrived at Northampton Castle and dismounted, he took his archiepiscopal cross from its bearer and carried it himself. Several bishops tried to take it from him.

Gilbert Foliot asked Becket how he would respond if Henry bore his sword in such a fashion. Becket was unmoveable. He and Henry were not speaking. They were not even in the same room. Henry sat upstairs, Becket downstairs, and the barons and bishops got a lot of exercise on the stairs acting as go-betweens. The bishops, desperate to avoid passing judgement on Becket, agreed they would seek his deposition in Rome if excused. They withdrew, and the remaining laymen went downstairs to pass sentence. The archbishop refused to listen and stormed out of the castle, once more carrying his cross in front of him. When Henry responded ambiguously to his message requesting a safe conduct to leave, Becket fled anyway. He found a ready place of exile at Louis VII's court.

The council at Northampton had shown Henry at his worst, petty and vindictive. He sent a mission to the Pope to seek a favourable verdict, but Alexander demurred. When Becket himself arrived at the curia shortly afterwards and put on a theatrical performance which ended with him tearfully handing the Pope his ring, Alexander handed it back. Thwarted, Henry took his rage out on Becket's followers in England. The next six years were basically a stalemate with Becket out of England, where he was not particularly missed, both king and archbishop fighting to get the Pope to bless their preferred course of action. Becket and Foliot engaged in a bitter and lengthy exchange of insults by correspondence.[8] Once Becket was in exile, Henry pushed the quarrel out of his mind for much of the next six years. Far from being 'largely the story of Henry's conflict with the Church', rather the 'story of the 1160s is the story of Henry II's attempt to consolidate his authority as a ruler'.[9] In England, the machinery of government continued to function smoothly even as he spent most of the decade out of the kingdom. He was always in touch with his key officials, who if necessary would travel to the Continent to meet and consult him. Men as significant as the King of Scotland travelled to Henry wherever he was, as happened when William I (William the Lion, 1165–1214) headed to Mont Saint-Michel in 1166.

In 1165, Henry turned his attention to the Welsh uprising. Troops were summoned from his continental lands and Scotland, and a fleet brought over from Dublin, meticulous preparations which suggested the king was intent on conquest. However, Henry's military sense suddenly failed him. Rather than use the sea and coastal routes, the key to Edward I's later success, he opted for a tricky overland route where it was hard to adequately provision his army. Mountains and the Welsh weather undid him and he retreated. It is hard to know what might have happened had Henry been able to devote more time and energy to Wales: 'Like Edward I he was a masterful king whose mastery was not lightly challenged; like Edward I he had the determination and resourcefulness to confront and overcome daunting military problems; unlike Edward I, his preoccupations elsewhere were so many that he could not afford to give Wales other than very brief attention'.[10] The Welsh now had the upper hand and Henry did not return to them until the early 1170s.

Early in 1166, Henry issued one of the most important legal documents of his reign. Proclaimed at the same Wiltshire manor as the Constitutions of Clarendon two years earlier, these twenty-two articles are known as the Assize of Clarendon.

('Constitution' and 'assize' seem to have been terms used interchangeably to describe legislation promulgated in Henry's reign.[11]) The intention was to deal with those guilty of serious criminal offences, for which the penalty was death or mutilation. Before this point, defendants in criminal cases had submitted themselves to what contemporaries viewed as the judgement of God. A common method of asserting innocence was to swear an oath on the gospels or a holy book. The alternative method involved submitting to an ordeal.[12] In ordeal by battle (or trial by combat), the accuser and defender or their champions fought it out, the assumption being that God would give the innocent party victory. Ordeal by iron involved the accused walking a set distance holding a heated piece of iron, having their hand being bound for three days and then inspected, with innocence declared if it was healing cleanly. Ordeal by water saw the accused thrown into a pool of cold water, being declared innocent if they sank and guilty if they floated. While ordeals continued to be used into the next century (and trial by battle was not officially abolished until 1819), the Assize of Clarendon began a fundamental shift in the process of criminal trials.

The most significant change was the introduction of jury trials. Juries were not new in Henry II's reign, but it is only from this point that they begin to be used regularly and systematically. At this stage, a jury did not consist of a group of people weighing the evidence impartially to determine guilt or innocence, as in the modern English understanding. They were rather juries of presentment, the ancestor of grand juries in the modern United States. Under the Assize of Clarendon, twelve men of every hundred (a subdivision of a county) or four of every township had to provide the names of all those accused or suspected of murder, robbery or theft since Henry took the throne, and of all those suspected of harbouring anyone guilty of these crimes. Under oath, the juries made these indictments before the sheriffs, who were then charged with capturing suspects and presenting them to the justices (after 1176, the juries were required to make or repeat their indictments directly in front of the justices). Importantly, the usual exemptions for special jurisdictions did not apply, so everyone was subjected to royal justice in this process. Unless the accused confessed, or had stolen goods in his possession, or had a particularly bad reputation, they underwent trial by water. If they floated and were thus found guilty, they had a foot removed (and after 1176, their right hand as well). If they floated but had a bad reputation locally, they were banished, God's views on their innocence notwithstanding. The lands of any convicted felon reverted to his lord, his goods were sold by the sheriff and the profits given to the royal treasury. While not justice by modern standards, it demonstrates a particular desire by Henry II to tackle a backlog of serious, unpunished crimes and to involve local communities in doing so.

Having crossed to France in March 1166, the king had entrusted these proceedings to his reliable officials. He would not return to England for another four years. His time would largely be occupied in the power struggle against France and combatting increasingly restless vassals. It was becoming more of a challenge to hold his disparate French lands together. King Louis had been emboldened by the birth, at last, of a son (the future Philip II) in 1165. He took to causing mischief in Henry's territories, which caused Henry to take increasingly firm action to shore up his position. Unrest in Brittany brought a particularly strong response in summer 1166. Henry stormed into the duchy and deposed Duke Conan, whom he held responsible for the collapse of order. He had his 7-year-old son Geoffrey engaged to Conan's daughter, Constance, who was aged around 4 or 5, once more using one of his children as a diplomatic pawn. The Bretons unhappily swore allegiance to their new, *de facto* lord, but it did nothing to diminish the dissatisfaction. There was also unrest in the south. Henry headed from Brittany to Aquitaine in 1167 to subdue discontented barons, but had to dash to Normandy to deal with diversionary raids from Louis. Henry attacked and burned Louis' arsenal, while Louis sacked Norman border towns. Peace with the French was eventually agreed in August, after which Henry marched off to deal once more with the problematic Bretons. The raid ended abruptly when Henry received news of his mother's death.

It was twenty years since Matilda had given up her struggle for the English crown. In that time, Henry had matured from a hopeful teenager into one of the most powerful kings in Europe, but he continued to respect his mother and her death on 10 September 1167 was a blow. In the autumn of 1167, Eleanor crossed to Normandy with their daughter Matilda. Matilda had been betrothed to Henry the Lion, Duke of Saxony and Bavaria, in one of her father's diplomatic schemes, this latest to put pressure on Pope Alexander III over Becket. As ever, King Henry showed little regard for his child's happiness when it came to the politics of marriage; Matilda was 11, Henry in his late thirties and already divorced. After Eleanor had brought Matilda to Normandy, ready for her to head east for her marriage (which took place in Minden Cathedral in February 1168), the queen went to England to pack, then returned to spend Christmas 1167 with Henry at Argentan. Here, they agreed to separate, with Eleanor returning home to Poitiers. Eleanor continued to act on behalf of Henry for some years, and they continued to spend Christmases together, so the split was not initially acrimonious.

There was no question of divorce. Louis VII and Eleanor's marriage ended because there had been no son from the union, then he watched Aquitaine fall straight into the hands of a rival. Henry had four healthy sons by Eleanor, so no dynastic worries. He was never going to formally end their marriage and lose her duchy. Naturally there are plenty of salacious rumours about why they split at this stage. Henry's extra-marital relationships were no secret and there were lurid stories about prostitutes and night-time activities at court, with the king even having a whoremaster in both England and Normandy.[13] Eleanor's fidelity is a harder matter to prove either way, but there were certainly rumours about her love life. Henry acknowledged illegitimate children, among them Geoffrey (later made Archbishop of York by his half-brother, Richard I) and William Longspee (created Earl of Salisbury by Richard). It is hard to see that Eleanor suddenly objected to Henry's infidelities. For all the strictures of the Church, and the official condemnation of clerics, medieval kings had affairs and this was largely accepted, unless a liaison had damaging political consequences or was especially scandalous.

Later legend has linked the split to Henry's infatuation with his most famous mistress, Rosamund de Clifford, later the romantic folklore figure 'fair Rosamund'. One version of the story, from much later and entirely fictitious, tells of how Henry and Rosamund used to meet secretly in a special underground labyrinth in the park of Woodstock Palace. Eleanor one day found her way through the labyrinth, confronting Rosamund and forcing her to choose between a bowl of poison and a dagger. She chose the poison and died. The reality is far less exciting. Henry and Rosamund certainly had an affair, living openly together for a period in the mid-1170s. She died around 1176, Henry investing heavily in her burial place of Godstow Abbey in Oxfordshire. Crucially, their relationship did not begin until sometime in the period 1170–73, well after Henry and Eleanor had effectively separated. The likelihood is that two strong-willed people simply couldn't live together all the time, while Eleanor felt marginalised. As Queen of France, Eleanor had acted almost as co-ruler with her husband. As Queen of England, she was politically irrelevant. Henry had set up a system of government in England which did not require the queen (or anyone) to act as a strong regent during his lengthy spells away from the country, since his officials could run the show. Back in Poitiers, Eleanor could be in charge, administering Aquitaine for her husband.

This sowed the seeds of major future problems for Henry. Eleanor took her 10-year-old son, Richard, to Aquitaine with her. She raised him as her successor in the duchy. Spending his formative years there meant that southern France was always home for Richard and he would later resist his father's attempts to deny him the rulership of Aquitaine. Yet, if Richard was his mother's favourite, she managed to stay on good terms with all her children. Even John, the youngest and Henry's favourite, would find Eleanor a major support in the early years of his reign, achieving one of his rare, brilliant military feats to rescue her from a siege in 1202. Henry would certainly not qualify for any modern parenthood awards (although this was true of nearly all medieval kings and nobles). Eleanor took pains to keep her children on her side.

1168 had been a year of fighting, sieges and abortive truces between the kings of England and France. In early 1169, Henry and Louis met at a peace conference at Montmirail. Chroniclers focussed on Becket's theatrics. The Pope had made him legate for England, leading Becket to gleefully excommunicate several of Henry's key servants at Easter 1166. Henry had threatened to withdraw his allegiance from Alexander III at a point when the Pope was under considerable pressure, so a worried pontiff overruled the archbishop. These issues had continued to rumble in the background as Louis and Henry engaged in hostilities, but now their peace talks expanded to include Becket. It looked like peace between king and archbishop had been achieved until, unable to help himself, Becket once again qualified everything he had said by the disclaimer 'saving the honour of my God'. Henry was furious and even Louis was thoroughly exasperated.

More importantly than the ongoing drama with the tiresome archbishop, at Montmirail Henry laid out plans for his succession which indicated that his 'empire' would cease to have a single ruler after his death, assuaging Louis' fears about the Angevin threat to France. Henry II faced the problem of a variety of inheritance customs in various territories, but the succession was to give him a headache for the next twenty years. At this stage, his eldest son, Henry, was to have the English crown along with Normandy, Anjou and Maine. Geoffrey would be Duke of Brittany, as a vassal of young Henry. Richard was to become Duke of Aquitaine, held directly from the King of France and thus independent of his older brother. No provision was made for John, the youngest, until Henry became seriously ill in 1170 and made a will. Then, the 3-year-old John was assigned the county of Mortain.

The 1169 Christmas court was kept at Nantes. March 1170 brought a moment of tragedy, when the king's personal physician, Ralph de Beaumont, drowned with some 400 others on a Channel crossing to Portsmouth; a rather heartless chronicler noted that he became 'food for the fish of the sea'.[14] Although Henry crossed the Channel some twenty-eight times, it was a perilous voyage in the twelfth century. His own path to the throne had begun with a Channel shipping disaster before his birth, the loss of the White Ship in 1120. Being a cross-Channel king was not without serious risks, and Henry took the risks seriously. There is evidence of his praying at shrines before crossings and giving thanks at them after safe arrivals, and making the voyage on major Church feast days if possible.

Meanwhile, tussles with Louis continued and in 1170 Henry determined to ensure at least one part of his succession plan could not be challenged. He revived the plan to have his eldest son crowned in imitation of French custom. In 987, following the death of Louis V and the extinction of the royal line, Hugh Capet was elected king. Almost immediately after his coronation he began a successful campaign to have his son, Robert II crowned. Robert's son, Henry I, and Henry's son, Philip I, were likewise crowned in their fathers' lifetimes. These coronations made the heirs into a king, albeit one junior to their fathers, and once they succeeded there was no new coronation. This practice made it almost impossible to challenge the succession of an already crowned king. While established in France, King Stephen had failed in efforts to introduce the practice into England, the bishops refusing to carry out a ceremony in the face of papal opposition. However, Henry was in a much stronger position than Stephen had been. There was logic in Henry II securing the future of the Plantagenet dynasty in England by having his own eldest son crowned in his lifetime.

Coronation of English kings was the accepted prerogative of the Archbishop of Canterbury, but Henry wanted Becket nowhere near this occasion. Eleanor and the Seneschal of Normandy were deployed to make sure the archbishop was kept out of England. Tight security was also necessary to keep out any papal representatives, as the Pope had explicitly forbidden anyone else to preside at the coronation. There were precedents for coronation by other bishops, but excluding Becket on this occasion was an intentionally political act. In a further snub, this one to the King of France, Henry was crowned alone, without his wife Margaret. (At King Louis' insistence, they would be crowned together at another ceremony in Winchester Cathedral in August 1172.) The coronation took place at Westminster Abbey on

14 June 1170, presided over by Archbishop Roger of York. Thereafter, the younger Henry was known as the Young King.

The coronation was not the king's only business in England. Henry had returned to a chorus of complaints about abuses and malpractice by royal officials, notably sheriffs. His response was to launch what became known as the Inquest of Sheriffs, a far-reaching inquiry into officials which showed the reach and authority of the English crown. The transformation since Stephen's reign was remarkable. Sheriffs were investigated for failure to administer the Assize of Clarendon correctly, while their financial affairs and management of royal manors was probed. The result was extensive change, the 1170 pipe roll revealing the replacement of twenty sheriffs. Rarely did a medieval king deal quite so energetically and ruthlessly with complaints against his officials.

After his son's coronation, Henry returned to France and fell sick, confined to bed for almost two months in the late summer. It was Eleanor who largely oversaw matters during Henry's illness. Predictably, there was a lot of anger about the coronation, not only from Becket. The Pope was furious that his commands had been flouted and began threatening interdicts and excommunications. Henry decided some conciliatory gestures were in order. He met Becket at Frétval not long before he fell sick, and there was a superficial reconciliation and promises that Becket could perform a second coronation for the Young King, this time with his wife. Mollified, Becket crossed back to England. Despite what his fawning hagiographers say, it appears that he was received very badly. He had done nothing to endear himself to anyone in England, and even young Henry refused to receive him. Undaunted, and unmoved by any notion of humility, Becket ostentatiously and proudly excommunicated the Archbishop of York, and the Bishops of London and Salisbury, during his Christmas Day sermon in Canterbury Cathedral.

King and queen were spending Christmas together with their sons at Bur-le-Roi in Normandy when Henry received the news. Exactly what he said in his rage is uncertain, but four knights took it as licence to hasten to Canterbury where, as evening fell on 29 December 1170, they hacked Becket to death in his cathedral. Whatever his many faults, the archbishop met his death with considerable courage. The news reached Henry at Argentan on 1 January 1171. The distraught king shut himself away from everyone for three days, his courtiers fearing for his sanity. Unsurprisingly, the murder of an archbishop shocked Christendom. Pope Alexander III apparently refused to speak to any Englishman for a week (rather overlooking the fact that Henry was not English). Louis VII and several other French rulers tried to capitalise on the situation, but it was not nearly as perilous for Henry as it seemed. While nobody could admit to relief that Becket was dead, many must secretly have felt it; he was infinitely more popular dead than alive. Notably, Alexander held back on immediately excommunicating Henry or placing his realm under interdict. He held those sentences in reserve. The Pope was an astute politician and realised this was a perfect opportunity to wrest concessions from Henry. Although he made the king sweat for a while, he sent legates from Rome in 1171. Henry, however, had removed himself from the scene.

He had been contemplating invading Ireland for years, intermittently interfering in Irish politics. The situation in Ireland was fiendishly complex, but Henry had actually been invited to intervene a few years earlier. In 1166, he had been asked by Diarmait Mac Murchada, exiled King of Leinster, to help Diarmait regain his kingdom. On that occasion, Henry simply authorised Diarmait to recruit troops. One man Diarmait enlisted for his successful campaign was Richard FitzGilbert, known as Strongbow, a powerful baron from the Welsh Marches. He married Diarmait's daughter and succeeded as King of Leinster when his father-in-law died in May 1171. There was no way Henry was going to allow one of his subjects to have an independent kingdom, and he forced Strongbow to surrender his Irish possessions, granting them back to be held as a vassal of the English crown. Now Henry wanted to see the latest extension of his lands. Securing control of Ireland would give his youngest son, John, an inheritance. Above all, however, Henry crossed the Irish Sea in October 1171 to escape the fallout from Becket's murder and allow heads to cool. The papacy had long been concerned about the state of Christianity in Ireland, so Henry hoped to gain currency with Alexander by bringing a degree of order there.

The trip was largely successful. Setting up administrative centres in Dublin, Waterford and Wexford, Henry reserved the south-eastern quarter of the island as royal territory. A Church council at Cashel in February 1172 introduced reforms to align the Irish Church with the rest of Western Christendom. Almost all the native Irish rulers submitted to the King of England, the major holdout being the High King of Ireland, Ruaidrí Ua Conochobair (Rory O'Connor). Needing to return to France, Henry left further action to his more warlike Anglo-Irish nobles. Henry and Ruaidrí eventually reached terms in the Treaty of Windsor in 1175. By then, the king had too many concerns elsewhere and the Becket issue had died down, so he would never return to Ireland, although he did designate John as future King of Ireland in 1177. After 1171, Ireland was firmly considered to be part of the Angevin and English orbit by the English Crown, even if only two other medieval kings would cross the Irish Sea in person and the extent of English control ebbed and flowed, never encompassing anything like the entire island. Whether this was an achievement or not, given the tragic contours of Anglo-Irish history ever since, it showed Henry's insatiable desire to extend the reaches of his dynasty. As a diversion tactic, the visit to Ireland worked. Returning to the Continent in 1172, he was able to settle more favourably with the Pope than might have otherwise been the case.

Strong winds hampered communication in the winter of 1171–72, leaving Henry largely incommunicado in Ireland. Even when he learned, in February 1172, that papal legates had arrived in Normandy, he was unable to cross from Wexford to St Davids until mid-April. Not until mid-May was he finally in Normandy to negotiate with the legates. Negotiations began at Savigny on 17 May. After some hard bargaining, the result was the Compromise of Avranches. Henry released the bishops from the oath to uphold the Constitutions of Clarendon and promised to withdraw all 'evil customs'. All the possessions of the archbishopric of Canterbury were to be restored,

Henry would send 200 knights to the Holy Land, and both Henry and his son swore to be faithful to Alexander III and his successors. Yet Henry was not subservient. The compromise laid the ground for future discussions about his relationship with the papacy rather than resolving everything immediately. With Becket removed from the scene, the relationship between Church and state was no longer reduced to stand-off by tantrum. Henry had been shocked by the murder, and no one else provoked him like Becket. Both king and Pope were willing to work towards a more constructive relationship. Henry did formal penance at Avranches on 21 May and was absolved from complicity in Becket's murder. There were then additional ceremonies of penance, at Caen on 30 May and again at Avranches on 28 September.

At the time, most viewed it as a humiliation for Henry, especially as Becket quickly became a miracle-working saint, his shrine at Canterbury a popular place of pilgrimage. The king had to abandon his hopes of bringing criminal clergy to secular justice. On the other hand, Henry's interpretation of 'evil customs' was very different to Rome's and he evaded a lot of what the legates surely intended. He had survived the period of danger and reconciled with the Church. Even with Becket on his conscience, he was never seen as impious and irreligious like his youngest son. If he had to give up on his hopes of subjecting the Church to secular justice and authority, he began to reassert himself against the ecclesiastical powers once the dust had settled. The death in 1171 of Henry of Blois, King Stephen's brother, had left the bishopric of Winchester vacant. Writing to the monks responsible for electing his successor, Henry allegedly told them: 'I order you to hold a free election, but I do not wish you to elect anyone except Richard, my clerk'. Richard of Ilchester, Archdeacon of Poitiers and Henry's loyal clerk, was duly elected Bishop of Winchester. It gives an insight into how Henry viewed ecclesiastical liberty – the monks were at perfect liberty to obey the king. Yet there was no repeat of the clashes of the 1160s. As one modern historian has aptly put it, while 'Henry and Becket were both alive, they could see the issues only in terms of victory or defeat. With Becket gone, Henry neither won nor lost'.[15]

At peace with the Church, Henry agreed with Eleanor that Richard should now be invested as Duke of Aquitaine. Two investiture ceremonies took place in June 1172, at Poitiers and then Limoges. However, Henry had no wish to surrender his title as Duke of Aquitaine, so Richard became known as Count of Poitou. Unlike the younger Henry in England, Richard was allowed, thanks to Eleanor, to take a significant role in Aquitaine. This caused considerable resentment between the two brothers. Geoffrey was also unhappy, as his marriage to Constance of Brittany had not yet occurred, even though her father had died in 1171. It is easy to forget, given all that had happened in his reign, that Henry was not yet 40, but his sons were aware that their father had been invested as Duke of Normandy in his own right at just 17. His refusal to share power in the same way as his father frustrated his impetuous children. Eleanor and Henry spent Christmas 1172 together at Mirebeau in Anjou, but family relations were strained. They were about to get far worse, as Henry proved himself an adept political diplomat and a terrible family one.

Seeking to isolate the Count of Toulouse, Henry arranged a marriage (which never happened) for his son John with the daughter of one of the count's neighbours. The gambit worked and in February 1173 the count swore homage to Henry and Richard, but not Eleanor, whose ancestral duchy this was. This insensitive move offended the queen. Equally upset was young Henry, as the marriage settlement gave John three castles in Anjou, which Henry felt were part of his inheritance. He and his father fell out spectacularly. All the Young King's grievances emerged as Henry removed from the Young King's household men he suspected of encouraging his son in his ambition and disloyalty. Henry took his eldest son, a prisoner in all but name, towards Normandy. In early March, young Henry managed to escape from Chinon Castle, riding to a warm reception at Louis' court in Paris. Geoffrey and Richard headed to join their older brother, all three swearing allegiance to the French king. Eleanor was captured on the road to Chartres while trying to flee to Paris, disguised as a man, and was promptly imprisoned in Chinon Castle, while far more gruesome punishments were meted out to her supporters. This was now an outright family war, but it would affect far more than just the family. With the scale of Henry's territories and wider influence, most of north-western Europe was about to be dragged into the conflict.

Louis summoned his leading nobles and declared Henry had been deprived of his French lands. Young Henry swore not to make peace with his father without Louis' permission, then the two started the process of assembling an army and a coalition along Normandy's eastern border. The Young King enticed King William of Scotland onto his side. The nobility in parts of Brittany, Maine and Aquitaine, where Henry II had asserted his rights especially forcefully, backed the younger Henry. Discontented earls in England also lent him their support. Chief among them Hugh Bigod, who was still holding a grudge against the king from 1157, and he was joined by the Earls of Chester, Derby and Leicester (the last the son of Henry's former co-justiciar, who had died in 1168). Most in England, however, held back from declaring their hand either way. The Young King found considerably more noble support in Normandy. Despite English uncertainty, a formidable range of foes was arrayed against Henry II. It was the most serious challenge he had faced and it had the potential to destroy him.

The initial assault in May 1173 was on Normandy, attacks launched at different points by Louis VII, Count Philip of Flanders, and a group of Bretons. Henry held his nerve, crossing briefly to England to stock up with money from the royal treasury, to hire mercenaries. The Norman war started going his way. Matthew, Count of Boulogne, died from an infected crossbow wound, which caused Count Philip, his brother, to return grief-stricken to Flanders. In August, Henry marched his army towards Verneuil, which Louis was besieging, to confront his enemy in battle. This prompted the less than heroic French king to flee and leave his rearguard to be slaughtered. Henry returned to Rouen and sent his mercenaries to deal with the Bretons, who showed equally little stomach for a fight and retreated to take refuge in the town of Dol, north of Rennes. They thought Henry was still tied up in eastern Normandy, so were unpleasantly surprised when he performed one of his spectacular materialisations from nowhere, having covered the 150 miles from Rouen in just two days. The rebels had no option but to beg for mercy, which Henry granted, although he imprisoned the ringleaders.

With the continental campaign not going to plan, and after brief and unsuccessful peace talks at Gisors, the Earl of Leicester tried to revive opposition fortunes by diverting attention to England. He landed on the Suffolk coast and joined forces with Hugh Bigod. The heart of rebel strength was the North and East Midlands. Henry's cause in England was being ably defended by the surviving justiciar, Richard de Lucy, who had recaptured Leicester but not its castle. He had had to break off that siege to repel a Scottish attack by King William's forces in the North. De Lucy now raced back to Suffolk. Although his army was smaller than that of the rebel Earls of Leicester and Norfolk, it won a convincing victory at the Battle of Fornham, near Bury St Edmunds, on 17 October 1173, where Leicester was captured.

With England and Normandy safe for the moment, Henry turned to deal with his southern lands. He strengthened Anjou's border with Blois, then headed to deal with the rebels in Aquitaine, led by Richard. From Chinon, he went to Poitou and launched a surprise attack to capture Saintes, Richard's base, which forced his son to take refuge in a baronial fortress. Aside from the odd ineffectual attempt at a surprise attack by Louis, little happened in the war in the opening months of 1174. Having failed so ignominiously the previous year, despite the odds being heavily stacked in their favour, Henry's continental opponents were unwilling to risk any more military efforts while he was in Normandy. To address this, William the Lion was engaged to launch a diversionary front. The Scottish king and his brother attacked northern England after Easter, supported by Roger de Mowbray (an old supporter of King Stephen who had been captured with him at the Battle of Lincoln in 1141) and northern rebels. At first, the attack failed to draw Henry across the Channel, as he travelled to Anjou and Maine to secure key fortresses there. More pressure was now applied. Philip of Flanders sent Flemish troops to East Anglia to join with Hugh Bigod, declaring his own intention of invading in July. This force captured Norwich, while in the North the Scots had taken some royal castles and were besieging Carlisle.

Now, Henry decided the situation was grave enough to require his presence in England. He took Eleanor with him on the crossing from Barfleur to Southampton, dispatching her to imprisonment in Salisbury Castle. Meanwhile he went to Canterbury, submitting to a public scourging at the tomb of Thomas Becket as penance. This gesture prevented the rebels associating the newly canonised Becket with their cause. The events which followed suggested to contemporaries that the saint had forgiven the king. Henry's subjects had rallied to his cause. His illegitimate son, Geoffrey, had besieged Roger de Mowbray; although de Mowbray escaped, he was captured by some peasants as he tried to reach Leicester. Northern earls and barons, with the sheriff of Yorkshire, were leading resistance to King William in the North. They met at Newcastle on 12 July and headed towards Alnwick the following day. Making swift progress, they surprised and captured the Scottish king outside Alnwick Castle, marching him back to Newcastle and sending him to imprisonment at Richmond until he could be sent to Henry. A messenger dashed to give Henry the good news, which he received at Westminster late on 17 July.

Huntingdon and Northampton were still in rebel hands, so Henry marched north to relieve them. Faced with the formidable king outside their gates, neither town resisted. The English part of the rebellion was over, allowing Henry to return to Normandy on 8 August, after just a month in England. Louis VII and Philip of Flanders had capitalised on Henry's absence to move against Rouen in late July. Henry's rapid success in England meant he was at the Norman capital before they had finished laying the siege. Once more, Louis chose to run away rather than engage Henry in battle. The war was over.

The events of 1173–74 confronted Henry II with a terrifying array of enemies on multiple fronts which would have toppled another, less able king. While usually termed a rebellion, because it began with the defection of his sons, they actually played very little part in the fighting, instead serving as a convenient excuse for the many enemies Henry had built up to seize the chance to launch a war to humiliate him. The result, however, was humiliation for his foes, who saw Henry emerge triumphant against a coalition which should have overwhelmed him. Yet Henry chose to be merciful in victory, astute enough to realise that the rebellion had been a result of widespread and deep grievances. When peace was agreed at the end of September 1174, Henry opted to be magnanimous and return to the status quo of early 1173. Young Henry was reconciled with his father and compelled to recognise the grants to John, but given an allowance and two Norman castles. Richard had prostrated himself at Henry's feet to beg pardon, which was granted along with confirmation of his title as Count of Poitou and an allocation of half the county's revenues. Geoffrey was likewise granted half the income from Brittany. There would continue to be arguments, tearful reunions and family conferences in the years ahead, but there were no fallouts on the same scale for the rest of the 1170s. The king's clemency had limits. Eleanor continued under house arrest in various royal residences in England. The Earls of Chester and Leicester were kept captive until January 1177, and although then restored to their titles, some of their castles were retained in royal hands. William the Lion was forced to sign the Treaty of Falaise in December 1174. The cost of his freedom was accepting English overlordship of Scotland. He was required to submit publicly to the King of England at York, and give five Scottish castles to Henry, while still paying to garrison them.

Henry now made a greater effort to use his sons in governing his territories. The main beneficiary was Richard. With Eleanor imprisoned, he was entrusted with tackling rebellion in Aquitaine, although as he had started the trouble originally, it is not impossible Henry was punishing him as much as trusting him. At first, Richard made little headway, but he was being useful to his father, unlike his elder brother. When Henry planned to return to England in March 1175, he had to extract the younger Henry from yet more intrigue at Louis' court. The two were reconciled, travelled together to England, and at the end of May visited Becket's tomb. They spent much of the next year together, although the Young King grew eager to return to his friends and enjoyment of tournaments in France. Henry saw his son's professed desire to go on pilgrimage to Santiago de Compostela as a desire to get back to his more enjoyable continental life. For all he railed against Henry giving him no power or responsibility, it is debatable how much genuine interest he had in the hard work of actually governing. After a family meeting at Winchester in the spring of 1176, Richard was given money to hire mercenaries and offered the support of his older brother. It was support not worth having, as young Henry idled in Paris and then made only the briefest journey to Aquitaine before returning north to spend the next three years on the tournament circuit, which at least kept him quiet. In contrast, Richard routed the Count of Angoulême and watched resistance crumble. He was able to send leading nobles to submit to Henry at Winchester in September 1176, having proved his military credentials and served his father infinitely better than the playboy Young King. Over the next few years, Richard tirelessly worked away at destroying the power of recalcitrant Aquitanian nobles.

It was just five years since Henry II had been the outcast of Christendom, but 1176 was possibly the zenith of his reign. He was one of the most powerful and renowned rulers in Europe. Outstanding issues with the papacy were settled, with none of the contrition of Avranches. There were matters where he reasserted royal control; clergy accused of forest law offences were to be tried by royal officials, not ecclesiastical courts. Envoys flocked to his court, including a visit from the representatives of the Byzantine Emperor, Manuel Comnenus. Henry's daughters also made good diplomatic matches. Matilda married Henry of Saxony in 1168. Eleanor wed Alfonso VIII of Castile in 1160, and in 1176 Alfonso was seeking his father-in-law's arbitration in border disputes with Navarre. In 1177, the youngest daughter Joan (or Joanna) married the king of another Norman kingdom, William II (William the Good) of Sicily. Anglo-Sicilian links are still evident in the dedication of Marsala Cathedral to St Thomas of Canterbury, and a mosaic of Becket in the resplendent interior of Monreale Cathedral, one of the earliest images of the saint. These marriages are testimony to what Henry had become: Western Europe's problem-solver and marriage broker, called upon from Portugal to Saxony.

Back in England for his longest stay for a decade, Henry once more turned his attention to legal matters. A great council at Northampton in 1176 resulted in the Assize of Northampton. This gave instructions for six judicial circuits of three judges each. The procedures outlined in the Assize of Clarendon a decade earlier were tightened up, and stricter punishments imposed. In addition to criminal law, Henry also addressed civil issues during his reign, especially around land and inheritance law. Various standardised writs became available, for a fee, to speed up such cases, as Henry sought to provide access to the king's justice without needing access to the king. He was still reasonably diligent in hearing cases himself – all justice was theoretically the king's justice – but he laid the foundations for regular judicial circuits and separate courts. The exchequer was hearing civil cases in addition to its financial duties, which led to the emergence of the court of common pleas in the following reign. One of the most remarkable and important procedural manuals of the Middle Ages emerged from the pen of an exchequer official in the late 1170s. Richard FitzNigel, treasurer from 1159 to 1196, was the son of his predecessor. His *Dialogue of the Exchequer* is a treatise examining the workings of the exchequer, set out as a series of questions and answers between teacher and student. Meanwhile, Henry's final justiciar, Ranulf Glanvill, wrote a hugely influential book at the very end of the reign which is the oldest surviving codification of English law: the *Treatise on the Laws and Customs of the Kingdom of England.* Of course, these had nothing to do with Henry directly, but they demonstrate the culture he had created. There seems no reason to doubt that Henry himself was interested in and drove judicial and institutional reform, but he also had the ability to choose high-quality officials and delegate the minutiae to them. If he was an engaged and active king, Henry was not an interfering one, trusting his officials to do their jobs.

In the spring of 1177, Henry summoned the Welsh leaders to Geddington in Northamptonshire, and subsequently to Oxford. There, they swore homage and oaths to keep the peace. Having asserted his claims over Wales, Henry's thoughts turned back across the Channel. He had neither forgotten nor forgiven Louis VII's role in the events of 1173–74. Dynastic concerns also played a part. During 1177, the Young King's wife, Margaret, heavily pregnant, returned to her father's court in Paris, where she gave birth to a son, William. The infant lived just a few days and was the only child Henry and Margaret were to have. In June 1177, the month of William's birth and death, Henry demanded that Louis hand his daughter Margaret the whole Vexin (the French part as well as the Norman) as her dowry for marrying the younger Henry. He further asked Louis that he honour the marriage which had been arranged in 1169 between another daughter, Alice, and Henry's son Richard, giving Alice the city of Bourges as her dowry. These claims were unjustified, but they did persuade Louis to the negotiating table. Overseen by a papal legate, the discussions on the Norman border led to the Treaty of Ivry. Louis and Henry agreed to respect each other's rights, and to prepare a joint crusade to Palestine.

Louis VII was now in his late fifties and had been king for more than four decades. His mind had turned to the future and he wanted to avoid unnecessary conflict with his English counterpart. He planned to have his son Philip crowned on his fourteenth birthday in August 1179, but when Philip fell seriously ill, the ceremony had to be postponed. Advised in a dream to seek the aid of Thomas Becket, Louis crossed the Channel, the only time a reigning French monarch voluntarily visited England in the entire Middle Ages. He was hosted by Henry for five days and went to Canterbury to pray at Becket's shrine. However, he suffered a stroke on the way home and was an invalid until he died in September 1180. Philip meanwhile recovered and was duly crowned at Reims on 1 November 1179, although Louis' condition meant that a power struggle had broken out at the French court. The intervention of Henry II was sought. Once Louis had died, the new Philip II renewed the Treaty of Ivry.

In 1182, Henry was once again called on to arbitrate by Philip, this time in a dispute with the Count of Flanders. Just shy of his 49th birthday, before setting sail Henry made his last will, copies of which were sent to Canterbury Cathedral and the treasury at Westminster. It made the kind of conventional bequests to religious orders and foundations expected of a royal will, although a considerable number were to benefit. In France, he oversaw the peace negotiations between France and Flanders, in the presence of four kings: England's two Henrys, Philip of France and William of Scotland. Henry was the undisputed elder statesman of Europe, but the last seven years of his life and reign were to be ones of bitterness and recrimination.

Once more, the cause was his children. Henry had learned some of the lessons of the 1173–74 revolt and was allowing his sons a greater share in government, at least in the case of those who could be trusted. Geoffrey governed Brittany himself from 1181. Richard was still allowed a free hand in Aquitaine, although his methods were often seen as oppressive and Henry had to help him crush a rebellion in the Limousin in 1182. The problem was the Young King. He lacked both the interest and the talent that his two younger brothers had when it came to governance, but he still resented the fact that he had nowhere to administer himself. He had been summoned to assist Richard and the king at the siege of Perigord in 1182, but made his way very slowly and arrived late. He gave his father no cause to trust him in the way Richard and Geoffrey had earned their roles, but at the end of the summer the younger Henry demanded control of Normandy or another territory. Unsurprisingly, and with some justice, Henry II refused, at which point his son once more headed for Paris in high dudgeon. The king offered Henry a very generous allowance for him and his wife, which seemed to resolve things, at least until drama erupted at the Christmas court at Caen.

It was here that William Marshal, who had been tutoring young Henry in military skill and chivalry, burst in, angry and indignant. Marshal was to provide loyal service to Henry II and both his sons as kings, and after John's tumultuous death to be instrumental in securing the throne for Henry III. Right now, however, he demanded to be allowed to challenge the Young King to trial by combat, to prove his innocence against charges that he had been having an affair with Henry's wife, Margaret. The king refused and banished Marshal, but he was concerned about what he strongly suspected his son and his household were up to. Everyone moved on to Le Mans, where the younger Henry and Richard had a huge falling out. Henry admitted that he had been plotting with the Aquitanian barons against his brother. The king now tried to resolve matters. At Angers, the next destination of what was turning into a touring family circus, he made his three older sons swear obedience to him and peace with each other. Unwisely, however, he also ordered Richard and Geoffrey to swear allegiance to their oldest brother as the future head of the family. An outraged Richard refused, was reluctantly persuaded to agree, then furiously refused again when the Young King demanded he take the oath on the gospels. Richard argued that he held Aquitaine of Eleanor, not Henry II, and stormed back there. The younger Henry convinced his father to allow him to go to make peace with Richard, but once safely out of Anjou he conspired with the barons in Aquitaine to remove Richard.

Not trusting his son, the older Henry had followed him towards Limoges, ostensibly to provide backup if needed. Here, in February 1183, the king learned about the latest betrayal. He discovered the Young King engaged in discussions with rebel leaders inside Limoges, and was appalled when he was fired on, an arrow tearing through his cloak. Worse still, Geoffrey then arrived with a group of Breton mercenaries to support his brother. Geoffrey had a reputation for hypocrisy and double-dealing, but it was still a blow to the king, as was the appearance of King Philip and the intervention of other local rulers. However, if there were disconcerting echoes of 1173, a decade later there was one critical difference. Henry II had Richard on his side, and in these circumstances, the militaristic Richard was easily the best son to have fighting for him. He obliterated Geoffrey's Bretons and laid siege to Limoges.

The younger Henry escaped Limoges and headed to Angoulême, before commencing a rather aimless wander south. He must have realised that he was no match for the combined forces of his father and brother. Moreover, he had no money to pay his troops, so he took to plundering monasteries to do so. Chroniclers saw what happened next as God's judgement for such iniquity. In late May, he contracted dysentery, and by early June it was obvious that he was dying. The last rites were administered and Henry sent a message to his father requesting a visit. The king was understandably suspicious of a trap. Instead of going in person, he sent his son a ring as a token of forgiveness. The Young King died at Martel on 11 June. His body was taken north towards Rouen, but when it reached Le Mans, a group of citizens abducted the body and buried it in the cathedral. The outraged citizens of Rouen demanded that the body be exhumed and handed over to them, but it was more than a month before the Dean of Rouen and the Archbishop of Canterbury managed to reclaim the body for burial in Rouen Cathedral on 22 July.

The news of his eldest son's death had been broken to Henry II while he was still at the siege of Limoges. His son had caused him no end of trouble, but the king was grief-stricken; all the evidence is that despite everything, he had genuinely loved the young Henry. Yet he was too seasoned a monarch not to attend to duty, with Limoges surrendering on 24 June. Philip and the other regional rulers no longer had a cause to support and had to withdraw, leaving Henry and Richard to easily clear up the last of the revolt. Yet with the younger Henry removed from the picture, the result was not peace but a reconfiguration of the family feud. In September 1183, Richard was designated as heir to England, Normandy and Anjou as the oldest surviving son. Clumsily, though, Henry told him to surrender Aquitaine so that could become John's inheritance. Culturally a southerner, who had invested considerable effort into the duchy, Richard asked for time to consider, then escaped and rode to Poitou, sending a message back to his father that he would never surrender Aquitaine.

When Henry returned to England in the summer of 1184, Geoffrey talked John into an invasion of Poitou. Richard retaliated by attacking Brittany. Exasperated by his endlessly squabbling sons, Henry ordered them all to England, where in December he forced them into a public peace agreement. Troublesome offspring notwithstanding, Henry remained the elder statesman of Europe, 'held in high regard internationally, evidenced by the willingness of former enemies to turn to him for mediation'.[16] In January 1185, he was visited at Reading by the Patriarch of Jerusalem, who laid the keys to the city and the Church of the Holy Sepulchre at Henry's feet, offering him the throne of Jerusalem. The armies of Saladin were threatening the Crusader states in the Holy Land, where the heirless King Baldwin IV was suffering from leprosy. Count Fulk V of Anjou had abdicated his Angevin title to become King of Jerusalem half a century earlier, so there was logic in approaching his grandson, the most renowned sovereign of the age. Henry, however, had no desire to abandon his hard-won lands for a risky venture in the Middle East. He was a shrewd politician and did not share Richard's lust for romantic adventures, especially while the future division of his lands remained unresolved. The king summoned a council to meet at Clerkenwell in March 1185, where his barons reminded him of his coronation oath to protect his kingdom and subjects; if they had not been told what to say by the king, they must have known what he wanted to hear. Instead, they advised him to consult the King of France about a crusade. Between them, they agreed to offer men and money to the patriarch.

In the spring of 1185, John was dispatched on an expedition to Ireland, while Henry crossed back to Normandy to deal with reports that Richard was mustering troops. For the first time since he had put her under house arrest in England more than a decade earlier, Henry took Eleanor across the Channel with him. Her presence was necessary for the king's strategy, to demand that Richard surrender Aquitaine back to his mother. In May, Richard did just that, yielding to his father in yet another peace accord. Yet each of these family agreements simply papered over cracks which were growing far too large to conceal. Worse, Philip Augustus was asserting himself as King of France, his aim of increasing French power leading him to interfere more in Henry's domains.

Initially, Philip was not hostile to Henry. He sought his aid against Flanders more than once, and when Henry was ill at the end of 1185, Philip visited him and stayed three days. When the two met at Gisors, a traditional venue for conferences between the King of France and Duke of Normandy, in March 1186, things still seemed amicable. Philip agreed that the Norman Vexin, the dowry of the Young King's widow Margaret, should now be given to Alice when she married Richard. For Henry, this was an incentive to make the marriage happen, but he still held back. Richard was sent to deal with the troublesome Count of Toulouse, while Henry and Eleanor sailed back to England. Geoffrey now became the problem. He headed to Paris and spent the summer at Philip's court, conspiring with the French king. But on 19 August, during a Parisian tournament, he fell from his horse and was trampled to death. Philip's grief was allegedly such that he had to be forcibly restrained from throwing himself into the grave when Geoffrey was buried in Notre-Dame Cathedral.

Philip turned against Henry with steely determination. In September, the French king demanded that Brittany be entrusted to him, along with custody of Geoffrey's two daughters. A truce was agreed between Henry and Philip in October 1186, but it lasted only until the next round of discussions in February 1187. Here, Philip complained that Alice had still not married Richard. There were persistent rumours that Henry, in whose care Alice had been since the betrothal, had seduced her, which gave Philip an excuse to demand that Henry hand back the Norman Vexin. Both sides brought mercenaries into the area and began arresting foreigners in their territories. When Philip took an army into the county of Berry, it provoked Henry into raising his own army. In late June 1187, the two armies faced each other outside Châteauroux. War was averted by Henry diplomatically backing down.

Meanwhile, another war temporarily necessitated cooperation between Henry and Philip. The Patriarch of Jerusalem's fears had come true. On 4 July 1187, the forces of the kingdom of Jerusalem had suffered a catastrophic defeat to Saladin's army at the Battle of Hattin. Jerusalem fell in October. In response, Richard impulsively took the cross (signed up as a crusader) in November. The kings of England and France reflected rather more on the question before following suit in January 1188. Henry held a council at Le Mans in late January, with a similar meeting in England, at Geddington, on 11 February. These councils set out the conditions for the crusaders and organised the raising of money. Both Henry and Philip imposed a tax on subjects who did not enlist as crusaders, known as the Saladin tithe. Plenty of men took the cross, but there was considerable resentment about the tax from those who did not. The fate of the Saladin tithe demonstrated the differing control of the two kings in their realms. In France, Philip was forced to abandon collection and apologise. In England, Henry successfully collected the money. We have a vivid account of the atmosphere of this time in Gerald of Wales' *The Journey Through Wales*, in which he describes travelling through his homeland in the company of Archbishop Baldwin of Canterbury, trying to rouse crusaders. In the end, Henry would die before he could go on crusade and Richard would be the beneficiary of his father's efficiency.

This was a distraction from the problems faced by an ailing king, confronted with a determined King of France and a gullible, treacherous son. Philip was dripping poison into Richard's ear and Richard was susceptible. Philip had succeeded brilliantly in separating Richard from Henry. This was shown when Richard gave credence to baseless rumours that his father had provoked Lusignan rebellion against his rule. He defeated them, but then turned his sights once more on the Count of Toulouse, against the agreement reached at Châteauroux. Cunningly, Philip complained to Henry, even though Richard was responsible. In June 1188, Philip invaded Berry and seized some Aquitanian lands. Henry retaliated against French lands, forcing Philip to withdraw, but repeated negotiations proved futile. In a fit of temper in August, Philip ordered the tree at Gisors, marking the place where French king and Norman duke traditionally met to negotiate, to be cut down.

In October, Richard offered to submit to the judgement of the French court in the struggle against Toulouse. Rumours began to circulate that Henry was intending to give the English crown to John. How much substance these rumours had is very hard to determine, but the idea is certainly not impossible. At a further meeting in November, Richard demanded that Henry confirm his succession to the kingdom. When the king refused, Richard did homage to Philip for Normandy and Aquitaine, and the conference broke up in chaos.

Henry was unwell in early 1189, but it suited Philip to treat this illness as a cover, and he started raiding along the border, supported by the treacherous Richard, who seemed to have little awareness that he was assisting in the attempted destruction of his own inheritance. Negotiations at Easter achieved nothing, and it took a papal legate (wanting to end the fighting so the promised crusade could begin) to bring the warring kings together. At the meeting, around Pentecost, Philip demanded that Richard and Alice should marry, that Richard should be confirmed in the succession, and that John should join the crusade. Richard added that he would only go on crusade if John went too. No agreement was reached and the sides descended back into war. Richard and Philip took arms against Henry, and on 12 June they forced him to flee from Le Mans. Henry watched his birthplace go up in flames. He raged angrily at God, purportedly telling the almighty that since he had taken the city the king loved most in all the world, Henry would withhold the thing God most loved: his soul. Richard pursued Henry, only to encounter an ambush from the king's rearguard. The less than courageous Lionheart pleaded with William Marshal not to kill him. Marshal, unlike Richard a man of honour who understood what loyalty was, purportedly replied, 'I won't kill you – I'll leave that to the Devil!'[17] The combined forces of Philip and Richard now swept through Maine and Anjou. There was resistance, but Henry was now clearly struggling. After Tours fell on 3 July, Henry had little option but to agree to a meeting. He had to be held up on his horse, even the sceptical Philip shocked into offering him a cloak to sit on the ground, an offer the proud old king refused. He had no choice but to consent to a list of humiliating concessions.

At the end of the meeting, Henry exchanged the kiss of peace with Richard, but as he did so apparently whispered into his son's ear a prayer that he would not die before he had his revenge. Despite this typically spirited utterance, the exhausted king knew he was dying. He retreated to Chinon Castle and demanded the names of the other rebels. When the first name he was given was that of John, Henry refused to hear any more and turned to the wall in despair. For forty years, since he had first landed in England to challenge Stephen as a headstrong teenager, his will and energy had been legendary, but the betrayal of his favourite son broke him. In lucid moments over the next few hours, he had himself carried into the chapel and set down in front of the high altar. He made his confession and took communion. The following day, 6 July 1189, King Henry II died in the chapel at the age of 56. The final words attributed to him were ones of defeat: 'shame, shame on a conquered king'.

The king's attendants stripped the body and made off with what they could, afraid they would get nothing from the new king. The ever-dependable William Marshal took charge. The next day, once some suitable regalia had been acquired or fashioned and the king appropriately attired, Henry's body was carried along the banks of the River Vienne to Fontevraud Abbey. He originally intended to be buried at Grandmont Abbey, but it would have been impractical in the circumstances. He had also been a notable patron of Fontevraud, where he had finally asked to be interred. Richard, having refused to believe the reports that his father was close to death, arrived at the abbey at nightfall on 7 July and stood looking at Henry's body, staying as long as it took to say the Lord's Prayer, then walked out to get on with claiming his inheritance. The next day, the Archbishop of Tours presided over the funeral.

It fell to Eleanor to support her two remaining sons and deal with Richard getting a taste of his own medicine from John. Once she had reconciled her sons, after Richard returned from crusading, Eleanor retired to Fontevraud in 1194. Richard's death in 1199 forced her to emerge from seclusion to aid John, before she returned to retirement in Fontevraud, where she died and was buried in April 1204. She was responsible for the effigies which were erected over the tombs of Henry II and Richard I, with a matching one placed over her own grave. The trio lay together in a peace they had rarely shared in life, later joined by John's second wife, Isabella of Angoulême. She had originally been buried in the abbey churchyard, but when Henry III visited he had his mother moved inside to join his grandparents and uncle, and a suitable effigy commissioned. After his death in 1272, Henry's own heart was sent to join this family mausoleum.[18]

This tranquillity in death would not last. Fontevraud was sacked during the French Wars of Religion, and again during the French Revolution. The royal remains were dug up and thrown into the river by rabid revolutionaries, the effigies consigned to the crypt, where they were rediscovered in 1816. King Louis-Philippe (1830–48) had them sent to Versailles, which he was turning into a huge museum of French history. After his abdication, the effigies were returned to Fontevraud. In the new spirit of Anglo-French royal cooperation of the later nineteenth century, Emperor Napoleon III (1852–70) offered them to Queen Victoria, but although she initially accepted, the idea faced strong opposition in France and was dropped. England had to make do with full-scale, painted plaster casts of Henry II's and Richard I's effigies, created in the 1850s and given to the Victoria and Albert Museum in 1938. Napoleon I had turned Fontevraud, including the church, into a prison, but by the early twentieth century work was underway to restore the historic church interior, even though the prison remained in the surrounding buildings until the 1960s. The Plantagenet effigies were reinstalled in the abbey church, finally returned to more or less their original locations in the 1990s.[19] Even if his mortal remains no longer lie beneath, the tomb of Henry of Anjou once more rests in the peace of an Angevin abbey, the calm stillness of his effigy a strange contrast to the restless turbulence of his life.

Henry through the Centuries

> Such is Fortune, alas, alas! From such a height! She brought so great a man so low – a king of such might, so honoured and so feared! It's well worth asking how a lofty prince, possessed of such a vast domain, could have fallen so soon into poverty. Once Fortune turned against him, rightly or wrongly, She wouldn't let him be till She'd delivered him to Death; and once Death had him in Her clutches She stripped him of all power, of everything.[20]

Henry II died in defeat and failure. A great king brought low by the judgement of God was a theme developed with glee by Gerald of Wales, who saw 'the saddest state of the unfortunate man is that he once knew happiness'.[21] He was an embittered witness, annoyed by Henry's refusal to confirm his election as Bishop of St Davids. Even in his bitterness, however, Gerald recognised Henry was a 'great prince', indeed would argue that 'if he had to the very end remained a chosen vessel to the Lord and had turned himself to his obedience, he would have been beyond comparison among the princes of this world for his many natural gifts'. In his less aggrieved moments, Gerald had much that was positive to say about the king, especially after encountering his successors; the chronicler is scathing about the ingratitude and faults of Henry's sons.

Indeed, although Henry died unpopular, opinions about him changed quickly as people experienced the rule of his son. Writing under Richard, less than a decade later, William of Newburgh declared of Henry that 'the experience of present evils has revived the memory of his good deeds, and the man, who in his own time was hated by almost all men, is now declared to have been an excellent and profitable prince'. For all the sadness of his end, for all they deplored some of his vices, the chroniclers recognised that Henry had been a great king who had transformed the English monarchy after the troubled years under Stephen. His final years saw a chronicle output unequalled in the Middle Ages: 'If we can speak of a golden age of historiography in England it was probably the last twenty years of the twelfth century'.[22] Thanks to the sketches of courtiers like Gerald of Wales and Walter Map, Henry comes alive like no other king before him and few other (medieval) ones after him. True, their character sketches draw heavily on Biblical, classical and mythological models,[23] but Henry emerges as far more than a stereotype.

Simply reading these descriptions of his life can be exhausting, and it is easy to see why men were astounded at the boundless energy of this king: 'he taxed his body with excessive hardship, thus, as it were, fomenting civil war in his own person'. Here was a man 'distinguished for many virtues and infamous for some vices'. The vices Gerald and Walter record are relatively few: Henry had a reputation as someone who did not keep his word; he could be slow in settling his subjects' business when they came to him in person. Interestingly, with more than a hint of misogyny, Walter blamed Henry's mother, Matilda: 'I confidently impute to her teaching all his unattractive qualities'. For Gerald, Henry's policy towards the Church was an additional cause for censure (not least because he thought the king talked too much during Mass, when he should presumably have been listening to the sermons of Welsh archdeacons), as were his extramarital affairs. Walter was more concerned that 'impatient of repose, he did not scruple to disturb almost half Christendom'.

Yet the scales tipped heavily in favour of the positive. Here was a king who for Gerald was 'easy of access and condescending, pliant and witty, second to none in politeness, whatever thoughts he might conceal within himself', while Walter echoed that he was a man 'lacking no courtesy [...] easy of approach, modest and humble'. He was a 'prince of great eloquence [...] polished in letters', one 'well-read to a degree both seemly and profitable'. Notably, Henry 'dreaded the doubtful arbitrament of war, and with supreme wisdom [...] he essayed every method before resorting to arms'; Henry II never had the reckless love of fighting for the sake of fighting that characterised his successor. Alongside this, 'in making laws and in ordering the affairs of government, he showed discrimination, and was clever in devising new and undiscovered legal procedures'. Gerald wrote that Henry was 'liberal beyond comparison in almsgiving', which is echoed by Walter. In contrast to his two sons, Henry 'never laid any grievous burden on his realm of England or on his lands overseas, until the recent tithe for the purpose of an expedition to Jerusalem, which was in fact also levied in other countries'. Though he exploited his rights to the full and restored the power of the English Crown, becoming wealthy, Henry was never guilty of the relentless financial oppressions of Richard I and John. Henry hoarded wealth but knew how to give generously. For the churchmen of the twelfth century, this generosity was extended too far: 'to the perfidious nation and enemy of Christians, the Jews, he gave undue encouragement on account of the liberal and advantageous terms he received from their usurious transactions'. One cause of the violence which broke out after his death was resentment at Henry's protection of the Jewish community. Even if he was not motivated by modern ideas of religious tolerance, we would today commend what the chroniclers of his own day condemned.

In contrast to other periods, the chroniclers were not primarily monks. All were still in holy orders of some form, but several were active participants in the history about which they wrote. Ralph of Diceto, Dean of St Paul's Cathedral, and Roger of Howden were both in Henry's service, and their histories are full of documents and details.[24] On the other hand, there were monks who managed to write works of great help to later historians without leaving the safety of their religious houses, such as William of Newburgh and Gervase of Canterbury. There has been plenty of debate about what prompted such a rich era of historical writing, but the fascination of the times and the king were surely a factor.

Naturally, the spectre of Thomas Becket was omnipresent in discussions of Henry II's reputation. Plenty of clerical writers told the tale of a blameless, saintly archbishop cut down by an evil, tyrannous king; more than a dozen hagiographical lives were published in the first twenty years after Becket's death. His cult became one of the most successful of the Middle Ages. Yet from very early on, opinions were never quite as universally in favour of Becket as is often portrayed. There is a record of a debate in Paris, written in the early thirteenth century.

> The blessed Thomas, archbishop of Canterbury, who in our time fought even to the death, did not shine with miracles, and after his death there was much disagreement about him. Some said that he was a damnable traitor to his kingdom; others that as a defender of the Church he was a martyr. This question was debated at Paris among the masters. For master Roger, judging the constancy of the man as obstinacy, he had been worthy of death, even if not such a death.[25]

There were views from Becket's own lifetime, not least the acerbic writings of Bishop Gilbert Foliot, which could be used to construct an alternative narrative to the hagiographies. Ralph of Diceto and William of Newburgh both offer versions which argue the king had a just cause. One line of argument ran that if the rebellion of 1173–74 was Henry's punishment, his ultimate triumph after praying at Becket's tomb showed that the saint had forgiven him. For Ralph, the capture of the King of Scotland was evidence of divine forgiveness that allowed Henry to triumph once more.

Later medieval chroniclers could do little to improve on the wealth of writing from Henry's own time. Not until three centuries later did a new approach take shape. Polydore Vergil, in the early Tudor period, was exercised by Henry's infidelities. Soon, however, such judgements would seem distinctly quaint – Henry VIII made it hard to dwell upon the adulteries of kings. When it came to the Reformation, the struggle between Henry II and Becket was deployed as a precedent in the debates over Church-state relations, and Henry VIII and Thomas Cromwell were only ever going to take one side. In 1532, Archbishop William Warham of Canterbury cited the death of Henry II as an example of what happened to princes who acted against the Church. Henry VIII had a different view: 'Becket was seen as "stubbornly" withstanding "the wholesome laws" that Henry II, the king's "most noble progenitor", had established against the "enormities" of the clergy'; indeed, the archbishop was a defender of 'the detestable and unlawful liberties of the church nothing concerning the common weal but only the part of the clergy', and who was basically responsible for his own death.[26] Becket's shrine was comprehensively destroyed and his feast days removed from the liturgical calendar. Interestingly, there seems to have been little overt resistance to the suppression of the cult, as in missals 'the feasts of St Thomas Becket appear more aggressively and more consistently defaced than the prayers for the pope'.[27] The king who had opposed Becket and sought to challenge the power of the Church was naturally seen as a good, strong monarch, although never attained the same heroic status as his son John in Reformation eyes.

The view of Henry remained largely positive throughout the seventeenth and eighteenth centuries. In the years of Church of England dominance, Protestant writers had little good to say about Becket, but plenty of positive things to write about the king. Under James I, Samuel Daniel would write about 'this mighty King of England' who was 'the greatest of all the Christian World in his time, or that the Kingdom ever saw'.[28] Yet there were still echoes of Gerald of Wales' moralising to be found. In 1700, James Tyrrell would see Henry as 'a Valiant and Magnanimous King, but an unfaithful Husband, an unkind Brother, and a Father too jealous of his Power; And if he had not stained his own House with Adulteries, and perhaps with Incests […] he had been an Excellent Man, and an Incomparable Prince'.[29] On the other hand, David Hume's Enlightenment views were entirely unconcerned by questions of adultery. In a short, matter-of-fact paragraph at the end of his chapter on Henry II, he wrongly attributes the king's illegitimate sons to Rosamund de Clifford, but then makes a sensible point ignored by many ever since: 'All the other circumstances of the story commonly told of that lady seem to be fabulous'.[30] Hume's Henry was 'the greatest prince of his time for wisdom, virtue, and abilities, and the most powerful in extent of dominion of all those who had ever filled the throne of England'. In a similar vein was the first biography of the king in 1767 by George, Lord Lyttelton. A man at the very heart of the British establishment, who served as chancellor of the exchequer under the Duke of Newcastle in 1755–56, Lyttelton went to lengths to demonstrate Henry's greatness that weary even the most committed reader; the intimidating four volumes expanded to six by the third edition in 1788. Lyttelton makes no attempt to hide his admiration for the king, concluding with a comparison between Henry I and Henry II in which the first Henry is judged to have had 'a temper of king more exempt from disorderly passions' and 'fewer faults', but the second ultimately emerges the better through his 'more generous and more benignant nature' and 'greater virtues', 'a cordial love of his people and an active benevolence towards all mankind'.[31]

One reason Hume and Lyttelton so admired Henry was that he stood up to Becket, who emerges as the villain standing for all that eighteenth-century sceptics and establishment men alike despised: papal pretensions and the evils of the Roman Church. Moreover, their Henry was a king for an increasingly imperialistic Britain in the mid-eighteenth century. Hume and Lyttelton wrote as Britain defeated (Roman Catholic) France in the Seven Years' War and asserted her dominance in North America. Henry represented a king who had opposed the iniquities of both France and papacy, establishing a proto-empire, an ideal historical example for the mood of the times. That he was both French and Catholic himself was conveniently overlooked.

Writing about Henry in this era was heavily influenced by religious affiliation. To Church of England historians, Henry's inconvenient Catholicism could be sidestepped by making him an honorary Anglican who had opposed the machinations of Rome. To Roman Catholic historians, he was the evil tyrant who had killed their sainted Becket. A taste of this can be found in the long title of Joseph Berington's 1793 volume: *The History of the Reign of Henry the Second, and of Richard and John, his Sons; with the Events of the Period, from 1154 to 1216. In which Thomas à Becket is vindicated from the Attacks of George Lord Lyttelton.* In the nineteenth century, with Catholic emancipation and the Oxford Movement, Roman Catholics and high Church Anglicans followed in this vein. The age of John Keble and John Henry Newman was not willing to be dismissive of the 'superstitions' of the twelfth-century Church in the same way as David Hume. William Cobbett, a radical involved in campaigning for the Great Reform Act of 1832, argued that Becket died as a martyr to English liberty, trying to preserve Magna Carta. This was a mightily impressive achievement for someone who died forty-five years before Magna Carta first appeared, but it showed the extent to which Henry's reign had become a polemical weapon. Becket was not the only, never mind the most important aspect of that reign, but it suited the writers of late Hanoverian Britain to make him so. Many of the arguments had little to do with Henry and Becket and an awful lot to do with divisions in nineteenth-century churchmanship.[32]

Moreover, Henry became caught in the tides of nineteenth-century nationalism. During and after the Napoleonic Wars, as Britain and France asserted their imperial dreams, it was hard to conceive of a past where the English Channel might not have been a barrier between the two nations. Then and ever since, too many have assumed that the modern versions of France and England/Britain are somehow inevitable. To English writers, Henry became a French tyrant, a foreign oppressor who prevented the English enjoying their inherent liberties. While relatively few French writers bothered with the Plantagenets at this time, seeing an inconvenient interlude in the French national story, those who did saw Henry as a different kind of foreign tyrant. In 1825, Augustine Thierry opined that 'although the husband of the Count of Poitou, Henry was a stranger to the Poitevins, and they suffered from seeing officers of a foreign race violate or destroy their country's customs by ordinances written in Angevin or Norman language'.[33] Such was the genius of Henry II: too French for the English, too English for the French, too Norman for the Poitevins, too Angevin for the Normans. In reflecting nineteenth-century nationalist prejudices, historians never considered that people just might not have liked strong rulers who interfered with their lives, or that the modern form of nation states is neither inevitable nor permanent.

Much of this reassessment of Henry was based on the voluminous records, now becoming available in printed form, about the Becket affair. Once historians began to delve into the administrative records, things began to change. A thawing and warming of relations between France and the United Kingdom allowed records from both sides of the Channel to be printed. Chronicles, exchequer records and all other manner of sources were edited for publication. It is no surprise that while they disapproved of his promiscuity, Henry II was greatly admired by Victorian constitutional historians. William Stubbs edited several of the chronicles for Henry's reign, producing editions which are still used by historians today. For Stubbs, Henry was 'the first of the three great kings who have left on the constitution indelible marks of their own individuality' (with Edward I and Henry VIII). He viewed him as 'a young man of keen bright intellect, patient, laborious, methodical; ambitious within certain well-defined limits, tenacious of power, ingenious even to minuteness in expedients, prompt and energetic in execution; at once unscrupulous and cautious'. The bishop cannot help himself deploring the later years when Henry 'gave way to violent passion and degrading licence', but even here cannot hide his admiration that 'his private vices made no mark on his public career, and he continued to the last a most industrious, active, and business-like king'. Henry was 'one of the greatest politicians of his time', to the extent that 'the whole of the foreign relations of England during the middle ages may be traced directly and distinctly to the result of his alliances and his enmities'. Although he thought the king was hardly motivated by any sense of great benevolence, Stubbs opines that the 'English nation may gratefully recognise his merit as a ruler in the vastness of the benefits that resulted from the labours even of a selfish life'. The Victorian moralist disapproves of Henry's later private life, but the Victorian constitutionalist approves wholeheartedly of his legal and administrative efforts. It is the latter which wins out in a portrait which, while not without caveats, is ultimately favourable.[34]

Historians still struggled to present a rounded picture of the cross-Channel king. One sentence in Stubbs' assessment perhaps betrays why Henry became something of an overlooked figure, at least outside specialist circles, in the twentieth century: 'There was nothing in him of the hero, and of the patriot scarcely more than an almost instinctive knowledge of the needs of his people'. While the reign was breathless and full of incident, there is no single event which could be used to create later legends, nothing like Agincourt for Henry V. Henry II was a very competent and largely successful warrior, but he never fought a major battle which has lodged in popular consciousness, so has never been viewed in heroic terms. Unlike Edward III and Henry V, whose victories against the French feed a historical Francophobia on the northern shore of the Channel, Henry II is impossible to appropriate for English nationalism, for all eighteenth- and early twentieth-century historians tried to turn him into a proto-imperialist. He may have been King of England, but he was culturally French and spent more time on the Continent than in England, governing and seeking to expand his territories there. A man at home on both sides of the Channel, whose interests were in the consolidation and growth of his own dynasty rather than any 'national' advancement, does not fit easily into a nationalistic telling of the English story. Consequently, despite the importance and undoubted fascination of his reign, Henry has never been a popular subject for biographers. Perhaps the scale of the task is too daunting. To write the story of his reign is incredibly difficult, for so much happened simultaneously in so many different places that a straightforward narrative is impossible. It requires some courage, or perhaps foolhardiness, to take on the challenge of such a reign.

One who did was L. F. Salzmann. His relatively short biography of Henry appeared in 1914. His summing up is a good insight into Henry's nature.

> We see a strong, clear-headed man, controlling his emotions but occasionally clearing off accumulations of irritation and annoyance by tremendous outbursts of mad rage; a methodical man with a keen sense of justice, but arbitrary and unscrupulous; a skilled general who never engaged in warfare if it could be avoided; a keen and restless sportsman with a sense of humour and a passion for literature; a free-thinking adulterer with a genuine appreciation of purity and true religion; a king who could manage the affairs of half-a-dozen principalities but could not rule his own house; an acute judge of men, who lavished affection and benefits upon ungrateful and unworthy sons; a mass of contradictions; in other words, an entirely human man.[35]

As the twentieth century progressed, historians struggled to move on from the Victorian Henry. General histories were largely admiring. John Harvey thought he could 'discern a very human soul, a very real man and true King, who despite the faults of his temper and his passions was a loyal friend and pillar of justice, the greatest of his time'.[36] For A. L. Poole, he was a 'remarkable character' whose 'natural abilities, his immense capacity for work, his sound business instinct, his accessibility combined with an easy faculty for remembering facts, all contributed to make him a statesman and diplomat of the first rank'.[37] Winston Churchill, having proclaimed Henry II's reign 'one of the most pregnant and decisive' in English history, went on to give an appreciative, rather jingoistic and decidedly idiosyncratic account. It leads to a bizarre and not entirely clear comparison with bishops being sent to concentration camps as proof that modern civilisation is no better than Henry's age, before disposing of the eighteen years after Becket's death ('years of glory') in a single page.[38] A much more critical note was sounded by the acerbic J. E. A. Jolliffe, who in the course of some extremely long sentences returned to the nineteenth-century view of Henry the foreign plunderer.[39] One important contribution came from a Frenchman, Jacques Boussard, although *Le Gouvernement d'Henri II Plantegenêt* [sic] (*The Government of Henry II Plantagenet*) is restricted to readers of French with a serious interest and a lot of time on their hands. (In French writing, Henry II is always given the additional 'Plantagenet' to distinguish him from the sixteenth-century Henry II of France.)

A revived interest in Henry II saw two biographies published in the 1960s. John T. Appleby began by describing Henry as 'the greatest king of the Europe of his time and one of the greatest kings that England has ever had'. His remains a readable account of the reign, providing the kind of solid narrative framework which modern biographers often eschew when it comes to Henry. He notes that 'such talk as is here written was reported by Henry's contemporaries', although his translations have a dated feel and are used rather uncritically. In the end, the conclusion is ambiguously positive: if 'in centuries to come men would count his name among the greatest kings of England', it would be because they 'would forget his faults, his passionate temper, his cruelties and injustices to his wife, his sons, and his subjects'. Instead, they would remember that 'he had rescued England from feudal anarchy and established a strong and capable government of almost unbelievable efficiency' which was 'manned by servants so well trained in law and finance and administration that it could function smoothly for ten years with hardly a glance from his successor' (the focus of Appleby's next work).[40] Richard Barber's *Henry Plantagenet* has aged better than Appleby. It is another good narrative, giving due weight to the years after Becket. If not uncritical, Barber is certainly admiring. That Henry 'chose to devote both his power and his energy to a better ordering of the affairs of his realm, rather than to frivolous wars and crusaders or to exploitation and tyranny [...] was his outstanding virtue'.[41] Some would view this as too generous, but it is notable that both Appleby and Barber link their praise of Henry to barbed, veiled comments about Richard I. In 1978, Barber also wrote *The Devil's Crown* to accompany the BBC drama series of the same name, a shorter and well-illustrated volume covering all three Angevin kings. He returned to Henry II in the Penguin Monarchs series in 2015, but the shorter format and lack of any new thinking makes this a less satisfying work.

1973 saw the most significant single contribution to twentieth-century scholarship about Henry's reign, with the publication of W. L. Warren's *Henry II.* It is a majestic work on an epic scale, which despite its daunting thickness is engaging and well-crafted. It immediately became the standard biography and remains so more than half a century later. Part of its lasting impact is the memorable way in which Warren wrote.

> Great men, be they barons or bishops, quailed before his sudden surges of anger, and ran for harbour like fishing smacks before a storm. [...] The abbot of St Albans, a man accustomed to exercising dictatorial authority, behaved like a schoolboy who had stolen apples when the young king asked to see the charters and bulls of privilege which the abbey claimed. [...] Beside Henry of Anjou, even the young Henry of Anjou, everyone else seemed small. The only man who ever dared to pit his will against Henry's was Archbishop Becket, and even he soon lost his nerve and fled across the sea to fight the king from a safer distance.

It is a book in which people come alive – Becket was described as a 'theological dinosaur', although Warren later repented of the phrase. Even if some parts are necessarily technical, Warren did his best to make the technicalities as accessible as possible. And although it relies upon a knowledge of the ancient Greek poet Homer that can no longer be taken for granted, it is hard to better Warren's admiring conclusion, which captures well the picture which emerges from the twelfth-century chronicles.

> He overflowed the bounds of ordinary men's comprehension. He bewildered them with his contradictory qualities. He baffled them by his disregard of contemporary wisdom. He astonished them by his tireless energy and resilience. He attempted the impossible and achieved the improbable. It seemed hardly credible to contemporaries that he should weather so many storms, and even escape shipwreck on the rocks strewn by Thomas Becket. Yet Henry of Anjou was not superhuman. He had all the frailties and passions of ordinary men – but in larger measure. He was no god-like Achilles, either in valour or in wrath; but in cunning and ingenuity, in fortitude and courage, he stands not far below the subtle-souled Odysseus.[42]

Although Warren was criticised in some quarters for being too sympathetic to Henry, overall he did his job too well. Some interpretations have changed since 1973, but the work still stands as a masterly starting point for study of the king. No scholar has dared to produce an academic biography since – Warren remains *the* standard work on Henry II. Most subsequent work on Henry has been specialised. Overwhelmingly, the popular interest has been on Thomas Becket and how Henry fits into that story. Tellingly, the Ladybird children's book, published in the same year as Warren's biography, is entitled *Henry II and Thomas Becket*. There have been several good biographies of Becket, most notably the carefully-studied one by Frank Barlow and the racier volume by John Guy.[43] Anne Duggan examined Becket's reputation and produced a critical modern edition of his correspondence, while Michael Staunton produced an excellent, affordable translation of some of the key sources for the archbishop's life.[44] Eleanor of Aquitaine has likewise been the subject of plenty of modern biographies, albeit of very variable quality, the best being those of Jean Flori and Ralph V. Turner.[45] Even the Young King has been the subject of Matthew Strickland's excellent biography, which seeks to rescue him from the negative reputation he has generally had since his death.[46]

The non-specialist is not nearly so well served when it comes to Henry, which says much about where popular interest in the reign lies. Most of the available chronicles are still those published in the nineteenth century, supplemented by the excellent new, multi-volume edition of his letters and charters,[47] all inaccessible to a general reader not schooled in Latin or medieval French and without very deep pockets. There has been a lot of additional research, but most of this is found in academic journals and books. The best drawing together of the post-Warren research is a 2007 volume of essays, *Henry II: New Interpretations*.

While his later years attract less interest, two volumes have examined how Henry initially established control in England. Emilie Amt observed how many 'pitfalls faced Henry II in his new kingdom in the first few years of his reign', pitfalls 'of daunting complexity and difficulty, requiring both great skill on the king's part and the cooperation of many other individuals and groups'. 'Henry had a household of loyal and familiar followers whom he would want to reward now that he had won his crown; many a king, in his position, would have been tempted to rely on such men in governing the new kingdom. Henry knew better than to follow the latter course, and he found plenty of men willing and competent to serve him in local government.' Looking at his national and financial reforms show a clear 'relationship between the presence of the king in his kingdom and the activities of the exchequer', as 'the king exerted a lively influence on the exchequer when he was in the country but did not, in this early period, when he was overseas'. Her research supports the image of an activist, reforming king: 'Henry II's pledge to restore the days of his grandfather was couched in grand and formulaic language and evoked awed memories, but his real achievement in that respect was accomplished in large part by the daily grind of exchequer business, the accumulation of small debts for small benefits, the careful husbanding of resources and the piecemeal extension of royal claims'. The verdict is that the 'achievement of Henry II in addressing these problems is considerable', as the 'kingdom he ruled in 1159 was stable and well governed; the uncertainties and distresses of 1149 had faded into the past'.[48]

Graeme J. White, meanwhile, traced the story into the 1160s. Examining how Henry reestablished royal control in the 1150s, he explored how this gave way to a reforming impetus in the following decade, as Henry began to make efforts to transform access to justice. Crucially, it challenged those who had questioned how interested Henry really was in judicial reform and whether he was personally responsible: 'if further proof were needed as to the king's importance as the driving force behind reform, one has only to look at his itinerary'. There is a strong correlation between times when Henry was in either England or Normandy, and when reforms were enacted in each place. If 'detailed framing of legislation, as well as its implementation, was probably left to others', Henry was the one who pressed the issue and saw his role as fount of justice as one which 'chimed in with his more general concern to uphold the dignity of kingship'.[49]

While Henry's judicial successes have long been recognised, little attention has been paid to his success as a soldier. Noting how Henry has traditionally been overlooked as a warrior, or even seen not to be one at all, John D. Hosler demonstrates that Henry was not only a soldier, but a very successful one.

> In the context of twelfth-century warfare, Henry II was an extraordinarily successful leader. [...] He was never entirely successful in his strategic pursuits. His trust in family loyalty was his weakness, and an inability to bring his enemies to battle ultimately checked his ability to dominate them fully. When hostilities did commence, however, Henry was usually the victor.[50]

An appendix on Henry's military campaigns runs to three pages, with one almost every year of the reign until 1174.

Recent scholarship has moved on from seeing Henry as a king of England who happened to be a French duke and count (or vice-versa). British and French scholars now work together to examine the Angevin 'empire' in more realistic terms, a group of territories which had a common cross-Channel ruler. Since the 1980s, there have been conferences which bring together scholars from both sides of the Channel to engage in study of the broader picture. Several works have addressed the broader Angevin 'empire' and dynasty, including those by John Gillingham, Martin Aurell and Jean Favier, while significant volumes have appeared looking at the wider Plantagenet court. More specialised works have looked at Normandy and Brittany, although there is no similar synthesis for Aquitaine. Many of the French sites associated with the Plantagenet kings see the tourist potential in promoting these links; the Pays de la Loire Region, the modern administrative unit incorporating the old counties of Anjou and Maine, recently funded a lavishly-illustrated colour volume about the Angevin kings and their family in the Loire Valley. A similar volume, under the same lead author, soon followed for Maine.[51]

The twenty-first century has seen popular biographers start to take an interest in Henry. In *Henri II Plantagenêt*, Christian Thevenot interweaved a brisk, staccato narrative of the reign with a wider look at the architecture and cultural context. For readers of French, it contains a lot of helpful information lacking in most books about Henry, such as a list and map of where he held his Christmas courts, and diagrams of some of the complex feudal links. Overall, the verdict comes down strongly in Henry's favour.

> Few reigns have been so full of transformations and improvements as that of Henry II Plantagenet. Not only was England born with him, but the political, administrative, civil, fiscal and legal solutions which he implemented have been copied and still affect most of the Anglo-Saxon countries of the Commonwealth, including on the other side of the earth, such as New Zealand.

Many historians would be sceptical about the direct link between Henry II and the twenty-first century government in Wellington, but this reflects a lingering tradition of Henry as the founder of the English legal tradition. Unsurprisingly, Thevenot concludes positively.

> One can only admire the genius and the courage of a man torn between two heritages, the one continental, the other insular, crossing the Channel twenty-eight times, running all his life from one end of his 'space' to the other and succeeding in such a task.

Seeing the dispute with Becket as Henry's one real failure, Thevenot nevertheless argues that the Church-state conflict has never been resolved, and that even today, 'nowhere in the world is there true independence between the two domains, neither in England nor in our hypocritical republics'.[52] While this might say rather more about his approach to his native France than Henry II, it is a valid point. Neither in an England with an established Church demanding exemption from equality legislation, nor in the avowedly secular United States where religion nevertheless exercises such a massive influence, has the conflict ever really been resolved. The arguments and contexts may have changed, but the underlying theme of Henry II versus Thomas Becket continues to be played out more than eight centuries later.

Claudia Gold presents Henry as 'the classic tragic hero', his the 'story of a great hero whose life traces an arc from ascent, to glory, to defeat, and who is brought down by a tragic flaw in his own character'.[53] She consciously echoes the prominent place given to the wheel of fortune theme found in several of the twelfth-century chronicles. This is fair enough, but there is little appreciation of the realities of the twelfth century or critical engagement with the chroniclers, especially when it comes to religion. It is simply not possible to impose the secular framework of the twenty-first century into the twelfth and make Henry some kind of anachronistic hero for the cause. It may be that someone other than the author wrote the blurb on the dust jacket that includes the cringeworthy notion that Henry 'pursued the tenets of reason over religious faith'. He did no such thing; that is a post-Enlightenment line of thinking. Yet Gold herself is responsible for the worst example of anachronistic modernism in the book, which concerns Henry's 'threat' to convert to Islam in 1168.

This was developed in a February 2020 article for *BBC History Magazine*, which prompted a considerable degree of ill-founded excitement, showing how dangerous it is to try to fit twelfth-century people into twenty-first-century moulds.

The 'threat' is an indirect one reported in a letter by one third party to another, not found in any letter from Henry to the Pope, which immediately raises questions. If there is any truth in the report, then it must surely be taken as a joke or a letting off of steam by the king that merits no more than an aside about Henry's sense of humour or temper. It is absolutely inconceivable that a king in the twelfth century, the crusading era when Christian control of the Holy Land was so precarious, would have ever entertained such an idea. Henry was a competent realist who would have known how quickly that would lose him his throne, even in the unlikely event such a thought ever really crossed his mind. Yet it is treated seriously by Gold as an excuse to prove the real point that she wishes to make.

> Although a superstitious man, Henry was not a religious one. The chroniclers railed against his lack of piety, blaming that he never sat still in church. Henry found himself so bored at mass that he doodled and met petitioners. His threat to convert to Islam is indicative of how little religion meant to him…'[54]

This is nonsense. It imposes modern ideas about superstition onto medieval religious practice and totally fails to analyse the chronicles on their own terms. It is true enough that they complained about his restlessness at Mass, but Henry was generally restless at everything, and the Victorian notion of everyone sitting still and dutifully listening was not one familiar to the colourful liturgical practice of the Middle Ages. In general, Henry was viewed as more than conventionally pious. One reason that the murder of Becket caused such shock was that Henry was not seen as impious; had it been John, it would not have stunned people in anything like the same way. Such an approach is the latest example of trying to appropriate the Henry-Becket conflict for modern ends, making Henry a hero of modern secularism. Any work which tries to divorce the king from his Christian context, or impugn his own faith, says far more about modern agendas than about Henry II.

Much more satisfactory is the most recent popular biography, by Matthew Lewis, which takes the unusual form of being an explicit dual biography of Henry and Eleanor. This means that the story begins and ends with Eleanor. While she is still absent from the story for pages at a time, reflecting the fact that the (male) chroniclers were not often interested in what she was doing, Lewis successfully charts Henry's reign as a political partnership between the two. As he notes, the depth and complexity of their relationship is often 'obscured by the tales of Eleanor's disloyalty and Henry's imprisonment of her that begins to sound more like a Grimm fairy tale'. Yet importantly, after everything, 'she elected to be buried beside Henry', not 'in her beloved Poitiers, nor even in Aquitaine, but at Henry's side'.[55] Placing Eleanor, so often overlooked, at the centre of the story in this way is a reminder of how crucial she was to Henry, how they continued to spend time together and how he used her in diplomacy even after their estrangement. This helps to support Lewis' positive view of the king in a lively yet sensible narrative.

These popular works notwithstanding, Henry is still far better known in the academic world than in popular consciousness. He did make it onto the list of 100 Greatest Britons in the 2002 BBC poll, but at number ninety-two, directly below Donald Campbell. If historians recognise the importance of his reign, that is not reflected in a popular context where he rates immediately below a twentieth-century water speed record challenger.

Henry in Popular Culture

Study of a map reveals where the popular sympathy of the centuries lies. There are several streets or squares in France named after Eleanor of Aquitaine, along with schools, the maternity unit at Bordeaux Hospital and (bizarrely) several veterinary clinics. Thomas Becket lends his name to churches and schools on both sides of the Channel. In contrast, just one street, the rue Henri II Plantagenêt in Rouen, has been named for their adversary, and even this lies outside the historic centre of the Norman capital. 'Rue Plantagenêt' is found more generically in several French towns, notably Angers and Chinon, as well as rather more unexpectedly in Montreal in Canada (where the context suggests no connection to the Angevins), but with no direct reference to Henry. The scattering of equivalent street names in England and Wales similarly have no apparent link to the twelfth-century kings.

No Shakespeare or Marlowe gave Henry a place upon the Tudor stage, although it was during the sixteenth century that stories and ballads about Rosamund de Clifford gained in popularity. It was the Victorians who first began to tackle his reign in fictional form. The place of Henry II as a player in the Thomas Becket story, rather than an interesting protagonist in his own right, is most prominent in the work of two of English literature's most notable poets and playwrights. Alfred, Lord Tennyson wrote an 1884 play, *Becket*, which in 1924 was made into a silent film at Cricklewood Studios. Despite being by a poet laureate, the work is no *Charge of the Light Brigade*. Perhaps the kindest thing to say about the play is that it has been forgotten with good cause. Much better, from a literary standpoint, is T. S. Eliot's verse play, *Murder in the Cathedral*, first performed in Canterbury Cathedral in 1935. It is entirely set in December 1170, with the murder based on the eyewitness account of Edward Grim. The play was one of the earliest BBC television broadcasts in 1936, which brought Robert Speaight to prominence as Becket, and was also made into a film, including Eliot's voice, which won an award for best production design at the 1951 Venice Film Festival. The Italians were clearly impressed, since in 1958 an operatic adaption, *Assassinio nella cattedrale*, premiered at La Scala in Milan in 1958. However, while it is a fine work, Henry himself is absent from the cast list.

The king featured prominently in Jean Anouilh's *Becket*, first performed in Paris in 1959, with English versions following on Broadway (starring Laurence Olivier and Anthony Quinn) and in the West End (with Christopher Plummer and Eric Porter). This French play was the basis for the more famous 1964 film, in which

Richard Burton as Becket was cast opposite Peter O'Toole as Henry II. O'Toole also took the part of Henry in the 1968 film version of *The Lion in Winter*, the star-studded cast including Katherine Hepburn (Eleanor of Aquitaine) and Anthony Hopkins (Richard the Lionheart). Originally a play by James Goldman which premiered in New York in 1966, the story was unusual for being set in Henry's later years; it focuses on the family squabbles at Christmas 1183. Oddly, although it was staged several times in the United States and even at the Vienna English Theatre in 1979, the play was not professionally performed in the UK until 1994. The film, however, was a commercial success which won three Oscars, including Best Adapted Screenplay. In 2003, a new version was released as a TV film, starring Patrick Stewart and Glenn Close as Henry and Eleanor.

In 1978, the BBC screened a thirteen-part dramatisation of the Angevin era, with Henry II played by Brian Cox. Even though Henry's reign was longer than those of both his sons combined, he is dead by episode six, and the Becket story occupies a fair amount of the episodes covering his time on the throne. It is an enjoyable example of historical drama that would probably not be commissioned in a twenty-first century saturated with reality shows and talent contests. Otherwise, however, Henry has never been a subject to interest filmmakers, and his rare appearances are not memorable. A bizarre 2013 film, *Richard the Lionheart*, has Henry choose Richard as his heir and send him off to a prison where the captives must continually fight enemies and overcome challenges to survive, some unfathomable twelfth-century remix of *Battle Royale*. As one reviewer aptly summarised this travesty of history and cinema, the only redeeming feature is that they managed to get the names of Henry's sons correct. Scarcely better is the director's 2015 follow up, *Richard the Lionheart: Rebellion*, which liberally reinterprets the 1173–74 war.

Henry is not an especially popular subject for authors of historical fiction, although there are a few epic works which reflect an epic reign. Few of the earlier novels have stood the test of time and most are largely forgotten today. Thomas Miller's *Fair Rosamund; or The Days of King Henry II* (1839) is practically unreadable, but is an early work in a continuing tradition of writing about Rosamund, who seems to bewitch novelists as much as they claim she bewitched the king. The handful of late nineteenth- and early-twentieth-century novels touching on Henry attracts few modern readers. There has, however, been a revival of interest in the period since the 1970s.

Jean Plaidy, one of the pen names of Eleanor Alice Hibbert, wrote a series of fourteen novels on the Plantagenet monarchy. The first, *Plantagenet Prelude* (1976), begins with the story of Eleanor and Louis VII and moves through the Henry and Becket years, while *The Revolt of the Eaglets* (1977) starts with Becket's murder and ends with Henry's death. Plaidy interweaves the complex rivalries between English and French royal families, along with the internecine strife within Henry's own family. While inevitable liberties are taken to enhance the Rosamund de Clifford story, the basic chronology is otherwise followed fairly accurately. Yet Henry does not emerge as a very attractive character. He is a schemer, one who is totally insincere in his repentance for Becket's death. Eleanor is just as much a schemer in her encouragement of her sons and Henry's opponents. The problem is that neither they, nor anyone else, really develops into a character with whom the reader can sympathise or emphasise, which makes what should be a dramatic tale feel rather leaden.

Far more satisfying are the novels of Sharon Penman. *The Plantagenet Trilogy* which begins with *When Christ and His Saints Slept* (1994) continues through *Time and Chance* (2002) to *Devil's Brood* (2008). The first covers the civil war of Stephen's reign and Henry's successful fight for the throne, the second the period from 1156 to Henry's embarkation for Ireland in 1171, and the third the remainder of the reign. Penman treats her characters sympathetically, and Henry is neither saint nor demon, but rather the complicated man who has perplexed so many historians. The trilogy delves into episodes many novelists ignore, such as Henry's relationship with his brother Geoffrey, and is easily one of the best fictionalisations of the reign. Henry's last days are captured well, and there is a poignant scene when Eleanor is brought the news of his death, in which the conflicting good and bad memories swirl around her mind, the memories of a man who was so kind and so cruel, who treated her so well and so badly: 'We've schemed and fought and loved until we are so entangled in years and minds that there is no way to set us free. God help us both, Harry, for we will never be rid of each other. Not even death will do that'.[56] Rather than the tired, easy story of love turned to hate, any novelist trying to portray something of the reality of the relationship between Henry II and Eleanor of Aquitaine has to account for why she chose to construct the effigy for and be buried with the husband who had imprisoned her for years. Penman understands the contradictions and complexities of such relationships, which is why her version of the story succeeds where so many others fall flat.

Henry appears more obliquely as a minor character in novels focussed on others, usually Eleanor, although almost no one can resist including sensational elements of the Rosamund de Clifford legend in the story. Elizabeth Chadwick has set several books in the reign where Henry has a part, including *The Time of Singing* (2008), *The Winter Crown* (2014) and *The Irish Princess* (2019). Henry's role is limited, as he is viewed in relation to those who must necessarily relate to him as king. Chadwick does not seem to be particularly enamoured by the king, who comes across as somewhat sex-crazed and prone to seducing young women. It is a case which could be built on a reading of certain chronicles, but it is not an especially fair or rounded portrayal.

An intriguing twist on the reign is provided by Diana Norman in *Fitzempress' Law* (1980). Three youths are sent back in time, where they find themselves confronting Henry II's new legal system. It's something of a niche novel – the process and writ of *mort d'ancestor* is not something which grips the average reader of historical fiction – but it is an unusual angle. More appealing is a series, set in Henry II's reign, written by Norman under the pen name Ariana Franklin.[57] The main character, a Sicilian named Adelia, is a female doctor, accompanied by a Muslim, Mansur, who for appearances' sake must pretend to be the actual doctor schooled in Arab medicine, with Adelia posing as the interpreter and assistant. After she successfully helps the king with a case, Henry forces her to stay in England. At first, something jars about the idea of a Muslim and a Sicilian woman existing peacefully in twelfth-century England, although the novels draw out the prejudice they face. But on deeper reflection, this is a very clever portrait that says something important about the king. As the novels demonstrate well, Henry's primary interest was in how useful a person could be to him. He was far too intelligent to avoid employing someone for prejudicial reasons if they could serve his purposes; his was a reign in which the Jewish community flourished because he was much more interested in their economic productivity than in the Church's antisemitic doctrines. Henry was an equal opportunities exploiter. The first novel, indeed, translates disturbing but real events into a fictional setting. The monstrous promotion of child 'martyrs' as victims of Jewish ritual murders did indeed happen, with the example of William of Norwich (1144) the basis for the story set in Cambridge in *Mistress of the Art of Death*.[58] It explores to good effect a theme not usually given much prominence by historians.

The Assassin's Prayer has Adelia accompany Henry's daughter, Joanna, to Sicily for her marriage to King William. In one scene early on, at a banquet in Southampton Castle prior to Joanna's party setting sail, Henry keeps the whole assembly on their feet as he attends to business, everyone else restlessly watching the food go cold. It is hard to tell whether this is the king's famed indifference to luxury and dining, or whether he is being intentionally mischievous, which is a convincing echo of a king who could drive his court to distraction in such ways. The king who exhausts the world around him is found throughout the series.

> In your impatience, you outstrip everybody – your wife, your son, Becket – and expect them to love you. They are people of our time and you are not; you see beyond the boundaries they set; you see me for what I am and use me for your advantage; you see Jews, women, even heretics, as human beings and use them for your advantage; you envisage justice, toleration, unattainable things. Of course nobody keeps up with you.

This might be a little too generous, especially when it comes to heretics, but the basic idea stands.

It is this ability to capture something of the king and his world which makes the series such enjoyable reading even for the historian who might wince at the factual liberties taken. There are plenty of invented details, yet something rings true about the overall picture. Henry comes to life here in a way that is perhaps more 'realistic' than in many a history book, colourful and larger than life, a powerful ruler: 'Henry Plantagenet's was the ultimate command; you could squirm under it, but you disobeyed it at your peril'. He has the presence of a king, majestic yet also intensely human, overbearing yet captivating: 'although the Plantagenet was a crafty, hot-tempered, parsimonious swine, he was still a great king, a very great king, and not just because he ruled an empire stretching from the Scottish border to the Pyrenees'. Adelia is often frustrated and infuriated by Henry – 'there was still an underlying savagery that marked him as a man of his time when she'd hoped for more' – yet cannot help admiring and liking him in spite of herself: 'when the Church would have put Adelia on trial [...] it was this busy king who'd found time to step in and exonerate her'. Indeed, she has absolutely no doubt of her loyalties in the clash between Church and state, king and 'that intransigent archbishop [who] had deliberately sought martyrdom by opposing every reasonable reform Henry had tried to introduce for his people's good'.

It is Henry's humanity and energy, for all those faults, which captivates Adelia, giving him a majesty which defies his appearance.

> The ruler of an empire that stretched from the border of Scotland to the Pyrenees was in worn hunting leathers – she'd never seen him in anything else; few people did. He walked with the rolling bandiness of a man who spent more time in the saddle than out of it. Not tall, not handsome, nothing to distinguish him except an energy that drew the eye. When Henry Plantagenet was in the room, nobody looked anywhere else.

And something is captured of the tempestuous relationship between Henry and Eleanor, lovers and rivals at war, never quite able to let one another go.

> Adelia, crouched in the stern, saw two people who had known one another too well and too long to surprise each other now; they had conceived eight children and seen one of them die, they'd ruled great countries together, made laws together, put down rebellions together, quarrelled, laughed and loved together, and if, now, all that had ended in a metaphorical attempt to disembowel each other, it was still in their eyes and hung in the air between them.

For all the liberties taken with the background details, this series is probably the most sympathetic and satisfying portrayal of Henry in fiction, one which echoes true to the chronicles of his own time but presents him for a modern readership.

Away from fiction, the ubiquitous king, renowned for his unexpected materialisations, made his most unpredictable appearance in Washington, DC on 8 June 2017. On that day, former FBI Director James B. Comey was testifying before the US Senate Intelligence Committee, being questioned by Maine's Senator Angus King.

> **Senator King.** But when you get a – when a President of the United States in the Oval Office says something like 'I hope' or 'I suggest' or 'would you', do you take that as a directive?

> **Director Comey.** Yes. Yes, it rings in my ear as kind of, 'Will no one rid me of this meddlesome priest?'
>
> **Senator King.** I was just going to quote that. In 1170, December 29, Henry II said, 'Who will rid me of this meddlesome priest?' And then, the next day he was killed, Thomas a Becket. That's exactly the same situation. We're thinking along the same lines.[59]

The use of 'meddlesome' rather than the more usual 'turbulent' is interesting. We do not actually know what Henry said, and it almost certainly was not that in either form, but 'meddlesome' is perhaps telling about the relationship between Comey and the president who fired him, Donald Trump. The comparison – between a king who enhanced the Crown and transformed access to justice, and a president who degraded his office and showed disdain for the rule of law – is a deeply unfair one. Nevertheless, it is a reminder of the place Henry occupies in the popular mind of the Anglophone world. Never mind that in a loose sense, the origins of parts of legal process in the United States can be traced to him. For those on Capitol Hill that day, he was simply Thomas Becket's opponent.

Verdict

> All the world's a stage,
> And all the men and women merely players;
> They have their exits and their entrances,
> And one man in his time plays many parts,
> His acts being seven ages.

So wrote Shakespeare in *As You Like It*. Henry II acted his part on a vast stage, entering and exiting in the most unpredictable places at times he was least expected, constantly refusing to follow anyone else's scripts. And while he was indeed a man of many parts, it is impossible to separate them into stages. His life, as so many have despairingly realised when trying to narrate it, can seem a mass of contradictions. He was a successful soldier and general who has left almost no impression on popular imagination as a warrior. As far as possible he avoided warfare, yet he spent long periods successfully asserting his rule by force where necessary. He transformed access to justice and oversaw some of the most significant legal reforms in English history, while doing his best to deprive other rulers and vassals of their rights. He was a deeply religious man who opposed ecclesiastical encroachment and was at least partly responsible for one of the most infamous clerical murders of the Middle Ages. A statesman of international reputation to whom others turned to help with their problems, he was unable to keep his own family in order. Having been so successful against so many odds for so long, he died a failure, defeated and reviled.

His cause is not helped by the way in which he constantly appeared involved in everything, everywhere. He was ubiquitous. Few kings have had the ability to exhaust others like Henry II. Even reading about him more than eight centuries later is exhausting. He has modern students in England pouring over maps, trying to work out where exactly the Norman Vexin is located, or how he managed to travel between places at a rate that would put some twenty-first-century train services to shame. It is simply impossible to write a straightforward narrative of his life, which is why so few have ever tried. Yet it is that very complexity which makes Henry an appealing character. If at times he appeared (and appears) superhuman, at others he comes across as profoundly and intensely human, with all the contradictions that entails. He had a hot temper, he could on occasion be spiteful and petty and vindictive, he had a cruel streak of humour, and he could certainly be avaricious and dishonest. But he could inspire loyalty, he could be amazingly generous, he found and trusted the right people, he was not remotely pompous, and he could laugh at himself. Of the three Angevin kings, Henry comes across as easily the most likeable.

Likeable kings did not always make good kings. What is remarkable is that he was also by far the most successful of the trio, and one of the most successful kings of the Middle Ages, if not in English history. Stephen too had been a likeable man, distinctly more even-tempered than Henry, but his reign was a failure. Henry benefitted to an extent from the war-weariness he inherited, but we should not downplay his achievement. He comes across as a powerful personality, even as a young man, who could eschew some of the pomp of monarchy because no one doubted his kingly presence. For all the efforts of some modern historians to temper his achievements, Henry II was largely a success. After years of civil war under his predecessor, in which the authority and reach of the Crown had been sorely tested and diminished, Henry rapidly and effectively reasserted royal power. He was an energetic, active king whose vision was broad and influence widespread. Militarily, he was extraordinarily successful for much of his reign, strong but with a merciful streak sorely lacking in his sons. While his motives might be debated, there is no doubt that he transformed the legal system, gave speedier access to justice to many, and introduced the measures which would develop into what became common law.

Naturally he did not do all this himself or create every point of detail, but it is ludicrous to expect that he would. A king had far too many responsibilities to engage in such minutiae. Henry's genius was in recognising the need for reform and in choosing the right men to achieve his aims. Kingship was about leading and inspiring, something at which Henry excelled until the final years of his reign. The chroniclers realised that they were living in interesting times that were worthy of recording. It matters little exactly how interested the king was personally in learning and literature. The point is that he created a culture in which they could flourish, one which compares favourably with other, less tolerant times. It is worth reiterating, in view of the terrible events of the century after his death, the relative tolerance Henry showed to the Jewish communities of England. While he was a pious Christian, we might well doubt how committed he was to the crusading ideals which so bewitched his son. Henry was far more concerned with pragmatic rule in Western Europe than quixotic adventures in the Middle East. He had commendably little interest in proving his Christian virtues by slaughtering Jews and Muslims.

Of course, there were negatives. Henry reigned for thirty-five years and, despite occasional doubts about the fact, was only human. There were bound to be mistakes. At times he overreached himself. His behaviour towards Eleanor was at times appalling, although she was by no means an entirely innocent party. He was certainly not a faithful husband, but we might question why Henry would be singled out for that failing in the history of a monarchy which includes Henry I, Edward IV, Henry VIII, Charles II and William IV. The greatest error, of course, was Becket. The twenty-first century might have considerable sympathy with the king, whose cause was (in modern terms) far more just than the archbishop's. Even contemporaries recognised the injustice of allowing criminal clergy to evade sanction. Thomas Becket could (and did) try anyone's patience, and he may well have courted martyrdom. Nevertheless, Henry allowed himself to be goaded, he behaved pettily and at times extremely badly, and there can be no excusing the murder, which destroyed Henry's efforts by allowing the Church to bury any attempt at reform with the archbishop. On the other hand, his contrition seems to have been genuine, and that he was able to survive the incident is testimony to his strength, to the fact that everyone's life became much easier without Becket, and to the fact that his Christian credentials were not generally in question. The tragedy is that it is this episode which has, unfairly and disproportionately, come to define Henry in popular memory.

Henry has faced criticism for not handing over more responsibility to his sons. It is not entirely fair, given the latitude he gave Richard in Aquitaine and, to a lesser extent, Geoffrey in Brittany. Henry's various schemes show that he never envisaged his 'empire' surviving him as a single territorial unit. Yet Henry, that shrewdest judge of men who employed so many fine servants to enact his will, knew what his sons were like. They would have tested the patience of the most placid of saints, which Henry certainly was not. They had inherited his temper and cunning, but little of his administrative ability. All were incorrigible schemers, always dissatisfied with their own lot and seeking more. It was fortunate that by the time Henry actually did die, there were only two sons left and that one of these was John. The younger Henry, despite attempts to rehabilitate him, seems to have had little aptitude for governing, let alone an interest in doing so. Geoffrey is the most enigmatic of the four, but what we do know suggests a slippery, unpleasant young man who would never have successfully governed on his father's scale. Richard and John were actually tested as kings, and both fell short. It seems unlikely that trusting any of his sons more would have made much difference. Henry cannot be judged a failure by their failings.

Overall, those who regard Henry as one of England's greatest kings have a valid point. It is not simply that he successfully managed to hold together such a diverse range of territories for so long. Nor is it just that he restored and then enhanced the authority of the English crown, doing so at 21 while simultaneously ruling half of France. His greatness lies in more than surviving setbacks which would have destroyed others, from Becket to the rebellion of 1173–74. Transforming the legal system and the exchequer plays a big part, but nor is that on its own sufficient. It is the sum of all these elements, that Henry managed to hold all this together until almost the very end. England and the continental lands did not change around him, they changed because of him, because he was a king who actively pursued that change and had both the determination and ability to bring it about. England in 1189 was a very different place to the war-ravaged, broken country Henry had inherited, able to survive the almost total absence of his successor, and that was the legacy of a great king.

Chapter 2

Richard I: A Wild King?

> Richard I was a hairy King with a Lion's Heart; he went roaring about the Desert making ferocious attacks on the Saladins and the Paladins, and was thus a very romantic King.[1]

> [Philip II of France was] a contrast to Richard the Lionheart, who to modern minds would appear as a kind of maniac, frequently risking his life for the least cause, and who eventually not surprisingly perished as a result of carelessness.[2]

The legend of Richard the Lionheart is encapsulated by his name. He is the only sovereign to be honoured with a statue outside the Houses of Parliament. That Richard has such a major place in English consciousness is baffling. He was on the throne for just under a decade, of which he spent a mere six months in England. Indeed, as king, Richard was a prisoner in the Holy Roman Empire for more time than he was in England. Sellar and Yeatman continued their satirical summary of the reign, 'Whenever he returned to England he always set out again immediately for the Mediterranean and was therefore known as Richard Gare de Lyon'. There is more than a grain of truth in the idea that Richard visited England only to leave. The statue outside parliament appears ironic, honouring the king who spent the smallest proportion of his reign in his realm of any English sovereign. During the nineteenth and twentieth centuries, his near-permanent absence and perceived plundering of the country's wealth brought criticism from many historians. For all that, he remains the romantic hero in popular thought, who appears to save the day from his evil brother in the Robin Hood stories. Tales of his feats and his struggle against Saladin have turned him into a legend as much as a historical figure. Does the actual king really deserve to be so lauded and counted among the great monarchs of English history?

Richard's Life and Reign

Richard was born in Oxford on 8 September 1157, the third son of Henry II and Eleanor of Aquitaine. He was not even 2 when his father engaged him to the daughter of the Count of Barcelona in 1159. It was a short-lived betrothal, the name of Richard's intended bride never recorded. He spent his early years in England, not seeing much of his parents; as king, Richard would give his wet nurse a generous pension. Eleanor took him to Normandy in 1165. In 1169, Richard swore homage to Louis VII of France as successor to the duchy of Aquitaine, and was betrothed to Louis' daughter, Alice.

Aquitaine would be Richard's preoccupation for the next twenty years, especially after he was installed as duke in 1172. His story intertwines with that of his father in the previous chapter. Despite the endless squabbles with his brothers that exasperated Henry, in the decade 1174–83 Richard caused Henry fewest problems and was most useful to his father. He made Aquitaine his home and forged a reputation as a warrior. Much of his time was spent in warfare, keeping order and subduing repeated rebellions. Problems with his father resurfaced in 1183. After the death of the Young King, Richard resented Henry II's clumsy attempts to make him hand over Aquitaine to his youngest brother, John, in return for succession to the young Henry's former inheritance. He refused to yield. Following the death of his brother Geoffrey in 1186, Richard assumed he now had a right to inherit all his father's titles. By declining to make a clear statement on the succession, Henry frustrated both Richard and John.

Philip II of France needed a new member of the family to take Geoffrey's place as treacherous conspirator against Henry. From 1187, Philip skilfully courted Richard and turned him into a useful ally. In Paris, the closeness of Philip and Richard was noted, Philip seducing Richard, but not in a sexual sense. He wanted an agent in his plans to diminish Angevin power in France. Despite their new alliance, however, Richard resisted Philip's attempts to conclude the marriage with Alice. At a conference in November 1188 involving Richard, Henry and Philip, Henry refused to confirm Richard as his heir in England. Richard promptly swore allegiance to Philip for all his French territories. From then on, Richard aided Philip in the fight against his father, who by 1189 was a sick man. Philip and Richard swept into Maine and Anjou, forcing Henry into humiliating concessions shortly before he died on 6 July. Richard shed no tears over his father's death. His visit to see the body seems to have been to check he was really dead. After a stay measured in seconds rather than minutes, he left.

An old superstition held a body would bleed in the presence of its murderer and some chroniclers noted that in Richard's presence, blood began to gush from the corpse's nose. Although Richard had not literally murdered Henry, he had hounded a sick man to his death. The continual treachery and rebelliousness of his sons finally wore Henry down. John has been heavily criticised for treachery and colluding with Philip against his brother, but he learnt the art of betrayal from Richard. The man who was so easily swayed by Philip into conniving with an enemy king and taking arms against his father could hardly complain if his brother proved equally susceptible to Philip's wiles. Moreover, John was not alone in believing that Richard could not expect absolute loyalty himself. Richard had seemed oblivious to the fact that he was helping Philip destroy his inheritance and creating many of the problems he then had to address as king.

For now, all passed smoothly into Richard's hands. He had already been invested as Duke of Aquitaine and fifteen years of unrelenting struggle meant the duchy was largely subdued. He stayed a short while in Anjou, where there was no tradition of an investiture ceremony. He did not need to hurry to Normandy and England; his father's competent servants would prepare his succession. His mother Eleanor, immediately released by Richard from captivity, took charge in England. Richard was invested as Duke of Normandy on 20 July, then met briefly with Philip II, transformed overnight from friend into foe, on the Franco-Norman border to resolve outstanding issues, including Richard's marriage to Philip's sister, Alice. Richard insincerely promised it would go ahead. Sailing to England from Barfleur, he landed at Portsmouth on 13 August. He met his mother at Winchester before proceeding to his coronation in Westminster Abbey, which began his reign on Sunday, 3 September 1189.

The festivities were marred by the first in a series of ugly antisemitic incidents. Richard had banned women and Jews from the coronation banquet. Nevertheless, a Jewish group tried to gain entry to present him with gifts. They were expelled by the king's sergeants, which a crowd took as licence to attack them. Soon Londoners were roaming the streets hunting Jews, offering them a choice between conversion and death, looting and burning their houses. While Richard ordered punishment for the perpetrators, he was not nearly as strong a protector of the Jews as his father. Once the king left the country, anti-Jewish riots and further attacks occurred elsewhere, including Lincoln, Norwich and Stamford. The worst episode took place in York on 16 March 1190. Around 150 Jews, including women and children, had been trapped inside the keep of York Castle by an angry mob. Rather than face slaughter or forced baptism, most committed suicide; the few who did not were murdered. Most of those responsible escaped to Scotland and the punishments meted out were light. Although the stone building which survives on the site as Clifford's Tower dates from the following century, it stands as a symbol of one of the darkest days in English history.[3] Richard was not directly responsible, but his crusading zeal created a climate in which antisemitism flourished. A crusade made people aware of non-Christians among them; with no Muslim communities in England, Jews became an easy target. In that sense, Richard does stand condemned. Henry II would not have tolerated such atrocities.

The exact physical appearance of the new king is unknown. Descriptions from after his death portray him as taller than average, elegantly built although more corpulent in later years. He had inherited his father's red hair and temper. Just shy of 31, he probably seemed a dynamic change after Henry's thirty-five-year reign, but he was a stranger to the English. He had rarely visited since leaving as a boy in 1165. His heart belonged south of the Loire; he spoke the northern French of his father and the southern Occitan of his mother. The quality of his Latin is debatable, but unlike Henry, he seems to have had no knowledge of English. Nevertheless, he was now ruler of lands stretching from the Scottish border to the Pyrenees, with their myriad of languages and dialects, although he wanted to leave them all as soon as possible. Back in 1187, Richard had taken the cross and he was now eager to go on crusade and heroically reclaim the Holy Land.

He began his reign with liberal grants. Henry II had started by revoking Stephen's grants, to reassert control and reclaim lost royal lands and revenues. So successful had Henry been that Richard was able to dispense considerable patronage, although risked undoing his father's work by the amount he granted away. The principal beneficiary was his surviving brother, John. Their half-brother, Geoffrey, posed a challenge since he had been zealously loyal to Henry. Recognising his abilities and determination, and fearing these might develop into ambition, Richard had Geoffrey elected Archbishop of York. Henry II had earlier appointed him Bishop of Lincoln, but Geoffrey had had no desire to enter holy orders. Richard gave him no choice. One modern historian notes that Richard may have further tried to tame Geoffrey by making York Minster 'a hornet's nest of jealous churchmen'.[4]

While the dependable William Marshal received generous grants, most had to pay for anything they desired. Richard wanted to leave swiftly, but crusading was an expensive business. The Saladin tithe, a crusading tax levied late in Henry II's reign, combined with his father's treasury, gave Richard a good start, but was insufficient. To make up the shortfall, the king began to sell everything he could conceivably auction off and plenty previously inconceivable: offices, castles, lordships, lands and anything which could fetch a price were all sold. As one chronicler sardonically noted, the king 'most obligingly unburdened all those whose money was a burden to them, and he gave to whomever he pleased whatever powers and possessions they chose'.[5] Richard jested that he would sell London itself if only he could find a buyer. In fairness, Richard does appear to have sold offices only to those competent to fill them, but the venal precedent set was a dangerous one. To many at the time, and plenty of historians since, none of this suggested a king with any interest in his kingdom as anything other than a bank.

The longstanding dispute between the Archbishop of Canterbury and the monks of his cathedral was resolved. New bishops were appointed.[6] As well as setting ecclesiastical affairs in order, Richard wanted to ensure that his territories would not be threatened by rebellious family members during his absence. Given his own history of disloyalty, it is easy to see why he was worried. The untrustworthy John was made to swear an oath not to enter England while Richard was away. Eleanor had John released from the oath, but subsequent events proved Richard's misgivings fully justified. The Queen Mother herself received additional grants. Bishop William Longchamp of Ely, chancellor and justiciar of England, was given the preeminent role in the regency arrangements.

Richard also took pains to secure England's borders. At Worcester in late September 1189, he met the Welsh princes, who agreed not to attack England during the crusade. The only holdout was Rhys of Deheubarth. John was sent to deal with him, and duly brought him to Oxford in October, where Richard refused to meet him; Rhys responded by resuming his attacks. However, the other princes kept their promise, and not even Rhys joined John in rebellion in 1193. Meanwhile, in November 1189, William the Lion of Scotland travelled to meet Richard at Canterbury. This resulted in the Quitclaim of Canterbury (5 December 1189), by which William paid 10,000 marks to undo the humiliating concessions he had made to Henry II in the 1170s. Berwick-upon-Tweed and Roxburgh Castles were returned to him, and Richard recognised Scotland's independence. Like the Welsh, the Scots avoided involvement in John's rebellion. Scottish writers would look favourably on Richard for his concessions. Edward I would be rather less appreciative of his great-uncle's efforts.

Coffers full and regency arrangements in place, Richard sailed from Dover on 12 December 1189. He was met in Calais by his fellow crusader, Count Philip of Flanders, who accompanied him to spend Christmas at Caen. Here, Richard named men to rule his continental lands in his absence. Richard and Philip II met and agreed terms to protect their lands against attacks from each other's supporters while they were on crusade. Tensions between the two kings were eased by the death of Philip's wife, Isabella, on 15 March 1190, which focussed Philip's mind elsewhere. With preparations taking longer than expected, several other rulers departed for the crusade some time before the kings of England and France. Richard was also delayed by his concerns about Aquitaine, his favourite but most troublesome territory. He summoned most of the Aquitanian lords to a council at La Réole in February 1190. In late spring he acted against bandits in the area. Concerned about the threat of Count Raymond of Toulouse, he strengthened his alliance with King Sancho VI of Navarre. Aquitaine now as secure as possible, Richard returned to Anjou. From Chinon, he officially proclaimed the crusading ordinances, the rules which would apply at home while the crusade was underway. At Tours, he gave orders for his fleet to sail around Spain to Marseille. Meanwhile, the Archbishop of Tours gave the king his pilgrim's staff, which rather ominously broke when Richard leant on it.

Richard and Philip Augustus met at Vézelay on 2 July, where they agreed that they would share conquests and profits of war equally, an agreement both were to interpret differently. On the 4th, the kings finally set out. Reaching Lyon ten days later, they separated to take different routes to Sicily: Philip via Genoa, Richard through Marseille. When Richard arrived in Marseille on 31 July, there was no fleet. Unbeknown to the king, most ships had been waiting in the River Tagus for the stragglers, when their crews decided to indulge in the loutish behaviour which has earned English tourists in Europe such a bad reputation. They rioted in Lisbon, attacking the city's Jews and Muslims, raping women and stripping vineyards, until a furious Portuguese king threw several hundred drunken rioters into prison. This meant the fleet did not leave Lisbon until 26 July; when Richard arrived in Marseille they had not even sailed through the Straits of Gibraltar. Richard was too impatient to wait any longer. Hiring ships, he sent half his troops with Archbishop Baldwin of Canterbury directly to the Middle East. He and the remainder made leisurely progress along the French and Italian coasts, including a stop at Genoa to see Philip, who was ill and had also failed to embark for Sicily on time. Richard called at several Italian ports on his way south. Notably, he declined to visit Rome and Pope Clement III, for whom he had very little regard, even though he could afford to spend ten days in Naples and five in Salerno. At Salerno, Richard learned his fleet had been spotted on approach to Messina and eagerly set out to join it.

An incident just before he crossed the Straits of Messina on 22 September gives an insight into the king's character. Riding through a Calabrian village with a companion, Richard heard a falcon calling inside a house. In his view, only nobles should have hawks, so he barged inside and took it. An angry mob of villagers surrounded him and attacked him with sticks when he refused to give the bird back, one villager even drawing a knife. Richard's sword snapped in the altercation, so he resorted to throwing anything within reach at the villagers to make good his escape. The situation was entirely of Richard's making, his arrogance exposing him to considerable risk. As a guest in a foreign land, it was not up to him to impose his views on hawk ownership on the locals.

The same evening, Richard arrived in Messina, entering the city the following day in a splendid ceremony. This irritated Philip, who had arrived in much more lowkey fashion a week earlier. However, the French king had been installed in the royal palace, whereas Richard and his men had to camp. While initial meetings were cordial, relations between the two kings deteriorated rapidly. Philip wanted to set out quickly, but was forced back into harbour by the winds, leaving the two armies trapped together in Messina. Richard's troops had already proved their thuggish nature in Lisbon, which gave Messinian Muslims cause to be wary. Both armies were responsible for disorder, although the chronicles suggest that whereas Philip kept his head down, Richard made efforts to deal with the disturbances and punish offenders.

The crusaders had arrived during a turbulent time. William II of Sicily, husband of Richard's sister Joan, had died without issue in November 1189. He had nominated his aunt, Constance, as his successor, but she was married to Henry of Hohenstaufen (from 1191, Emperor Henry VI). Few Sicilians liked the idea of a German king, an antipathy shared by the mainland part of the realm in Calabria and Puglia, as well as by Pope Clement III. Their preferred candidate was Tancred, an illegitimate cousin of William. He was the *de facto* ruler and was keeping Joan in captivity, having no desire to release her dowry. William's will had left a considerable sum of money to Henry II, but Tancred viewed this as void since the English king had predeceased the Sicilian. Richard's magnificent entry into Messina convinced Tancred to send Joan from Palermo to Richard, but no money.

Richard resolved to obtain Joan's dowry by force. The citizens of Messina shut Richard's forces out. During negotiations, Richard's army was attacked. With Philip refusing to get involved, Richard conquered the town and handed it over to the Knights Templar and Hospitaller. Tancred decided surrender would be wise, so in early October an agreement was reached, giving Richard a sizeable sum of gold. Tancred now had Richard as an ally, while Richard had additional funds for his crusade, but it was well into October. Winter storms in the Mediterranean made the voyage to the Middle East too risky a prospect, so Richard and Philip settled down for Christmas in Sicily. It is possibly at this point that a strange episode occurred, related by the chronicler Roger of Howden (he gives no date and some historians place it in 1195), with Richard apparently doing penance for his moral failings.

As the stay dragged into 1191, people became restless and relations between Philip and Richard worsened. Those between Richard and Tancred were little better, because Philip was up to his old tricks and poisoning Tancred's mind against Richard. At Catania, Richard sought Tancred's permission for a fleet carrying his mother Eleanor to come to Messina. Eleanor's imminent arrival caused further disharmony between the kings of England and France, for she brought Berengaria of Navarre, Richard's intended bride. It had long been clear that Richard had no intention of marrying Philip's sister Alice, yet now his repudiation of Alice was public. Richard neatly sidestepped the truth by claiming he could not marry Alice as his father had had a son by her. It was a convenient fiction to gloss over the awkwardness of the moment, for he could have raised this objection on any previous occasion. Philip, hampered by the discovery of his conspiratorial correspondence with Tancred, accepted Richard breaking off the engagement with Alice, while Richard pretended to believe Philip's protestations of innocence. Richard paid 10,000 marks for the formal end of the betrothal, and the two officially became friends once more. In reality, their relationship was now mistrustful and cold. Philip and his men left Messina on 30 March, hours before Eleanor and Berengaria docked.

The redoubtable Queen Mother was now in her late sixties, but stayed only four nights before sailing home. As it was Lent, the marriage could not take place, so Richard began the eastward voyage on 10 April 1191. It should have taken around a month. However, a storm hit the fleet on Good Friday (12 April). While most ships reached the meeting point of Crete, those missing included that of Berengaria and Richard's sister Joan. Richard dispatched ships to find them and went to Rhodes. He learned that the missing ship was at anchor off Limassol, while other ships had been wrecked and the survivors imprisoned by the ruler of Cyprus, Isaac Comnenus. Berengaria and Joan were still aboard their vessel, refusing Isaac's invitation to come ashore. Richard asked Isaac to release his men and goods plundered from the shipwrecks. Meeting a predictable refusal, Richard equally predictably prepared to get his way by force.

Isaac, appointed governor of Cyprus by the Byzantine emperor, had declared it an independent kingdom and installed himself as emperor. Among his allies was Saladin, making him a hate figure for the crusaders. Richard and his men arrived on 6 May and routed the Cypriots on Limassol beach, but Isaac's army fled. Richard launched a surprise attack on Isaac's sleeping men, and though Isaac himself escaped, his treasure and goods were captured. On 11 May, a ship docked in Limassol carrying Guy of Lusignan, King of Jerusalem, and several other prominent lords from Outremer (the crusader states). Guy's brother Geoffrey, originally from Aquitaine, had had plenty of differences with Richard in the past. Now, however, the brothers promised Richard assistance and homage in return for backing Guy in his struggle against a rival for the throne of Jerusalem, Conrad of Montferrat. This was a fiendishly complex dispute, but Richard accepted, seeing the value of the additional warriors and a chance to strike a blow against Philip II, a supporter of Conrad.

Next day, 12 May 1191, Richard and Berengaria were married in St George's Chapel in Limassol. Immediately afterwards, Berengaria was crowned by the Bishop of Évreux. She would become the only queen of England never to set foot in England as consort, although she outlived Richard by thirty-one years and probably visited Canterbury in 1220. The newly married king was not inclined to enjoy nuptial bliss; this was no love match. Richard did all he could to avoid spending time with his wife over the following eight years, failing at a core duty of a medieval king, fathering an heir and securing the succession. We can never be certain why, but this failure had serious consequences for the Angevin dynasty when the 'empire' ended up in John's hands.

Isaac declared himself ready to submit, came to Richard's camp, changed his mind when everyone was having the afternoon nap necessitated by the Cypriot sun, and ran away. This 'treachery' gave Richard a perfect excuse to conquer the island. Guy of Lusignan took charge of the land forces, while Richard commanded naval attacks. The combined efforts of the kings of England and Jerusalem were too much for the Cypriots. Isaac realised the hopelessness of his position and surrendered on 1 June, his lone condition that he should not be put in irons. Richard obligingly had him held in chains of silver. Cyprus was sold to the Templars, from whom Guy purchased it in 1192. His brother, Aimery, became King of Cyprus in 1196, the dynasty ruling the island until the last sovereign was forced to sell Cyprus to Venice in 1489. The rapid conquest thus won an important strategic base for Latin Christendom; for Richard personally, it resulted in considerable riches and a further enhancement of his military reputation. Indeed, so favourable was the whole episode that some have questioned whether the storm and shipwreck were handy cover for a plan Richard had already conceived.[7]

Yet he was anxious to reach the Holy Land. Setting sail, he landed on the coast of modern Syria, imprisoning Isaac in the Hospitaller fortress of Margat (Marqab). He continued to Tyre, where he was refused entry as it was held for Conrad, so carried on to Acre, taken by Muslim troops in 1187. Since 1189, it had been under siege from Guy's forces, supported by a Pisan naval blockade, while the besieging force found themselves besieged by Saladin's forces. Philip Augustus had reached the Christian camp in April 1191. It was into this stalemated double siege that Richard now plunged. Approaching Acre, Richard's fleet encountered a very large ship (it was almost the size of Noah's Ark by the time some chroniclers had finished exaggerating) laden with supplies for the besieged garrison of Acre. Through a combination of skill and luck, Richard's ships managed to sink this vessel. His triumph allowed Richard to enter the crusader camp as a hero, bringing reinforcements the Christian forces had been awaiting, received with open arms by those who had experienced a siege dragging on for two years. However, disputes quickly began.

Richard paid knights more than Philip. Philip wanted to attack Acre straight away (despite having held back for three months). Richard refused until he had his equipment ready for action. Eventually, a complex battle for the town began. Most action occurred in the absence of the two kings, struck down by fever and only occasionally brought to watch. Assaults dragged on throughout late June, without any breakthrough, but supplies were running low in the town and morale was sinking. An offer from the garrison to surrender with conditions was rejected; Richard and Philip wanted total surrender. Saladin unsuccessfully attempted to break the siege on 4 July. With parts of the walls about to collapse and following a near-successful assault by Richard and the Pisans on 11 July, the garrison surrendered the next day. The Muslims had to hand over the entire town with everything inside, and in return for their lives they had to pay a sizeable sum and release over 1000 Christian prisoners. Saladin agreed to give back the relic of the true cross captured in 1187.

An incident now occurred which seemed minor but subsequently had grave repercussions. Duke Leopold of Austria had his standard raised next to those of the kings of England, France and Jerusalem, but Richard had his men throw it down. An angry Leopold sought restitution, and when he failed to obtain it, stormed off home. He was hardly a political heavyweight, but the action was gratuitously offensive. Leopold had become leader of a bedraggled German crusading contingent after the Holy Roman Emperor, Frederick Barbarossa, drowned on route to the Holy Land. He had been at the siege of Acre longer than both Philip and Richard. According to some English chroniclers, with so few men he had entered Richard's service, which would have given him no right to have his banner displayed alongside those of the kings. This argument is pushed by John Gillingham when he claims Leopold was 'an unimportant outsider in a camp which had split into two factions', whose action in raising his standard was 'totally unrealistic'.[8] Even if that is strictly accurate, Jean Flori is surely correct that Richard's attitude was 'neither adroit nor prudent', demeaning and undervaluing all those who had been maintaining the siege far longer than the two kings.[9] It was another display of the arrogance to which Richard was prone, for which he would pay a heavy price.

Acre was Christian once again, and with typical impetuosity, Richard swore to stay three years or until Jerusalem was recaptured. Philip declared he wanted to go home. Both kings had been seriously ill, but Philip was not recovering nearly as well. Relations between the two were poisoned by rumours and suspicions swirling around the crusader camp. Philip was jealous. Richard had eclipsed him in battle, success, wealth and diplomacy. Richard and the French barons entreated Philip to stay, but he was adamant. Having agreed the succession to the throne of Jerusalem on 28 July – Guy was to hold it for life, after which the crown would pass to Conrad – Richard made Philip swear on the gospels not to attack his lands or intrigue with any of his subjects while he remained in the Holy Land. Philip set sail from Tyre on 3 August. English chroniclers had a field day; Philip was a coward who had put his own interests ahead of those of God, leaving the heroic Richard to continue the struggle alone. French chroniclers were reduced to unconvincing special pleading. In hindsight, Richard's reputation profited far more from Philip's departure than it would have done from his remaining. The Lionheart was now the unrivalled star commander. Philip did his reputation further harm when he called at Rome on the return voyage and tried to persuade the new Pope, Celestine III, to release him from his oath not to interfere with Richard's lands. An unmoved pontiff refused.

The agreement with Saladin after Acre involved an exchange of prisoners, but many Muslim captives were being held in Tyre, under the control of Philip's ally, Conrad, who refused to hand them over. Richard was all for besieging Tyre to compel Conrad to do so. Duke Hugh of Burgundy, now in charge of the French troops, had to deploy all his diplomatic skill to dissuade the hot-headed English king. With Richard and Saladin both having problems, the original date for exchange was postponed. The crusaders waited for Saladin's ambassadors but none appeared. Fearing a Muslim trick, Richard had the captives beheaded. Christians justify the act, while Muslim sources concede Richard's dissatisfaction but lament it caused the conflict to become even bloodier. Saladin naturally had the Christian captives executed in retaliation. Today, this seems barbaric, 'a chilling act of slaughter that in the modern era would be classed as a war crime'.[10] Mass execution of prisoners did still occur in Western Europe, Richard taking similar action against rebel garrisons in Aquitaine. Yet there was a difference between punishing those who rebelled against their feudal lord, and slaughtering enemy prisoners during a truce which had not been broken. Even some Christian writers struggled with the ethical conundrum. Were it a unique episode, it might be easier to dismiss, but it is part of a broader pattern which points towards a hot-tempered man who resorted readily to violence and had little compunction about brutality. Richard's brother, John, has rightly been held to account for his cruelty, and we might wonder if the romantic legend which enfolds the Lionheart has obscured the fact that morally, he was little better. Perhaps the difference is that Richard was on occasion (albeit very rarely) capable of mercy, a concept almost entirely alien to John, but the distinction between the brothers is not as sharp as often depicted. Ironically, Richard was at his most merciful when it came to John, whom he treated with baffling indulgence.

Richard was in a hurry. While most in the army were keen to march on Jerusalem, Richard opted to secure more of the coast, to allow for better provisioning of a future siege of Jerusalem. Marching south towards Jaffa, the crusading army was constantly shadowed and harried by the Muslim one. There were skirmishes and small battles, Richard even suffering a minor javelin wound on 3 September, and conditions on the march were intolerable in the summer heat. Saladin gave battle on 7 September 1191, choosing an advantageous site on the plain outside Arsuf, which did not save him from defeat. Richard's victory dealt a blow to Saladin's reputation and further enhanced his own. Saladin dismantled the fortress further south at Ascalon, despite its strategic significance, to concentrate on defending Jerusalem. Richard arrived in Jaffa on 10 September and began to fortify it. His victory gave him an excess of confidence; he took unnecessary risks in the search for further glory, personally leading raiding parties into Muslim territory. During one of these, in late September, four knights were killed in an ambush, Richard only escaping because a loyal companion pretended to be the king and let himself be captured instead. Even supportive chroniclers criticised the king for such foolishness. His capture or death would have been a mortal blow to the crusade.

Arsuf brought differences of opinion about how to proceed. Richard decided to secure the coast and the army spent two months at Jaffa. The decision had strategic merit for a battle-weary force, but it was frustrating for those wanting to press on to Jerusalem. There was much grumbling. As Jaffa was rebuilt, Richard spent October and November engaged in planning and diplomacy. He put out feelers to Saladin to see if an agreement might be reached, but their aims were too far apart to be reconciled. (Although their armies did battle, Richard and Saladin never met in person.) The troops left Jaffa on 31 October and reached Ramla in mid-November. There they camped for six weeks in near-constant torrential rain. Only a few miles from Jerusalem, many crusaders began to sense glory. Yet those more familiar with the Holy Land were sceptical about the chances of success. These sceptics won out at a council in January 1192, and the army headed back to the coast. Now, the aim was to fortify Ascalon. Turning away from Jerusalem, having come so close, was a blow to Richard's prestige. When it had come to the critical attack, the purpose of the whole crusade, Richard had faltered, and his earlier victories could only compensate so much for that failure. In strategic terms, the decision is entirely understandable and defensible. Yet for a warrior whose reputation was built on military success and courage verging on recklessness, it was a devastating setback. Crusader morale plummeted, and as Richard headed to Ascalon, many of the French troops returned north to Acre and Tyre.

Richard spent early 1192 fortifying Ascalon, but concerning reports were reaching him from England. Equally worrying was the squabbling among the crusading forces. The Pisans and Genoese were at each other's throats again. Guy and Conrad were still implacable foes, but Richard now recognised Guy's isolation and reluctantly accepted Conrad as King of Jerusalem, compensating Guy by allowing him to buy Cyprus. This resolved matters for only a short time, since on 28 April Conrad fell victim to a fanatical Islamic sect, the Assassins. Two men disguised as monks infiltrated his household and stabbed him as he was on his way to dinner with the Bishop of Beauvais. His 21-year-old widow, through whom he had his claim to the throne, was pregnant with his child, but remarried just a week later. Her new husband, Henry of Champagne, took on the troubled role of King of Jerusalem, albeit without using the title. Meanwhile, Richard began asserting control over the coast, capturing the strategic fortress of Darum (Deir al-Balah, in what is now Gaza) on 22 May, raising hopes that he was finally going to launch an assault on Jerusalem.

On 29 May, Richard received further alarming news from England, where John was fomenting opposition with the connivance of Philip Augustus. With his throne in jeopardy, he determined to return to England. To his consternation, the barons declared they were going to Jerusalem regardless. When Richard asked his chaplain what the troops now thought of him, he received an honest answer, too much for the king's pride. He changed his mind and announced he would stay until Easter 1193. On 6 June, the army set off towards Jerusalem. It is possible that Richard even set eyes on the holy city while he was chasing some enemy soldiers, but this was as close as he was to get. Richard's army managed to capture a baggage train on its way from Egypt to Jerusalem, but the city itself remained beyond their grasp. Recognising the weakness of their position, with Saladin potentially able to block off access to the coast, Richard called another council which recommended an expedition against Egypt instead of Jerusalem.

Most crusaders were horrified. Hugh of Burgundy, who had hardly been noticeable by any active part in the campaign, spread stories accusing Richard of cowardice. His crowing was to be short-lived, as he would die in Acre in late August. The divisions were too deep to make the besieging of Jerusalem a realistic option, and Richard returned to Acre on 26 July, his forces sullen. Two days later, he was about to launch an attack towards Beirut when he learned that Saladin was besieging Jaffa, which the defenders had agreed to hand over if they were not rescued by 1 August. Richard reached Jaffa at the last possible moment, the night of 31 July. He initially held offshore, causing many defenders to surrender, but a priest swam out and begged the king to intervene. They waded ashore under a hail of arrows and attacked the Muslim troops who were busy looting the town. In a confusing, bloody encounter, Richard's force emerged victorious. On 5 August, Saladin attempted an early morning attack on the Christian camp outside the town, but the Muslim force was spotted and Richard was able to organise a hasty repulsion of the assault.

Defeating Saladin's men in combat twice in five days disguised the vulnerability of his position. His army was badly divided, his money running low, and problems were mounting back home. It was time to go, deal with the trouble at home and then (hopefully) return with a fresh army. For the rest of August, negotiations took place with Saladin. The treaty ratified on 2 September, to take effect from the following Easter, concluded a truce of more than three years (Muslims were not allowed to make conclusive peace with the infidel). The Christians were given control of the coast and allowed to fortify the towns. Christians could freely visit the Church of the Holy Sepulchre in Jerusalem as pilgrims. Many crusaders took advantage of this agreement before returning home, but a bitterly disappointed Richard refused to do so. Having promised to remain in the Holy Land until Easter 1193, he set sail from Acre on 9 October 1192.

On its own terms, the crusade was a failure for Richard. Its unachieved objective had been to recapture Jerusalem. Despite memorable victories, the Christian position in the Holy Land remained vulnerable and much of inland Palestine remained in Muslim hands. Whether Richard would have achieved more had he stayed until the following Easter is an unanswerable question. Saladin died on 4 March 1193 (Easter that year fell on 28 March) and his family immediately fell to infighting. Perhaps Richard might have capitalised on this and secured a decisive victory. Yet his own force was divided and demoralised, and he could hardly have known Saladin had just six months to live. His lands were under threat from John and Philip. The decision to leave was justifiable and sensible, but sat oddly alongside the developing legend of a courageous, reckless warrior. In truth, the crusade had shown that this trait combined in Richard with a certain indecisiveness and occasional excess of caution. While the slanders and criticisms of Philip of France and Hugh of Burgundy, men bitter at being overshadowed by Richard and who played little constructive role in the campaign, can safely be dismissed, praise in the chronicles is tempered by hints of bewilderment and disappointment at Richard's abandoning of the struggle. However, Richard became widely known as a formidable warrior and general.

October was late to be setting off, the prevailing winds against the king. After calling at Cyprus and Corfu, a storm put him off course. Exactly what happened is unclear, as fact and fiction have become inseparably intertwined. It seems Richard intended to travel, disguised, via the Veneto and through Austria and Bohemia to Saxony, where his brother-in-law, Henry the Lion, was duke. Instead, he ended up shipwrecked with a few companions on the Dalmatian coast. At Zadar, in modern Croatia, Richard posed as a merchant, sending a request for safe conduct to the local lord, accompanied by a ruby ring. Unbeknown to Richard, he had landed in about the worst place possible. The local lord was Count Meinhard of Görz (Gorizia), a vassal of Leopold of Austria, the duke Richard had insulted at Acre. He was also the nephew of Conrad, whom Richard had opposed as King of Jerusalem. Whether or not he recognised the ruby, the count quickly realised that the man was no merchant but King Richard of England. Despite being no friend of Richard, Meinhard magnanimously returned the ring and allowed the king to continue. His brother, however, chased after Richard, who had immediately departed with his small retinue. They escaped, but had little idea where they were and wandered rather cluelessly until they ended up in one of the few places even worse than Zadar: Vienna. Worse still, Duke Leopold was in residence.

Richard moved into a house on the city's outskirts. According to the most colourful version of the story, one of Richard's servants was recognised in the marketplace after behaving too flashily, and under interrogation betrayed the king's location. Leopold learnt that his enemy was on his doorstep, and on 21 December 1192 he took Richard prisoner. The duke had his vengeance for Acre and sent the king to Dürnstein Castle. Leopold was not the only ruler interested in the ransom the King of England might attract, for Richard had made various enemies. The duke's action was a violation of the protection afforded to crusaders on their journey to and from the Holy Land, and Leopold was duly excommunicated by Pope Celestine. English chroniclers were outraged and dwelt gleefully on Leopold's death after a horse fell on his foot at a tournament in 1194, which resulted in a botched amputation, gangrene and an agonising demise. Nevertheless, that Richard took pains to travel undercover suggests he knew how unpopular he was with several European rulers.

Leopold promptly informed the Holy Roman Emperor, Henry VI. Philip II was delighted and swiftly wrote to Leopold begging him to keep hold of the English king. Richard's brother, John, came to Paris to capitalise on the situation. As Richard had feared, John had wreaked havoc in England. In fairness, the initial problem was not John, but what turned out to have been an unwise choice of *de facto* regent by Richard. Richard seems to have had doubts about William Longchamp from the start, as in early 1191 he sent the Archbishop of Rouen, Walter of Coutances, to England from Messina, accompanied by William Marshal. They carried authorisation to depose Longchamp should he start to act arbitrarily.

Among the actions through which Longchamp overreached his authority was besieging Lincoln Castle in the spring of 1191. The castle was held by one of John's supporters, and the siege caused John to seize Nottingham and Tickhill Castles and force Longchamp to withdraw. In July, Archbishop Walter oversaw an agreement between the two at Winchester.

However, Longchamp soon went too far. Archbishop Geoffrey of York was prohibited from entering England during Richard's absence, but with John's encouragement he returned in September 1191. Longchamp had him besieged in Dover Priory for five days, after which he was dragged out in full Mass robes and imprisoned in the castle for eight days. It was only twenty years since Thomas Becket had been murdered, and mistreatment of another archbishop in Kent caused outrage. Longchamp quickly realised he had made a disastrous error, but his enemies now had the ammunition they needed. At a great council outside St Paul's Cathedral on 8 October, Archbishop Walter and William Marshal deposed Longchamp. John now became effective regent, with Walter as his deputy. His enemy vanquished, power in his hands and recognised as heir by most in England, John had been raised to a powerful position and capitalised on this during 1192, but it was the news of Richard's capture that gave him his opportunity. After his conference with Philip in Paris, John returned to England and spread rumours that Richard was dead. Most English barons refused to believe this, as did the Queen Mother. Eleanor successfully led the defence of her elder son's kingdom against her younger son, although Philip (blatantly breaking the oath he had sworn) invaded Normandy. The news of Richard's imprisonment reached Archbishop Walter in England in late January or early February 1193, and he immediately informed the council, who sent an embassy to secure the king's release.

Meanwhile, Richard had been transferred to the custody of Emperor Henry VI, who had paid Leopold a huge 75,000 marks (£50,000) for the prisoner. Aside from the insult the banner incident had been to the German forces, Henry had an additional grievance against Richard, who had backed the emperor's rival, Tancred, for the Sicilian throne. Having received him from Leopold at Speyer on 28 March 1193, Henry transferred him to Trifels Castle. Diplomatic wrangling commenced, with Philip trying to ensure Richard was kept captive while he conquered Normandy. There were considerable advantages to Henry in playing the two kings against one another, but agreement was reached at Worms at the end of June. The Emperor agreed to free Richard upon receipt of 100,000 marks. This was an enormous sum which his lands could ill afford. It fell to Eleanor to lead efforts for Richard's release. She pressured officials across Richard's territories to work hard to raise the ransom. A levy could legitimately be imposed on vassals to cover the ransoming of a feudal lord, but the sum involved was vast. Even without the initial, heavy financial burden imposed for the crusade, 1193 would have been a difficult year, coming after a harsh winter. Money came in slowly and corruption was widespread, forcing the king to send repeated messages begging Eleanor and other officials to hurry up. Eleanor set off for Cologne with the money in December. Henry announced that he would release Richard on 17 January 1194, but Philip and John tried to bribe the Emperor to keep the king captive. Tempted, Henry delayed. However, at a council meeting in Mainz on 2 February, a majority of princes of the Holy Roman Empire voted to release Richard. On 4 February, Richard was freed for the 100,000 marks Eleanor had brought, although hostages were taken until a further 50,000 marks were paid. Richard and Eleanor left Mainz for Antwerp, where they set sail for England, arriving at Sandwich on 13 March 1194. For Philip and John, it was disastrous news; as one chronicler put it, the devil had been loosed.[11]

As the price of his support, John had promised Philip sizeable chunks of the Plantagenet lands. Philip was doing his best to take as much of Normandy as he could. John's supporters were running riot in England and holding several castles. Richard's first task was to regain control of his lands. In England, this was not hard. Following Eleanor, most English barons had remained steadfastly loyal to Richard, the amount he had just cost them notwithstanding. Militarily, John was no match for his brother. After riding to Canterbury to give thanks at Thomas Becket's shrine, then being joyously received in London, the king quickly quelled John's rebellion. Acting as warrior rather than churchman, the new Archbishop of Canterbury, Hubert Walter, besieged the two remaining rebel castles, Tickhill and Nottingham. Tickhill fell, and Richard himself appeared to besiege Nottingham. It was a formidable, supposedly impregnable castle, but it held out for just a few days against the king's onslaught and the garrison surrendered on 28 March. A fortnight after landing in England, Richard had regained control of his kingdom with ease.

His next priority was to reassert his kingship. In April, he held a council at Northampton, then went to Southwell to meet William the Lion. At Winchester on 17 April, he held a solemn crown-wearing ceremony in the cathedral to erase the humiliation of captivity. While the Norman kings had habitually held crown-wearings two or three times a year, with Winchester a common venue, the ceremony had not been used since 1158. Notably, while Eleanor and King William were in attendance at Winchester, Berengaria was not. We are not even certain where the queen was; Richard had not seen her since they left the Holy Land nearly eighteen months earlier. That he made no effort to have her join him for this ceremony strongly suggests that he had no interest in her, nor did he want her sharing his spotlight. Richard had more than a streak of narcissism.

He had easily reasserted himself in England, but his continental lands would prove harder to tame. With his sovereignty ritually affirmed, Richard set to recruiting mercenaries to help him across the Channel. On top of all the demands for the crusade and the ransom came further taxes and (re)sale of offices, the English receiving little thanks for their loyalty as the king extracted yet more money from them. After a short break to go hunting, then a storm delay, Richard sailed from Portsmouth to Barfleur on 12 May 1194, having been in England for just two months. He would never set foot in the country again.

From Barfleur, Richard headed to Lisieux, where Eleanor orchestrated a reconciliation between her two sons. The Queen Mother had no illusions about

John, but she far preferred him as heir (as long as Richard remained childless) to her grandson Arthur, with whose mother she was on distinctly frosty terms. Richard indulgently forgave John, although he was stripped of his lands, then carried on to relieve Verneuil from Philip's siege. In short order, he then reclaimed Tours and Loches. John promptly demonstrated his treacherous nature by returning to Évreux, entrusted to his keeping by Philip, slaughtering the French garrison, and handing the fortress back to Richard. Philip, having abandoned Verneuil, chased John out of Évreux. In early July, at a standoff at Vendôme, Philip lost his nerve and fled, narrowly avoiding capture by hiding in a church. The booty from his camp, including the French royal archives, fell into Richard's hands.

Richard was to spend the rest of his life trying to reassert his control over the Angevin territories in France, the problem largely of his own making. Yes, Philip was perfidious in attacking the land of a fellow crusader and John was opportunistic and treacherous, but these and other problems were foreseeable. While going on a crusade might have appeared to be a heroic Christian venture, it left the Plantagenet lands very vulnerable. No matter how good the arrangements for governance, nothing could act as a substitute for the personal presence of the king when trouble arose. Richard's diverse continental lands were linked only by complex and competing ties of lordship and allegiance, at the mercy of neighbours with avaricious eyes. The financial demands of the crusade, made far worse by the need for a ransom payment, seriously depleted the resources of England in particular. Above all, Richard had shown John (and others) the path of treacherous collusion with Philip against Henry II, so had little reason to expect that the skilful, manipulative French king would not similarly tempt others into rebellion against Richard himself when the opportunity arose. Despite the longer-term factors, the five years of continuous conflict after Richard's release from captivity were primarily the consequence of his own past actions and choices.

For now, with Philip subdued, Richard turned to Aquitaine, taming some of the main rebels there before returning to Normandy. A truce had been agreed with Philip by envoys at Tillières on 23 July 1194, which would maintain the status quo until November 1195. In reality, the next year was marked by repeated, confused skirmishing and attempts to seize castles. Open conflict broke out again in July 1195 after Philip broke the truce and destroyed several Norman castles, only for another ceasefire to be agreed in August. As part of this, Richard finally returned Alice to her brother, who instantly married her to the Count of Ponthieu. The level of tension is shown by a meeting between Philip and Richard at Vaudreuil, during which the castle collapsed in the background after the French undermined the walls. Philip fled across the Seine and destroyed the bridge after him, while a furious Richard went on the rampage. Another meaningless truce was agreed, during which Philip destroyed Dieppe before being chased away by Richard. A further truce was agreed in December 1195, ratified at a full peace conference at Louviers in January 1196. The French king very quickly broke this peace agreement as well, leading to full-scale war.

Both kings made early gains. Richard's attempts to win the support of Brittany led to Arthur, his nephew, taking refuge with Philip in Paris, significantly easing John's succession after Richard's early death. Throughout 1196, the war ground on, 'a dreary succession of castles destroyed, taken and retaken, of villages burned, of massacres of garrisons considered disloyal, of prisoners blinded and sent back to the enemy to discourage him, all to no avail'.[12] The castle at Gisors was a major strategic advantage for Philip which Richard, fearful of the threat posed to posed to the security of Normandy, decided to counter by building a huge castle at Les Andelys, twenty-five miles south-east of Rouen and only seventeen miles from Gisors. Even today, it is possible to appreciate what an undertaking Château Gaillard ('Impudent Castle') must have been, perched dauntingly on its outcrop above the Seine. The impressive and complex fortress was competed in just two years, testament to the importance Richard attached to it, as was the immense £12,000 it cost to build. However, its construction came at more than a financial cost. The local lord was Archbishop Walter of Rouen. Despite his record of loyal service to Richard, Walter was extremely unhappy at the king appropriating the land to build his castle, and placed the duchy of Normandy under interdict. That Richard was prepared to go ahead with Château Gaillard regardless demonstrates how important the fortress was to his plans.

Richard also built diplomatic bridges. At the end of 1194, an old nemesis, Count Raymond V of Toulouse, had died. In October 1196, his son and successor, Raymond VI, married Richard's sister Joan, widow of William of Sicily. Raymond stands in company with Henry VIII of England: married six times (Joan was wife number four), in the early thirteenth century his perceived tolerance of heresy led to him being an early target of the Albigensian Crusade. Richard was less interested in Raymond's love of weddings and doubtful orthodoxy than in a match which ended a long-running dispute and made his position in Aquitaine more secure. He also managed to tempt the Counts of Boulogne and Flanders onto his side. As campaigning got underway in the spring of 1197, another succession of complex sieges, attacks and atrocities commenced. Richard's force, under the redoubtable William Marshal, made progress in eastern Normandy. Meanwhile, the Bishop of Beauvais, a cousin of Philip who hated the King of England and had been a prime mover in the campaign to delay his release from prison, was captured while leading an army and handed over to Richard. The bishop appealed to the Pope, claiming that a cleric could not be so treated. When Celestine tried to intervene, Richard sent him the bishop's military tunic. The pontiff got the message and ruled accordingly; the bishop had been captured as a soldier in arms, not a churchman, and could be imprisoned and ransomed as such. Despite being offered a large ransom, Richard preferred to keep him imprisoned.

Richard's new ally, Baldwin of Flanders, captured Douai, besieged Arras and trapped Philip's army by destroying the bridges and opening the sluices around the town. In September 1197, acting on Richard's instructions, Baldwin agreed a sixteen-month truce with Philip, which was disregarded as blatantly as the lengthening list of predecessors. At the same time, the proxy war spread even further afield when Emperor Henry VI died on 28 September 1197. The Imperial Crown was elective, not hereditary. Philip of Swabia, Henry's brother and candidate of the Hohenstaufen faction, was backed by Philip. The opposing Guelf faction offered the crown to Richard himself. While flattered, Richard showed the same realism that his father had demonstrated when offered the crown of Jerusalem, preferring to stick with his own territories and problems. Instead, he suggested his nephew, Otto of Brunswick, who was finally elected after a controversial contest in July 1198.

Open fighting recommenced in France in late summer 1198. Baldwin invaded Artois and took Saint-Omer on 4 October. Philip was preoccupied with a failing campaign elsewhere. Richard routed Philip near Vernon; with the English king in hot pursuit, the French king had to flee to safety in the castle. Richard then began to make gains in the French Vexin. Philip, on his way to help Courcelles, was defeated and again had to flee, this time to Gisors. Two ignominious flights in quick succession did little for Philip's reputation. Worse, a bridge at Gisors collapsed and the king was thrown into the River Epte, only being rescued from drowning by the quick reactions of his attendants. Philip regrouped and sacked Évreux. Richard retaliated with an attack on Abbeville. After a merciless season of campaigning, in November 1198 the two kings sought yet another truce. Richard, in a stronger position, agreed only to a ceasefire until January 1199. The new Pope, Innocent III, seeking to promote a new crusade, sent a legate, Peter of Capua, to try to reconcile the two kings. The legate went first to Richard and dwelt on the damage being done to Christendom by the war. Richard received the lecture icily, reminding the legate that the Church had done little to protect his lands or act against Philip while Richard was previously on crusade. He did agree to a five-year truce, only for the legate to foolishly push his luck and seek the release of the Bishop of Beauvais. Richard went into a rage worthy of his father and sent the legate away, his ears ringing with the king's angry outburst. The legate now went to Philip, who asked him to secure the five-year truce regardless. Terrified after his verbal mauling, he refused, and the Archbishop of Reims was sent in his stead. Meanwhile, William Marshal had successfully cooled Richard's temper and persuaded him that a truce would be beneficial. On 13 January 1199, Richard agreed.

Loyal lords in Poitou and the Limousin had been pressing him for some time to come and deal with treacherous vassals, so Richard set off for Aquitaine. By March, he was taking part in the siege of Châlus-Chabrol, south-west of Limoges. For a long time, historians believed Richard was motivated by greed, having heard there was hidden treasure there for the taking. Avarice and foolishness, a quixotic quest typical of the Lionheart's whole career, was what led to his fateful appearance at a minor castle in central France in March 1199, where there was no political or strategic merit to his presence. It was a story which John Gillingham matter-of-factly told in 1973.

> A peasant in the Limousin found some buried treasure and took it to his lord, Achard of Chalus. Richard heard about this and decided that by rights the whole of the treasure should be his. In March 1199 he besieged the little castle of Chalus.[13]

In 1979, however, Gillingham published a detailed article which showed that Richard actually went to the Limousin for sound strategic reasons, to deal with rebellious vassals in Aquitaine. It was possible that 'Richard may have marched into the Limousin to deal with the rebellion and then been drawn to Chalus-Chabrol itself by a report that treasure had been found', but 'the treasure was of subsidiary importance'.[14] If the treasure story has refused to die completely, since 1979, historians of Richard's reign have accepted that the king had good political reasons for going to Châlus. Yet it was not enough to save him from his fate.

On 26 March, after dinner, Richard rode up to the castle ramparts without armour. He intended to inspect the defences, a generous term for something which that Friday evening consisted of a man using a frying pan as a shield. Unfortunately, he also had a crossbow, and he let off a bolt which embedded itself in the careless king's left shoulder. Richard returned to his tent and, with typical impetuosity, tried to remove the crossbow bolt himself. All he managed to do was snap off the wooden shaft. Only with great difficulty did a surgeon manage to extract the iron bolt. Twelfth-century Muslim doctors were appalled by the unhygienic ignorance of Western medicine, but a surprising number of soldiers managed to survive battlefield wounds despite the ministrations of their doctors. Richard himself had survived his fair share, but he was a terrible patient who refused to listen to his doctors. The wound became septic and gangrene set in. Aware he was dying, he sent not for his wife, but instead to Fontevraud, where Eleanor of Aquitaine had retired to a life of peaceful seclusion. She immediately dashed to his side.

Meanwhile, the castle surrendered. All the defenders were hanged except one. Richard had the man who had mortally wounded him brought into his presence. The king forgave him and ordered him released, although after Richard's death, his orders were probably disobeyed. He made provision for his lands, which were to pass to John, along with various other bequests, and received the last rites. In the early evening of 6 April 1199, Richard the Lionheart died at the age of 41. His mother was at his side. The grief at the loss of her favourite son must have been especially acute. She took his body back with her to Fontevraud, where it was interred beside Henry II. Richard's entrails stayed in Poitou, while his heart went to Rouen Cathedral. The fate of the Fontevraud effigies and bodies is related in the previous chapter. At Rouen, a full body effigy was also erected in the thirteenth century. The tomb was demolished during rebuilding works in 1734, but the effigy was found, along with the casket containing the heart, in 1838. The restored effigy was placed back in the cathedral in 1869 and moved to its current location in 1956. The slab table on which it lies bears the Latin inscription 'Here is the embalmed heart of Richard, king of England, called Lionheart, [who] died in the year 1199'. On the other side of the cathedral, there is a similar effigy of Henry, the Young King, where the opening words of the nineteenth-century inscription identify him as the Lionheart's brother before getting to his own name. Richard would have been happy. Everyone took second place to him.

Richard through the Centuries

'To deprive a hero of a hero's death was the most terrible punishment that God could inflict.'[15] Had Richard died in battle in the Holy Land, it would have been noble or fitting. It seemed scarcely credible that the mighty crusader king, who had so often flirted with danger and emerged unscathed, could be brought low by a single crossbowman at an obscure castle in central France. To several chroniclers, the manner of Richard's death was a punishment from God. Acerbic as ever, Gerald of Wales drew an explicit connection between William II, shot dead while hunting in the New Forest by an arrow directed by the hand of God, and Richard being killed a century later by a similarly directed crossbow bolt. The cause was his financial demands on the Church. William of Newburgh, who had been critical of Henry II, found himself revising his opinion in the light of Richard's reign, pointedly observing that Henry had never burdened his people in such a way. Although some modern historians dispute that England had been 'bled dry' by Richard, there was surely considerable resentment at the amount Richard had extracted from England. While there might be more nuance than the outraged chroniclers allowed, Richard's demands were hefty and unpopular. Against those who claim Richard was universally admired in his own day, it is worth quoting the chronicler who deemed the king 'bad to all, worse to his friends, and worst of all to himself'.[16]

Yet many of these same chroniclers were awed by Richard's military achievements and heroic reputation. With a lack of impartiality flagrantly breaching modern civil service standards, one scribe headed an official record, 'Ninth Regnal Year of King Richard the Good'.[17] He was called Lionheart during his own lifetime. For the most part, aside from criticism of the hefty financial demands, chroniclers praised Richard's eagerness to fight for Christianity in the Holy Land and recover Jerusalem. That he failed in the second of these goals was a partial disappointment, but writers nevertheless gushed about his soldierly qualities. A note of caution is necessary, however. 'Contemporaries were unanimous in believing that Richard's highest duty was to attempt the recovery of Jerusalem', asserts Richard's greatest modern champion.[18] That is not quite true, but even overlooking that, it is important to remember that on this subject, we cannot uncritically see the churchmen who wrote the chronicles as representative of opinion. We have no access to the thoughts of the mass of ordinary people, but it is unlikely that a Lincolnshire fisherman or Shropshire farmer thought in these terms. Their resentment of royal exactions, though unrecorded, was probably heightened by the fact that the cause for which so much was demanded had little meaning for their everyday lives. Chroniclers may have lauded Richard, but their verdicts must be read as representing a relatively narrow interest group.

While French chroniclers also have tales of Richard's courage and military skill, they naturally downplay his achievements. Sources associated with the Parisian court were in a tricky position since Philip's crusade exploits and vow-breaking left them with some explaining to do. Although Philip's legacy as King of France was immeasurably greater than Richard's as King of England, Richard was the undeniable victor in the battle of legends. Yet the hostile French sources provide nuances often ignored by the English, their depiction of some of Richard's actions as deceitful or brutal a useful counterpart to the more uncritical glorification. Richard also features prominently in Muslim chronicles. These Islamic chroniclers admired Richard's valour and military record. It is true that they considered him deceitful, both a true reflection of Richard's character and a required belief about a non-Muslim, enemy king. Unlike western sources, the Arabic ones have plenty to say about Richard's diplomacy, much of it positive. Of all their opponents in the Third Crusade, they respected the Lionheart as the most valiant and able of the infidel leaders.

Popular songs and ballads of the later Middle Ages took Richard as the shining example of a glorious warrior. 'England boasts in the valour of Richard', according to a song from the reign of his nephew, Henry III. After Henry's long and tempestuous reign, the new king, Edward I, was lauded for his deeds: 'while Edward flourishes, look, he glows like a new Richard'.[19] England once again had a king, Richard's great-nephew, in whose accomplishments the country could take pride. When the author of the *Vita Edwardi Secundi* lamented that in the opening six years of his reign, Edward II had 'achieved nothing praiseworthy or memorable', his lament drew on Richard I's example: 'How different were the beginnings of the reign of King Richard, who, before the end of the third year of his reign, scattered far and wide the rays of his valour'.[20] Edward III's collection of family memorabilia included the helmet Richard I was supposed to have taken from Saladin.[21]

In the fourteenth century, Ranulf Higden placed Richard in illustrious company, alongside Alexander the Great, the Emperor Augustus and Charlemagne, as a source of English pride.[22] The focus was on Richard's reckless valour, not on the questions of governance which would occupy later historians. It was an approach which held for a remarkably long time. If he was far less useful to Henry VIII's anti-papal struggles than a reinvented John (Richard had, after all, led a crusade promoted by the papacy), his warrior legend could still appeal in Tudor times. Not until the Stuart era did doubts surface with Samuel Daniel. Richard 'exacted, and consumed more of this Kingdom, than all his predecessors from the Norman had done before him, and yet less deserved than any, having neither lived here, neither left behind him Monument of Piety, or of any other public work, or ever showed love or care to this Commonwealth, but only to get what he could from it'.[23] Because it was a crusade, and because of the already legendary tales around his exploits, Richard managed to get away with this extortion with minimal complaints being raised. His agents were able to do far more to exploit the English in his absence than he could ever have done in person.

Richard was viewed with some suspicion in the Age of the Enlightenment. Edward Gibbon talked of the 'sanguinary Richard', then damned the king with barbed praise. In a comparison with Philip Augustus, Gibbon opined that 'the king of England, though inferior in dignity, surpassed his rival in wealth and military renown; and if heroism be confined to brutal and ferocious valour,

Richard Plantagenet will stand high among the heroes of the age'.[24] David Hume took a similar line. While no one 'carried personal courage and intrepidity to a greater height', and Richard 'possessed every talent necessary for acquiring' the military glory that he 'passionately loved', his 'resentments also were high, his pride unconquerable; and his subjects as well as his neighbours had therefore reason to apprehend from the continuance of his reign a perpetual scene of blood and violence'. Moreover, 'his reign was very oppressive and somewhat arbitrary'.[25] While Richard's military talents and courage were still recognised, there were by now questions about how much he enjoyed violence for its own sake and the cost in human bloodshed.

By the end of the nineteenth century, the ambivalence had disappeared. William Stubbs gave an unambiguous verdict on Richard: 'He was a bad king'. For Stubbs, Richard's 'military exploits, his military skill, his splendour and extravagance, his poetical tastes, his adventurous spirit, do not serve to cloak his entire want of sympathy, or even consideration, for his people'. Here was a king who made no contribution to the development of English government and institutions, and who was never even in England to try, a cardinal sin in the eyes of Victorian constitutionalists. 'His ambition was that of a mere warrior: he would fight for anything whatever, but he would sell everything that was worth fighting for. The glory that he sought was that of victory rather than conquest.' The bishop skips through the reign, Richard himself largely absent from the story as it is about an England in which the king was scarcely present: 'His subjects, fortunately for themselves, saw very little of him during the ten years of his reign'.[26]

Nevertheless, the story of Richard and Saladin had continued to resonate in the Anglophone world in the nineteenth century, one biographer of the eighth president of the United States bizarrely making a comparison when writing about his subject's time as a lawyer; as a more modern biographer observed, in a line we might consider superfluous, 'Van Buren was not Richard the Lionheart and never would be'.[27] Yet the Lionheart's fame ensured that, unlike Martin van Buren, he was not forgotten. The result has been a large quantity of biographies of distinctly variable quality, a fair few so valueless that they do not merit comment. Amidst some very dubious histories, an honourable mention must go to the sober, reliable Kate Norgate. *Richard the Lionheart* (1924) was the last of her major works on the period and has stood the test of time remarkably well, remaining readable and eminently sensible a century later.

In 1948, John Harvey defended the king's absence from England: 'that he was almost wholly a foreigner, when such is generally the nature of kings, is insignificant; to blame him for failure in bringing material prosperity to England would be unfair and irrelevant'. However, 'in what goes to make a hero his vices, his anger, his vengeful cruelty even, count for as much as his chivalric virtues'. Ultimately, 'his qualities were more than life-size', which is where 'the secret of his lasting fame still lies – he would not be bound down by the chains of the average, the mediocre and the reasonable, and died because the merely possible was not enough for him'.[28] The portrait is more sympathetic than most of this era, but Harvey made one novel contribution which opened a contentious debate never subsequently resolved. He outed the Lionheart.

The French historian, Paul de Rapin, had possibly hinted at Richard's homosexuality in the early eighteenth century,[29] but the argument really began with Harvey, who chose to break 'the conspiracy of silence'. Even in 1948, this remained something of a taboo area; not until 1967 would homosexuality be decriminalised in Britain. Despite having been a 1930s member of the Imperial Fascist League, Harvey's views on sexuality come across as remarkably enlightened for the time. While still constrained by the prejudices of his age into seeing homosexuality as a 'profound psychological problem', he condemns outright the persecution of same-sex attraction in England by 'penalties so ferocious as to seem incredible'.[30] Harvey seeks to out Richard in order to humanise him, to show him as a tormented man constrained from being himself by the moral code of his age. Several opinions in Harvey's book are decidedly eccentric, and he would not ordinarily be considered a serious authority, but this claim has proved immensely influential. After 1948, Richard's homosexuality took on the guise of accepted fact until John Gillingham challenged it in 1980. It continues to be repeated, influencing reference works and fictional portrayals.

Four principal arguments are used in the case for Richard's homosexuality: his sharing a bed with Philip Augustus in Paris in the 1180s; the exclusion of women from his coronation banquet; his penance; and the fact that his marriage to Berengaria was childless. The debate about the shared bed misunderstands the past, or even a present where bed sharing is mandated by financial or other necessity. Making this about sex projects modern obsessions back into periods when cultural habits were entirely different. Henry II and the Young King had also shared a bed in the mid-1170s,[31] which no one has ever considered meant that they were engaged in an incestuous relationship. The spurious link between bed sharing and a sexual relationship has even been made for the likes of Abraham Lincoln, compelled by financial circumstances to share a bed for nearly four years when he first moved to Springfield.[32] To use this as evidence that Richard was gay is to build on very dubious foundations indeed. Excluding women from his coronation banquet was more puzzling. John Gillingham claimed this was 'not in any way unusual', but Jean Flori observed it is unlikely that 'the exclusion of women really was traditional'.[33] It does seem unusual, but it is quite a stretch from that to the gay orgy some seem to imagine. The penance episode is mysterious, especially as it apparently involved a hermit warning Richard to repent, but it is certainly not clear evidence of homosexuality. It is true that he spent very little time with Berengaria, although it would not be the only time in history that such a political marriage involved little in passion. Aside from one illegitimate son, the obscure Philip of Cognac (the Bastard of Shakespeare's *King John*), Richard left as little legacy outside his marriage as within it.

The whole debate around Richard's sexuality says much about the twentieth century's need to apply labels. Modern writers have tended to frame the debate in binary terms, straight or gay, often tied up in outdated and offensive notions about the connection between masculinity and heterosexuality. More recently, bisexuality has been considered, but there is still some pressing need to accord Richard the sexual appetite of his father and brother. For all the lurid tales about nuns and whores in some chronicles, there is remarkably little specific in these stories, which read like a general idea of how chroniclers felt an Angevin king should behave. Richard's primary interest was fighting, and the lack of any identifiable sexual partners beyond generic types could suggest a tendency towards asexuality. There is simply not enough evidence to say one way or the other, nor does it really matter. Beyond the fact that he left no heir, a major failing in any medieval king, there is nothing to suggest that his sexual antics (or lack thereof) negatively affected his rule. Who he slept with, if anyone, was his business, and not something we will ever know for certain. However, the debate continues, as evidenced in the opposing conclusions reached in the 1999 biographies by John Gillingham (a straight Richard) and Jean Flori (a gay Richard).

Mid-twentieth-century writers could never quite get a handle on Richard, accepting his military qualities while condemning his plundering of England's resources. The king had 'all the failings and some of the virtues of his race', opined A. L. Poole, being 'hot-tempered and irresponsible, generous and accomplished'. He 'used England as a bank on which to draw and overdraw in order to finance his ambitious exploits abroad', and that 'the country stood and survived the strain is the highest proof of Henry II's constructive work'.[34] Winston Churchill, the former war leader, admired Richard the warrior, arguing that in calling him Lionheart, his contemporaries 'paid a lasting compliment to the king of beasts'. However, the former chancellor of the exchequer could not approve of his financial exactions for foreign gain: 'Little did the English people owe him for his services, and heavily did they pay for his adventures'. The former prime minister and party leader, meanwhile, observed that Richard was 'in politics a child, lacking in subtlety and experience', and that his 'political alliances were formed upon his likes and dislikes; his political schemes had neither unity nor clearness of purpose'.[35] Far more than he realised, as he traced the unevenness and contradictions of Richard I's career, Sir Winston Churchill could have been writing about himself.

John T. Appleby produced a study of England during Richard's reign in 1965, the king intruding into the narrative only during his two visits and then as a spectre from afar. It is, Appleby argues, 'almost meaningless to say that Richard was a bad king; for all practical purposes he was king in name only'. He 'took little interest in England', which 'gave him a crown, so that he could take his place amongst the rulers of the world', and which he treated as 'an inexhaustible source of money to fund he his crusade, his ransom, and finally his defence of Normandy'. Yet 'Richard's neglect was England's good fortune', since 'the barons of England developed a sense of collective responsibility for the good governance of their country' that led to Magna Carta. This is highly dubious, but Appleby reflected a common line of thinking that Richard did most for England by leaving it alone.[36]

Into the 1970s, views of Richard remained negative. John Julius Norwich saw a man whose 'ambition was boundless and, nearly always, destructive', who 'could be faithless, disloyal, even treacherous, in the pursuit of his ends' and who would 'ignore the responsibilities of kingship for the sake of personal glory'. He seems to have taken it for granted that Richard was gay, but in tune with changing social attitudes in Britain, he noted cheerily that 'if his tastes ran in other directions they never appreciably affected that shining reputation'.[37] Such tolerance was notably absent from James A. Brundage's biography, today brazenly offensive, referring to 'Richard's emotional instability and immaturity, manifested by his homosexuality'. We might perhaps explain Brundage's homophobia by the fact he taught in Wisconsin, which only decriminalised homosexuality in 1983, but his amateur psychologising makes his book very dated. His conclusion is that 'Richard remains ambiguous to the end', it being the 'combination of great courage and great strength with common failings that endows him with perennial appeal'. Yet this masks a largely hostile previous discussion, which concludes starkly that Richard was 'one of the worst rulers England has ever had'.[38]

However, a challenge to this came in the later 1970s. By far the most prolific modern, academic writer on Richard and his reign has been John Gillingham.[39] His opinions are scattered throughout this chapter because no study of Richard I can ignore his work and insights; carefully researched and often opinionated pieces have done much to counter many unwarranted assumptions about Richard. Asserting that contemporaries valued Richard's military prowess and crusading efforts, Gillingham has also attacked the idea that Richard neglected England or that he was uninterested in government. Invaluable though this is, however, he sometimes takes his partisanship too far. Behaviour or actions that Gillingham would criticise in Henry II or John are excused when it comes to Richard. John's inheritance in 1199 was not as perfect as Gillingham sometimes seems to suggest. Gillingham's critique of the agendas of modern historians is valid, but he does often seem reluctant to face the negative contemporary judgements about Richard, or question how representative the chronicles really are. Trying to turn a king who was never in his kingdom into a perfect exemplar of kingship is a tricky exercise and a hard line to sell. For all these caveats, Gillingham's work is fundamentally important, his 1999 biography the standard life of the king.

The 1990s saw efforts to reassess the relative merits of Richard I and Philip II. English historians have tended to condemn Richard for his absence from England, but see Philip as cowardly and devious. Such an assessment is not entirely unfair, but it is usually made by overlooking the faults of Richard I and John, ignoring Philip's natural interest in defending the Capetian monarchy. That he was a remarkably successful king of France is not usually acknowledged in English histories. A rare exception is Jim Bradbury's 1998 biography, asserting there is 'no doubt that Philip II had been a great king'. He was 'not the king we in England have come to think him', that is, he 'was not feeble, treacherous or double-dealing', but 'a truly brave king' and 'the sort of man the modern world should admire: intelligent, diplomatic, effective, successful, but generally modest, peace-loving and hard-working'.[40] Bradbury goes too far; while Philip Augustus is among the great kings of France, he was certainly guilty of double-dealing, and 'peace-loving' is a stretch for someone who repeatedly started conflicts during the 1180s and 1190s. Nevertheless, it is an important corrective, looking at Philip's relationship with Richard from the French perspective. When compared in terms of achievement and long-term legacy, rather than glamour and renown, Philip emerges as far superior to Richard.

French historians have tended to be as blinkered about Richard as English ones about Philip, whose poor military record against the Lionheart rather spoils their story. However, one of the best recent biographies is by a French author, Jean Flori. He examines Richard against the emerging code of chivalry. Half the book is devoted to a study of the king's life, the other half looking in more detail at his military career in this chivalric context. Flori thus takes a broader view of Richard the soldier that avoids simply seeing him as a man obsessed with violence, rather examining the ways in which his militarism can be understood against the developing ideas of the warrior. This leads him to take a more favourable view of Richard than most French historians, and while not uncritical, the overall verdict is a positive one, that 'Richard was truly a "roi-chevalier": he was a knight who was also a good monarch; he was a king who was and wanted to be a model of chivalry'.[41]

By no means everyone agreed with this or the extravagant claim that since 1978, 'medieval historians have acknowledged in Richard a king of exceptional ability and extraordinary success'.[42] Michael Markowski argues that the fundamental aim of the Third Crusade was the recapture of Jerusalem, and by allowing himself to become distracted and not even making an attempt on the city, Richard I 'was a failure as a crusade leader'. This failure meant Richard 'was a bad crusader who avoided the main goal of the Third Crusade, prolonged and increased warfare'. Cuttingly, 'he was no hero, but a man who merely wanted to fight hand-to-hand forever'. Richard's 'misuse of crusade forces' is a reminder of the distinction 'between the limited goals set by the Church, and the actual hostilities carried on by secular leaders'.[43] The point certainly merits consideration. One of the defences of Richard's crusading is that he was simply serving the Church and doing a Christian duty, but does that hold if he deviated from the Church's stated aim? The failure of the crusade on its own terms is too often overlooked and, having set himself up as its leader and hero, Richard cannot escape judgement for that. A crusade undertaken for reasons other than the goals of the Church is surely very hard to defend as an expression of medieval piety and religious fidelity.

Ralph V. Turner and Richard R. Heiser judge Richard a success in keeping the administration of his territories running and managing an effective government: 'Richard largely fulfilled much of his contemporaries' criteria for good kingship'. They argue that 'war was a medieval monarch's vocation, and Richard could hardly have ignored either Philip Augustus's threat to his continental possessions or Saladin's menace to the Holy Land'. While Richard certainly couldn't ignore Philip threatening his lands, plenty of other monarchs did ignore Saladin to concentrate on matters at home. Their assertion that scholars 'writing today should be more tolerant of Richard's warfare [...] than were nineteenth-century nationalist writers' would certainly not command universal acceptance. However, they do acknowledge that Richard 'viewed England mainly as an inexhaustible treasure house'. And in the end, their final verdict on his legacy is condemnatory: 'Richard left not only a disputed succession, but a legacy to his brother John in 1199 that was otherwise flimsy'.[44]

No full academic biography of Richard has appeared in the twenty-first century, the closest being a short volume by Thomas Asbridge in 2018, approaching Richard from the perspective of chivalry and knightly valour. As the author of a history of the crusades, Asbridge is generally admiring of Richard's crusading achievements. Rather than one who neglected his realm, he sees Richard as halfway between the French kings Philip II, 'prioritizing his role as a monarch above that of a crusader', and Louis IX, who 'in pursuit of his victory in the East, neglected his duties at home'. Richard 'never truly turned his back on the kingdom of England, or the Angevin realm as a whole', but 'he was clearly captivated by the prospect of leading the Third Crusade to a successful conclusion, and thus proved willing to dedicate the early years of his reign to this cause'. For all that, the greater skill was demonstrated against Philip II: it is the period 'between 1194 and 1198, that rightly should be regarded as the pinnacle of Richard I's military career'. The portrait is not, however, entirely uncritical. 'His failure to adequately address the issue of succession must be recognized as a significant blemish on his record.' He can be 'accused, first and foremost' of working 'not for the betterment of his realm, protection of his kin or defence of Christendom, but for himself', his 'eyes fixed on the creation of a legend, rather than the foundation of a legacy'. It was 'the quest for this hollow prize' that 'placed the Angevin realm on the path to destruction'.[45]

Richard continues to divide opinion sharply. Some maintain the legend of the great warrior and general, often with great knowledge about military strategy and tactics and very little about the twelfth century. Others denigrate this reputation and view his crusade as an expensive, selfish neglect of his kingdom. There are works which lapse into the bizarre, such as the assertion that Richard's 'legend originated as a PR campaign orchestrated by Queen Eleanor to blackmail the citizens of the Plantagenet Empire into stumping up the enormous ransom demanded for his release from prison that was all of his own making and had nothing to do with religion'.[46] The comparison with Goebbels in the next sentence only emphasises the foolishness of such a ridiculous claim, but when it comes to Richard the Lionheart, it is harder than normal for writers to cast aside the prejudices of their own day. In a secular age, many popular writers barely mention Christianity and the Church when writing about the Middle Ages, erroneously projecting modern indifference backwards. However we judge his crusade, we cannot do so apart from the standards of his religious time, but as one writer has recently observed, the 'issues that he was at the heart of are embarrassing ones in the modern world'.[47] Richard wanted to project himself as a great hero, larger than life, and he succeeded to the extent that in the hands of the historians he has become a famous mass of contradictions: success and failure, lionised and despised, vindicated and condemned, hero and villain.

Richard in Popular Culture

'Alas, I think I am becoming a god' were the humorous last words attributed to the Roman Emperor Vespasian. In Christian medieval England, such notions were blasphemous, but if Richard I was not deified after death, he ascended to the heights of legend. In life he had straddled the border between reality and legend, in death he crossed firmly into mythological realms. 'It is impossible to separate the Richard of history from the Richard of legend', for 'Richard both attracted and encouraged legends in his own lifetime'.[48] While many stories focussed on his deeds as a warrior, some of the earliest and most evocative legends are about his time in captivity. A thirteenth-century French writer, known as the Minstrel of Reims, relates one of the most famous, of Richard and the minstrel Blondel.[49] Not knowing where the king was being held, Blondel sang a song they both knew beneath his prison window, Richard responding with the next verse. The story grew over time, having the minstrel wandering from castle to castle as he searched for the missing Lionheart. It is all romanticised fiction, there never being any secret about where Richard was held. Nevertheless, the legend has exercised a powerful grip on popular memory, one of the few tales showing a softer side to Richard.

A very different approach is taken by a medieval verse romance, *Richard Coer de Lyon*.[50] This survives in fourteenth- and fifteenth-century Middle English versions, based on a (lost) thirteenth-century French original. There are deeply disturbing elements to this poem, not least the portrayal of Richard as a cannibal. During his illness at the siege of Acre, Richard finds himself craving pork. None could be found, so the king is fed a broth made with a young Saracen, restoring his health. The crusaders serve the boiled heads of Saracens to Saladin's envoys, who report back to their master that Richard will not leave the Holy Land until he has eaten every Saracen. Scarcely less palatable is the scene during Richard's captivity, which in this version happens after he has been to scout out the Holy Land but before the actual crusade. He falls for the daughter of the fictitious king holding him prisoner and takes to sleeping with her every night. Learning this, the king has a starving lion released into Richard's cell, which Richard battles and predictably kills. He then tears out the lion's heart, which he takes to the banqueting hall with him. In front of the king, he dips it in salt and eats it raw. Perhaps a medieval audience might have found these exploits in which Richard takes to eating enemies of various species to be evidence of his manliness and martial prowess. Today, we are more likely to feel queasy and see this fictional Richard as a psychopath with a lot of issues.

Richard's was a legend which spread across medieval Europe, found in both German and Spanish literature, and took many forms.[51] In the eighteenth century, the legends worked their way into the opera hall. Handel premiered *Richard the First, King of England* at the King's Theatre in London in November 1727. The opera was based around Richard's conquest of Cyprus, but ran for only eleven performances in 1727–28, with additional performances in Hanover and Braunschweig in 1729. Thereafter, it was forgotten until revived by the Handel Opera Society in London in

1964, and was performed in Cyprus in 1991, on the 800th anniversary of the events it portrays. *Richard Cœur-de-Lion* by André Grétry received its first performance in Paris in October 1784, with the British premier at Covent Garden in October 1786 and a rather surprising US one in Boston in January 1797. One reference book sees this as 'one of the greatest *opéras comiques* of its century'.[52] It tells of Blondel's search for Richard in captivity, where music naturally has a major role. Although it was taboo during revolutionary periods of anti-monarchism in France, it continued to be performed when the political climate allowed, and a recording from a performance at Versailles was released as recently as 2020. In 1841, a new orchestration was provided by Adolphe Adam, who three years later would release his own, considerably less successful, *Richard in Palestine*. Operatic adaptions of the Walter Scott novels *Ivanhoe* and *The Talisman*, which feature Richard, were also popular in the nineteenth century, among them a pastiche opera of *Ivanhoe* using music by Rossini (1826) and a version of *Ivanhoe* by Arthur Sullivan (1891).

With his brother, Richard has become inextricably linked with the Robin Hood legends, Scott's *Ivanhoe* securing the roles of hero and villain for Richard and John in the oft-reworked myths. There is no historical basis, but reality has long been banished from popular ideas about Robin Hood. The legend has proved popular on the screen, lending itself well to cinematic versions. Often, Robin himself is a current or former crusader. Playing Richard in films based around the Robin Hood stories is typically an easy gig, the actor usually only appearing at the end to save the day. Often the physical characteristics of the role are carefully chosen to be an obvious contrast to those of John. Hence in the Disney version of *Robin Hood* (1973), Prince John is a slender, suspicious, unregal lion, whereas King Richard is drawn as a corpulent, jovial, avuncular lion with a prominent mane. John does not appear in the 1991 film *Robin Hood: Prince of Thieves*, but Richard makes a similar last-minute cameo. Sean Connery was 60 at the time, almost twice Richard's actual age when he returned from crusade, the broad Scottish accent unintentionally highlighting that Richard was not English. Plenty of actors have taken on the role of Richard to appear, briefly, in some version of *Ivanhoe* or a Robin Hood story, and there is a degree of monotony across the decades. Occasionally there are different angles, such as Patrick Stewart in the 1993 parody *Robin Hood: Men in Tights*, but generally the part adheres to a tired formula.

On the other hand, that formula highlights Richard the absentee king. A heroic resistance movement led by an outlaw would be unnecessary with a king who was present. The standard narrative is thus an indirect indictment of Richard, and a few retellings take this further by portraying the Lionheart in a much less flattering light. *Robin and Marian* (1976) is set twenty years after Robin Hood's resistance against the sheriff of Nottingham. Robin (Sean Connery) is now an ageing captain in the army of Richard the Lionheart (Richard Harris), his reign extended long beyond historical reality, and the treasure story is the loose basis for the opening part of the film. There is little heroic about Richard here, Harris portraying a brutal, murderous obsessive rather than the chivalric hero. Ridley Scott's 2010 *Robin Hood* similarly begins with Robin (Russell Crowe) as a former crusader in France. An ageing and cantankerous Richard (Danny Huston) does not appreciate Robin's honesty. In the ITV series *Robin of Sherwood* (1984–86), Richard (John Rhys-Davies) turns against Robin when he refuses to do the king's bidding, and unsuccessfully tries to have him killed. While Richard's appearances in a negative light are almost as brief as his heroic ones, they do subvert and refresh tired stereotypes.

Richard's popular fame extends beyond fictional Sherwood Forest. While nineteenth-century historians were growing increasingly critical of Richard, culminating in William Stubbs' blistering condemnation, the bishop's sovereign and many of her subjects had a very different view. In 1853, a letter in *The Times* argued that the effigies of the Plantagenets should be given to England, as recompense for Napoleon's body (exhumed on St Helena and returned to France in 1840).[53] At this stage, Richard was enjoying popular acclaim. In 1851, a clay statue by the Italian sculptor, Carlo Marochetti, had been displayed outside the Crystal Palace at the Great Exhibition. Two years later, an appeal was launched to fund a bronze version, Queen Victoria and Prince Albert among the notable subscribers. Finished in 1856, it was installed in 1860, after lengthy arguments over where to put it. In the end, it was placed in Old Palace Yard, outside the Palace of Westminster. There were those who criticised the placement of Richard outside the Houses of Parliament, among them the architect of the building, Charles Barry, and plenty since have noted the strange juxtaposition of an absentee king and the 'mother of parliaments'. The statue has had some close calls, especially when a Luftwaffe bomb fell nearby during the Blitz and showered Richard with shrapnel, perhaps appropriately for a man who enjoyed being under fire.

Through the nineteenth and early twentieth centuries, the crusades were a popular, romanticised subject,[54] but Richard became especially topical during the later stages of the First World War. As General Edmund Allenby prepared to march on Jerusalem and seize it from the Ottomans in November 1917, the Press Bureau of the British Department of Information advised the press to avoid making any connection between the campaign and ideas of a modern crusade. Mindful of the large number of Muslim subjects in the British Empire, including ones fighting for the imperial forces, the government was very nervous about allowing this to be portrayed as a religious war. Nevertheless, eight days after Allenby had entered the captured city on 11 December, the satirical magazine *Punch* published an inflammatory cartoon. Richard, in full crusading garb, stands on a rock looking towards Jerusalem. The caption reads: 'THE LAST CRUSADE. CŒUR-DE-LION (looking down on the Holy City). "MY DREAM COMES TRUE!"'[55] This was precisely what the Department of Information had warned against, yet by March 1918 it had itself issued a film called *The New Crusaders: With the British Forces on the Palestine Front*.[56]

The Third Crusade is fertile territory for filmmakers, yet they often cannot help projecting anachronism into their characters, as was the case in Ridley Scott's *Kingdom of Heaven* (2005), where the lead character Balian (Orlando Bloom) toys improbably with very modern sentiments. In 1965, in a four-part *Doctor Who* serial, the First Doctor (William Hartnell) takes his TARDIS into Palestine during the Third Crusade and interacts with both Richard and Saladin. In the late 1990s and early 2000s, Richard became a character in video games of warfare and strategy, such as *Age of Empires*, *Medieval: Total War* and *Assassin's Creed.* Few English monarchs have been so employed, and it says much for Richard's continuing popular appeal as crusader and warrior.

Elsewhere, uses of the crusade are far more ominous. Without delving too deeply into a murky area, Richard's story has been used in far-right, Islamophobic rhetoric in the twenty-first century. Even far more noble attempts to link the twelfth century with the modern situation in the Middle East (such as David Elridge's 2014 play, *Holy Warriors*, performed at The Globe) enter dangerously unhistorical territory in directly connecting Richard with the post-9/11 world. A post-religious age likes to see religion (especially, in the West, Islam) as backward and 'medieval', rather than intelligently wrestling with the very different causes of conflict between the twelfth and the twenty-first centuries. Richard was not fighting the twenty-first century's battles and should not be made to do so. This is bad history, and as one historian of the subject sensibly notes, 'the crusades must also be placed where they belong: in the past'.[57] Whatever Richard's faults, we cannot hold him accountable for this grotesque misuse of his name in hate-filled corners of the internet and social media.

Outside Robin Hood and the crusaders, Richard's story does not feature heavily on stage and screen. In James Goldman's play *The Lion in Winter*, he was portrayed in the original, 1966 Broadway run by James Rado. Notably, this is one of the earliest fictional works to assume Richard's homosexuality. Anthony Hopkins took the role in the 1968 film and Andrew Howard in the 2003 TV film remake, and the play has continued to enjoy relatively frequent performances. Four actors were needed to cover Richard's progression from child to adult in the 1978 BBC drama *The Devil's Crown*, Michael Byrne taking the adult role for the relevant episodes. However, there is a certain one-dimensionality to Richard's reign, which was overwhelmingly one of warfare, which limits the opportunities for creative exploration of other angles.

This is also true of novels which take Richard as their subject or a main character. In 1791, James White published *The Adventures of King Richard Cœur-de-Lion*, which begins with Richard leaving captivity. From the opening pages, when Richard addresses his 'favourite and famous steed Arlino' ('Companion of my triumphs, of my travels, of my captivity, collect all thy swiftness, and bear away thy master from this hated principality!'), it is all far too florid for most modern readers.[58] Many details of old legends are changed, but it shows how the romantic stories continued to find an audience in the Georgian era and beyond. *Winning His Spurs: A Tale of the Crusades* (1882), by G. A. Henty, is another romanticised story, about a young nobleman who accompanies Richard to Palestine. The author is controversial, heavily criticised for his jingoism, and his books continue to be promoted on homeschooling websites because the values he espoused (which most today would view as racist, sexist and extremely nationalist, among other things) accord with the views of those in the United States who see minority rights as something to be regretted, if not actively opposed. Unfortunately, a fictional

Richard fighting the Saracens can easily be appropriated into that agenda. The late nineteenth and early twentieth centuries saw several novels published that would now go into the category 'young adult', but which were primarily and unashamedly targeted at boys. As the twentieth century progressed, plenty of adult novels appeared portraying Richard as a swashbuckling hero, very few of which are worth reading today.

Gore Vidal's 1950 *A Search for the King* takes the story of Blondel as its theme, as did *Sir Scoundrel* by John Jakes (originally published under the pen name Jay Scotland) in 1962. Jakes' work was one of the earliest fictional portrayals of a gay Lionheart. The British author Graham Shelby wrote *The Devil is Loose* (1973) about the tussle between Richard and John. Sharon Penman's lengthy *A King's Ransom* (2014) takes the story from Richard's capture until after his death, presenting a more rounded Lionheart than in most fiction, while *Cruel as the Grave* (1998) had looked at England during the imprisonment. The heroic knight, or the poetic captive, are the two dominant themes of most literature about Richard, and few have managed to bring a memorable or original perspective.

Some books fictionalise the story from the perspective of others, in which case Richard rarely emerges well. Ariana Franklin's series is about Henry II, but comments about Richard are unfavourable.

> He has that about him. His father believes in treating with rebels once he's defeated them – anything else is sowing dragon's teeth – but I doubt Richard sees the sense of it; the boy has the touch of the butcher in him.[59]

Likewise, novels written from Saladin's side highlight Richard's brutality and blood lust, the mass execution of Muslim prisoners the prime example. In *The Knight Templar* (1999), by Swedish author Jan Guillou, the protagonist, Arn Magnusson, encounters Richard the 'slaughterer'. The British-Pakistani author, Tariq Ali, treats Richard with some derision in *The Book of Saladin* (1998). Here is a reminder that from some angles, Richard does not appear nearly as heroic as he does in the western legend.

One unusual series was begun by Bernard Knight in 1998. A former Home Office pathologist involved in several high-profile cases, including that of Fred and Rosemary West, it is perhaps unsurprising that the hero of Knight's *Crowner John* series is the fictional coroner for Devon, Sir John de Wolfe. Although the duties were not new, the office of coroner was an innovation of Richard's reign, dating from 1194. Richard himself appears significantly only in the first half of the 2012 prequel, *Crowner's Crusade*, in which Sir John accompanies the king as far as his capture in Vienna. Otherwise, since Richard never visited Devon, he remains in the background for the series. Yet this gives the novels a backdrop while allowing them to develop as local murder mysteries. By largely avoiding the two usual subjects of novels about Richard, and choosing instead to focus on this theme, Knight manages what so few achieve and brings a different perspective to the fictionalisation of the Lionheart's reign.

That little of the fiction about Richard's reign is satisfying or enduring is hardly a surprise. As several historians have noted, here was a man who became a legend in his own lifetime, and the stories have simply been told too often. There are only so many ways to relate the story of Richard the crusader, Richard the warrior, and Richard and Robin Hood. Beyond that, he is not an especially interesting protagonist. There are no sordid love stories, no tempestuous relationships, no great achievements. Strip away the soldier, and there is not much left for the novelist or filmmaker to work with. Beneath the superficial military glamour, Richard the Lionheart is rather dull.

Verdict

'We should not read the Vikings backwards from our own time, but anyone who regards them in a "heroic" light needs to think again', notes the author of a recent history of the Vikings, reminding us that 'no one should look away from what we would see as their less palatable sides, particularly the aggression'.[60] A similar approach is required to assess Richard the Lionheart, for too often he has been condemned as a monster by modern ideologies, or else turned into a heroic, 'ideal' king. We should not judge him by standards which would have made no sense in the twelfth century, or project the ideologies of our own day onto that distant era. However, that does not mean, as many are still inclined to do, that we must accept the legend uncritically and make him a hero. We cannot shy away from the brutality. To understand is not to excuse.

Central to any assessment of Richard is always going to be the thorny question of the Third Crusade. The crusades either get tangled up in the battles of modern religious fundamentalism, or else get lost in the disapproval of secularist fundamentalism that makes no effort to understand the medieval religious world. Where the twenty-first century seeks ownership of places for nationalist reasons, the twelfth sought it for religious ones. That is why so many writers of the twelfth century saw the struggles for Palestine as a noble cause, and why so many warriors responded to the call. Modern condemnation does not get us very far in analysing the twelfth century. Far more important are the questions of whether Richard's crusade was a success and whether undertaking it was a wise idea. In both cases, the answer is probably no. There were some spectacular victories. Richard emerged with his martial reputation reaching great heights. However, the purpose of the crusade was to recapture Jerusalem. It was not achieved and to the immense frustration of many, Richard never even tried. However good the strategic arguments, it was a failure. That Richard sulkily refused to go to the Holy Sepulchre, the holiest of Christian sites, raises serious questions about how far he was motivated by the quest for personal glory rather than the piety so often used to defend his crusade. If the capture of Cyprus was beneficial in the long term, it was one of a series of distractions which turned Richard from what should have been his main purpose. Richard was following his own agenda, hiding behind that of the Church.

Going on crusade was seen as an honourable venture, but was it sensible for Richard to do so when he had only just inherited the large, complex Angevin 'empire'? By the time he returned, his territories were diminished and under serious threat. His defenders are quick to observe that had he not been captured on his way home, the governance arrangements he had put in place would have held firm. Yet crusading was an inherently risky venture. Had Richard been killed in the Holy Land, there were no practical arrangements in place for the succession and civil war would have been a very real possibility. Part of the reason he was captured and held for so long was that his brazen pursuit of personal fame and renown had led him to trample ruthlessly on the sensibilities of other rulers. Above all, it is hard to justify the immense financial burden he placed upon his subjects. Politically, the crusade was a reckless venture, costing huge sums across the decade of Richard's reign. It is a very debatable point how much longer England could have afforded to support Richard's endless campaigning, even had there been a desire to do so. He may not have bled England dry by the time he died, but he was doing his best to ensure a fatal haemorrhage.

When considering Richard's chivalric reputation, few tend to remember that Richard was in many ways no better than Philip II. English writers are exercised by Philip's bad faith in conspiring with John and attacking Normandy during Richard's absence. The criticism is valid, but in the matter of Philip's sister Alice, Richard had been equally deceitful. He knew that he was never going to marry her, yet continued to make dishonest promises, then hid behind a pathetic excuse. Meanwhile, John is frequently and heavily criticised for his treachery against Richard, but Richard's treachery against Henry is usually explained away or overlooked. John learned about conspiracy from Richard, and Richard was no political genius as he dismantled his own inheritance with Philip because Henry wouldn't give him his own way. Nor can we forget Richard's brutality, manifested most obviously in his slaughter of the prisoners at Acre, but evident too in his love of fighting for its own sake.

The criticisms levelled at Richard for the time he spent in England are unfair, at least in the Anglocentric way they are normally framed. England was but one of several lands over which he ruled, albeit the wealthiest and the one which gave him his crown. The gravest threats during his reign were to his French lands, so it is natural that he spent his time on the Continent. However, accepting that does not mean that we must also accept that he was a good king. He paid attention to administrative matters because he needed England to be peaceful in order to harness its resources. Richard had little interest in England for its own sake and he did neglect the kingdom. If anyone emerges vindicated from Richard I's reign, it is Henry II. Had Henry left England to go on crusade four months into his reign, chaos would have ensued. There would certainly have been no money to allow any such venture. That Richard could raise the money he needed, and that England survived his absence largely unscathed, was testimony to Henry's enormous achievement in creating a stable, solvent and well-governed kingdom. The crusade was only possible because of Henry's legacy. Richard left no comparable legacy, and we should not turn him into a great administrative genius simply because he was able to use effectively what his father bequeathed.

Beneath the glamorous stories, the tales of heroic deeds and feats of arms, there lies at the heart of the legend of Richard I a sad, curious emptiness. If there were victories, the crusade failed in its ultimate objective and Richard turned for home without even trying. If he was winning the war against Philip Augustus, he was only edging things back towards the situation he had inherited. If robust government continued, it says far more about Henry II and Richard's officials than it does about Richard himself. Behind the legend, there is nothing of substance. Perhaps on his own terms he succeeded, for he narcissistically wanted to be famous and achieved that aim. But there is no achievement, no lasting legacy, and had Richard lived longer this might have become glaringly obvious even in his own lifetime. Romantic stories and elaborated myths can conceal this only so far. Richard the Lionheart was not a great king. He was not even a good one.

Chapter 3

Edward I: A Strong King?

To what shall we compare the noble Edward?
Perhaps he will be rightly called a leopard.
If we divide the name, it becomes a lion and a pard [...]
He is a lion by his pride and ferocity;
by his fickleness and inconstancy
he is a pard, changing his word and promise,
excusing himself with pleasing speech.[1]

In comparing the future Edward I to a leopard, the author of the *Song of Lewes* was not being complimentary. Leopards were believed to be the offspring of a lion and a mythical creature called the pard; these beasts had a reputation for cunning, dishonesty and brutality. Edward's courage was acknowledged, but when this was written in the 1260s, the prince was seen as slippery and untrustworthy. When he died as king more than forty years later, he was still regarded as slippery and untrustworthy by many, but none would have accused him of hiding behind pleasing speech. His reign was one of the most aggressively transformative in British history; he left few in any doubt about his intentions as he forthrightly pursued his aims.

Edward changed the history of the British Isles. He had a vision of English overlordship besides which the efforts of Henry II and John pale into insignificance. Had he achieved his aim, the King of England would have ruled across the whole island of Britain. Edward conquered Wales and is known as the 'Hammer of the Scots'. Many in Wales and Scotland might curse his ambition rather than salute his greatness, but his impact is undeniable. Past generations were also awed by the legal achievements of his reign. He was undoubtedly, as Sellar and Yeatman called him, a strong king, or in the title of a modern biography, a 'great and terrible king'.[2] This last hints at elements of darkness, stains on his reputation, not least a brutality in which he seemed to take pleasure, and the grim story of the expulsion of England's Jews. Like Shakespeare's Julius Caesar, he may at times have seemed to 'bestride the narrow world like a Colossus', but do those dark stains blot out his claims to being one of the greatest of kings?

Edward's Life and Reign

Edward was born in the Palace of Westminster on the night of 17/18 June 1239, the oldest son of Henry III and Eleanor of Provence. Although the royal family and nobility remained culturally French, Henry was an English speaker with a devotion to Anglo-Saxon royal saints, especially Edward the Confessor. His eldest son was named after the Confessor and became the first heir since the Norman Conquest to have an English name. Although known to us as King Edward I, he was not the first Edward to rule in England. Prior to 1066, there had been three Anglo-Saxon kings with this name: Edward the Elder (899–924), Edward the Martyr (975–78) and Edward the Confessor (1042–66). Regnal numbers were not unknown, but during Edward I's lifetime he could easily be identified as 'King Edward the son of King Henry'. Likewise his son, Edward II, was readily identifiable as 'King Edward the son of King Edward'. By the time of Edward III, however, 'King Edward the son of King Edward the son of King Edward' was a little cumbersome. Hence regnal numbering became more common in England, but rather than being styled Edward VI, Edward became 'Edward the third after the Conquest'. 1066 was seen as a definitive break, resetting the system, so Edward's grandfather became 'Edward the first after the Conquest', Edward I rather than Edward IV.

In 1239, all this lay in the future. Henry could be relieved that the future of the dynasty was more secure. In a further link with the Confessor, Edward became the first future king baptised in Westminster Abbey. In 1240, Henry had everyone in the realm swear allegiance to Edward as his heir. Edward would have four siblings, including the crucial 'spare', a brother, Edmund (named after the canonised Anglo-Saxon king interred at Bury St Edmunds) in 1245. The royal family was unusually close for the time, his parents far less remote than most monarchs, as shown by one episode in Edward's early years. While visiting Beaulieu Abbey in 1246, Edward fell ill (he suffered several childhood illnesses). Breaking every rule of the Cistercian order, which banned women from the monastery, Queen Eleanor insisted on staying with her son for almost three weeks, until he recovered. The prior and cellarer of the abbey, consequently dismissed for allowing this breach of regulations, perhaps felt more ambiguous about this demonstration of parental love.

Edward's English name belied the French culture in which he was raised. French was his first language, although he also became proficient in Latin and could speak English; there is no evidence he could read and write, but it is unlikely he was illiterate. His mother was the daughter of the Count of Provence, and her sister was married to Louis IX of France. The queen's Savoy relatives would become key players at the English court from the late 1230s, which was largely accepted. By contrast, when Henry III's half-brothers, issue of his mother's remarriage to Hugh de Lusignan after King John's death, were brought to England in 1247, there was considerable resentment at the patronage they absorbed and the influence they exercised. Another key Frenchman in court circles was Simon de Montfort, Earl of Leicester and husband of Henry's sister Eleanor. In 1248, Montfort was made lieutenant of Gascony, all that was now left of the duchy of Aquitaine. He continued in this role when Gascony was assigned to the 10-year-old Edward (without the title 'Duke of Aquitaine') the following year. It was not a successful appointment. By 1252, Gascony was in turmoil.

This unrest led to Edward's marriage at the tender age of 15. In 1253, the unmilitary Henry was forced to campaign in Gascony to quell the disorder. Among those supporting the rebels was Alfonso X of Castile (1252–84), whom the English government were seriously concerned might invade the duchy. Alfonso was the great-grandson of Henry II of England and claimed Gascony. It was a weak claim, but Henry III wanted to remove any potential threat. Alfonso agreed to renounce his claim if Edward married Eleanor, his half-sister. In February 1254, in preparation for the marriage, Edward was granted estates worth £10,000 annually: Gascony, Ireland, the Channel Islands, Cheshire, Bristol and lands in North Wales were the key elements. Known honorifically as the Lord Edward, he was afforded no formal title to accompany his extensive lands. Henry was adamant that Gascony would remain fully attached to the English crown, denying a frustrated Edward free rein in the duchy.

Edward sailed to Bordeaux in May, joining in the last military action against the rebels. Henry returned to England while Edward went to Castile. His wedding to Eleanor, two years his junior, took place in Las Huelgas Monastery in Burgos on 1 November 1254. Although conceived as a political match, this turned into one of the most successful marriages in the history of the English monarchy. They would later become almost inseparable. Highly active in the marriage bed, Edward is not known to have had any illegitimate children or mistresses. The couple produced at least fourteen and possibly sixteen children between 1255 and 1284.[3] However, of the four boys, only the last, the future Edward II, survived into adulthood. The girls were scarcely more fortunate, just three outliving their father.

Edward returned to Bayonne to deal with Gascon affairs, growing increasingly exasperated by his father's interference from a distance, before heading back to England at the end of 1255. Yet as he began to assert himself and seek a greater political role, Edward's relations with his father grew tenser. The prince connived behind the king's back. Stories tell of loutish and scandalous behaviour by Edward and his household. An arrogant prince with a gang of disorderly followers suggested trouble to come.

In November 1256, Llywelyn ap Gruffudd, ruler of Gwynedd, overran the Four Cantrefs, the area of Wales between the Rivers Dee and Conwy that had been given to Edward ahead of his marriage. Henry wanted a diplomatic solution, Edward wanted war. Dreadful weather and a lack of money favoured the king's strategy. In the winter of 1256–57, Llywelyn pushed into South Wales. Edward planned to use his castles at Carmarthen and Cardigan to fight back. Instead, on 2 June 1257, Edward's troops suffered a catastrophic defeat in Carmarthenshire. Henry reluctantly accepted that he would now have to act and in August, he and Edward set out from Chester and reached Deganwy, Henry's castle overlooking the Conwy, which was still in royal hands. Henry then called off the campaign on 4 September on the risible grounds of the approaching winter. The king looked weak and ridiculous. Edward became embroiled in violence in the Welsh Marches. In March 1258, Llywelyn used the title 'Prince of Wales' for the first time. The following month, Wales faded into the background as Henry's reign fell apart.

By the 1250s, parliaments had become an accepted part of the political scene, although at this stage they were still essentially assemblies of the barons and upper clergy. The one which met in April 1258 did so with elements of the nobility feeling mutinous. Resentment at the king's Lusignan half-brothers, and bemusement at an expensive and unrealistic scheme to put Henry's son Edmund on the Sicilian throne, were two of the major factors in the baronial revolt which followed. In the face of an armed march on Westminster Hall by key lords, Henry and his heir were forced to accept a plan for reform of the realm. Notably, the queen sided with the rebels, in part to end the influence the hated Lusignans had begun to exercise over Edward. A new parliament met at Oxford in June. The barons embarked on a programme of sweeping reform, the results of which became known as the Provisions of Oxford. These imposed severe restrictions on the king and his freedom of action, placing a council in effective charge of running the country. Edward escaped to Winchester with his half-uncles, where after a standoff with the barons in early July, he caved and swore to accept the new arrangements, while the Lusignans went into exile.

The problems in Wales gave Edward an excuse to continue associating with other belligerent friends, while tournaments in England and France provided combat training for him and his associates. By the late summer of 1259 he had decided he needed to align himself with the reformers' cause, if only to repair his badly damaged reputation. Reform had proceeded apace, but neither quickly nor universally enough for some. There were divisions among the earls. At parliament in October 1259, an enigmatic group addressed a protest to Edward about the lack of meaningful reform for the lower orders, and the prince immediately swore to support them. Whether or not Edward was behind the petition, the barons had to act, issuing further reforms which became known as the Provisions of Westminster. The king was with Louis IX in France, a visit which resulted in the Treaty of Paris. It was a rare success of these years for Henry, bringing an extended period of peace between the two realms.

The king's eldest son, meanwhile, was moving closer to the reformers, in particular Simon de Montfort. Although Montfort was Edward's godfather, the two had not had much to do with each other before this stage. Now mutual self-interest drew them together. Personal feuds intermingled with high ideals at this time: 'what was arguably more important during these years than any clash of principle was the series of bitter feuds at the heart of the royal family'.[4] Edward saw the potential for Montfort to help him regain control of the lands and castles surrendered to the council, Montfort sensed Edward could aid him in his disputes with other barons. Both opposed the Treaty of Paris, albeit for different reasons. With the king and queen in France, Edward seized back his castles. Provocatively, he spent Christmas 1259 in Bristol Castle, also claimed by another leading reformer, Richard de Clare, Earl of Gloucester. In February 1260, Edward and Montfort arrived in London for parliament, which according to the Provisions of Oxford should meet three times each year. However, Henry was still in France and had written to forbid parliament to convene in his absence. Edward and Montfort's attempts to hold a parliament regardless led to a breach between the king and his son. Henry sent the Earl of Gloucester back to England to investigate, an unfortunate choice given the bad feeling between Edward and Gloucester over Bristol. Both sides began to assemble forces.

Richard of Cornwall, the king's younger brother, calmed matters down until Henry returned at the end of April 1260. Richard then mediated between his brother and his nephew, until Edward was formally reconciled with the king and queen at a special ceremony in St Paul's Cathedral. Edward's appointees were evicted from his castles and replaced. Henry had no desire to reach a similar accord with Montfort, who was placed on trial in the parliament of July 1260. By now, Edward was his only real ally, unable to help after his own submission. It was Llywelyn ap Gruffudd who saved Montfort, news arriving in the middle of the trial that he had destroyed Builth Castle. The trial collapsed immediately as the royal councillors argued about how to respond. Edward had no doubts. Builth was one of his fortresses and he raced to Cheshire to prepare a counterattack. After some indecision, however, Henry agreed with the peacemakers and a truce was negotiated, frustrating Edward's desire for revenge.

Incredibly, given they had been on the verge of armed conflict just months earlier, Edward and Montfort now made common cause with the Earl of Gloucester. The unlikely trio appeared at the Westminster parliament of October 1260 and staged a coup. The realm's main officials and key councillors were replaced. Having seized control, Edward then left England with a large group of knights. Stopping in Paris to see his exiled half-uncles, he travelled through France to Lyon, participating in tournaments. Christmas and the early part of 1261 was spent in Gascony, until news reached Edward in March of developments in England. Henry and Eleanor had taken refuge in the Tower of London and were involved in a standoff with Montfort and Gloucester, both sides now claiming to be the true reformers.

Hurrying back, Edward brought with him one of his Lusignan half-uncles, Aymer de Valence. Soon after returning to England, however, Valence defected to the king. Edward's loyalties were now torn between Montfort and Valence. Financial considerations were the deciding factor. Edward had been spending extravagantly and was almost bankrupt. In May 1261, he returned to his parents. At Winchester in June, Henry staged a counter-coup, revealing a papal letter which countermanded all reforms since 1258 and released the king from his oath to uphold the Provisions of Oxford. As England stood on the brink of civil war, Edward went back to Gascony. By the end of 1261, Montfort had been outmanoeuvred and he was in exile in France, isolated. So too was Edward as he spent Christmas and the New Year of 1262 in Bordeaux, accompanied by very few of his friends. In England, his parents were dealing with his financial affairs, which prompted him to return in February. A deal was reached in June, whereby Edward surrendered some of his lands for three years in return for badly needed money. He crossed the Channel again at once and began a rather aimless drift through the tournament circuit.

In Paris, Henry and Eleanor were engaged in fruitless negotiations with Simon de Montfort. When these collapsed in December, Henry returned to England to learn that Llywelyn and the Welsh were causing serious damage in the border counties. By April 1263, Edward was in the Welsh Marches preparing to retaliate, but he unintentionally started a different war. Henry's regime was unpopular, the queen and her relatives especially blamed for the overthrow of the reforms. Now Edward's old friends were infuriated that he came accompanied by yet more foreigners. The opposition rallied around Montfort, who returned to England. At Oxford in May, the rebels swore to uphold the Provisions and called on the king to denounce all those who did not do likewise. Henry's predictable refusal resulted in an attack on the lands of the queen and her allies. Edward rapidly abandoned Wales and dashed to join the king and queen in the Tower of London.

As Henry considered his options, Edward seized the initiative. On 29 June, he and his associates plundered the New Temple, English headquarters of the Knights Templar. This treasure was taken to Windsor Castle and augmented by supplies stolen from the surrounding area. The Londoners responded to Edward's brazen act by looting the houses of royalists and foreigners. On 4 July, Henry capitulated to his enemies' demands, which had descended to vindictive xenophobia, as Montfort demanded the permanent expulsion of all foreigners from the kingdom of England. 'It is', notes a modern commentator, 'one of the more telling ironies of English history – one apparently lost on contemporaries – that this self-consciously English political movement, brought together in part by common resentment of foreigners, should be led by a Frenchman'.[5] The demand was unacceptable to Queen Eleanor, a foreigner herself, who set out by boat along the Thames to join Edward, but was stopped by a hostile crowd at London Bridge. Soon the king and queen, along with Dover Castle, surrendered, leaving Edward the lone holdout at Windsor. In late July, with Montfort marching to besiege the castle, terms were agreed and Edward rejoined his parents. Eleanor crossed to the safer surroundings of France.

Montfort was now in control of the kingdom, yet as had been the case in Gascony more than a decade earlier, he was unequal to the task. The legend that has grown up around his name obscures the reality of a man who was ambitious and vindictive, achieving his ends through xenophobic rabble-rousing, primarily motivated by his own interests rather than the reformist cause he used as a fig leaf. This made him unable to act as a source of unity and the country rapidly descended into chaos. The situation was twice submitted to Louis IX for arbitration. On the first occasion, at Boulogne in the autumn of 1263, the French king upheld the terms agreed between Henry and Montfort in July. A second judgement in January 1264, the Mise of Amiens, reversed this position and ruled almost entirely in favour of Henry III and royal power. Violence erupted in the Welsh Marches and civil war began. A period of sieges and counter-sieges across southern England, castles captured and surrendered, led the two sides to Sussex.

There, in the Battle of Lewes on 14 May 1264, Montfort emerged victorious. That he did so was largely due to a major error by Edward. The prince had begun the battle with a bold and successful charge, but a thirst for vengeance got the better of him as he and his contingent chased the defeated enemy several miles from the battlefield. By the time he returned, the situation was hopeless. His uncle, Richard of Cornwall, had been captured. Edward joined his father in the refuge of Lewes Priory. A settlement was negotiated whereby Henry and Edward surrendered, the king once again submitting to rule by council and the Provisions of Oxford. In practice, Montfort had set himself up as king in all but name. Henry was kept in London, officially free but actually an open prisoner. Edward was imprisoned at Dover and then Wallingford.

Montfort's regime held together uneasily through the rest of 1264. Wales and the Welsh Marches remained tense. Most worryingly for Montfort, one of the key lords in that region was far from a resolute ally. Gilbert de Clare, the new Earl of Gloucester, had resented Henry III's delays in letting him inherit his lands, prompting him to align with Montfort. His commitment to Montfort and his cause was lukewarm at best, especially because he had grave doubts about Edward's incarceration. On 11 March 1265, in an ostentatious ceremony in Westminster Hall, Edward was freed. In reality, this simply meant he was no longer officially imprisoned, as Montfort kept him under his control. However, it gave hope to the growing coalition against Montfort. Sensing the greatest threat to be in the Welsh March, Montfort made for Hereford, taking Henry and Edward with him. Here Edward made a daring but carefully planned escape on 28 May. He was permitted to exercise his horses, and proceeded to ride them one by one until they were exhausted, galloping away on the final horse. With Roger Mortimer, one of the Marcher lords, Edward rode swiftly to Ludlow, where the Earl of Gloucester was waiting.

For Montfort, this was a disaster. He was in the worst possible place as a formidable coalition built against him, and needed to get to less hostile territory in the South East. Recognising this, his enemies broke all the bridges over the River Severn. A trapped Montfort, with a small army and the captive Henry III, was shadowed around South Wales by Edward and his allies. The end of July found Montfort back at Hereford, waiting for the arrival of reinforcements under his son, another Simon. Edward was in Worcester, guarding the Severn line. On 1 August, he received intelligence that the younger Simon had reached his father's castle of Kenilworth. Inexperienced and complacent, the army was enjoying the town rather than safely behind the fortress walls. Edward immediately set out from Worcester to travel overnight, speeding the thirty-five miles to Kenilworth, where his forces fell upon the sleeping enemy. Montfort junior escaped by rowing naked across the castle moat, but Edward's return to Worcester with a large number of prisoners was a triumph. His brief absence had allowed the elder Montfort to cross the Severn on 2 August, either by ferry or ford at Kempsey, only around four miles south of Worcester. Hoping to unite his forces with what remained of his son's, Montfort and his army set out on the evening of the 3rd. Early the next morning, they paused at Evesham for breakfast. Shortly afterwards, there was jubilation when the banners of the younger Montfort were sighted. It turned to despair when it became clear that the army was in fact Edward's, having shadowed them through the night and made good (if deceptive) use of the standards captured at Kenilworth.

Montfort was a dead man. Evesham is a dreadful place to be trapped and forced into battle, for the loop of the River Avon surrounds it on three sides. While there is some debate about the exact scenario, Edward had essentially cut off the only way out, to the north, and his superior army now approached from this high ground. The prince and his allies were so determined to see Montfort dead that a special squadron was specifically tasked with finding and killing him. The job was undertaken with glee and savagery, Montfort's body hacked apart and his genitals placed in his mouth before his head was sent to his luckless wife. The royalist victory was absolute and a bloodbath, a massacre rather than a battle. 'Within the town, the abbey courtyard, the cemeteries and the monastery church the dead bodies lay thick and dense on the ground like animals', wrote one commentator, adding additional gory details, that 'the choir of the church and the inside walls and the cross and the statues and the altars were sprayed with the blood of the wounded and the dead, so that from the bodies that there were around the high altar a stream of blood ran right down into the crypts'.[6]

The Battle of Evesham undid the humiliations of the previous decade. In contrast to his bloodthirstiness on the battlefield, Edward was afterwards inclined to be merciful to former adherents of Montfort. Henry III had other ideas. At the parliament of September 1265, he declared that his supporters could keep the lands they had seized from his opponents in the aftermath of Evesham. Londoners received especially heavy punishment. Richard of Cornwall, recently released from imprisonment and with cause to support such vengeance, nevertheless saw how unwise the policy was; he was not alone in refusing to support his brother and withdrawing from court. His own inclinations notwithstanding, Edward backed his father rather than his uncle. Perhaps he was more concerned in rebuilding his family ties. He was reunited with his wife, from whom he had been separated during his captivity. In October, he met Queen Eleanor as she docked at Dover after two years in French exile, accompanying his mother to a reunion with her husband at Canterbury. Edmund, Edward's younger brother, had also been in exile and now returned to England to be granted Montfort's lands and then his earldom of Leicester.

At Northampton in December 1265, plans were laid to subdue dissenters and malcontents, but the king's vindictiveness proved counterproductive. Kenilworth still held out. The younger Simon de Montfort had based himself in the inaccessible Isle of Axholme in Lincolnshire. Edward was tasked with dealing with this band of rebels and opted for negotiation, bringing Montfort to trial in Northampton, where he was sentenced to a year in exile. Yet the royalists, above all Edward after all his changes of allegiance, were not trusted. Consequently, Edward worked hard at conciliation and gradually won people and communities over. Through the first half of 1266, he brought rebels to heel, but opted for clemency rather than bloodshed. His reputation was beginning to change as he showed evidence of the political and military qualities, as well as the statesmanship, a king would require, in noted contrast to his father.

July 1266 brought a moment of happy respite, as Eleanor gave birth to the couple's first son, who was named John after his great-grandfather, a rather pointed choice in the circumstances. The following month, parliament assembled at Kenilworth to reach terms with those still holding out in the fortress. At the end of October, a committee headed by the papal legate issued what became known as the Dictum of Kenilworth, whereby the rebels would be allowed to regain their lands in return for large fines, although they would only receive their lands back when they had paid in full. The most zealous continued to hold out, but just before Christmas, worn down by a long siege and the prospect of starvation, Kenilworth's garrison surrendered. In March 1267, Edward dealt successfully with a rising based around Alnwick in Northumberland, while his father failed to end the rebellion based in the fens around Ely. The Earl of Gloucester had defected back to the rebels and seized London. Edward brought a large army with him from the North, joining Henry at Cambridge in late April. Together, they began a march on London. At this point, Richard of Cornwall and other moderates intervened to secure an amendment to the Dictum of Kenilworth, allowing rebels to recover their lands immediately. Bloodshed averted, Henry III was reinstalled in London. Edward mopped up the final resisters in Ely. Almost two years after the Battle of Evesham, England was finally at peace. In September, peace was also assured in Wales by the Treaty of Montgomery, whereby Henry and Edward conceded the title 'Prince of Wales' to Llywelyn, along with possession or overlordship over many of his territorial gains, in return for the promise of homage.

The war years had transformed Edward from a mistrusted, wayward young man. Now 28, he had shown himself a skilful general, a courageous warrior and a level-headed, realistic statesman. Henry III reigned, but the stability of England depended on Edward. The problem was that despite having been on the throne half a century, already far longer than any previous king of England, Henry was only sixty. It was entirely possible Edward had several more years to wait before the crown became his. The heir therefore wanted to avail himself of the opportunity provided by the papacy's latest call for a crusade, to which Louis IX had signed up (despite already having one crusade on his CV). Henry III and many others were appalled by the idea, fearful of what might happen in England with Edward's stabilising presence removed from the scene. Edward was adamant. At Northampton on 24 June 1268, Edward, his brother Edmund and hundreds of others took the cross. Their number included Edward's wife, Eleanor; while women were discouraged from such actions, there were precedents for queens and noblewomen accompanying their husbands. Now the problem was finding the money. The papacy had none to offer. Parliament was not going to fund him. Legislation to reform Jewish moneylending and its abuse by rich Christians was passed and then ignored. A loan from the King of France helped, but the crusade and fundraising efforts began to cause tensions among the English nobility as 1269 advanced. The Earl of Gloucester took offence again. Henry III was far more concerned with the translation of Edward the Confessor's body to its new shrine, a ceremony which took place in Henry's remodelled but unfinished Westminster Abbey in October

1269, with the king, his brother and his two sons shouldering the saint's coffin. At the start of 1270, Edward's planned departure on crusade in the summer looked distinctly unlikely.

Fortune changed course suddenly. The parliament of April–May 1270 granted a tax for the crusade. After Henry III got carried away and wanted to join in, Edward presumably enormously relieved when this plan proved nothing more than a brief period of deluded enthusiasm, the prince had to scramble to assemble his knights. This was achieved by early August. At Winchester, Edward put Richard of Cornwall in charge of his lands and made him guardian to his children while he was away, since Eleanor would accompany him. On 20 August 1270, Edward and his crusading force set sail for France. They reached the Mediterranean coast in France at the end of September, to discover Louis IX had departed two months earlier. Bewilderingly for the English, they discovered that the French had headed not to the Middle East but to North Africa.

Louis' younger brother, Charles of Anjou, had succeeded in installing himself as King of Sicily and now had ambitions to rule over parts of the African coast. Charles persuaded Louis, in what must have been a truly ingenious argument, that attacking Tunis would be the best way to help the Holy Land, so the French crusaders sailed south. The bemused English had little choice but to follow the French to North Africa. Arriving on 9 November, they discovered that Louis IX had died on 25 August and been succeeded by his son, Philip III. Charles had reached accommodation with the Tunisian ruler and the French were already starting to withdraw. Again, the English had little choice but to accompany them back to Sicily. Officially the Eighth Crusade, the campaign was a bizarre venture which had seen no action and was a naked vanity project for Charles of Anjou, which suited him very well but was catastrophic for the French. In addition to losing Louis, much of their fleet was wrecked in a storm off Trapani while returning to Sicily. Philip III left for France with his father's body in January 1271. In the spring, refusing to be diverted from their aim, Edward and the English sailed for Palestine.

The Christians were barely clinging on in the Holy Land. Edward's fleet arrived in Acre just weeks after the imposing crusader fortress of Krak des Chevaliers, in modern Syria, had fallen. The English force was too small to provide anything but symbolic hope to the beleaguered Christians in Acre, especially when the summer heat and unfamiliar diet finished off a fair number of the new arrivals within a short time of their arrival. To improve his chances of emulating his great-uncle, the Lionheart, Edward set about making alliances with the Knights Templar and Hospitaller, and the King of Cyprus. In September, his brother Edmund arrived. Edward's most daring appeal was to the Mongols, who responded positively and swept from modern Iran into what is now Syria, evicting the Muslims from Aleppo. With the Sultan's forces heading north in response to this threat, the Christian forces seized the opportunity to leave Acre and attack Qaqun, a castle around halfway to Jerusalem. The attempt failed and the disillusioned crusaders found themselves back inside Acre, facing further dismay when news reached them that the Mongols had turned back. In April 1272, the Christians agreed a ten-year truce with the Muslims.

While contemporary accounts of what followed are muddled and difficult to disentangle, it seems Edward grew reckless. A Muslim messenger managed to secure a private audience with him in June, at which he attempted to stab the prince. Edward killed his attacker but was wounded himself. The concern was that it was a poisoned dagger. A later story, romantic but sadly entirely fictional, told how Eleanor courageously and lovingly sucked the poison from her husband's wound. In reality, the main worry was infection, no one needing a reminder that Richard I had succumbed to gangrene. The incipient infection was cut away, the painful process saving Edward's life. The crusade, however, was over. In September, Edward and Eleanor left Acre, sailing for the kingdom of Sicily. Arriving in November, they spent Christmas with Charles of Anjou. There, at the start of 1273, Edward learned he had become king.

Henry III had died on 16 November 1272. He had been on the throne for fifty-six years, beyond the living memory of most of his subjects. The realm now had a problem. Before 1272, it was the coronation which ended an interregnum and began a new reign. There were several precedents for the heir to the throne being in France when their predecessor died. Edward, however, was much further away and any interregnum would be far longer than normal or desirable if traditional practice were followed. Where in previous times others might have come forward to seize the crown, the rules of succession were now fixed and there was no question that Edward was to be the new king. The nobility innovated. After Henry's funeral in Westminster Abbey on 20 November, they swore allegiance to Edward at the high altar, despite being (as one chronicler put it) 'entirely ignorant whether he was still alive'.[7] It was an approach which fundamentally changed the theory of accession; thereafter, in normal circumstances the new king acceded the day after his predecessor's death, coronation following at a later date.

Edward's eldest son, John, had died in 1271. His uncle, Richard of Cornwall, had gone to the grave a few months ahead of Henry III. Though England, having lost three senior royals in short order, would have welcomed Edward's swift return (if only to prove he was still alive), he took an extraordinarily long time coming back. He visited Pope Gregory X, stayed with his Savoy relatives, took part in a tournament in France, and in July 1273 went to Paris to swear homage to Philip III of France for the duchy of Aquitaine. Edward finally had the title his father had denied him, Duke of Aquitaine, along with actual power in Gascony. Already on the Continent, he took the opportunity to spend a year dealing with Gascon affairs, including the perennial rebellions, before eventually landing back in England on 2 August 1274, more than twenty months after his accession. Yet if he had been slow in returning, from his coronation on 19 August onwards Edward seemed in a great hurry to impose himself on his realm. His barons might have wondered whether they were quite so keen to have him back after all, as he embarked on a determined campaign to reassert the royal authority and rights he felt had been lost by his father. No sooner had the Archbishop of Canterbury crowned him than

Edward took the crown off and vowed not to put it back on until he had recovered all the crown rights granted away by Henry.

The new king was physically imposing. At 6ft 2in, his height was notably above average, leading to the contemporary nickname Longshanks ('long legs'). Edward was never to shed his hot temper and proclivity for violence, his more noteworthy tantrums including beating a squire with a stick at the wedding of one of his daughters, and throwing another daughter's coronet into the fire. There was 'a streak of character which could turn Edward from a legalist to a vicious street fighter'.[8] Old and new kings were very different in significant ways. Ascending to the throne as a crusader with a military reputation, Edward's reign was to show that he almost lived for warfare. Henry had poured vast resources into Westminster Abbey, but his son would be remembered for castles, not abbeys. Henry 'liked the comfortable life', staying as much as possible in his palaces in the South of England, which he decorated lavishly. He was distinctly unmilitary and a reluctant campaigner, with 'a genuine desire for peace between rulers and peoples'.[9] Edward, by contrast, was a much more itinerant king. His favourite pastimes were active ones, hunting and falconry. As Henry's biographer notes, the 'contrast between Henry's inertia and Edward's drive is extreme'.[10] On the other hand, Edward inherited something of his father's piety when it came to almsgiving, touching for scrofula, pilgrimage and visits to religious centres. Despite more than one clash with the Church and having his last Archbishop of Canterbury exiled, Edward was viewed as a pious Christian king by his contemporaries.

Almost immediately, Edward showed his determination. He named as chancellor a cleric from his household, Robert Burnell. The new chancellor was a man of great administrative ability but distinctly limited spiritual gifts, his mistresses and illegitimate children causing the monks of Canterbury to reject him as a candidate for archbishop in 1270. However, Edward managed to appoint him to the bishopric of Bath and Wells when it fell vacant at the end of 1274. Until his death in 1292, Burnell was Edward's loyal right-hand man. King and chancellor embarked on making good Edward's coronation vow to reassert royal authority. In October, they replaced most sheriffs. Commissioners were appointed to investigate corruption by royal officials and encroachment onto royal rights in the shires. These commissioners travelled the country in pairs, taking evidence from local people. These endeavours have become known as the Hundred Roll Inquiry of 1274–75, because the unit of investigation was the hundred (a subdivision of a county), and the commissioners compiled hundred rolls.

The voluminous data these contained helped to shape the agenda of the first parliament of the new reign at which the king was present in person, which assembled at Westminster in April 1275. From this assembly came the first Statute of Westminster. It is a lengthy, wide-ranging piece of legislation, fifty-one chapters concerning the governance of the realm and the localities, the conduct of royal officials and all manner of administrative reforms. In addition, Edward solved some of his financial worries by persuading parliament to agree to give him a customs duty of half a mark (6s 8d) on every sack of wool exported. More sinister was the statute which was published by another parliament in the autumn. Among its provisions were a ban on Jews practising usury (moneylending with interest), and an order that Jews live only in royal towns, Christians unable to live among them. Most ominously in the light of later history, a clause stated that Jews over the age of 7 had to wear a yellow badge, six inches by three inches, showing the 'two tables joined' (the stone tablets on which the Ten Commandments were given to Moses). Jews were also expelled from the dower lands of his mother, which has led some to see her as the driving force behind the measures, although as Eleanor's biographer has observed, Edward 'had respect for his mother's views on matters concerning her own affairs or concerning the family', but 'his expulsion of the Jews is readily explained without any reference to her influence'.[11] It was politically popular in the antisemitic context of England and Europe at the time, and it was not the first time Edward had acted against Jewish communities.

In the eyes of contemporaries, Edward had made a bold and successful start to his reign, a welcome change from the dithering of Henry III. He now turned his attention to Wales. Llywelyn ap Gruffudd was in considerable arrears, the payment schedule agreed at Montgomery in 1267, in return for recognition as Prince of Wales, having proved distinctly optimistic relative to his income. Edward might have overlooked this, but Llywelyn failed to attend his coronation, then more than once refused to appear to pay homage to the king. The late summer of 1275 found Edward at Chester for Llywelyn to perform this overdue duty, but the prince failed to turn up and Edward left in a rage. Still, he held back from war. Then, at the end of the year, Eleanor de Montfort, daughter of the man Edward had vanquished at Evesham, set out from exile in France. Her ship was captured by the English, who discovered Montfortian banners hidden onboard, along with the purpose of her voyage. She was travelling to marry Llywelyn. A furious Edward imprisoned Eleanor in Windsor for three years, while her accompanying brother, Amaury, had six years in captivity at Corfe. Preparations for war with Llywelyn began.

Llywelyn was given one last chance, summoned to Westminster to perform homage in April 1276. While he was not seeking war, Llewelyn's successes of the past two decades made him confident he could repel the threat. At parliament in November, Edward and the magnates declared Llywelyn a rebel and resolved to bring him to heel militarily. As no sane man would consider invading Wales in winter, there was a lull, which the prince filled with statements of his grievances and peace proposals that the king deemed unacceptable. In January 1277, Edward travelled to Worcester to begin preparations. Once he was satisfied these were in good hands, he left his local leaders to carry on. The spring found him in Norfolk, involved in a strange juxtaposition of pilgrimage to the shrines of Bromholm and Walsingham while ordering supplies for warfare. Spiritual and military preparations complete, Edward held parliament at Westminster in May, before returning to Worcester at the start of July 1277.

In his absence, his lieutenants had performed admirably. Payn de Chaworth had subdued South Wales and secured the allegiance of the local lords. Roger Mortimer had taken Dolforwyn Castle and secured the central March. Earl William de Beauchamp of Warwick had spearheaded the reconquest of Powys. These successes meant that when Edward arrived in Worcester, he could concentrate on the campaign against Gwynedd and Llywelyn himself. From Worcester, one force set out for Carmarthen under the command of the king's brother Edmund, Earl of Lancaster since 1267. A much larger force marched behind Edward to Chester, where they joined those who had already assembled in that city. After a week of provisioning and organising, this army headed into Wales. Llywelyn had no chance of matching the military resources of the English king, and to confront Edward's army would be suicidal. Yet plenty of previous English armies had come unstuck in the hostile terrain of North Wales, which would allow the fearsome Welsh troops to take advantage. Edward was determined to avoid this.

From the very start, he recognised the importance of new, improved castles. Work began on Flint Castle, on the River Dee, and proceeded rapidly. The army proceeded considerably less rapidly. Edward was still at Flint, only twelve miles from Chester, at the end of July. On around 9 August, he acted on a vow he had made years earlier to found a Cistercian abbey, and a splendid ceremony was held in Cheshire to lay the foundation stone for what became Vale Royal Abbey. Returning to Flint, he found workmen had made considerable progress on clearing and widening the roads that would take the troops into North Wales.

Edmund's army was advancing with greater ease in South Wales. Having left Carmarthen, by the end of July they had reached Aberystwyth, where a new royal castle was commenced. Edward, meanwhile, was having to reassure Llywelyn's brother Dafydd, a rather volatile presence on the English side, about plans for the future. The army marched on to Rhuddlan, where another castle was begun beside the River Clwyd, then to Deganwy and the ruins of Henry III's castle overlooking the River Conwy. By this stage the army had shrunk considerably, although whether through desertion, death or a conscious decision by the king to send them away is unclear. In early September, using ships and sailors from the Cinque Ports, Edward sent some 2000 troops across the Menai Strait. They occupied Anglesey with ease, instantly depriving Llywelyn of the island that was his granary and providing Edward's men with grain instead. The fall of Anglesey was a blow the Prince of Wales could not absorb and he sent word of his willingness to surrender to the king.

Edward returned to Rhuddlan and dismissed most of his commanders and troops. Edmund was permitted to send his southern army home as well. Under the terms of surrender, agreed at Conwy on 9 September 1277, Llywelyn was allowed to keep Gwynedd, and Anglesey was handed back in return for an annual payment of 1000 marks. Dafydd was given two of the Four Cantrefs, the English crown keeping the other two and all other war gains. Llywelyn was brought to Rhuddlan, where he submitted to Edward, after which the king magnanimously waived the annual payment for Anglesey. However, Edward took Llywelyn back to Westminster with him, where in a suitably magnificent assembly on Christmas Day 1277, Llywelyn finally swore homage. Llywelyn returned home (with strict conditions) early in 1278. That Easter, Edward took the court to Glastonbury and had the bones of King Arthur and Guinevere exhumed. The miraculous 'rediscovery' by the monks of the grave of a non-existent king in 1184 had made the abbey a major pilgrimage centre, but Geoffrey of Monmouth's entirely invented story also claimed that Arthur had only been wounded and retired to a mythical island called Avalon, from where he would return to lead the Britons to victory. It was a story popular with the Welsh, the descendants of the Britons, so Edward's public celebration at Glastonbury was intended to show that Arthur was dead and would be making no miraculous returns to save the Welsh. The very real King of England would not suffer any insubordination on behalf of fictional, undead kings of the Britons. On 13 October, the marriage of Llywelyn and Eleanor de Montfort took place in Worcester Cathedral, in the king's presence and ostentatiously on his terms, in an English cathedral and on the feast of the translation of Edward the Confessor, patron saint of the English kings.

In May 1279, Edward crossed to France with Eleanor for a successful meeting with Philip III at Amiens. The king also addressed his need for money. The Welsh war had been expensive and he did not wish to try parliament's patience by requesting a tax. Edward's Italian bankers, the Riccardi of Lucca, had lent him a considerable sum of money. He used an archaic process called distraint of knighthood, whereby all men owning land above a set value (here £20) had to become knights by a set date. Most men paid a fine to avoid the expensive obligation of knighthood, Edward's revenue-raising aim. He also initiated a recoinage. As part of the process of issuing new coins, throughout 1278 agents investigated coin clipping and other monetary offences, as a result of which offenders were rounded up and hanged in early 1279. A disproportionate number of these were Jews, around half the adult male Jewish population executed. Soberingly, this was 'the single biggest massacre of Jews in British history'.[12]

One of Edward's innovations was to take 'care to have his laws promulgated as statutes, generally in parliament'.[13] When parliament met at Gloucester in August 1278, the legislative momentum continued with the Statute of Gloucester and the establishment of the Quo Warranto proceedings. A writ of quo warranto ('by what warrant') was used to inquire into a landowner's rights and the evidence of title to lands. The process was deeply unpopular, incorporated some manifest injustices and favouritism, and ground on slowly and bitterly over the following twelve years, until the king was forced to make concessions in 1290 and abandon it altogether in 1294. Yet in 1278, Edward was still successfully driving forward his stated aim of reasserting crown rights. All manner of inquiries had been instituted and legislation promulgated in the first years of the reign, and this would continue throughout the 1280s. There was a second round of Hundred Roll inquiries in 1279–80. It was this onslaught of activity and laws which earned Edward the nickname the 'English Justinian' in the seventeenth century, after the Roman Emperor renowned as a legal reformer. Not all his reforms were unpopular; Edward made parliament a place where petitions could be regularly and systematically brought by his subjects, who took full advantage of the opportunity.

In March 1282, Wales suddenly returned to the top of Edward's agenda. Building work had continued on castles at Aberystwyth, Flint and Rhuddlan, which were also being turned into administrative centres with adjacent towns populated by English settlers. Llywelyn's grievances had been mounting and the Welsh were starting to resent English subjugation. In 1281, Reginald de Grey was named justiciar of Chester and implemented a much harsher regime in the region. Dafydd ap Gruffudd, whose lands bordered the royal parts of the Four Cantrefs, felt oppressed by the new justiciar. Some southern Welsh lords likewise felt themselves victims of English injustice. On the night of 21 March 1282, a group of armed Welshmen led by Dafydd kidnapped Roger Clifford from Hawarden Castle, near Chester, killing several of his men and torching the fortress. Similar attacks were launched against Flint and Rhuddlan the next night, Aberystwyth Castle being destroyed a couple of days later. There were also attacks on castles in South Wales, along with an assault on the Shropshire border town of Oswestry.

It does not appear that Llywelyn was involved in what must have been carefully coordinated planning. He faced an unenviable choice between supporting his brother and backing the king. As he agonised, the news reached Edward. In early April, summonses were sent out to ready troops, ships and money. The muster point was Worcester once again, but the king faced problems when he arrived in the city in mid-May. Rather than use the traditional summons, based on obligation and limited to forty days' service, Edward had asked people to serve for pay. This idea proved unpopular, and a new summons had to be issued, in the traditional format, for Rhuddlan in August. Edward headed for Chester, and after he arrived in June he sent forces which recovered Hope, Ewloe and Hawarden Castles. This success was tempered by the Earl of Gloucester's failure in the South, where his army fell victim to a Welsh ambush. Edward dismissed Gloucester and had to alter his plans, diverting the knights of South West England to muster at Carmarthen, and those of the western Midlands to Montgomery. Meanwhile on 19 June, Llywelyn's wife, Eleanor, died in childbirth. As the prince was around 60, he now had little hope of fathering a son to carry on his dynasty, which meant he had less to lose in a fight against the English.

Edward moved to Rhuddlan, followed by his troops. William de Valence was securing the south, in a competent operation which left Edward free to focus on the primary goal, the north. Once again, men were dispatched to seize Anglesey and its harvest. This time, with Anglesey conquered, the English force began to build a bridge of boats across the Menai Strait to link island and mainland, an alternative attack route into the Welsh stronghold of Snowdonia. The land forces, proceeding slowly and methodically to negate the risk of attacks by guerrillas, gradually worked towards the Conwy, recovering the Four Cantrefs. On 22 October, Edward arrived at Dafydd's base, Denbigh, to discover that the Welshman and his force had slipped into Snowdonia. These mountains had always been a fearsome prospect for the English and no king had ever successfully enforced his sovereignty there. Edward I, determined to assert the power of the English crown once and for all, was not one to be daunted by history.

First, he had to contend with the Archbishop of Canterbury. John Pecham wanted to negotiate a peace. The king refused the Welsh safe conducts to his court and told Pecham not to go to them. Pecham defied the king, to find Llywelyn equally implacable. Edward authorised Pecham to try to find a suitable solution, only for English troops to bring idiocy into the pervasive atmosphere of stubbornness. With Llywelyn based near Bangor, on 6 November forces charged across the boat bridge in search of glory and were promptly massacred by Welsh troops pouring from the mountains. After this, neither side was prepared to negotiate.

Edward returned from Denbigh to Rhuddlan, and on 24 November sent writs across England to declare his intention of dealing with the Welsh problem once and for all. Llywelyn, needing to act before Edward could raise troops or additional men, left Dafydd in command in Snowdonia and headed for Builth. Near Cilmeri to the west of Builth, Llywelyn ap Gruffudd was killed in the Battle of Irfon Bridge on 11 December 1282. The circumstances are murky and his body was not recognised until the following day. His severed head had a grotesque afterlife; it was sent to Edward, who dispatched it to be paraded through London and placed on a spike at the Tower, where it rotted for many years. The English were delighted, the Welsh crushed. Dafydd lacked his brother's stature and authority, and sought peace terms from the king. Unfortunately for him, Edward was in no mood for compromise. His mind was set on conquest and submission.

In January 1283, William de Valence recaptured Aberystwyth. At the same time, Edward boldly marched out of Rhuddlan into the middle of Snowdonia, in midwinter, and besieged Dolwyddelan Castle. The place had significance for the Welsh as the birthplace of Llewelyn ab Iorwerth (Llywelyn the Great), who had built the castle. The siege was brief. By the end of January, Edward was back at Rhuddlan, having captured Dolwyddelan. In England, large assemblies at Northampton and York granted taxes to fund Edward's final push. On 13 March, Edward sailed across to the western bank of the River Conwy and set himself up in the hall Llywelyn had built. Orders went out for the English troops to muster at Carmarthen and Montgomery. Dafydd ap Gruffudd had taken refuge in the remote Castell y Bere, although he slipped away before it fell to the English in late April. Snowdonia was now assaulted by armies from four directions. Edward established his headquarters at Dolwyddelan, as thousands of troops roamed the mountains in search of Dafydd. He was finally captured near Llanberis in June, although by then an impatient king had returned to Rhuddlan. Jubilant, Edward spent two months on a hostage-gathering tour of Snowdonia. In August, after a year in Wales, the conquering king returned to England. It had been very expensive, financially and in numbers of war dead, but he had achieved something of which his predecessors could only dream.

Edward was not vindictive, avoiding executions of the defeated. The exception was Dafydd. Parliament met at Shrewsbury at the end of September; no clergy were summoned as a capital sentence was to be passed. In a novel and strained definition of treason, the assembly predictably deemed Dafydd a traitor deserving death. On 2 October 1283, he was dragged through Shrewsbury before being hanged, disembowelled alive and quartered. His head was sent to keep his brother's company at the Tower of London. Edward set off for a thanksgiving tour of the cathedrals and religious houses of Herefordshire, Gloucestershire and Worcestershire, spent Christmas at Rhuddlan, then did a round of thanksgivings in Lincolnshire and Yorkshire before returning to Rhuddlan.

On 19 March 1284, the Statute of Rhuddlan was promulgated. It made the conquest official. Welsh law was allowed to continue to operate in civil cases, but English criminal law was imposed, along with English-style shires and a full range of royal officials. Edward was also imposing his authority on Gwynedd in stone – three new castles being constructed under the guidance of the king's chosen architect, James of St George. Among the most iconic physical legacies of medieval Britain, the audacity and scale of these can still amaze visitors seven centuries later. All were carefully sited so they could be supplied by water as well as by land. Harlech, loftily perched above Cardigan Bay, watched over Snowdonia from the south-west. Conwy sat beside the river of the same name. Most extravagant of all was to be the base of the new justiciar of north-west Wales, Caernarfon. Built near an old Roman fort, beside the River Seiont, this fantastical fortress was constructed in a style which consciously echoed Constantinople. It was at Caernarfon, in the middle of a building site, that Queen Eleanor gave birth for the last time on 25 April. The boy was given his father's name, and by August, the death of the king's only other surviving son, Alfonso, meant that the baby was now heir to a significantly expanded realm.

There was little time for the king and queen to grieve as Alfonso was buried in distant Westminster. They travelled to Edward's foundation of Vale Royal, then from Cheshire embarked on a royal progress of Wales in October. Christmas 1284 was spent at Bristol, as Edward's thoughts turned to another crusade, which the papacy was very eager for him to undertake. The venture was thwarted by a volatile situation on the Continent. On Easter Monday 1282, the Sicilians had risen up against Charles of Anjou in a revolt known as the Sicilian Vespers, triggering a conflict which brought in the kings of Aragon and France, along with the Pope. Edward raced to Kent in January 1285, probably aiming to cross to France and try to prevent war in order to save the crusade, but Philip III was not amenable to this intervention. Instead, Edward toured the shrines of East Anglia, before parliament assembled at Westminster in May. It was another busy legislative session. The second Statute of Westminster dealt with land law, and there was a new Statute of Merchants. The king took action to deal with lawlessness in London and assert royal authority against a city which had traditionally caused problems for the kings of England. After the king had a few weeks at leisure, hunting and pilgrimage, a meeting at Winchester later in the summer enacted the Statute of Winchester, dealing with further questions of public order. During this visit, it is possible that Edward commissioned the Round Table which now hangs, in restored form, in the city's Great Hall. Crossing to the Isle of Wight, Edward received the news that Philip III of France had died in eerily similar circumstances to his father, of plague in a disease-ridden army engaged on an ill-advised military campaign, this one against Aragon.

By the time Edward reached Exeter for Christmas 1285, all four leaders involved in the continental conflict – Charles of Anjou, Pope Martin IV, Philip III and Peter III of Aragon – were dead. In stark contrast to his aggressive conquest of Wales, in European politics the Edward of the 1280s was a conciliatory diplomat. His services were suddenly required as peacemaker, while he needed to do homage for Gascony to the new French king, Philip IV (Philip the Fair). Parliament met in April 1286 for Edward to appoint Edmund of Cornwall, his cousin, as custodian of the realm, before the king left Dover for France in May. With a sizeable retinue of earls, Edward travelled to meet Philip at Amiens, from where the two kings rode together for a stay in Paris. As Duke of Aquitaine, Edward did carefully worded homage for Gascony on 5 June. He had no hope of overseeing a peace between France and Aragon, as the situation was fiendishly complex, but he did spend several weeks negotiating a truce which would last from August 1286 to September 1287. Philip then conceded Edward's rights, as duke, over Saintonge, the northern part of Gascony between the River Gironde and Saintes. Added to the Agenais, the eastern part of the duchy centred on Agen which had been conceded to Edward in 1279, this meant that Gascony was now considerably larger than the territory Edward inherited in 1272.

He took a leisurely route to his duchy, via the tombs of his ancestors at Fontevraud, travelling through Saintonge and the Agenais. He spent Christmas and New Year 1287 on route to Bordeaux at St Macaire. After an itinerant and somewhat lethargic opening to the year, Edward was at Bordeaux to celebrate Easter. He had a lucky escape on Easter Sunday, when a floor collapsed beneath the assembled company and the king was fortunate to emerge with only a broken collarbone. It did not hold him back for long. In mid-May, he set out for Blanquefort, where in the presence of the Archbishop of Ravenna he took the cross once more. Unfortunately, it transpired that yet another Pope had died and the financial promises the deceased Honorius IV had made to fund the crusade would have to be renegotiated. Edward instead headed for the northern fringes of the Pyrenees, where in July he entertained Alfonso III of Aragon. Agreement was reached on the release of Edward's cousin, Charles of Salerno, who was in Aragonese captivity, although it could only take effect once a new Pope was elected to approve the accord. Unfortunately, a protracted conclave was abandoned because of disease and the death of several cardinal electors, so the papacy was vacant from Honorius IV's death on 3 April 1287 until Nicholas IV's election on 15 February 1288, the chosen candidate refusing to accept for a whole week. Edward had by then given up hope and returned to Bordeaux for Christmas 1287.

A bored king spent the opening months of 1288 founding the bastide, or new town, of Burgus Reginae ('Queen's Borough') at the confluence of the Dordogne and the Garonne. (Edward successfully created several bastides in Gascony, although New Winchelsea and Kingston [King's town]-upon-Hull were notable English examples of his new towns policy.) The new Pope vetoed the treaty with the Aragonese, which meant Edward had to give much of the summer to negotiating a new agreement which was not finalised, this time on the Aragonese side of the Pyrenees, until the end of October. In March 1289, Edward and Alfonso met high in the mountains at snowy Peyrenère, to exchange hostages. Returning to Gascony,

Edward spent until June on administrative matters. He and Eleanor returned to England, landing at Dover on 13 August 1289.

Edmund of Cornwall's government had successfully suppressed a revolt in South Wales, but the king's absence had led to a worrying increase in violence and lawlessness in England. The royal justices had been working hard on the Quo Warranto proceedings in these years, entangling many lords in tedious and expensive litigation as they tried to prove their rights to their lands. As a result, the nobles were unhappy. A story which may be apocryphal captures the mood of the time: asked by what warrant he had his rights, an earl brandished his sword and declared that his ancestors had come with William I and conquered his lands with the sword, and he would defend them by the sword. The atmosphere in England was faintly mutinous and Edward was heavily in debt. He needed to embark on a charm offensive.

As in 1274, he invited complaints against royal officials, but the response was much less enthusiastic. An attack on the judiciary brought some popularity and considerable income through fines, although there was dismay at the general lack of further punishment. As parliament convened in April 1290, Edward neutralised the opposition of Gloucester by marrying the earl to his daughter, Joan, showing little concern for the feelings of the 18-year-old princess compelled to wed a divorcee 28 years her senior. He also (eventually) made concessions on Quo Warranto, permitting landowners to retain their rights if they could prove continuous ownership of their lands since the accession of Richard I, which became the limit of legal memory. (Despite several attempts by fourteenth-century parliaments to change the date, 1189 has remained the limit.[14]) The lords were appeased, but if Edward wanted a grant of taxation, he also had to give something to the knights and lesser landowners. One last time, it was the Jews who were to suffer the consequences of Edward's insolvency and unpopularity.

By 1290, the Jewish community in England was tiny, oppressed and broken: 'it was now more profitable to expel the Jews than to protect them'.[15] While Jews were no longer officially allowed to practice usury, it persisted in secret. Wealthy Christians continued to profit by buying up debt-ridden estates from the Jews (foreclosing on the debts in the royal courts to secure the lands), the queen an especially resented culprit. Beyond the financial questions, there was the pervasive climate of fervent antisemitism, a sorry tale of intolerance and persecution which found its most disturbing expression in the stories of ritual child murder, episodes subverted to rouse hatred and inflame local mobs. Edward was no less anti-Jewish than his father or nearly everyone in Christian England, and with his Italian bankers, he was far less reliant on Jews financially. He resolved to expel the entire community. There were plenty of precedents for such action. The Jews had been kicked out of France by Philip II and Louis IX, out of their estates by Simon de Montfort and Eleanor of Provence, and out of Gascony by Edward himself just three years earlier. Far from being a pioneer, 'Edward I was a king of international repute, bearing and connection' who 'must have been aware of the prevailing European attitude'.[16] On 18 July 1290, Edward ordered that all Jews were to leave his realm by 1 November. Both the laity and the clergy responded gratefully with sizeable grants of taxation. Jews were not allowed to return until 1656. Today, this strikes us as an appalling episode of hatred and cruelty based in religious intolerance. At the time, it was 'the most popular act Edward ever committed'.[17]

Soon afterwards, the king suffered an enormous personal tragedy. At the end of October, Queen Eleanor fell ill at Clipstone in Nottinghamshire. The royal party made their way, in painfully small stages, towards Lincoln, seeking the intercession of St Hugh at his shrine in the cathedral. They made it only as far as the village of Harby, around six miles to the west of the city. In the house of a local knight, Eleanor of Castile died on 28 November 1290. Edward was devastated. Eleanor had been seen as greedy and made little effort to endear herself to the English, as the rather laconic treatment of her death in the chronicles shows, yet her husband's ostentatious response has served to conceal her unpopularity behind memories of a great love story. The queen's body was taken to Lincoln, where it was embalmed. Her viscera were buried in Lincoln Cathedral, while her heart would go to the Blackfriars in London, and elaborate tombs would be built over both. On 3 December, the funeral procession set out from Lincoln, accompanied by the king, ending with Eleanor's interment in Westminster Abbey on 17 December. It took two years to create the bronze effigy which still lies over her tomb. The most striking memorials were the twelve Eleanor crosses Edward later ordered to be constructed, one for each place her body lay overnight on the journey from Lincoln to Westminster. The three which survive, at Geddington and Hardingstone in Northamptonshire and Waltham Cross in Hertfordshire, are testament to the scale of Edward's pain. It was grief memorialised in stone, to an extent never attempted before or subsequently. After Eleanor's funeral, a heartbroken Edward retired for what must have been a lonely and miserable Christmas at Ashridge in Hertfordshire. 'After her death', mused one modern writer, 'the music seems to have faded'.[18]

Perhaps, as 1291 dawned in lonely solitude, the widowed king reflected on the fragility of his dynasty. Had he been killed by the accident in Bordeaux which broke his collarbone in 1287, he would have left a 3-year-old as king. Such troubling thoughts would have been exacerbated by the news which came from Scotland, where the ruling house had been wiped out. Death had taken a special interest in the family of King Alexander III in the years 1275–84, depriving him of his wife (Edward's sister) and all his children. He had no uncles, brothers or nephews, so remarriage was a matter of urgency. In 1285, he duly wed a French princess, Yolande. On 19 March 1286, the lovesick Scottish king was in Edinburgh, but wanted to join his wife at Kinghorn in Fife. Despite being strongly advised against the idea, with a dreadful storm sweeping in, Alexander crossed the Forth that evening and resisted pleas to pause overnight at Inverkeithing. He rode on overnight and over a cliff, at the foot of which his body was found the next morning. Scotland was plunged into crisis. Yolande claimed to be pregnant, but the child was either stillborn or never existed. The only remaining heir was an infant girl in Norway, Alexander's granddaughter Margaret, the 'Maid of Norway'. Guardians took over the running of Scotland, and tricky negotiations involving

England, Norway and Scotland led to an agreement that Margaret would marry Edward of Caernarfon, heir to the English throne. The Treaty of Birgham, agreed by English and Scottish representatives on 18 July 1290 and confirmed by Edward at Northampton in August, guaranteed that Scotland would remain an independent kingdom. How well this dual monarchy would have worked is an imponderable of history. On her way from Bergen to Orkney in autumn 1290, the Maid died.

The choice of successor came down to two men, Robert Bruce and John Balliol, but neither had a claim which was obviously superior to the other. In the circumstances, an arbitrator was needed, and the Scottish Guardians had only one real option: the King of England. Edward I and Alexander III had enjoyed an amicable relationship and Edward had not concerned himself with Scotland thus far, although it would dominate the second half of his reign. Yet the kings of England persisted in seeing themselves as above their Scottish counterparts, as shown by their successful opposition to the Scots turning the installation ceremony for their kings, which took place at Scone, into a coronation. Like Edward himself with Gascony, Alexander had been very careful when doing homage to his brother-in-law for his English estates. Naturally enough, the Scottish monarchs saw themselves as independent and the equals of the kings of England. Asking Edward I to arbitrate may have been the only option, but it was not without risks. Everyone remembered how Edward had treated Llywelyn.

Edward summoned parliament to meet at the Bishop of Durham's castle at Norham, in Northumberland, on 6 May 1291. Meanwhile, the king ordered a search of monastic archives and chronicles to find evidence of his right to be overlord of Scotland. Duly ignoring the lack of evidence they failed to find for a very tenuous claim, the monks informed the king that his interpretation was indeed correct. To the consternation of the Scots, who naturally expected a Scottish matter to be handled in Scotland, in May they found themselves ordered to join the king in Norham. There, Edward asserted his claim of overlordship and declared that far from giving a straightforward judgement between Balliol and Bruce, he would hear any claim to the Scottish throne. The meeting ended in acrimonious disarray, with the Scottish party retreating to Berwick-upon-Tweed.

Edward now changed tactics, essentially declaring that he would only entertain the claims of candidates who acknowledged his right to overlordship. Bruce did so at once, Balliol shortly afterwards. Several others, with claims ranging from flimsy to outrageous, likewise submitted. Downriver in Berwick, the remaining Guardians were unimpressed. So Edward devised another cunning plan, whereby he entered his own claim to the throne and then took charge of the kingdom and its castles on behalf of all the claimants. The subtle difference in this legal fiction, that the kingdom was being given to Edward in trust rather than surrendered by right, was acceptable to the Guardians, although they made him cross to the Scottish side of the Tweed to surrender their seal and the royal castles on 12 June 1291. The stage was now set for Edward's arbitration in what eighteenth-century writers would call the Great Cause.

There was a pause for the competitors to assemble their bids. Including Edward, who had no genuine intention of pursuing his claim, there were fourteen candidates. Some were never going to receive a serious hearing, such as King Erik II of Norway, who relied on the entirely invalid concept of 'ascendancy' (being the Maid of Norway's father). The other foreigner in the mix, Count Florence V of Holland, had a scarcely more credible claim. Another nine Scottish and English lords based their bids, with varying degrees of plausibility, on descent from long-dead kings and illegitimate lines. Balliol and Bruce remained by far the strongest (and only realistic) contenders. During the pause, Edward went to receive homage from the residents of the royal burghs in central Scotland.

Proceedings in the Great Cause began on 3 August 1291. This time, Edward and the tribunal were sitting in Scotland, at Berwick. There were 104 auditors or judges in the court (105 if Edward himself is included), 24 chosen by Edward, 40 apiece by Balliol and Bruce, tacitly acknowledging the superiority of their claims. However, the other claims had to be heard, which was an opportunity for a crafty English king to extend his time in charge. After just nine days, he allowed an adjournment for the Count of Holland to find documentary proof to support his very dubious claim. Moreover, proceedings were suspended for a lengthy ten months. It was hardly the swift resolution Edward had promised, and the Scots were understandably bewildered and angry, but there was little they could do.

Edward returned to England to bury his mother, who had died in June. Eleanor of Provence was not laid to rest next to her husband in Westminster Abbey, but at Amesbury Abbey in Wiltshire, where she had lived out her last years among the nuns. In October, he assembled the council at Abergavenny to deal with a dispute between the Earls of Gloucester and Hereford. Deferred to a meeting of parliament at Westminster in January 1292, the case saw both men imprisoned and deprived of their Welsh estates. As all Edward wanted was recognition of the Crown's superiority over Marcher law, the punishments only lasted a short time. Now that the Marchers, as well as the Welsh, were accepted to be subject to royal jurisdiction, Edward's supremacy over Wales and the Marches was at last complete.

The king returned to Berwick, where on 2 June 1292 proceedings to award the Scottish throne resumed. Count Florence was persuaded to stand aside, even though he had been the cause of the ten-month delay. This brought matters back to the two genuine competitors, John Balliol and Robert Bruce. Both were descended from Earl David of Huntingdon, younger brother of Alexander III's grandfather, William the Lion. David had had three daughters. Balliol was the grandson of the eldest, Bruce was the son of the second. In very simplistic terms, Balliol was relying on descent through the senior line (customary law), Bruce on the fact that he was closer in blood as David's grandson rather than great-grandson (ancient or imperial law, with the argument that customary law for estate inheritance did not apply to kingdoms). Both arguments had merit, which meant the court spent ten days going round in circles. Edward adjourned proceedings yet again, this time to seek advice from learned men at the University of Paris about which type of inheritance law should apply to the kingdom.

On 3 November, the English councillors ruled in favour of the customary law right, a verdict endorsed three days later by the Scottish auditors. Bruce had lost, but the lesser claimants still had to be heard. As a result, Bruce tried desperate schemes. He threw in his lot with the Count of Holland, who was dismissed because he had still not managed to produce a shred of evidence. Next, Bruce argued that if customary inheritance law did apply, then as it was through female lines the kingdom should be divided, with himself and John Hastings (grandson of David of Huntingdon's third daughter) each receiving a third. However, Edward was now bored. He had achieved his aim of demonstrating his dominion over Scotland and had spent long enough in the north. On 17 November 1292, the court finally ruled in favour of John Balliol. As agreed, he then swore homage to Edward for Scotland in explicit, unambiguous terms, a ceremony which Edward insisted occurred in England, back at Norham. The Scots then raced to Scone, where on 30 November, St Andrew's Day, John Balliol was invested as King of Scotland.

'No other Scottish monarch has suffered the same dreadful degradation of character inflicted upon John, the first Balliol king of Scots.'[19] Balliol had spent most of his life as an English magnate, his estates centred on Barnard Castle in County Durham, the deaths of older brothers bringing him an unexpectedly large inheritance, and that of his mother substantial Scottish lands in Galloway. His rise was thus meteoric and unexpected, and the way he became king has resulted in him being reviled, especially in Scottish historiography, as the puppet of Edward I. Such is his unpopularity that although officially King John I, he is rarely referred to as such. This is unfair. Bruce had been far quicker than Balliol to promise acceptance of Edward's overlordship at the start of the process, and in swearing homage the new king was merely honouring the pledge made by all the competitors. If the superiority of Balliol's claim was not clear-cut, a case can certainly be made that it was the strongest and he was the most popular candidate. The court's decision, even though heavily influenced by Edward, was an entirely reasonable one. Much less defensible was Edward's motivation. He had intentionally prolonged proceedings far beyond what was necessary, to assert his overlordship of Scotland. Almost immediately after King John was installed, Edward began hearing complaints from Scottish subjects, imitating the process whereby French kings heard complaints against the Dukes of Aquitaine from Gascon subjects, about which the English kings protested vehemently when it was their authority being challenged by an overlord. At Newcastle-upon-Tyne on 26 December, John swore homage to Edward in an official ceremony. As 1292 ended, the King of England made clear that he intended to be a dominant, interfering overlord of the King of Scotland.

It was the path of hubris. In November 1293, John was at parliament in England, meekly succumbing to a summons to respond to an appeal against him from a Scottish earl to Edward as overlord. The Scottish king accepted the loss of three castles and towns in punishment. However, around the same time, Edward found himself summoned, in his capacity as Duke of Aquitaine, to answer to Philip IV in Paris. There had been growing conflict between English and Gascon sailors on the one hand, and Flemish and French ones on the other hand, throughout 1292. On 15 May 1293, a Norman fleet had attacked an Anglo-Gascon one off the Breton coast, only for the French to be defeated and have several ships captured.

The Gascons had then sacked La Rochelle on their triumphant voyage home. Some modern French historians claim that 'Edward had deliberately launched his fleet against the French', but there is no evidence to support this.[20] By October, it had escalated into a major Anglo-French diplomatic incident, the refusal of Gascony to comply with Philip's wishes (Gascons preferred the largely hands-off rule of a duke separated from them by a sea) leading the French king to summon Edward as a disobedient vassal. England and France had been at peace, enjoying amicable relations since the Treaty of Paris more than four decades earlier. The two royal families were closely related. Edward thus relied on his brother, Edmund of Lancaster, to negotiate a deal whereby much of Gascony would be surrendered, with a secret addendum that it would soon be given back. Part of the deal was that Edward would also marry Philip's younger sister, Margaret. Philip and the French court, however, were not negotiating in good faith, and once they took Gascony under these terms in early 1294, they had no intention of giving it back. By the spring, Edward realised that he had been deceived. For one who was no stranger to using bullying, deceitful behaviour, he proved remarkably blind to what was happening when he was the victim. For once Edward was not the aggressor; responsibility for this war lay squarely with Philip IV.

The sudden lapse in judgement by a king normally so sure of touch led the English chroniclers to decide that he had been driven mad by carnal desires. Edward was now 54, his intended bride Margaret, a teenager. At the parliament which met at the end of May 1294, Edward had to swear publicly that he had acted not from lust but from a desire for peace with France. This was necessary to win over his furious lords, whose pique at not being consulted made them disinclined to help their unusually contrite king. His oath won them over, but the task against a determined and powerful foe was formidable. The Riccardi, his reliable Italian bankers, could not help him this time, and the king turned against them; in the autumn their assets were seized. Not until later in the decade did another Italian company, the Frescobaldi, take their place. This left parliament to take emergency fundraising action in June. All wool in England was ordered seized and churches searched for stashes of money (officially to find forged and clipped coins). Edward I headed for Portsmouth, as royal servants began rounding up supplies for the coming war. The plan was that an advance party would go to Gascony quickly, but it was delayed until mid-August by the delights of an English summer.

The endless torrential rain and generally awful weather caused the king to make a quick pilgrimage to Worcester to seek the intercession of St Wulfstan. He continued making arrangements, massively increasing customs duties instead of seizing wool. Gathering of troops continued apace. Then it turned out that the advance party had been scattered by contrary winds. Some were refusing to obey the summons to fight for the king, on the grounds that they were not required to do so overseas. The muster was abandoned. On 21 September, Edward met with the clergy, who were irate at the indiscriminate and heavy-handed way royal agents had plundered cash from churches. After the king pleaded with them, three days' deliberation brought an offer of a 20% tax. Edward saw this as an insult and dispatched troops to inform the clergy that he wanted 50%, or he would outlaw them. With no archbishop currently in post to lead them (Pecham had died in 1292), the intimidated clerics agreed to this huge tax. Having bullied the clergy, Edward next summoned the knights of the shires to come to Westminster to grant him a lay tax. Then, alarming news arrived from Wales.

A decade on from the conquest, Welsh resentment had boiled over. On top of all manner of other grievances, the Welsh found themselves subjected to taxation in the early 1290s and assessed at an unfairly high rate. Then they were summoned to fight the king's Gascon war. As Englishmen poured out of the new castles to respond to the royal summons, the Welsh seized their chance and revolted. Madog ap Llywelyn, a distant relation of Llywelyn ap Gruffudd, was the ringleader in the north, Morgan ap Maredudd his counterpart in the south. Edward's new fortresses at Conwy and Harlech were surrounded and besieged, as was the old Welsh castle that he had captured and improved at Criccieth. Caernarfon Castle, still unfinished, was successfully attacked and torched. Recognising the gravity of the situation, the king diverted the troops to muster at Worcester. Aware of his precarious position, Edward was atypically tactful and asked rather than ordered the lords to respond to a military summons. He sought a lay tax of a third, but the laity were not nearly as supine as the clergy and had the determined Earl of Gloucester as a leader. The king had to settle for a tenth and sixth before heading, via Worcester, to spend Christmas 1294 at the now-finished Conwy Castle.

The army assembled was considerably larger than that deployed for the conquest. Once more, there was a three-pronged strategy, attacking northern, central and southern parts of Wales simultaneously. In early January 1295, Edward marched west out of Conwy, lost his baggage train in an enemy attack, and retreated back to Conwy. Besieged there, the wisdom of having built his castles with sea access became apparent as supply ships were able to restock the depleted royal stores. The news from southern and central Wales was much more positive. On 5 March, in the Battle of Maes Moydog, the Earl of Warwick's army crushed that of Madog ap Llewelyn.

Edward had been unusually cautious after the failed sortie in January, remaining in Conwy until early April. At that point, he launched an assault on Anglesey, which had played a key role in the revolt. An amphibious operation quickly retook the island. The king went to Llanfaes, Anglesey's main settlement, and had it razed to the ground. The inhabitants were sent to a new town, Newborough. On the coastal marsh to the south of Llanfaes, Master James of St George began work on yet another new castle, the last in the great Edwardian sequence, to bring security to Anglesey. Named Beaumaris, this innovative fortress was designed with concentric symmetry enclosed within a moat, a dock giving direct access to the Menai Strait. Work petered out in the 1320s and it was never finished, but with its beautiful design and stunning location, it remains one of the most evocative castles in the British Isles.

In May, Edward ventured south, receiving surrenders and taking hostages. He inspected Criccieth and Harlech, which had withstood the revolt, and just north of Aberystwyth reunited with other forces. By the end of June, victory was complete and he was back at Conwy. Now, the king braved visiting Caernarfon, the only major fortress to suffer substantial damage at rebel hands, but still far advanced from when he had last seen it in 1284. Master James was allotted considerable sums to permit the rapid completion of both Caernarfon and Beaumaris. Edward went back to England, once more to face the Gascon crisis.

While Edward was entangled in the Welsh campaign, a small English force had been busy capturing towns along the Gironde estuary and River Garonne, only to lose most of them again. The situation was desperate. Parliament was summoned to start at Westminster on 1 August 1295, but the next day the French raided Dover. When parliament settled down to business, the mood was both sombre and restless. Royal agents were starting to collect the tenth granted by the previous parliament, but those lords who had voluntarily served in Wales clearly expected to be spared payment. Instead, Edward exempted some of those currently in Gascony, offering the same deal to those who agreed to serve in the duchy. When this had no effect, he started ordering magnates to fight there, only to meet with opposition from fourteen of them, who refused point blank to fight his overseas wars. They were second-order lords, the most significant being the new and relatively impoverished Earl of Arundel, but a livid king ordered them to be distrained (have their goods confiscated up to the value of their debts) on 23 August. Parliament broke up with the king angry, many of the lords angry, and no obvious plan to help Gascony amidst the surfeit of rage.

The French now attacked Hythe and Winchelsea. Militarily, these raids achieved nothing, but they fuelled panic about a French invasion. Wild rumours began to fly, including one about a Huntingdonshire prior raising the French royal standard. There was even a spy scandal: Thomas Turberville, a knight of the royal household, was executed for treason, having been captured by the French and sent back as a double agent, claiming to have escaped. In such volatile circumstances, Edward backed down. Large numbers of lords were exempted from the tax and settlement was reached with those who had refused to fight in Gascony. Another parliament was summoned for November to address the French threat. The writs of summons used Philip IV's desire to destroy the English language to justify the need for action, slightly ironic given that the writs were in Latin and the parliamentary discussions of the lords would be in French. At the time, it was an emergency assembly to respond to an urgent threat. In the late nineteenth century, William Stubbs saw the meeting of November 1295 as a 'great and model parliament'.[21] Parliament was developing and becoming more significant, but the importance Stubbs afforded that of November 1295 was a case of wishful thinking. It certainly did not achieve what Edward wanted. True, the laity granted a tax of an eleventh and seventh without demur. However, the clergy, led by the formidable new Archbishop of Canterbury, Robert Winchelsey (who on one later occasion was so ferocious in rebuking an abbot that the unfortunate victim suffered a fatal heart attack),[22] were much more combative, and conceded only a tenth instead of the higher tax the king sought.

The Scots had taken advantage of Edward's preoccupations. Once the lords had placed restraining measures on King John's freedom of action, an alliance was made with France. On the ostensible grounds that the Scots had failed to surrender the three places demanded under the judgement of November 1293, Edward decided on military action. In March 1296, he and a large army convened at Newcastle, from where they marched to reclaim and then spend Holy Week and Easter at Wark Castle, which the local lord had handed to the Scots. A failed Scottish assault on Carlisle on Easter Monday prompted Edward to attack Berwick. The surprisingly confident citizens refused to surrender to a dauntingly large English force, which led to many of them being slaughtered in the conquest and sack of the town which followed. Wisely, the castle garrison agreed terms of surrender and were spared. Edward spent almost a month at Berwick, working on improving the defences, and it was there he was notified of King John's formal defiance, in which he renounced his homage. It was a bold move, but events unfolded catastrophically for the Scots.

The Earl of Surrey had been sent to take Dunbar Castle. A Scottish attempt to lift the siege in late April led to a battle in which they were obliterated. Edward arrived in person for the surrender of the castle, after which he went to take Jedburgh and Roxburgh Castles. He headed to Edinburgh, which gave in after a five-day siege, then Stirling, which did not even bother to put up a fight. By mid-June, Scotland was falling into Edward's hands with embarrassing ease. The King of England sent the Bishop of Durham to the King of Scotland, offering him a chance to resign his throne and live peacefully on his English estates. John had spent four years being bullied from above by an insufferable Edward and from below by equally insufferable Scottish lords. He was thoroughly fed up with being king, and having no desire to end up as a rotting head keeping Llywelyn's rotting head company in London, leapt on the deal. For whatever reason, Edward withdrew the offer, so when John and his followers submitted at Montrose on 8 July, he was subject to ritual humiliation. He surrendered his regalia and had the royal arms torn from his tabard (which led to the mocking nickname 'Toom Tabard'). Thus unkinged and once again John Balliol, he was sent to imprisonment in the Tower of London.

As he had in Wales, Edward embarked on a victory tour, taking surrenders and hostages on the way. He travelled as far as Elgin, far further north than any English king had ever ventured, before returning to Berwick by the end of August. Large numbers of Scots came to swear allegiance to him there. Edward had no desire to install a new king of Scotland after the experience of Balliol; he crushingly dismissed the hopes of Robert Bruce, son of the now dead competitor. To avoid the Scots being tempted to make any more kings, he sent the Scottish regalia south, and removed the Stone of Destiny from Scone and had it sent to Westminster, where it was housed in a specially crafted new chair on which every English and United Kingdom monarch has been crowned since 1308. Rather than an independent kingdom, Edward now treated Scotland as an English colony, installing the Earl of Surrey as governor in Berwick, which was rebuilt as a major fortress town.

Edward returned to England in September 1296 in triumph, lauded by the English chroniclers as a conquering hero. No king had been so dominant across the British Isles since John, ninety years earlier, and in both Wales and Scotland, Edward had far surpassed his grandfather's achievements. Yet John had achieved his dominance as his financial exactions and failure to make any headway in France caused considerable resentment, a parallel which had some echoes in Edward's situation. The latest expedition to reconquer Gascony was going badly. The leader had been the king's brother, Edmund of Lancaster, who had died at Bayonne on 5 June 1296, leaving the floundering efforts under the command of Henry de Lacy, Earl of Lincoln. Edward honoured his brother by summoning his next parliament to meet in the town where lay interred the saint for whom he had been named, Bury St Edmunds, where it would be in session on 20 November, St Edmund's Day. The king desperately needed cash. His Scottish war had been expensive, and merely added to the burden of debt racked up in his previous wars, with a Gascon campaign ongoing, the king spending considerable sums bribing and buying allies on the Continent. Seeking a grant of taxation, Edward had tried to forestall some criticism by suspending all his building projects, except the castles at Beaumaris and Caernarfon, and the murals in the Painted Chamber at Westminster. It was unlikely to be enough of a concession to a country resenting the weight of a considerable financial burden.

The king had exacted two hefty taxes in recent years. His outrageously high customs duty on wool exports was bitterly resented and had been dubbed the maltolt ('evil tax'). Perhaps the greatest source of anger was purveyance (or prise), the system whereby royal officials could take food and other goods for use by the royal household, usually on credit with delayed payment. The amount Edward's officials had been seizing to provision entire armies had led even the collectors to object by the autumn of 1296. The laity in parliament granted a tax of a twelfth and eighth at the end of November. The clergy proved intractable. Back in February, Boniface VIII had issued a papal bull, *Clericos Laicos*, which prohibited the clergy paying secular taxes without the prior permission of the Pope; some of the provisions suggest it was directly aimed at Edward after his imposition of 1294. Archbishop Winchelsey asked the king for permission to postpone the clergy's decision, a reluctant Edward giving him until January.

As 1297 dawned, Edward's diplomatic endeavours were bearing fruit, albeit not necessarily in honourable fashion. Count Florence of Holland, the timewasting competitor of the Great Cause, had allied himself with Philip IV of France. He was kidnapped and then murdered, almost certainly with English involvement, possibly with Edward's direct knowledge. The new count, Florence's 12-year-old son, John I, was married to Edward's daughter, Elizabeth, at Ipswich on 7 January 1297, and the new regime in Holland reverted to an English alliance. Count Guy of Flanders was not finding the bullying Philip to his taste, so swapped an alliance with one overbearing king for a different alliance with a different overbearing king. Unfortunately, Edward was rather less diplomatic on the home front.

The clergy had assembled in London to consider the king's request for a tax, surrounded by knights sent to intimidate them. They were not to be intimidated. An irate Edward learned that they had refused and on 30 January 1297, he outlawed the clergy. The same day, in news which would not reach England until the following month, the Earl of Lincoln's forces suffered a major defeat in Gascony. Edward's agents instantly began seizing Church estates. The clergy were informed that the price of buying back royal protection was, funnily enough, exactly the same as the clerical tax would have yielded. Parliament was summoned for 24 February at Salisbury, but only the laity were invited. Excluding the clergy did not help Edward, the assembly revealing just how isolated he had become.

Purveyance had become an even greater burden as Edward tried to build up supplies for the French campaign. The lords were feeling the pressure and with the tax burden also enormous, they were not inclined to help the king. At parliament, the magnates were asked again by the king to fight in Gascony. Like the clergy, the laity had had enough. The most loyal earls and likely supporters were already occupied elsewhere in Edward's service, Lincoln in Gascony and Surrey in Scotland. Drained by three years of warfare, alongside the cost of taxation, the maltolt and purveyance on their estates, those at Salisbury refused to fight overseas. Warwick, who would ordinarily have been considered a loyalist, joined his fellow earls in refusing. Roger Bigod, Earl of Norfolk and marshal of England, had willingly served the king previously at personal expense, but had now had enough. He told Edward that he was obliged only to fight at the king's side, not be sent overseas on his behalf. According to one chronicler, whose reliability is admittedly questionable, the furious king informed the earl that he would either go or hang. An equally enraged Norfolk retorted that he would do neither.[23]

Edward was now in trouble, but he was incapable of backing down. He returned to an earlier plan and ordered the confiscation of all the wool in England, then commanded all debts to the Crown be urgently investigated. The king took some comfort from the fact that his bullying of the clergy had paid off. Hunger, theft, attack and Edward's threats led them to petition the archbishop. Winchelsey allowed that each cleric could follow his own conscience, and they settled with the king in droves. Only a handful, including the archbishop himself, held out. The lay lords were not minded to follow the clerical submission. The four main opposition earls (Arundel, Hereford, Norfolk and Warwick) met at Montgomery in the Welsh Marches and declared that the excessive taxation the king had imposed meant that they would not serve overseas with him.

In mid-June, Edward presented the Scottish regalia in Westminster Abbey, but it did not pass unnoticed that the audience was far smaller than the equivalent ceremony for Wales more than a decade earlier, many lords now in opposition and absent. Not until 7 July was everyone together again in London, the occasion a muster for the French campaign. Edward bluntly asked Norfolk and Hereford, hereditary marshal and constable respectively, whether they would do their duty and draw up the muster lists. When they refused, citing an irregular and invalid summons, the king stripped them of these roles and prepared to arrest them. They immediately left court again. Arundel and Warwick wavered and returned to the king's side. On 14 July, Edward gave a theatrical performance outside Westminster Hall, a reconciled Archbishop Winchelsey at his side, in which he accepted there had been suffering but claimed to be acting for the good of the kingdom and his people. At the end, he asked everyone to swear allegiance to his son, Edward of Caernarfon, in case he did not return from France. The king could rise to a public performance.

Still Norfolk and Hereford held out. They produced a document of grievances, the Remonstrances, in the name of the 'community of the land', which circulated widely. By now the king desperately needed money to pay his continental allies, so resorted to seizing 8000 sacks of wool. He claimed he would pay people back later from the tax just granted by parliament, but by now the king was in fantasyland; this 'parliament', as one chronicler derisively put it, was nothing more than the men standing around in the king's chamber.[24] In August, Edward went to Winchelsea to meet his fleet. His departure from the scene revitalised the opposition. Back in London, the Archbishop of Canterbury held an ecclesiastical council which ruled the latest tax incompatible with *Clericos Laicos* and threatened excommunication of all who dared touch Church holdings. Representatives from the lay opposition rode to the king with petitions he refused to hear. Edward fought back, announcing that the clergy would be taxed by royal authority. On 22 August, Hereford and Norfolk stormed into the exchequer at Westminster to reiterate their grievances and prohibit the seizure of wool and collection of the tax. Edward sailed for Flanders two days later with his kingdom possibly edging towards civil war, although it has recently been argued that there 'was no real danger of civil war' because 'neither side wanted one'.[25]

Nevertheless, this was a crisis, and one almost entirely of the king's own making. Whether he was brave or just plain stupid in leaving the country in August 1297 is an open question, although resolution was perhaps easier without his obstinate presence. On 21 September, Norfolk and Hereford convened a rebel assembly at Northampton, while at the end of the month parliament met under Prince Edward in London. News from Scotland brought everyone back to their senses. Resentful enough at the English occupation and the demands to finance Edward's French war, the Scots revolted at demands to supply fighting men. In May 1297, the sheriff of Lanark was assassinated by William Wallace and rebellion began. Among the ringleaders were the Bishop of Glasgow and the Earl of Carrick (Robert Bruce, grandson of the competitor). An English force crossed the border and brought the rebels to terms at Irvine on 7 July, but then complacency set in among the commanders, who returned to Berwick. Hugh Cressingham, treasurer of the English administration, was alarmed at their inability to see the dangers and wanted to march against rebels gathering further north, but others insisted they wait for the governor. John de Warenne, Earl of Surrey and officially in charge of the English administration, was absent. Now in his mid-sixties, the governor of Scotland did not like Scotland, never mind its weather, and spent his time as far south into England as he dared, desperately trying to persuade people to relieve him of his job. By the time he arrived at Berwick in August, northern Scots under Andrew Murray and southern Scots under William Wallace had joined together in the north of Scotland. Reluctantly, Surrey led his troops to the first point where they could cross the Forth – Stirling. Murray and Wallace were waiting across the river, and when the English tried to cross the narrow bridge on 11 September, the result was a predictable disaster, the Scots dividing them and massacring those who had already crossed, including Cressingham. A horrified Surrey watched from the southern bank until he ordered the bridge destroyed and rode full speed back to Berwick. The arrival of news about the Battle of Stirling Bridge brought the rival sides in England back from the brink of civil war.

The Archbishop of Canterbury brokered an agreement in parliament. Faced with some disturbing echoes of 1215, the political class turned to Magna Carta. Along with the Forest Charter, this had become a standard rallying point, but additional safeguards were demanded. New clauses abolished the hated maltolt and formally asserted that the 'common assent of the realm' was required for future taxation, although these were kept separate from Magna Carta. It was both confirmation and innovation, but the agreement between earls and regency government, sealed on 10 October 1297, became known as the *Confirmatio Cartarum* ('Confirmation of the Charters').

Edward was in Ghent. A day before agreement was reached in England, a two-month Anglo-French truce had been agreed. Although he hesitated, the king had the sense to realise that he had no real option. On 5 November, he ratified the Confirmation of the Charters and sent his treasurer, Walter Langton, back to England to announce this publicly. Edward's military prospects were not good, and on 28 January 1298 a two-year ceasefire was settled, along with agreement to submit the question of Gascony to papal arbitration. His expedition to Flanders had achieved very little, most of the fighting done by English troops against the Welsh and Flemish on their own side, but at least the truce allowed him to sail home and deal with Scotland.

Andrew Murray had died of wounds sustained at Stirling Bridge, leaving William Wallace as leader of the Scottish effort, a role his compatriots acknowledged by making him sole Guardian after Murray's death. Despite all manner of rumour, legend and outright invention over the centuries, almost nothing is known about Wallace before 1297, when he suddenly enters the history books in dramatic fashion. He oversaw an effort in the later part of 1297 through which the English presence in Scotland was reduced to isolated outposts, then in November led a looting raid into Cumberland and Northumberland which terrified the inhabitants and made him the top English target. Back in England, the earls had received the king's ratification of the Confirmation of the Charters and marched north. In early 1298, they relieved the sieges of Berwick and Roxburgh, but then received letters from Edward ordering them to pause until he could arrive to lead the campaign in person.

Edward landed back at Sandwich on 14 March 1298. At the end of May, parliament met at York (where Edward, in a pointed rebuke to London, also moved the government) to plan the Scottish campaign. It had the potential to be a tense occasion, the first time Edward and Norfolk had faced one another in person since their row at Salisbury, but it passed without incident. From York, everyone headed north to begin the military action. On the border, the king had to promise the suspicious Norfolk and Hereford that he would not renege on his promises and would address their concerns after defeating the Scots. Finding the Scottish army proved challenging. Wallace had no intention of engaging the enormous English force in battle. As they found themselves running short of supplies near Edinburgh, drunken English and Welsh troops brawling, Edward's campaign looked in trouble. Then, on 21 July, the Scots were sighted near Falkirk.

The English spent the night camped at Linlithgow. Fearful of an ambush, they slept on the ground with their shields as pillows, the horses of the cavalry stood beside their riders. Edward's horse showed its Scottish sympathies by treading on the king in the night, leaving him to face battle the next day with two broken ribs. When the battle lines drew up at Falkirk on the morning of the 22nd, the Scots occupied the higher ground, which may have given Edward a flashback to his defeat at Lewes. Indeed, Falkirk was only the third pitched battle Edward would fight, the first since Evesham, thirty-three years earlier, and would turn out to be the last in his fifty-year military career. At Evesham, he had been a dashing, blond prince of 26 with much to prove. Now he was a venerable, white-haired king of 59, still in good health and with a long record of military triumph behind him. Pitched battles brought inherent risks and Edward was cautious, but the Battle of Falkirk was, like Evesham, a massacre of the opposing forces. The rank-and-file Scottish troops were slaughtered, although Wallace and the nobility escaped, limiting the impact of the English victory. After sacking Perth and spending a fortnight retaking Stirling Castle, Edward tried to capture some of the earls, making Robert Bruce his prime target. Yet he reached Ayr to find Bruce had burned the castle and vanished. The English returned home, reaching Carlisle in early September.

Edward had won the battle, but the war continued. Scotland was not subdued and the Scottish nobility had lived to fight another day. The king also bungled the aftermath of the campaign. There had been resentment, after the conquest of Wales, at his distributing lands only to a few close favourites. The earls, not least Hereford and Norfolk, hoped that this time things would be different. Instead, the king made some bizarre decisions, such as giving Arran to an Irishman, which convinced the two men that their service would once again go unrewarded. They sped away from Carlisle, sulking. Too late, Edward realised his mistake and started to distribute Scottish estates, mainly to loyalists like Lincoln. The king's foolishness caused resentment for some time, but also missed an opportunity to give others a vested interest in helping him to final victory.

Edward's judgement was increasingly questionable and questioned. At the end of 1298, Humphrey de Bohun died, succeeded as Earl of Hereford by a son with the same name. That left Earl Roger Bigod of Norfolk as the solitary leader of the opposition, but if he thought the dissidents would quieten down or disappear, the king was fooling himself. Parliament met at Westminster in March 1299, ostensibly to consider Gascony, the Pope having ruled in Edward's favour over the question of control of the duchy. Instead, led by Norfolk, the opposition demanded that Edward honour his promise to confirm the charters in person. He stalled for several days, finally promised an answer the next day, then ran away. Unimpressed with his pathetic dawn escape, the king's opponents chased him and cornered him at Harrow, unamused by his claim that he was fleeing the foul air of Westminster. Back at Westminster, Edward made things worse. He did indeed confirm the charters, but when his confirmation was examined closely, there was an outcry. He had confirmed not the text of 1297, but his own version. To the whole thing, he had added the rider 'saving the rights of our crown', then removed the first five clauses of the Forest Charter. Parliament broke up acrimoniously, while the Londoners came close to rioting. Yet again, the king had created a crisis through arbitrary and unwise actions.

This time, he realised matters were grave. On Good Friday (17 April), he restored London's ancient liberties. When parliament met again in May, it did so in Stepney, the king presumably not confident of his reception or safety in London and Westminster. It consisted of another fortnight of futile argument between Edward and Norfolk, which ended with the king riding off to Dover and the earl heading in the opposite direction to his castle at Chepstow. The murmurs of discontent grew louder across the realm, accusations that the king did not intend to keep his word over the charters widespread. The criticism was now too strong. On 25 June, Edward issued a letter in which he promised a perambulation of the forest in the autumn; this was the part of the Forest Charter he had excised. The enormous efforts made to publicise his climbdown in every town and village – we know it was read aloud in English in Worcester – shows how low Edward felt his credibility had sunk.

His fortunes now turned. Ambassadors returned from France with the news that Philip IV had agreed to a permanent peace and the restoration of Gascony. As part of the treaty, Edward's son would marry Philip's daughter, Isabella, when she was old enough (he was 15 and she was only 3). The 60-year-old Edward himself would marry Philip's 17-year-old sister, Margaret. By summer's end, everyone was in a much better mood. Prince Edward and the Earl of Norfolk met Margaret off the boat at Dover on 8 September, and on 10 September Archbishop Winchelsey solemnised the marriage at Canterbury Cathedral. Amid the feasting and good cheer, it must have been evident in the autumn of 1299 that the guard was changing. Surrey, Norfolk and Lincoln were the only earls left of Edward's own generation. Hereford, Lancaster, Pembroke and Warwick were all in their twenties and had recently inherited their titles; these were to be the key men of the next reign.

Yet Edward had no intention of slipping into a quiet old age. After his wedding, he ordered the troops to muster at York on 12 November, ready for an ambitious winter campaign against Scotland. Although the Scots were allied with France, Edward had refused point blank to recognise their sovereignty or allow them to feature in the peace treaty; his lone concession was to release John Balliol from English custody into the Pope's. Despite an intense siege, Stirling Castle remained under English control. William Wallace was in semi-disgrace after Falkirk. Leadership was now in the hands of two young men: Robert Bruce, Earl of Carrick, and John Comyn. Comyn was the nephew of a namesake who had backed Balliol against Bruce's grandfather in 1291–92, so there was no love lost and the two had come to blows when they met at Peebles in August 1299. The Scottish leadership was thus divided in all but a desire to oppose the English.

At York, Edward was encountering problems. Unsurprisingly, there was no rush of volunteers to serve in Scotland in the middle of winter. Edward arrived at Berwick with his earls in the middle of December to discover a dearth of infantry (2500 instead of a planned 16,000) and a boycott by knights which meant there was no cavalry. Edward had totally misjudged the country's mood. Amidst his wedding festivities, he had failed to implement the perambulation of the forest. Because he had become so distant from public opinion, and not consulted properly, he had marched off without realising the anger in the country at his failure to uphold the charters. He had no choice but to call a full parliament for March 1300. He saw in the new century at Berwick, then journeyed back south, his temper not improved by the news that Stirling had fallen to the Scots.

'Do you think me a child, or a deceiver?' one chronicler has an irate Edward asking a fractious parliament when it assembled.[26] After three years of assurances and promises, none kept, many would have answered the second part of the question in the affirmative. People did indeed feel deceived and confirming the charters was no longer enough. Clergy and laity alike brought lengthy lists of complaints to parliament. As the clergy had made abundantly clear they would not give him any money, Edward simply ignored them. If he wanted a tax from the laity, though, he had to offer them something. After three weeks of intense negotiations, the charters were confirmed at the end of March along with additional concessions known as the *Articuli super Cartas* ('Articles on the Charters' or 'Articles in addition to the Charters'). Edward was determined that these new articles were kept separate from Magna Carta itself, as that would make any later alterations almost impossible. Yet still there was no perambulation of the forest, which the laity now made a condition of a grant of a twentieth, too small a sum for Edward to give way. He carried on with his military plans regardless, although a perambulation did eventually take place that summer. When the army assembled at Carlisle in June 1300, it was strong but not nearly as large as the king might have hoped or expected. The Scottish war was now unpopular and there was a deep reluctance to serve; one knight required to serve with a bow and arrow took the obligation literally, firing his arrow as soon as he saw the Scots and then heading home.

The strategy this time was different, with the focus on southwestern Scotland, but Edward's lack of money and resources made the campaign a dismal non-event. Caerlaverock Castle was captured in July, but this was hardly a great achievement, and as Edward headed to Dumfries and then an indecisive skirmish near Wigtown, his troops deserted in large numbers. By the end of August, the king and what remained of his army were camped forlornly at Sweetheart Abbey, where Robert Winchelsey found him rather bereft of ideas. The archbishop carried a letter from Pope Boniface VIII, telling Edward to stop interfering in Scotland. On top of everything else, this missive ended a futile, underfunded excursion and in late September Edward returned to Cumberland. The only piece of good news from this period had been the birth of a son, Thomas of Brotherton, to his new wife on 1 June, providing a crucial 'spare' should anything happen to Prince Edward.

Parliament met at Lincoln in January 1301 with Edward seeking to alleviate his financial plight through a tax of a fifteenth. A bill proposed by Henry of Keighley, representing Lancashire, was adopted to address the numerous perceived injustices. Had Edward not prevaricated for four years, he might have been able to negotiate on this point, but his endless delays and evasions had exhausted everyone's patience. The price of the tax was confirming the charters, righting wrongs, and accepting the verdict of the previous year's perambulation of the forest, which would dramatically reduce the extent of the Royal Forest. While suffering a setback, and a significant one, Edward remained in control. He was granted his tax in return. Attempts to remove his corrupt treasurer, Walter Langton, were angrily but easily resisted. The king also seems to have received backing for his position on Scotland. Edward of Caernarfon, his 16-year-old son, was endowed with the earldom of Chester and became the first heir to the throne to be given the title Prince of Wales. Though chastened, the king was by no means defeated. His opponents had cause to be nervous as they left Lincoln. Edward was not a man to forgive or forget. This was proved five years later, when he belatedly identified Keighley as the architect of the bill against him. The hapless knight was imprisoned.

Suddenly Edward's fortunes improved. The Pope, desperate to deal with the problem of Sicily, wanted to impose a 10% tax on the European churches to finance action against the island. English ambassadors struck a deal whereby the Pope could do so in England for three years, as long as half went to the king. Winchelsey's stance against clerical taxation, that it required papal consent, was totally undermined at a stroke. Edward was now in a position to renew his Scottish campaign, this time in a two-pronged attack with his son. For someone who would later be remembered as a disastrous military commander humiliated by the Scots, young Edward acquitted himself very well on his first Scottish campaign. In the summer of 1301, the prince set out from Carlisle and took the castles at Ayr and Turnberry, both attached to Robert Bruce's earldom of Carrick. The king made rather slower progress from Berwick to Glasgow. He did manage to take Bothwell Castle in September, but had to stop short of an assault on Stirling as the campaign fell apart. Prince Edward was back at Carlisle. Troops at Berwick had mutinied for lack of pay, and as the king sent ever more irate and unreasonable letters to the exchequer to demand officials send him money he didn't have, soldiers once again haemorrhaged away.

Edward settled down for the winter at Linlithgow; for Christmas 1301 and New Year 1302 he was joined there by Prince Edward, along with Queen Margaret and his latest son, four-month-old Edmund of Woodstock. Under pressure from Philip IV, the papacy had released John Balliol from custody, and he was now reported to be raising an army in France. The Scots were placing much hope in the French king's support, but the wily Philip simply saw Scotland as an excuse to avoid handing back Gascony. He had no intention of providing actual aid. During the course of that winter, disheartened Scots like Robert Bruce returned to English allegiance. The Franco-Scottish alliance had been exposed as a sham, Philip's cynicism apparent. Philip was unashamed and continued to insist that any permanent Anglo-French treaty also had to include Scotland.

Not for the first time, Edward found fortune deciding to favour him without his having to lift a finger. Philip IV and Boniface VIII fell out in spectacular style, with both the French king and the Pope suddenly wanting to be Edward's new best friend. Boniface immediately turned against the Scots, writing admonishingly to the Scottish bishops about their duty to obey Edward. Philip had other problems. His own behaviour in Flanders, where he had removed the count and occupied the county, was strikingly similar to Edward's in Scotland. Like the Scots, the Flemish rebelled. Bruges revolted and killed the occupying French force, prompting Philip to send a large army to subdue the unrest. On 11 July 1302, outside Courtrai (Kortrijk), the Flemish achieved a famous and stunning victory over the French in the Battle of the Golden Spurs. After this costly and humiliating defeat, and not wanting Edward to become too close to Boniface, Philip became much more amenable. Neither the Scots nor Scotland were mentioned in the Anglo-French truce agreed later in 1302, nor in the more conclusive Treaty of Paris the following May, which formally ended the war and restored Gascony to Edward.

Things were also looking up for Edward financially at the start of 1303. He still lacked anything like the resources his ambitious campaign plans needed, and the war was unpopular with large sections of English society called upon to serve or supply the royal army. The king called in every debt, including a customary aid granted in 1290 for his daughter's marriage, collected from November 1302 even though twelve years had elapsed and the groom had died before the wedding could take place. In early June, Edward was back at Linlithgow, from where he moved to Stirling to cross the Forth, the small Scottish garrison of the castle in no position to also defend the bridge. News came from Carlisle that the Scots had launched a counterraid in northern England and were harrying the English in southwestern Scotland. Edward had to dispatch a force to deal with that situation, which they did with the assistance of Irish troops who landed in August. Meanwhile, the king took aim at the heartland of John Comyn, currently Scotland's single Guardian and the biggest thorn in Edward's side. He proceeded to Perth, then to Montrose to meet the ships carrying artillery which allowed him to capture Brechin Castle, then to Aberdeen. It was now late August and the king was running out of money, with troops deserting yet again. Ships bearing vital coin arrived, so Edward could press on to the Moray Forth and Kinloss Abbey. In October, as Comyn continued to harass English forces in central Scotland, his castle at Lochindorb fell to the king.

Boldly, Edward decided to winter in an area where the Scots had previously been safe from him. He set up his own winter quarters in Dunfermline Abbey, the burial church of Scottish kings. Prince Edward settled in at Perth, next door to Scone Abbey, where Scottish kings had been installed on the stone now hundreds of miles away in Westminster. Father and son were making a statement. In February 1304, Comyn knelt and swore homage to Edward. The following month, at St Andrews, scores more followed his example. There were a few holdouts, but Edward now felt confident to turn to his greatest irritation, Stirling Castle. He threw tremendous amounts of firepower into this siege, battering the castle for twelve weeks and refusing to accept the garrison's surrender until he had tried out a new toy, the Warwolf, which was possibly the largest trebuchet (siege catapult) ever made. Once it had been tested in action, Edward accepted Stirling's surrender on 24 July 1304, honouring chivalric convention by sparing the defenders. He was in generous mood, making just one significant exemption to the general amnesty: William Wallace. The king headed south, via a lengthy stay in Yorkshire and Christmas in Lincoln, leaving the Scots to capture Wallace, which they duly did in August 1305. He was handed over to the English and tried for treason (a ludicrous charge for 'probably the only Scottish leader who had *not* sworn allegiance to the English king'),[27] and after the inevitable guilty verdict he was gruesomely executed and dismembered at Smithfield on 23 August.

At the start of 1305, Edward had a mastery of the British Isles far beyond the wildest dreams of any predecessor, and unequalled until the union of Scottish and English crowns in 1603. Yet things were far more fragile than appearances suggested. Scotland had been subdued, but there was hardly enthusiastic embracing of English occupation or overlordship, and it had experienced a decade of war and disorder. The area of Ireland under English control had contracted, in large part due to Edward's repeated summons to Anglo-Irish lords to serve in Scotland, which had led to a situation on which native Irish lords could capitalise. In modern parlance, it was verging on a failed state. Gascony too had spent ten years as a conflict zone. The financial cost of war had been mind-boggling by the standards of the time, the struggles over Gascony and repeated invasions of Scotland probably absorbing over a million pounds in the decade 1294–1304. The king had been out of England (and Wales) for a significant proportion of those years, which had taken its toll on law and order. This was shown most dramatically in the theft of the Crown Jewels from Westminster Abbey in 1303; a man named Richard Pudlicote was convicted and executed, but the monks may well have been complicit. More seriously for the general population, violent crime had soared. Armed gangs were roaming the country, known as 'trailbaston' because of the clubs they carried. Edward had to introduce a new judicial commission, also called trailbaston, in which judges went on circuit to deal with the offenders.

The trailbaston commissions were formally established in the parliament which met at Westminster from February to April 1305. As the first parliament in more than two years, there was a large volume of petitions to deal with in addition to other business. Learning some lessons from the past, Edward invited Scottish representatives to advise on the future governance of their country, among them both Robert Bruce and Bishop Robert Wishart of Glasgow, a man who had previously been among the king's severest critics. They were dispatched to choose ten men for full discussions later in the year. After parliament finished, Edward began a tour of southern England, and much of the following months would be occupied by a combination of hunting and pilgrimage. In June, the Prince of Wales fell out with the treasurer, Walter Langton. Edward backed Langton and dismissed his son from court.

Parliament met again at Westminster that autumn. One major item of business was future arrangements for Scotland. The new Guardian was to be John of Brittany, Edward's nephew. English judges were named, but with Scottish counterparts. Nearly all of the sheriffs were to be Scots. While there was no mention of Scotland being a kingdom, Edward had drawn back from a total colonial occupation and opted for a more pragmatic settlement. In October, reconciliation was effected between the king and his eldest son. Over the previous three years, Edward had also reconciled with his old foe Roger Bigod of Norfolk; the childless earl had named Edward his heir, and during 1305 was pardoned his debts. After the years of discord, harmony seemed to be settling over England and Britain.

Even better, from Edward's point of view, was his victory over his other implacable foe during the winter of 1305–6. Archbishop Winchelsey had been doing his best to provoke Edward by dredging up matters from the distant past in the archiepiscopal court, to which the king had responded with counter-proceedings in royal courts and a demand for unpaid taxes. Unfortunately for Winchelsey, who might have expected some support from Boniface VIII, the Pope had changed. Boniface's quarrel with Philip had led French thugs to beat him up in September 1303; he never recovered and died the following month. His successor, Benedict XI, lived less than nine months, and after eleven months of arguing, Archbishop Raymond Bertrand de Got of Bordeaux was elected by the conclave. Taking the name Clement V, the new Pope was a Gascon and thus previously a subject of Edward, which was good news for the king. Clement compliantly absolved him from the concessions of the previous years, in a letter which reached him in February 1306. Better still, the Pope then suspended Winchelsey. Heading towards his sixty-seventh birthday, Edward showed few signs of slowing down. His wife was even pregnant again.

Once more, it was Scotland that disturbed this joyful interlude. Robert Bruce had been secretly conspiring with the Bishop of St Andrews to reactivate his grandfather's claim to the throne. On 10 February 1306, Bruce and John Comyn met in the Franciscan church at Dumfries. The meeting ended with Bruce stabbing Comyn and his followers finishing him off in front of the high altar. Whether a quarrel got out of hand, or whether Bruce acted on a premeditated plan when Comyn refused to back his conspiracy, is hotly debated. Bruce certainly acted quickly in seizing castles on southwestern Scotland, then riding to Glasgow to obtain a dubious absolution and hidden regalia from Bishop Wishart. From there, he sped to Scone to be installed as King Robert I at the end of March. Yet not all were as willing to forgive unapologetic, cold-blooded murder as the Bishop of Glasgow, and Bruce certainly did not command the allegiance of a majority of Scots. His patriotic cause had been badly tarnished when he murdered his rival.

Edward's health finally began to collapse. He spent the period between March and May 1306 in Winchester, carried out in a litter when he left. Of the old guard, only Lincoln was both still alive and available for campaign leadership. The torch was instead passed to the next generation, Earl Aymer de Valence of Pembroke dispatched north with the first force. At Pentecost (22 May), Edward knighted his eldest son and several others, including a certain Piers Gaveston. The Prince of Wales was to command this Scottish war, although the king made determined noises about following in person. The prince set out for Carlisle, but it was the advance party under Pembroke who enjoyed considerable success as the main army travelled. He crossed the Forth, captured the Bishops of Glasgow and St Andrews and the Abbot of Scone, and reclaimed Perth. On 19 June, he attacked Bruce's camp near Methven at dawn. Although Bruce escaped, many of his men were killed or taken. Prince Edward set out from Carlisle and recaptured southwest Scotland, joining with Pembroke at Perth in early August. Bruce took refuge in the rugged coastline of the western seaboard, probably not seeking inspiration from spiders, whatever later romantic legends were weaved.

An ailing Edward had made very slow progress north and was in an even worse mood than normal. In early August, Pembroke's captives were brought before the king. Edward's patience was exhausted and there would be no mercy this time. The prelates were treated as warriors, and while their clerical status saved their lives, they were packed off south in chains. The knights captured at Methven were sentenced to be dragged through the streets of Newcastle and hanged. Even the exalted were not spared. Edward dispatched the Earl of Atholl to his death, albeit on higher gallows to take account of his status. These were 'the bloodiest reprisals seen in England [...] since the spate of executions and assassinations which had accompanied Cnut of Denmark's consolidation of power as king of England in 1017'.[28] The king moved into Northumberland, but at Hexham and Newbrough, it was clearly feared he was dying. He rallied and headed slowly towards Carlisle. At the end of September, the travelling court reached Lanercost Priory in Cumberland.

The war in Scotland was effectively over; all that remained to be achieved was the capture of Bruce, who escaped to Ireland. Edward, never the gentlest or most patient of souls, had now become a very grumpy old man, his health in ruins, lashing out at everyone and everything. A cantankerous, vengeful king insisted on widespread executions for Scottish 'traitors'. He raged against young knights who had taken off to fight tournaments on the Continent. His presence held little appeal, any more than did Carlisle in the middle of winter. When parliament met in the city in January 1307, an unusually large number of men opted to send proctors in their stead, rather than brave a moody king and the northwestern climate themselves.[29] Next in Edward's firing line was Edward of Caernarfon, whose dissolute behaviour and increasingly scandalous association with Piers Gaveston resulted in a mighty row, the king allegedly tearing his son's hair and physically throwing him out of the room. Gaveston was banished.

The bloodletting and severity had negative consequences in Scotland, where the English had started to lose ground and Bruce had resumed his role as leader of the resistance. Edward decided that once again, it was an army led by himself that was required. At the end of June, he rode out of Carlisle. Yet the king was no longer the fearsome warrior of a decade earlier. He had just turned 68 (no sovereign had lived to such an age, nor would again until Elizabeth I three centuries later) and his health was broken. In ten tortuous days, he advanced six agonising miles, to the lonely hamlet of Burgh by Sands. There, in the afternoon of 7 July 1307, King Edward I died in the arms of his attendants.

His death was not officially announced until 20 July, after the new King Edward II reached Carlisle. There is no truth in the evocative legend that on his deathbed, the king had his son swear to boil his body in a cauldron and take the bones into battle against the Scots; young Edward was hundreds of miles away when his father died. It is tempting to muse that Edward I's skeleton might have been more effective against the Scots than Edward II's living body, which may explain why the story arose. It would be more than three months before he was buried. The old king's corpse was sent to Waltham Abbey, where it rested while the new king attended to Scottish affairs. The first service for Edward was actually held at the papal curia, in Poitiers Cathedral, where Pope Clement V honoured his former master. The body finally left Waltham around 18 October, travelling in slow and solemn procession to Westminster Abbey. On 27 October 1307, following the funeral service, Edward was laid to rest beside the shrine of Edward the Confessor, next to his father and first wife.

He had commissioned fine effigies for Henry and Eleanor, but not for himself. Arguably one of the most successful kings to rule England is beneath a large, stern chest of plain black Purbeck marble, almost certainly a deliberate choice on his part rather than neglect by his son. The Latin legend painted on the side dates from the sixteenth century: 'Here is Edward the First, the Hammer of the Scots. Keep the Vow'. On 2 May 1774, with the Dean of Westminster looking on, a group of macabrely curious antiquarians opened the tomb and the Purbeck marble coffin within. There, richly vested in coronation robes, was Edward's body, the face in a state of remarkable preservation after the better part of five centuries. While they measured him, the antiquarians seem to have been too overawed to carry out a full examination. Even having been dead almost 467 years, Edward could still intimidate. The lids were replaced, and ever since he has rested undisturbed. Yet even today, more than seven centuries later, his successors continue to be crowned just a few yards away on the throne he crafted, atop the stone he purloined to show himself the 'hammer of the Scots'.

Edward through the Centuries

Edward I did not die unpopular and was genuinely mourned, at least in England. He had become a legend in his own lifetime, largely because he had outlived his own peers and was viewed as a heroic, conquering king by an overawed younger generation. The eulogies and laments for the king in 1307 were a far cry from what chroniclers had written about the leopard-like prince half a century before. Back then, Matthew Paris, the St Albans monk who had memorably written that Edward's grandfather defiled hell by his presence, despaired of the prince's loutish and violent behaviour. His subsequent reign and achievements meant that the chroniclers had very different things to say when Edward died. The chronicler Peter Langford eulogised the deceased king in florid verse.

> Speak of King Edward and his memory
> As of the most renowned combatant on steed. [...]
> Of chivalry, after king Arthur,
> Was king Edward the flower of Christendom.
> He was so handsome and great, so powerful in arms,
> That of him may one speak as long as the world lasts.
> For he had no equal as a knight in armour
> For vigour and valour, neither present nor future. [...]
> He reigned over England by established law,
> By reason and right he maintained the monarchy;
> Of vigour and worth, and full of understanding,
> He had no equal in ruling a lordship. [...]
> May the Prince who was punished for us under Pilate
> Receive king Edward into his mercy.[30]

Scottish authors had very different views, looking sceptically on the idea of Edward being received mercifully into paradise. Later in the century, John Barbour asked how 'could he safely call on Him who judges all things in truth to have mercy on the pleading of one who, through his wickedness, had no mercy at this extremity?'[31] John of Fordun was scathing.

> He troubled the whole world by his wickedness, and roused it by his cruelty; by his wiles, he hindered the passage to the Holy Land; he invaded Wales; he treacherously subdued unto him the Scots and their kingdom; John of Balliol, the king thereof, and his son, he cast into prison; he overthrew churches, fettered prelates, and to some he put an end in filthy dungeons; he slew the people, and committed other misdeeds without end.[32]

Edward was as great a villain to the Scots as he was a hero to the English. There was no chance of reconciliation between these views. As far as the English were concerned, he was in the pantheon of great kings and nothing could remove him, especially after the catastrophic reign of his son.

The view remained unchallenged for a very long time. Tudor writers uncritically echoed the opinions of the medieval chroniclers. The admiration was demonstrated when the Elizabethan and Jacobean jurist, Edward Coke, labelled Edward the 'English Justinian'. The title endured for several centuries, at least until modern times when it can no longer be taken for granted that people know who Justinian is. Through the seventeenth and eighteenth centuries, there was little significant change in opinions about Edward, who became a useful mirror for some of the later Stuart struggles over the relationship between king and parliament.[33]

It is no surprise that for later nineteenth-century historians, especially William Stubbs, Edward was almost an ideal king. Stubbs views Edward's shortcomings as strengths: 'Edward loved power. He would not have been so great a king as he was, if he had not estimated at its full value the kingly power that he inherited'. Yet 'Edward had, besides force and honesty, a clear perception of true policy, and such an intuitive knowledge of the needs of his people as could proceed from a deep sympathy with them'. What Stubbs most admired was that the 'improvement of the laws, the definite arrangement of rights and jurisdictions, the definite elaboration of all departments, which mark the reign and make it the fit conclusion of a period of growth in all these matters, was unquestionably promoted, if not originated, by the personal action of the king'. There is nuance and half-hearted criticism of some measures and arbitrary actions, but with little bite. When it comes to Scotland, 'Edward's designs were premature [...] whether or not the two countries could have benefitted by union, the time of union was not come'. A strong king who promoted active government and constitutional development, anticipating the United Kingdom, was Bishop Stubbs' idea of perfection.[34]

T. F. Tout's 1893 biography was published in a series called 'Twelve English Statesmen', which aimed to present 'the lives and work of those leading actors in our affairs who by their direct influence have left an abiding mark on the policy, the institutions, and the position of Great Britain among States'. The purpose was therefore to glorify those who had contributed to making what late nineteenth-century historians viewed as the constitutional perfection of Queen Victoria's United Kingdom. There is indeed something very Victorian about Tout's portrayal of a man on whom 'the home lessons of purity and piety took a deep root, and all through his life Edward was honourably distinguished by the uprightness of his private life and the strength and fervour of his religious principles'. For a medieval king to find such approval by the censorious standards of the late nineteenth century was rare indeed. There is also more than a hint of Protestant nationalism, with Archbishop Winchelsey's 'unpatriotic conduct' condemned on the grounds of his allegiance to the Pope. The overall verdict on Edward is gushing: 'after-ages agreed to recognise in him one of the greatest and wisest of her rulers', where 'the whole subsequent history of the land he loved so well bore daily witness to the strength and endurance of the great king's work'.[35] Less than a decade later, in an even less subtly titled series (*Heroes of the Nation*), Edward Jenks went further: 'if ever there was a national hero, it was Edward of England'.[36]

Tout, however, changed his mind. He laid stress on how 'conservative' was 'Edward I's general political outlook': 'a strong king, loving efficiency but dominated by very conservative instincts, strove to weld the administrative system into a coherent whole which would enable him to exercise to the uttermost his supreme authority'. Even his development of parliament was 'no yielding to a people crying for liberty, but the shrewd device of an autocrat, anxious to use the mass of the people as a check upon his hereditary foes among the greater baronage'. Edward was now a quasi-dictator locked in a conflict of ideals with his nobility, deviously manipulating the system to triumph over them. It was a very different view of Edward, which was to exercise considerable influence later in the twentieth century.[37]

While some of this more damning portrait was incorporated into subsequent writing, the overall tone remained positive. In his extensive study of Henry III and Edward, Sir Maurice Powicke saw Edward as 'a conventional man' who 'lived intensely in conformity with the ideas and passions of his time, and found independence in applying them with vigour and precision'. Although 'a hard man', he was also 'a very great king'.[38] Powicke developed this theme a few years later in writing about 'a conventional man in an age of change', with 'two outstanding qualities', being 'physically and mentally, a most active man' and 'a consistent and also a very conventional Christian in his outlook on life'.[39] In a study of Edward's legislation, T. F. T. Plucknett was unstinting in his praise: 'Edward I meant to be a great king, and he was. He was a magnificent monarch, an intrepid soldier, and at times a supple politician'.[40]

Predictably, John Harvey's portrait of Edward was eccentricity verging on fantasy. Edward 'realized that the future lay with the united national state, and sought to build up a union of such states within the geographical frontiers of the British Isles', although 'he had no intention of imposing a foreign rule upon subjected peoples' but 'allowed himself to be forced by opposition into this forlorn attempt'. Such an attempt to make Edward a benevolent federalist is a perverse reading of a man whose aim was to assert the supremacy of the English Crown and tried to obliterate Scottish kingship. Even more bizarrely, 'it is impossible not to regret that the peace-lover, the arbitrator, the fountain-head of his country's prosperity and justice, should have exhausted himself in constant war'. Only the most deluded could possibly see Edward I as a peace-lover.[41]

The Victorian Edward had his swansong in the 1950s, at the hands of Winston Churchill. Edward 'presents us with qualities which are a mixture of the administrative capacity of Henry II and the personal prowess and magnanimity of Cœur de Lion'. To 'a greater extent than any of his predecessors' Edward was 'prepared to govern in the national interest and with some regard for constitutional form'. He was 'the last great figure in the formative period of English law', the man who 'made parliament [...] the associate of the crown'. By the end of his reign, 'the foundations of a strong national monarchy for a United Kingdom and of a Parliamentary Constitution had been laid'. This was anachronistic nostalgia from a Victorian hangover, perhaps carried away by the unlikely Conservative achievement in securing over half the Scottish vote in the 1955 general election. Edward's idea of a 'united' kingdom had almost nothing in common with the twentieth century understanding.[42] There is also something Victorian in L. F. Salzman's 1968 biography, published when the author was 90. 'Had his son and successor resembled him in character and ability a despotic autocracy might have been established which would have altered the whole history of English constitutional history, and it is questionable whether we owe a greater debt to the strength of Edward I, which curbed the baronial oligarchy, or to the weakness of Edward II, which shook the power of the throne and saved England from a despotism'.[43]

This reflected a shift in Edward's reputation, in which Tout's harsher verdict of an autocrat locked in conflict with his nobility gained ground. K. B. McFarlane said in 1953 that Edward oversaw 'the restoration of the old community of interests between Crown and baronage', yet he too changed his mind. In a 1965 article about Edward I and his earls, McFarlane noted that the king 'did not keep within the bounds of his own law and there was no one to bring him to do justice to those whom he had wronged', a 'wilful abuse of power' which 'must however contribute to the historian's assessment of his greatness as a king'. In the end, 'Edward I preferred masterfulness to the arts of political management', hence 'he belonged less to the future than to the past'.[44] For many years thereafter, it was largely accepted that Edward had been stingy when it came to patronage.

A more critical approach to Edward also came with the revitalisation of Scottish history during the 1960s. The first edition of G. W. S. Barrow's biography of Robert Bruce was published in 1965, which naturally cast Edward I in a negative light as a cruel, bloodthirsty and vindictive king. While perhaps too indulgent towards Bruce, Barrow nevertheless highlighted the very different way in which the Scots remember a man who sought to destroy their kingdom. Welsh academics also found their voice in the later part of the twentieth century: J. Beverley Smith's important biography of Llywelyn ap Gruffudd was originally published in Welsh, with no translation for English speakers for more than a decade.[45] For parts of the British Isles beyond England, Edward's reputation and legacy was not one to be celebrated. Scottish historians were especially critical of 'bloodthirsty' Edward's 'cruel, vindictive and paranoiac' treatment of William Wallace: 'Edward I, the greatest of the Plantagenets, a king most admired and feared and one who could show nobility of character, appears small and mean'.[46]

The most prolific modern scholar of Edward's reign has been Michael Prestwich. His doctoral thesis was developed into a 1972 monograph about the conduct and financing of Edward's wars, while in 1988 he published what remains the standard academic biography of the king. In addition to more general volumes on the thirteenth and fourteenth centuries, he has also written a considerable number of articles on Edward and his times. At first, Prestwich reflected the negative approach to Edward common in academic thinking of the 1960s and 1970s, noting that 'Edward I left to the son he distrusted a government weakened by debt and a country threatened by disorder, with the problem of Scotland unresolved'. Yet he also acknowledged that Edward was 'without doubt one of the greatest rulers of his time'. In his biography, Prestwich remained more critical of Edward than some later writers, but it is a detailed, nuanced portrait which confronts Edward's failings at the same time as acknowledging his undoubted successes. Contradicting McFarlane, Prestwich notes that while Edward did not codify law in the way Justinian did, what he achieved 'was far more effective than any codification could possibly have been', as 'Justinian's legislation had preserved the past: Edward I's created openings for the future'. Importantly, 'Edward did not ride rough-shod over law and custom in many cases'. Prestwich has focussed considerably on Edward's military career, seeing him as an effective but not an innovative warrior, observing bluntly that 'Edward I failed in his Scottish wars', but that 'failure is perhaps less surprising than the degree of success which the king achieved'. Prestwich lays stress on Edward as a 'formidable figure', whose 'personality was central to his reign', 'a man who could not be diverted from his purpose'. Ultimately, the verdict is balanced: 'Edward I was a formidable king; his reign, with both its successes and its disappointments, a great one'.[47]

The later twentieth century saw scholars try to put Edward's policies towards Scotland and Wales into a broader context of medieval British history. It led to a slightly more nuanced picture, with Robin Frame observing that 'there is little to suggest that Edward himself was dominated by imperial dreams, devoted to the construction of a unitary monarchy of the British Isles, or even irredeemably hostile to regional custom'. Instead, 'throughout the tumultuous events of his reign he did no more in his own view than employ his existing rights; nothing was further from his mind than the creation of novel forms of rule'.[48] Yet as the Welsh historian Rees Davies noted, this ended up being the result, as the 'transfer of the regalia and holiest relics of the Welsh principality and the Scottish kingdom to Westminster [...] made it visually clear that the other kingships in Britain had been eradicated by, or absorbed in, the English kingship'.[49] This was one of Edward's legacies which was undone as the twentieth century ended. In 1950, a group of students had stolen the Stone of Scone from Westminster Abbey on Christmas Day, although it was left on the altar of Arbroath Abbey the following April and returned to Westminster. On 3 July 1996, Prime Minister John Major and Scottish Secretary Michael Forsyth announced that the stone would return to Scotland. In November, it was duly sent to Edinburgh Castle. The move was widely seen as 'a publicity stunt' and did nothing to save the Conservative Party from electoral annihilation in Scotland the following year.[50] Nevertheless, the stone stayed in Edinburgh, making a brief return visit to Westminster for the coronation of Charles III in May 2023.

The 1990s also saw important work on some of the figures around Edward, including biographies of the two Eleanors, his mother and his wife, and his nemesis, Simon de Montfort.[51] However, at the turn of the millennium, the king's own reputation was distinctly mixed. There was a general consensus that the reign divided around 1294, twenty-two years of triumph succeeded by thirteen of disappointment and failure; in the words of one historian, the continuing pageantry 'could not mask the fact that the later years of Edward's reign were played out in diminuendo'.[52] However, the historiographical tide turned once again in the early years of the twenty-first century.

In 2008, Marc Morris published a lively, largely admiring biography of the king. The title, *A Great and Terrible King*, is an apt summary of Morris' approach to a man with 'the character of a great king – brave, wise, eloquent, just, pious – combined with an abundance of good fortune and a restless venturesome nature'. He argued that the unkind views of the youthful Edward are 'unduly harsh'. When it comes to the Jews, Morris acknowledges Edward was a 'bigoted man, he lived in a bigoted age, and was king of a bigoted people', although reminds us that what we find abhorrent 'was regarded by his Westminster obituarist as one of Edward's most commendable achievements'. This distinction between medieval and modern outlook underpins some of the other conclusions: 'to thirteenth-century Englishmen [...] it was more important to have a warlike king than a peaceable one', but 'Edward's legacy [...] was one of profound disunity and lasting division'. For all his achievements, the most problematic part of his 'legacy, from which neither his son nor his successors could escape, was the use of extreme violence to solve intractable political problems'. Edward's undoubted greatness came at a price.[53]

Two monographs sought to redeem Edward's reputation further. Caroline Burt looked in detail at his governance of England, concluding that while the later years were problematic, taken as a whole the reign shows that 'Edward's beliefs and ability made him into one of England's most innovative, conceptually creative, focussed and successful rulers', who 'not only played the part of a good king well, he played it with aplomb'.[54] Andrew Spencer examined Edward's relationship with his earls and concluded that the 'reign stands as one of the clearest examples of what a medieval king could achieve when he worked in partnership with his earls'.[55] The negative verdicts of the later twentieth century were comprehensively challenged.

Biographers continued to endorse this more positive approach. Andy King's short volume is a thematic study rather than a biography. For King, the 'guiding principle behind his government and his reforms' was 'maintaining the rights of his crown undiminished, in keeping with the promise he had made at his coronation'. In warfare, Edward 'was not, in fact, a particularly daring or imaginative commander', rather 'his campaigns were won by the careful marshalling of resources and supplies, and by sheer, grimly relentless perseverance'. While he faced opposition, part of his political success was learning from the mistake of his father and being 'genuinely concerned to consult as widely as possible on issues which affected the realm' and 'to be *seen* to be consulting as widely as possible', which is 'why he so reliably held parliaments, which gave a voice to his subjects, and were a public demonstration of his willingness to take counsel'. He 'transformed the government of England, making it markedly more responsive to his subjects'. Above all, 'Edward was a king who appreciated the value of symbolism and political theatre', since 'medieval kingship was very much a performance; a king needed to be seen to be acting as a king'. And King's verdict, echoing that of the medieval commentators, is a positive one: 'In the panoply of English kings, Edward I came closer than most to fulfilling the medieval idea of a great king'.[56]

As the twenty-first century advances, Edward has thus come to be viewed in a much more positive light, at least in England. Historians have started to look at how Edward met contemporary ideals of kingship rather than condemn him according to modern standards. For all that, he remains something of an enigma who has never quite captured the popular imagination.

Edward in Popular Culture

'King Edward I', wrote Sir Maurice Powicke, 'stands apart in our history. We remember him, but not as a living man who stirs the imagination'.[57] The truth of his words is shown by the paucity of fictional works which have a role for Edward. There is a good reason that very few people know about the first – George Peele's 1593 play *The Famous Chronicle of King Edward the First*. It is lengthy, rambling and confused, a second (1599) edition and the efforts of modern editors doing little to redeem it into a work people might actually want to watch. In 2019, the Sam Wanamaker Playhouse did a version as part of its 'Read not Dead' series, 'script-in-hand performances of little-known and rarely or never-performed early modern plays'. However, this is a far cry from the continuing popularity of Shakespeare's history plays, and it looks set to remain in deserved obscurity.

Edward was a reasonably popular subject for historical novelists in the Victorian and Edwardian era. Most of these novels are romantic, swashbuckling affairs which hold little interest for the modern reader brave enough to tackle the often florid and quaint prose. Of considerably more interest is the nineteenth-century visit Edward's legend took to an unexpected venue: Hungary. In 1857, János Arany was asked to write a celebratory piece for the visit of Austro-Hungarian Emperor Franz Joseph I, the first imperial visit to Budapest since the failed 1848 revolution. What Arany produced was *The Bards of Wales* (*A walesi bárdok*), a ballad retelling the myth of Edward burning 500 Welsh bards who refused to sing his praises at Montgomery. In recalling the subjection of a people by a foreign king, Arany was obviously taking aim at the Emperor, and it was not published (in heavily disguised form) until 1863. It remains a core part of the Hungarian national canon, still learnt by schoolchildren today.

It is this theme, of a ruthless, brutal king obsessed by conquest and destruction, that is taken up by most modern novelists in the rare books which feature Edward. The general approach is the struggle of the Scots and Welsh against this tyrant king, seeking to obliterate their identity. It is no great surprise, since these campaigns make for good stories; it would be hard to write an engaging novel about the Quo Warranto proceedings. Yet this does mean that Edward largely becomes typecast as the irascible villain of the piece. Series by Edith Pargeter, Sharon Penman, Nigel Tranter and Robyn Young are all well-researched, readable novels, but while historically defensible, there is something predictable and tired about portrayals of Edward the anti-hero.

Rather different is the Edward of Paul Doherty's Hugh Corbett series, begun in 1986.[58] Corbett is a former soldier from the Welsh campaign, who becomes a chancery clerk and then the king's solver of mysteries. The series delves into the dark underworld and murky corners of Edward's reign, real events the backdrop for the stories, from murders in St Paul's Cathedral to the death of Alexander III to spy scandals in France. And here Edward is a much more complex, rounded character. He is hardly likeable, and the temper and stubbornness and brutality are fully on display. Edward is 'a conqueror' who has 'smashed the Welsh' and 'always wanted to do the same to Scotland'. Grief makes him more irate in later years: 'Edward's rages were becoming more frequent, the deaths of the beloved Queen Eleanor, his Chancellor and friend, Robert Burnell, Bishop of Bath and Wells, had loosened dark forces in the King's soul'.

Yet alongside that is the king who could be capable of kindness and compassion as well as bloodthirstiness and vindictiveness: 'Edward never forgot a favour or an injury'. He is a man of very human contradictions.

> Edward was a strange man, on the one hand, hard, ruthless, he would without any compunction order men, women and even children to be slain in a town which had resisted him. On the other, he was almost like a child, if he trusted someone he expected that trust to be returned and could never understand why people broke their word.

There are those who look on him with affection.

> Benstede worshipped Edward. He saw the English king as a living reincarnation of all that was good and proper in a knight and in a king. Benstede had read the Arthurian romances spread by the minstrels and troubadours of France and England and considered that if they were true, then Edward was Arthur come again. The English king had brought peace and good order to Wales, built roads, stimulated trade, healed the wounds of civil war and, through his use of Parliament, brought the whole kingdom and entire community of the realm into one coherent organisation.

This is an important reminder of the king who was genuinely mourned in 1307. For the novelist, the story is usually better from the perspective of the underdog, which gives a very skewed perspective on Edward. The Corbett series gives an insight into why he never faced a major revolt and retained the loyalty of his English subjects for more than three decades.

Edward I has very rarely been a character on screen, and in most cases his appearances are as the opponent of Robert Bruce or William Wallace which glorify the Scottish leader and demonise the English king, the actor playing the hero usually not Scottish. Most famous is the quasi-psychopathic portrayal by Patrick McGoohan in *Braveheart* (1995). The film is a historical travesty, factually inaccurate on multiple counts, but its portrayal of Edward in his declining years is an exception. McGoohan captures something of the ageing but still energetic king, irascible and violent, the angry relationship with his son probably an accurate enough reflection of the situation between them in the final years. The following year, Brian Blessed played Edward in *The Bruce*, although anyone familiar with Blessed's portrayal of the fictional Richard IV in the first series of *Blackadder* might see too much of that in his performance to be convinced by him as Edward I. In *Outlaw King* (2018), Stephen Dillane took the role of Edward. The film takes plenty of historical liberties (albeit far less egregiously than *Braveheart*), but this representation of Edward is more rounded, with more nuance in the relationship between father and son. Dillane captures the aloofness and hardness of the king, but there is also something more human and complex about this portrayal.

A more light-hearted take on Edward was provided by Donald Sumpter in the BBC comic drama *Heist* (2008). Very loosely based around the events of the Crown Jewels robbery of 1303, with Kris Marshall as Richard Pudlicote, there was considerably more emphasis on the slapstick than the drama, but it made a welcome change of theme for a programme featuring Edward. And while not a fictionalisation of the history character, Edward served as the inspiration for Tywin Lannister in George R. R. Martin's fantasy series *A Song of Ice and Fire*. When this was adapted by HBO under the title of the first novel, *Game of Thrones* (2011–19), the role was taken by Charles Dance, who would have made a convincing Edward.

The Edward I of contemporary popular thought has largely been cast as the villain in romantic stories of Scottish and Welsh identity. Modern nationalisms can be too easily projected back onto the complexities of a different era, the Edward who emerges an unsatisfactory caricature, especially when he becomes a vehicle for the Anglophobia of film directors in the United States. Yet the difficult legacy of Edward in Scotland and Wales can also be confronted in more creative, challenging ways. When Cadw undertook a restoration and improvement project on the King's Gate at Caernarfon Castle in 2020, they commissioned the artist Rubin Eynon to produce three bronze statues for the project. The third, entitled 'Legacy', sits on the new upper floor of the gate. It is a giant, shattered bronze head from an imagined statue of Edward l, perhaps evoking the memory of all the shattered statues torn down in Eastern European capitals when Communism fell. It is intended to show that the king's legacy has been destroyed. As the board beside it says, the 'Welsh national flag now flies over the turrets, and Wales once again has its own parliament'. The phrase 'once again' is interesting, for whatever Edward did, he certainly did not destroy a Welsh parliament, nor did one exist before 1999. Perhaps this underlines the truth of the concluding sentence: 'Imperial monuments like Caernarfon stand as a powerful reminder of bitter medieval divisions and a contested history'. The Welsh flag flies over the turrets, but as long as the castle ruins stand, it flutters over a visible legacy of Edward's conquest. His memory will always be contested.

Verdict

Edward I's contested memory and legacy cannot obscure the fact that he was a remarkable sovereign. King for thirty-five years, he was also the major political actor in England for a decade before his accession. His energy and achievements rivalled those of his great-grandfather, Henry II. Unlike his great uncle Richard I, in whose footsteps he followed as a crusader, he combined his warrior instincts with considerable attention to governance and reform, to great effect. The physical legacy he left in Wales, in the form of the iconic castles which still stand, is among the most tangible of any medieval king. Whether for good or ill, his reign fundamentally transformed Britain.

There is no denying that Edward, however remarkable, was a bully. His bullying behaviour was especially bad in the late 1290s, when he browbeat anyone who failed to do what he wanted, from the clergy to the Scots. He was stubborn and inflexible, and that caused him problems. His temper and will were fearsome, and rare indeed were those like Roger Bigod who had the courage and strength to stand up to the king. In this regard, King John's blood ran in Edward I's veins, even if Edward's infinitely greater military competence and achievements saved him from his grandfather's fate. Edward was not someone many of us today would find a convivial dinner companion. Yet conviviality was not something people expected of a medieval monarch. If he was clearly John's grandson in temper, arrogance and ferocity, Edward also used his undeniable abilities much more wisely and recognised the importance of consent.

While he faced dissent, opposition and criticism, Edward never suffered outright rebellion by either family members or English subjects, something of an achievement given the length of his reign and the force of his personality. Even at his worst moment, he was never in serious danger: 'Edward did not lose the allegiance of most of his subjects in 1297, though through his insensitivity and stubbornness, he put it to a considerable test'.[59] He avoided complaints about favourites and excessive patronage, showing a genuine concern for broad consultation. Parliament developed significantly during his reign, the rather unwieldy size of its membership on some occasions testament to the king's desire to have as broad a base of consent as possible. Given the problems both his father and his son provoked through favouritism and inability to take wise counsel, Edward's achievements in this regard are noteworthy. He made mistakes and on occasion acted unwisely, but in general he managed to rule by consent without there ever being any doubt who was in charge. That was the mark of a successful king.

In two further key measures by which contemporaries judged a king, Edward also succeeded. Even though he clashed dramatically with the Church and took the extreme step of outlawing the entire clergy, Edward was never viewed as impious. His piety was seen as conventional but authentic, not least because he was a crusader and because of the way he dealt with the Jews. Abhorrent though we find this antisemitism today, we cannot lose sight of how, in the thirteenth century, it was immensely popular. Meanwhile, his military achievements were enormous. He was no great innovator, but his stubborn determination and willingness to challenge common sense (sane men did not typically invade Wales or Scotland in winter) yielded spectacular results. His judgement could occasionally fail him, as it did over Gascony in 1294. The military achievements are also tempered by the fact that Edward bequeathed a deeply problematic legacy to his son. His endless campaigns had left the Crown with large debts and the treasury empty. Despite ferocious efforts, Scotland had not been subdued. It would have required a king of considerable competence and ability to take on this inheritance successfully.

Unfortunately, the new king was Edward II. Edward I should not be judged by Edward II's inadequacies, but his legacy must be acknowledged as a contributing factor in what followed.

Indeed, the real problem is that Edward succeeded militarily. Had he failed, like his predecessors, to defeat and conquer Wales, or to assert his overlordship over Scotland, his memory would not be nearly so divisive, but then we would scarcely remember him at all. While it is entirely understandable that Edward is not looked on fondly (to put it mildly) in Scotland and Wales, we need to remember he was a man of his time. Edward believed that he was asserting his rights to overlordship over those two places, in the same way that Philip IV of France believed he was asserting his rights over Flanders and Gascony. Edward fought for those rights forcefully and successfully, skilfully preying upon divisions among his opponents; it is worth noting that the Scots were never united against him. We might baulk at his brutality, his insensitivity and what was unleashed, we might criticise his failure to recognise Scottish identity, but asserting rights was what medieval monarchs did. It is rarely remembered that just thirty years earlier, Alexander III had asserted Scottish rights against the Norwegians, wrestling control of the Kingdom of the Isles from them in the conflict which led to the 1266 Treaty of Perth. Scotland too expanded aggressively in the thirteenth century. It was part of kingship. Edward was simply very powerful and very successful.

Edward I was a king of international standing who transformed his realm, imposing himself by force of personality and will for more than three decades. Unusually for a king who reigned so long, he did not die unpopular and many of his compatriots genuinely grieved his loss. This is testament to the fact that in English eyes, he had lived up to the ideals of kingship. Though the legacy Edward left is complex, controversial and contested, it was nevertheless immense, and he was indeed a great king.

Chapter 4

Edward III: A Romantic King?

> He governed gloriously his kingdom into his age. […] In no land under heaven has been brought forth so noble a king, so gentle and so blessed.[1]

> Here is the glory of the English, the paragon of past kings, the model of future kings, a merciful king, the peace of the peoples, Edward the third fulfilling the jubilee of his reign, the unconquered leopard, powerful in war like a Maccabee. While he lived prosperously, his realm lived again in honesty. He ruled mighty in arms; now in heaven let him be a king.[2]

> He lived too long, and ended his life a heroic failure.[3]

Atop his tomb in Westminster Abbey, the gilded effigy of Edward III depicts an old man with long, flowing hair and beard. In an era before official portraits, this is the most familiar image of the king, the elderly, sad figure of the 1370s. He had been on the throne half a century and in the final years watched his achievements crumble to dust around him, becoming a tragic spectator in his own reign. As the modern biographer cited above observes, he had lived too long, so people had the opportunity to forget the dynamic, younger warrior king and all his successes. Superficially, Edward's reign ended as it had begun, the English position in France weak and under threat, the court riven by discord and deeply unpopular, hope invested in a new king who was but a child.

Yet in the half century between tumultuous beginning and tragic ending lies a very different story. For three decades in the middle of his reign, Edward cut a dashing figure. He had been a renowned warrior who had atoned for the military catastrophes of his father, triumphing in battle against both Scots and French. His court was a dazzling centre of chivalry, epitomised by the founding of the Order of the Garter. Edward was seen as a monarch blessed by God, presiding over a golden age. The inscription on his tomb shows this to be the official memory his successor wanted to promote. Warfare dominated much of his reign and many modern historians have tended to see him as above all interested in war, yet for many years he oversaw one of the most constructive relationships with nobility and parliament of any medieval monarch. That Edward died in failure should not erase the undoubted achievements of his time on the throne, not least the dignity and pride he restored to a monarchy badly tainted by his parents.

Edward's Life and Reign

Edward was born at Windsor Castle on 13 November 1312. The arrival of Edward II and Isabella of France's first child was a moment of joy at a tense and difficult time. Five months earlier, the king's favourite, Piers Gaveston, had been executed by a group of earls opposed to what they perceived to be his malign influence over the sovereign. At least the birth of an heir showed Edward was doing his marital duty and securing the succession. The newborn infant was given the English name of his father and grandfather, and baptised on 16 November in St Edward's Chapel. At eleven days old, he was granted the county palatinate of Chester. He would receive his own household and a conventional education suitable for an heir to the throne.

Edward grew up against a backdrop of crisis.[4] The king was an abject failure against the Scots, most humiliatingly in the Battle of Bannockburn in 1314. Edward II's feud with his cousin, Thomas of Lancaster, and the growing influence of a new favourite, Hugh Despenser the Younger (supported by his father, Hugh Despenser the Elder), dominated the later 1310s and early 1320s. After Lancaster was executed following the Battle of Boroughbridge in 1322, the king and his favourite presided over a greedy, vindictive regime that caused widespread resentment. In September 1325, afraid of what might happen to the Despensers if he left England, King Edward sent his 12-year-old son to the court of the French king to swear homage for the duchy of Aquitaine. Queen Isabella was already in Paris with her brother, Charles IV. The prince duly swore homage to his uncle.

Isabella then announced that someone (clearly the younger Despenser) had come between her and her husband, so she was staying in Paris and keeping their son with her. Rumours, increasingly insistent, began that the queen had embarked on an affair with Roger Mortimer, a marcher lord and opponent of Edward II who had escaped from imprisonment in the Tower of London. As Edward desperately sought the return of his wife and son, Paris became a gathering point for prominent opponents of the English regime. Charles, however, was unimpressed by his sister's scandalous liaison with Mortimer, and whatever his feelings about his brother-in-law and his favourite, the French king was not going to permit his kingdom to be used as a launching point for an invasion of England. In summer 1326, Isabella took Prince Edward and other leading rebels to the Low Countries.

The queen struck a deal with the Count of Hainault. In August, Prince Edward was engaged to Philippa, the count's daughter, in return for money and troops to invade England. Despite the political motivation for the engagement, the marriage (celebrated in 1328) would be a happy one. Leaving Dordrecht, the invaders landed at Orwell in Suffolk on 24 September 1326. Edward II's regime collapsed with spectacular speed. By Christmas, the king was imprisoned in Kenilworth Castle, while nearly all his closest associates were dead. In January 1327, Edward II was deposed, although a delegation visited him at Kenilworth on 20 January and compelled him to renounce the throne the next day, providing the legal fiction of an abdication. While momentous, the removal of the anointed king was made easier by the existence of an undisputed son and heir. Still just 14, Edward had played no direct role in the events which brought down his father, although necessity meant that he had officially been keeper of the realm after the king's capture. On 25 January 1327, his reign as King Edward III began, his coronation following in Westminster Abbey on 1 February. Yet he was king in name only. The country was being run by his mother and her lover, Isabella and Mortimer's regime 'just as vindictive, despotic and unstable as that of the Despensers but a great deal less competent'.[5] For Edward, the next three years were to be ones of humiliation and frustration, as he could only look on at what this incompetent, avaricious pair did to England.

Parliament resumed in February and began the work of reconciliation. The 1322 sentence against Thomas of Lancaster was revoked, which allowed his brother Henry to be restored to the earldom of Lancaster. The judgement of the same year against Roger Mortimer was annulled. Dealing with the consequences of Edward II's rule and removal occupied much time. Given Edward III's age, a regency was avoided, but Isabella asserted that her son was too young to assume the full rights of an adult king. The Queen Mother herself does not seem to have been an especially malign figure, but her lover was, and Isabella eventually became deeply unpopular because of Mortimer. A major grievance for the new king would be the treatment of the former Edward II, now known once again as Edward of Caernarfon. Plots to free him or help him escape were uncovered throughout 1327, until the regime decided it was too risky to let him live. He died at Berkeley Castle on 21 September, almost certainly murdered on Mortimer's orders. Isabella and Edward III both attended the funeral and burial in Gloucester Abbey on 20 December, and in later years the king would promote pilgrimage to Gloucester and honour his father's memory. While probably seething as he spent Christmas in Worcester, he was in no position to take vengeance in 1327, but after Mortimer's downfall he acted against those he believed to be the murderers.

Edward and Philippa were married in York Minster on 24 January 1328, but the queen's coronation was insultingly delayed until February 1330. 1328 was thereafter a year of humiliations in foreign affairs. The Scots had capitalised on the unrest in England to launch damaging raids in the border counties, and an English expedition against them in 1327 was a costly failure. When parliament met at York in February 1328, the main business was negotiations with Scotland. The resulting peace treaty was signed by Robert I (Robert Bruce) in Edinburgh on 17 March, then ratified by the next English parliament at Northampton on 4 May. The Treaty of Northampton (or Edinburgh-Northampton) recognised Scotland as an independent kingdom, acknowledging Robert and his heirs as king, and restored the border to its position under Alexander III. Many in England saw the treaty as dishonourable and refused to endorse a 'disgraceful peace' which was blamed fully on Isabella and Mortimer.

Meanwhile, Charles IV of France died on 1 February 1328, and the House of Capet became extinct with him. There were two possible successors: Edward III of England was the grandson of Philip IV (Charles' father), while Count Philip of Valois was Philip IV's nephew and cousin of Charles IV. Under normal rules of succession, a grandson would succeed ahead of a nephew, but Edward's claim was complicated by being through a female line. The choice of Philip would later be justified by Salic Law, which debarred women from the throne; if Isabella could not be queen, it was reasoned, nor could she transmit a claim to the throne. In reality, the French nobility had no desire to give their crown to a foreign king and never seriously considered Edward. The English regime initially protested but after a few months quietly accepted the situation, and Edward was dispatched across the Channel in 1329, to pay reluctant and guarded homage to the new Philip VI for Gascony in Amiens Cathedral on 6 June.

Domestically, 1328 made clear how limited was Isabella and Mortimer's competence. There was a crisis of law and order which measures taken at the Northampton parliament did little to redress. The administration had exhausted the enormous surplus left by Edward II and had to borrow from the Bardi of Florence. Worse for Edward, his mother's approach was suffocating him, while her unbearable lover was humiliating him. Mortimer's arrogance increased as he held tournaments around his Herefordshire and Shropshire heartland and lorded it over the king. Parliament met at Salisbury in October, many believing the assembly had been summoned solely to raise Mortimer higher. He has already enriched himself and vastly expanded his lands, but it was now expected that he would have the king create him Earl of Shrewsbury. The reality was worse. The title Mortimer had the king award him was Earl of March, an unprecedented style which suggested authority over the whole Welsh March. Comparisons began to be made between Mortimer and the Despensers. Henry of Lancaster became an open opponent. From Winchester, Henry made public his accusations against the new Earl of March. He made for his Warwickshire and Leicestershire heartlands, while Edward was taken for the anniversary of his father's funeral at Gloucester, followed by a second successive Christmas at Worcester. Civil war threatened.

The Earls of Norfolk and Kent, the king's uncles, tried to broker an agreement. Lancaster and Mortimer met at Bedford in January 1329, where they agreed to submit to the queen's arbitration at a future parliament, although Lancaster had to pay a large surety and seventy names were excluded from pardon. It was humiliation dressed up as clemency. Opposition began to grow, and now included two bishops who had played a key role in Edward II's downfall, Adam Orleton of Worcester and John Stratford of Winchester. Oblivious to his unpopularity and the risk from the discontent he was causing, Mortimer continued to load himself with honours and rewards. Edward demonstrably turned against Mortimer in the autumn of 1329. He sent a trusted aide, William Montagu, to the Pope, and a code was worked out. At some point in early 1330, Edward sent a letter with the words *Pater Sancte* ('Holy Father') written in his own hand; in future, only letters containing this greeting in the king's handwriting were to be accepted by the Pope as Edward's own wishes.

By early 1330, Mortimer's paranoia was mounting. Rumours continued unabated about Edward II's survival. One of these reached Edmund of Woodstock, Earl of Kent and Edward II's half-brother. Kent went looking for Edward at Corfe Castle. When parliament met at Winchester in March 1330, Kent's dramatic arrest and show trial overshadowed everything else. On 19 March, Kent was executed outside Winchester Castle. He waited at the execution site for several hours; there were considerable problems finding anyone willing to act as executioner for a royal earl after a process of highly dubious legality for a trumped-up charge.

It was probably the judicial murder of his uncle which finally convinced Edward that he had to act. He would be 18 at the end of the year and needed to assert his independence, not least as 'a man who had engineered the murders of his father and brother might just countenance disposing of him as well'.[6] His first son, Edward of Woodstock, was born to Philippa on 15 June. (He was not called 'the Black Prince' until the sixteenth century, but the title is used here as an easy means to distinguish father and son.) As English relations with France worsened over the summer, so tensions grew between Mortimer and Edward. Gossip suggested that Isabella was pregnant with Mortimer's child and that he was planning to usurp the throne. Mortimer was increasingly suspicious, yet this only increased his disrespectful treatment of the king. In early September 1330, the couple moved into Nottingham Castle. The council met at Nottingham from 15 October to discuss Gascony, and it was during this gathering that Edward struck. Mortimer behaved arrogantly and high-handedly, interrogating Edward's friends to try to uncover evidence of a plot. The friends stayed loyal and Mortimer achieved nothing but hastening his overthrow. With a group of associates, including his close friend William Montagu, on the night of 19 October, the king sneaked into Nottingham Castle through a secret tunnel and made for the Queen Mother's apartments, where they found Mortimer hiding behind a curtain. Three Mortimer men were killed. Isabella pleaded for her lover in vain. Mortimer was arrested and put in chains.

Edward's coup at Nottingham was dramatic and brought about a rapid, painless transition of power. On 20 October, sheriffs were ordered to proclaim the arrest. The king set out for Leicester with his prisoners, but now had to decide how to act against Mortimer. Since the execution of Piers Gaveston in 1312, England had been plagued by a series of judicial murders, unsatisfactory legal processes and mob 'justice'. Edward now had a chance to end this bloody cycle of vengeance and begin his personal rule with a clear statement about the just nature of his kingship. Parliament was duly summoned to Westminster on 26 November. The trial that took place there hardly met modern expectations of a fair process, but by contemporary standards, the trial was 'both legitimate and seen to be legitimate', with 'the legitimacy of community consent – a consent that could only properly be sought in parliament'.[7] Mortimer was unsurprisingly condemned and suffered a traitor's death at Tyburn on 29 November. Few mourned a man who had been seen as a cruel, self-aggrandising upstart presiding over an illegitimate regime. Isabella was sent to her manor of Berkhamsted, before spending two years confined at Windsor. There is no truth in the popular legend that she was sent to live out her days in effective imprisonment at Castle Rising in Norfolk. It did become her home, but after 1332 she was rehabilitated into the court. If Edward was never close to her and probably never forgave her for Mortimer, he gave her proper status as Queen Mother until her death in 1358. Meanwhile, the king's co-conspirators were showered with rewards.

The events of 1330 in Nottingham 'provided the first example of something that was to be a recurring theme of Edward's kingship: his ability to seize the moment, to take decisive action and to win the day'.[8] Edward was now master of his own realm and determined his kingship would mark a break with the previous twenty years. In November 1330, he turned 18. He appears to have been around 5ft 10 or 11 as an adult, not the stature of his grandfather but tall for the time. Like most Plantagenet monarchs, he loved hunting and was also an aficionado of falconry and (more unusually) fishing, as well as taking great delight in tournaments. He enjoyed chess, chequers, and the likes of board games and dice in the evenings; the exchequer, which had to pay his gambling debts, presumably appreciated these pastimes rather less. The king was conventionally devout, aware of the importance of pilgrimage and the Christian nature of his role. Everything about Edward suggests a friendly, approachable man who was at ease with his common subjects, and who actively sought to build friendships and good relationships with his nobility. He adored staging masques and balls. Nor was he blind to the importance of ceremonial and performative kingship, and from the 1330s onwards he consciously encouraged a chivalric culture at his court, which was to blossom into the golden years of the 1340s and 1350s.

One of Edward's primary concerns was the restoration of law and order. There were plenty of initiatives in this respect in the 1330s, although the results were relatively modest. The king made serious efforts to address the problem in the early 1330s, although thereafter he became distracted elsewhere, before turning his attention back to the matter ahead of his departure for the Continent in 1338. The measures enacted then did largely preserve the peace during the king's absence, in contrast to the disorder which had marked Edward I's absence on campaign in his later years. It would be wrong to see Edward III as some great legal reformer, but he showed sufficient interest and did enough to ensure that he largely met expectations of the king as the preserver of domestic peace and order.

Revenue was a serious problem for Edward, becoming more acute during the 1330s. In his final years, his father's rapacious regime had built up a very large Crown surplus, but that had been rapidly squandered by Isabella and Mortimer. Heavy taxation in the early fourteenth century had made the English rather adept tax avoiders. From 1334, the government abandoned new lay tax assessments and decreed that collectors had to receive at least the amount each district contributed in 1332. The clerical taxation assessment had likewise been frozen in the 1290s, and both lay and clerical figures remained the same long beyond Edward III's reign, a maximum of around £19,000 from the clergy and £38,000 from the laity. As the years passed, £57,000 proved a woefully inadequate sum for the ambitious campaigns planned by monarchs, and it was not enough even in the 1330s. Like his predecessors, Edward made considerable use of loans from Italian banking companies, although he also employed bankers from the Low Countries and the German Hanse. English merchant communities in major cities like London and York helped secure loans, among the most notorious being Hull's William de la Pole. Control of the customs and the wool trade gradually allowed the Crown to compensate for its problems with direct taxation. Edward III needed large sums of money for his military activities, so setting his financial house in order was crucial to what followed. There were no dramatic reforms to excite anyone except fourteenth-century specialists, but by applying himself to these questions he convinced his subjects that he was a competent king, very different to the two regimes that had preceded his. It is easy to lose sight of rather mundane questions of finance and public order in the dramatic narrative of campaigns and battles, but Edward's success in conflict was built on his success in domestic management.

Ever since Edward I's death, the war against Scotland had gone badly for the English and the Scots had seized the upper hand. The Treaty of Northampton, while deeply unpopular in England, recognised this reality. Yet events conspired to favour Edward III reopening the conflict. Robert Bruce died on 7 June 1329 and was succeeded by his 5-year-old son, David II, so the realm was entrusted to a Guardian, Earl Thomas Randolph of Moray. By the time David was crowned at Scone in November 1331, his kingdom was under serious threat from the 'Disinherited'. These men had been awarded lands and offices during Edward I's occupation, before being cast out by Robert I. One of the provisions of the Treaty of Northampton was that they be restored, but this had not occurred. In August 1332, a small group of the Disinherited landed in Fife. They were led by Edward Balliol, son of the John Balliol who had reigned after being awarded the throne in 1292. Now in his late forties, Edward was the perfect figurehead for the cause.

The Scottish government was caught off guard, in part because of squabbling following Moray's death the previous month. A worrying number of Scots defected to Balliol. The new Guardian, Earl Donald of Mar, assembled an army which met Balliol's force near Perth on 11 August. The Battle of Dupplin Moor was a triumphant rout for Balliol and the Disinherited, who overcame a much larger army. As Lowland Scotland declared for Balliol, he made his way to Scone for investiture on 24 September. Balliol declared his allegiance to the English Crown and called on Edward III to assist him, while Bruce loyalists regrouped. On 16 December 1332, led by the latest Guardian, Archibald Douglas, they surprised Balliol at Annan in Dumfriesshire, just inside Scotland on the northern shore of the Solway Firth. Balliol fled, half dressed, to Carlisle. That might have been the end of the adventures of the Disinherited, but Edward III sensed an opportunity.

Ireland had moved to the top of the English government's list of priorities, with concerns about the state of the lordship, and during 1332 plans were being made for Edward to cross the Irish Sea in person. Now, however, the English king (with enthusiastic support from the parliament of September 1332) diverted his attention to Scotland. In March 1333, Edward led an army into eastern Scotland, while Balliol took the western approach. The two armies joined at Berwick and

Family Tree of Henry II and Richard I

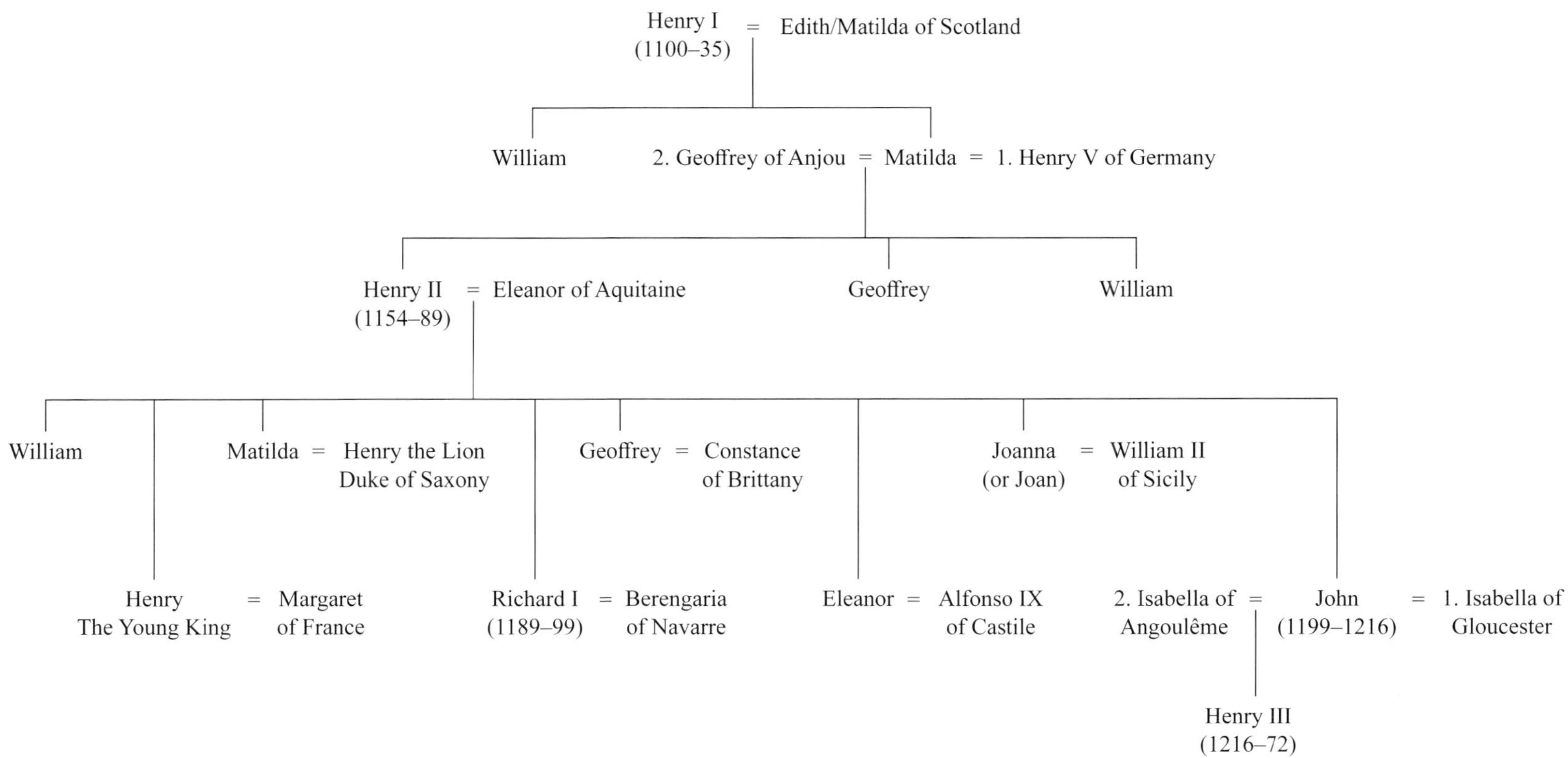

Family Tree of Edward I

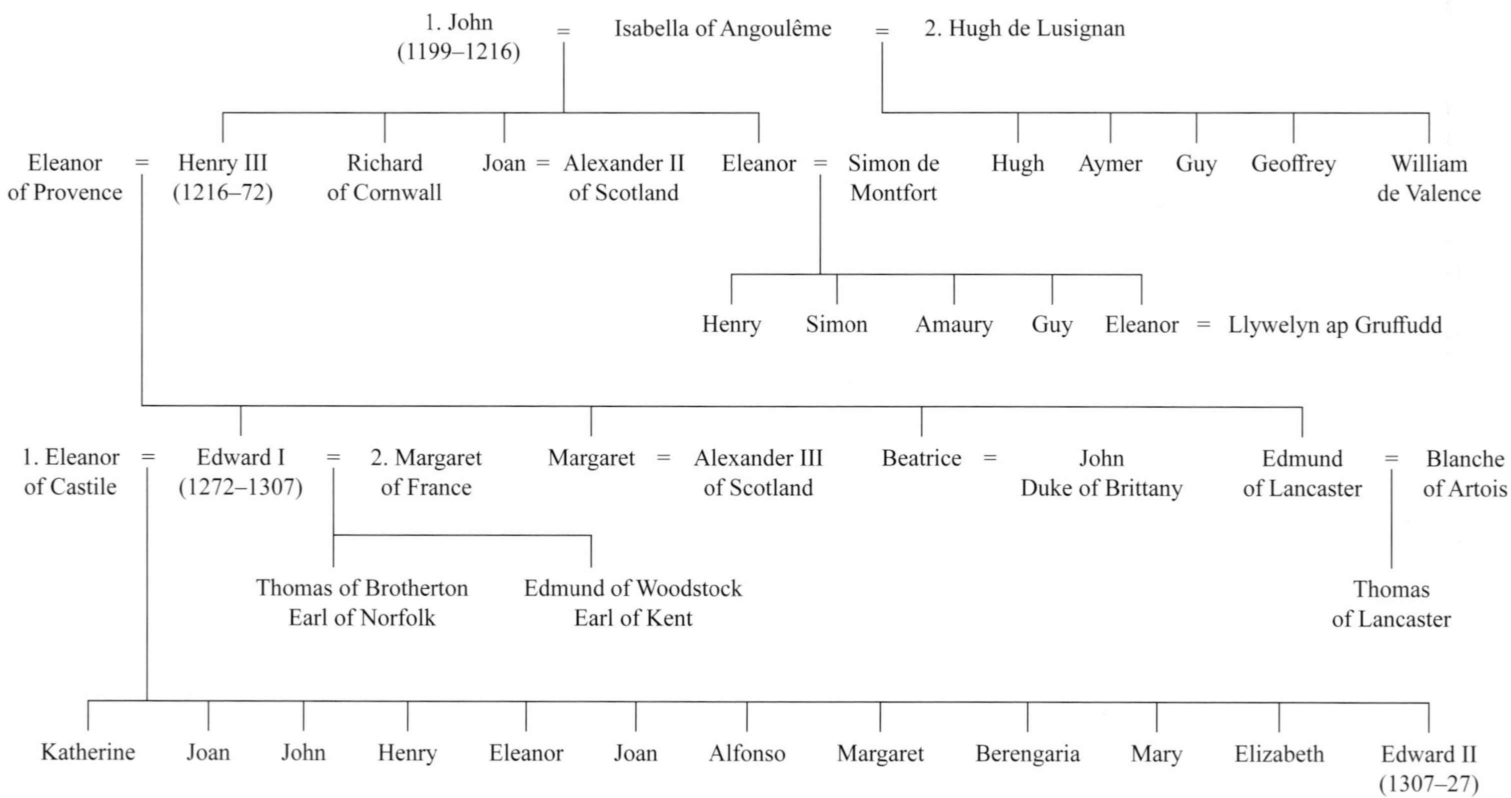

Family Tree of the Kings of Scotland

Simplified to show main lines of descent for claimants to the throne in 1290-92
Underlined names were claimants in the Great Cause

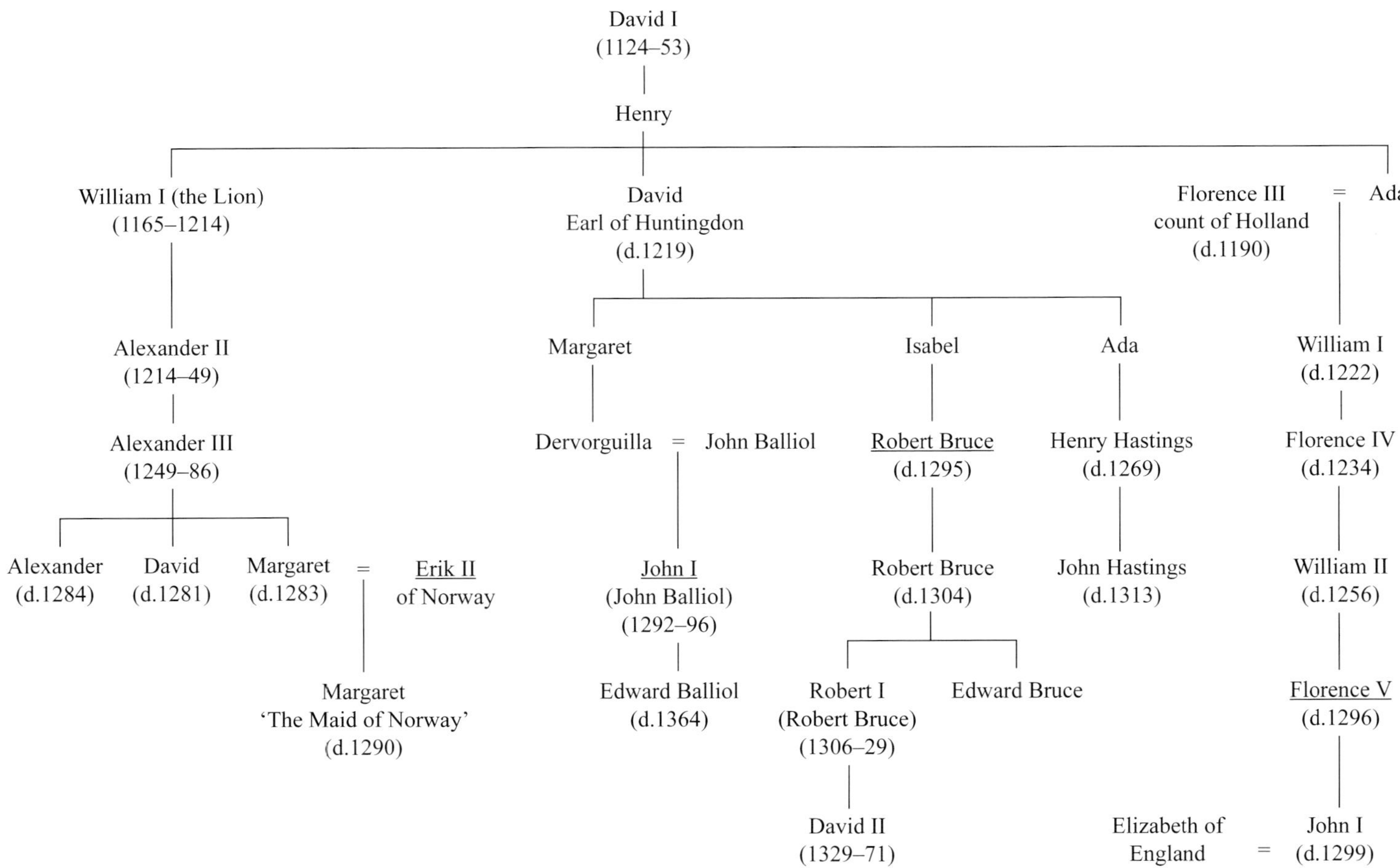

Family Tree of Edward III

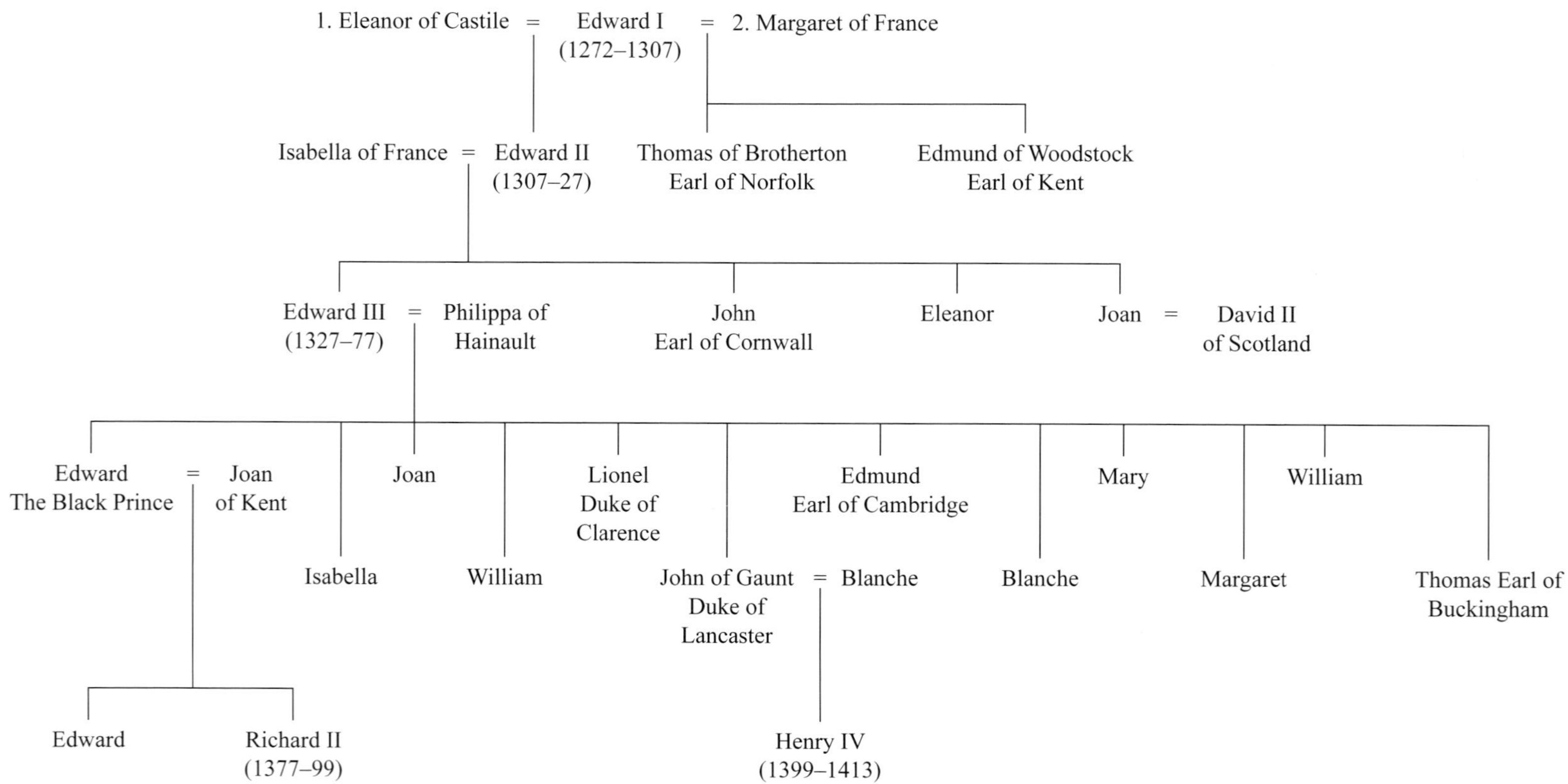

Family Tree of Henry V

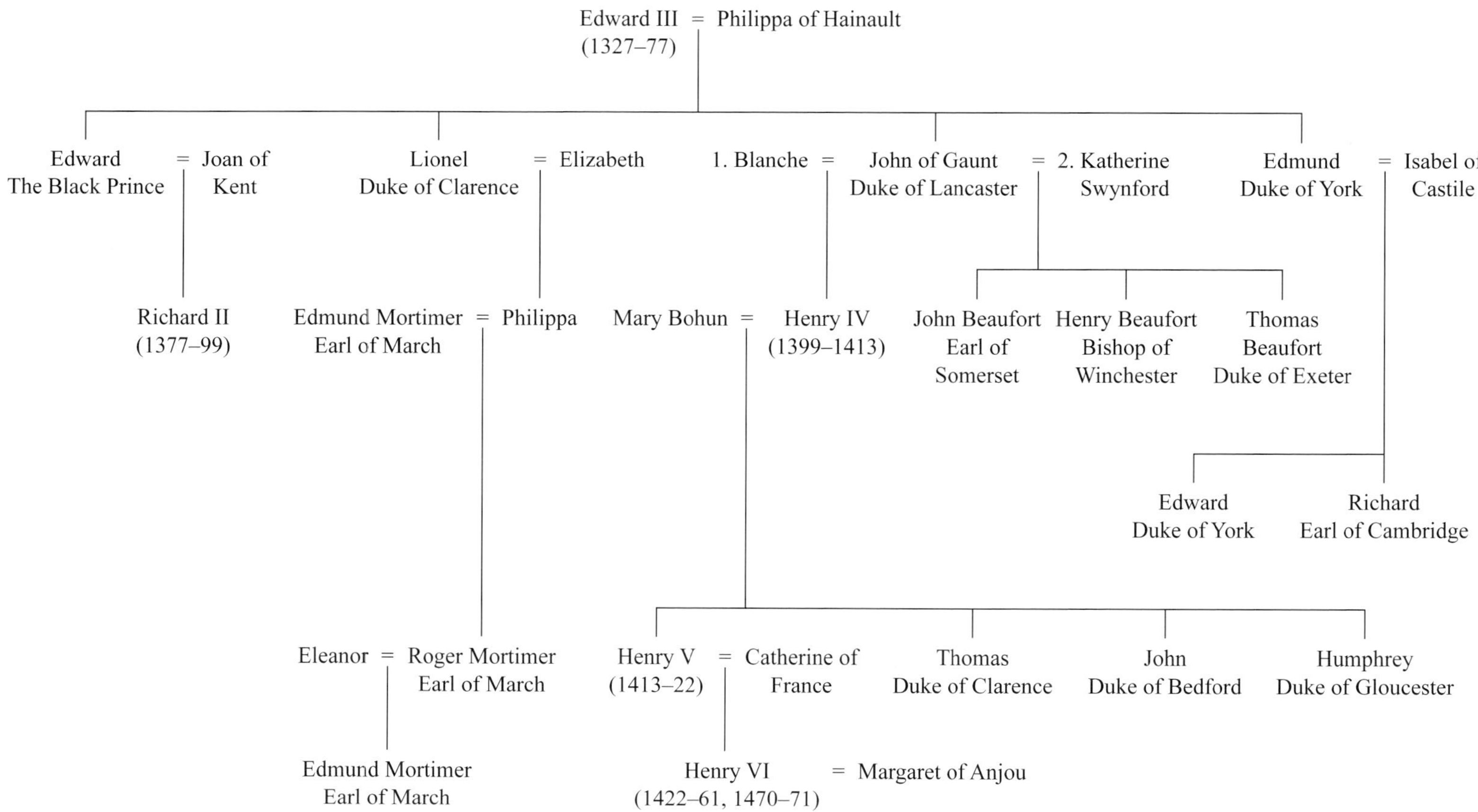

Above: Henry II and Richard I from a thirteenth-century manuscript (British Library, MS Royal 14 C VII f. 9, Wikimedia Commons).

Below: Poitiers Cathedral. It was here that Henry II married Eleanor of Aquitaine in 1152, and where the first requiem mass was held for Edward I by Pope Clement V in 1307.

Above: Portchester Castle in Hampshire, in the corner of an old Roman fort, was taken into royal hands and developed by Henry II. It was a useful embarkation point for him when travelling to his continental lands. The campaigns which saw Edward III's victory at Crécy (1346) and Henry V's at Agincourt (1415) both mustered here. On that last occasion, Porchester was where Henry confronted and arrested the protagonists of the Southampton Plot.

Right: An illustrated miniature from the 1180s of the martyrdom of Thomas Becket in 1170 (British Library, Harley MS 5102 f. 32*r*, Wikimedia Commons).

Above: Chinon Castle, on the bank of the River Vienne, was a major fortress for Henry II and Richard I in their capacity as Dukes of Anjou, and where Henry died in July 1189. Captured by Philip II of France in 1205, it became a French royal castle; here Charles VII first met Joan of Arc in 1429.

Below: The effigies of Henry II and Eleanor of Aquitaine in Fontevraud Abbey, Anjou. Henry was buried there in 1189, Eleanor in 1204.

Above: Clifford's Tower, the only remaining part of medieval York Castle. This stone structure dates from the mid-thirteenth century, but is built on the site of one of the darkest episodes in English history, the suicide and massacre of the city's Jews in 1190. In the fourteenth century, when frequent Scottish campaigns often saw the government moved to York, it acted as an administrative base, especially for the exchequer.

Right: Carlo Marochetti's statue of Richard the Lionheart, installed outside the Houses of Parliament in 1860 (courtesy of Doug Chaplain).

Two effigies of Richard I, built to mark the burial place of his heart in Rouen Cathedral (*top*) and his body in Fontevraud Abbey (*bottom*). Note the different appearance, especially the fact that only one is bearded.

Above: Las Huelgas Monastery in Burgos, Castile. Here the 15-year-old Prince Edward (later Edward I) was knighted by Alfonso X in 1254, before marrying Alfonso's half-sister. Edward and Eleanor of Castile's marriage became a famous royal love story.

Right: A painted image of a king, probably Edward I, on the wooden sedilia in Westminster Abbey (Wikimedia Commons).

Above: Beside the river of the same name, Conwy was one of Edward I's 'iron ring' of castles to maintain control and assert power after his conquest of Wales. It was at Conwy that Richard II was arrested before his deposition in 1399. Embarrassingly for the English, the castle fell into Welsh hands for a few months in 1401, during the Glyndŵr Revolt.

Below: Another of Edward I's 'iron ring' castles and deliberately echoing the walls of Constantinople, Caernarfon Castle was meant to be an impressive symbol of English power in Wales. The future Edward II was born in the building site here in 1284, but the castle was never finished.

Above: The mountains of Snowdonia form an imposing backdrop to another castle in the 'iron ring', Harlech. It was captured by Glyndŵr's forces in 1404 and held out until 1409, when it was recaptured in the English campaign headed by the future Henry V.

Below: Begun following the Welsh revolt of 1294–95, Beaumaris Castle on Anglesey was ambitious and innovative, but never came close to completion.

'Legacy', by Rubin Eynon, was commissioned by Cadw as part of the 2020 renovation and improvement of the King's Gate at Caernarfon Castle. It represents the shattered head of an imagined giant statue of Edward I, a reminder of the king's reputation among the Welsh.

Above: When his wife, Eleanor of Castile, died in 1290, Edward I was devastated. He later had Eleanor Crosses erected at each place her body rested on its journey from Lincoln to Westminster. Only three survive, in Northamptonshire at Geddington (*left*) and Hardingstone (*centre*), and at Waltham Cross in Essex (*right*).

Below: Portraits of Edward III and Duke Henry of Lancaster in the *Bruges Garter Book*, a fifteenth-century manuscript commemorating the original members of Edward's new Order of the Garter (British Library, Stowe MS 594, Wikimedia Commons).

Left: A statue of Prince Hal preparing to place his father's crown on his head, a scene from *Henry V*, overlooked by a statue of its author, William Shakespeare. These are two of the five statues in the nineteenth century Gower Memorial, near the Royal Shakespeare Theatre in Stratford-upon-Avon.

Below: Château de Vincennes, east of Paris. Henry V died here in August 1422.

besieged the castle. On 19 July, Douglas and the Scottish army approached to lift the siege of Berwick, and battle was joined. It was a crushing English victory in which Douglas and five Scottish earls died. The Battle of Halidon Hill was the first victorious battle for an English king against the Scots since Falkirk in 1298, going a long way to heal the memories of the Bannockburn catastrophe in 1314. It was Edward's first military triumph, showing him to be a general in the successful mould of his grandfather rather than the disastrous one of his father. Berwick was reclaimed. Edward Balliol was reinstalled as King of Scotland, basing his administration in Perth. In June 1334, Balliol transferred eight southern Scottish shires to the English, then travelled to Newcastle to swear homage in person to the King of England for the remnant of his Scottish realm.

The month before, David II had been put aboard ship at Dumbarton and sent into protective exile in France, where Philip VI housed him and his sorry party in Richard the Lionheart's imposing Château Gaillard in Normandy. Thanks to the Auld Alliance, Edward III's renewed interest in Scotland created further tensions in Anglo-French relations. Philip VI sent the resisting Scots money and arms, and refused to contemplate restoring captured parts of Aquitaine unless Edward III reached accommodation with David II. Philip repeatedly rejected the attempts of English embassies to reach terms. There was another revolt against Balliol in summer 1334, causing him to flee yet again. Edward responded by leading an army into Scotland in November, but the Scots had no intention of offering battle. During a terrible winter, the English spent three months ravaging the lowlands, but by February 1335 Edward was back at Newcastle. In July, he invaded Scotland again, this time with one of the largest forces he was to lead in his entire reign. The results were the same: the Scots resolutely avoided battle, the English army burned the countryside. Meanwhile, the French declared that they were going to forcibly restore David II, and by summer 1336 serious plans were underway. The strategy was for a landing between the Moray and Tay Firths, and a small advance French party even arrived in Aberdeen.

The invasion never happened. Edward's spies in Paris were keeping him well informed, and in June 1336 he swiftly made his way to the English garrisons at Stirling and Perth. Gathering a small army, he made for the Moray Firth and proceeded methodically along the coast, burning crops, rounding up and slaughtering animals, and seizing stores of food. Aberdeen was torched, only the churches spared. Deprived of ports and provisions, the invasion was impossible. Philip, however, now focussed on England for his assault. By the time Edward hurried south for a great council at Nottingham in September 1336, war fever was gripping the country and a tax was duly granted to defend the realm. Yet this French invasion also proved impractical and was abandoned. Instead, Philip turned his sights on Aquitaine and looked for an excuse to confiscate the duchy.

While the defence of the south coast was entrusted to others, Edward returned to Newcastle, and October found him at Bothwell Castle on the River Clyde. However, the remaining Balliol positions in the Highlands were embattled and Bruce guerillas roamed the Lowlands. Unable to make any impact, Edward left

Bothwell in December to spend Christmas 1336 at Hatfield in Yorkshire. The start of 1337 was a grim time for the king personally. His younger brother, John of Eltham, had died at Perth the previous September, aged just 20, and was buried in Westminster Abbey in January 1337. Queen Philippa gave birth to a second son, William of Hatfield, early in the new year, but he lived only a short time and Edward had the sombre task of arranging his interment in York Minster.[9] Amidst this personal grief, Scotland continued to be on Edward's agenda, and June found him setting out from Newcastle to relieve a siege of Stirling, although the Scots had melted away by the time he arrived and just days later he was back in Stamford in Lincolnshire for a council meeting. He would be briefly in the Borders again at the start of 1338, but his focus was now being drawn elsewhere.

For five years, with his attention on Scotland, Edward had moved all the offices of government (in effect, the capital) to York.[10] The city is considerably more central in Britain and was a much more obvious base when Scotland was the main focus of the English king. Had Scotland remained significant and France not become an issue, York and Westminster may have developed along different lines in the fourteenth century. As it was, Edward now needed to focus on Gascony and France, so shifted government back south. While Edward never abandoned his claims to Scotland, without active royal support the English there were left fighting a losing battle. Scotland had been a good place for Edward to earn a military reputation, but when it came to a choice between Scotland and Aquitaine, the king was more interested in his duchy, even if his involvement in Scotland was far from over.

In December 1336, Philip demanded that the seneschal of Gascony extradite Robert of Artois, the French king's brother-in-law and a fugitive from his justice. It was a slightly feeble demand, since as Philip knew full well, Robert was in England, where Edward as king did not answer to Philip. Parliament met at Westminster in March 1337, granting a tax to fund an army to fight the French. As part of preparations, there was also a revolution in the peerage. Edward, the king's 6-year-old son and heir, was created Duke of Cornwall, the first time a ducal title had been used in England. Six new earls were created from among Edward's companions, including the loyal William Montagu, who was made Earl of Salisbury. Along with his fellow new earls (Derby, Gloucester, Huntingdon, Northampton and Suffolk), Salisbury was to be at the forefront of Edward's military and diplomatic efforts against France in the following years. The contrast with Edward II could not be starker. There would be some muttering about the 'new men' in the troubled next few years, but Edward III consciously avoided the accusations of favouritism which had made his father so unpopular, spreading patronage widely and generously, and including a large segment of the nobility in his government and military endeavours.

In May 1337, Philip VI declared war. In July, a large army led by the constable of France marched towards Bordeaux. Although the French took several minor fortresses, they failed to take Bordeaux, which with Bayonne was the only truly defensible place in Gascony. In September, the army returned north and disbanded. Edward's strategy was to divert the French by attacking northern France. Royal diplomats brought German princes into a coalition against Philip with generous (and ultimately unaffordable) bribes. The Hundred Years' War is conventionally held to have started with the declarations and manoeuvres of 1337. A dubious scheme, hatched by the merchant William de la Pole, involved seizing the 1337 wool crop (on credit), then selling it at an inflated price in the Low Countries, thus paying the producers the market rate and financing Edward's bribes out of the surplus. This plan failed badly. The parliament of February 1338 involved some hard bargaining over finances, and the king eventually had to abandon schemes in both Scotland and Gascony. When Edward reached Antwerp in July 1338, he did so having raised a far smaller force than anticipated, and there was 'no wool, no money and no German army'.[11] He scrambled to raise funds to pay the Holy Roman Emperor, Louis IV, to supply troops, and after the king had visited the shrine of the Magi in Cologne, the two men met ostentatiously at Koblenz in September, with Edward named imperial vicar general. Yet the invasion of France was put back again, to May 1339. Edward retreated to Antwerp for the winter, where he did little except consume his resources; parliament in February 1339 was especially critical of his hosting a tournament at this time.

The French continued to harry the English coastline, the sack of Southampton in October 1338 particularly bad for morale. Portsmouth, Plymouth and the Isle of Wight were also attacked, and the Channel Islands were occupied. Throughout the early months of 1339, Edward tried desperately to raise funds. He sent frequent messages home cajoling and rebuking his ministers. The problem was that the campaign had achieved nothing, and back in England it was being viewed as a failed (and costly) vanity project. Parliament rebelled against the king's increasingly exorbitant demands. He received no grant of taxation from either 1339 parliament. In January 1340, parliament granted no money, only 30,000 sacks of wool with stringent conditions attached. There was widespread resentment that the king was trying to use parliament as a bank to cover his military costs, while failing to attend to his responsibility to provide justice. In the minds of his subjects, the king had an obligation to hear petitions in parliament in return for taxation. A king repeatedly absent from sessions could not uphold his side of the bargain, and parliament therefore refused to fund him.

Edward eventually invaded France in September 1339, but it was a frustrating campaign. The English and their allies torched villages and crops in the hope of bringing the French to fight, but Philip knew Edward's finances meant he could campaign only a short time. There was no incentive for the French king to satisfy his English counterpart's desire for a battle, and Edward ended up back in the Low Countries with nothing to show for his efforts. In late 1339, Flanders allied itself with Edward, and the rhetoric of war changed. At Ghent in January 1340, Edward had himself proclaimed King of France, a title that his successors would use in the face of all reality until it was abandoned under George III in 1802. Arguably, having already paid homage to Philip VI, Edward had forfeited his claim (although the counterargument was that Edward had been underage and not a free agent in 1328–29). It is unlikely Edward seriously intended to make his claim a reality;

it was rather a useful bargaining counter, especially at a stage where he needed Flemish support, but he could never officially admit that. It seems that the idea had first been discussed in diplomatic channels in 1337, but kept secret from most in England; the announcement of January 1340 took nearly everyone by surprise. As one modern historian notes, for 'a king who set such obvious store by securing common consent for his wars, it is to say the least odd that Edward III never seems to have allowed the English polity the opportunity formally to approve his title to the French throne'.[12]

Edward briefly returned home for funds in early 1340, although he owed so much to creditors that he had to leave his wife and son as security in Flanders. On 24 June 1340, the English fleet obliterated the French in a naval battle off the port of Sluys (today Sluis in the Netherlands). Victory in the Battle of Sluys was a triumphant moment for Edward after years of disappointment, but it did not lead to further success. His land force was small and he had no money to pay mercenaries. Heavy borrowing to meet expenses had consequences for the Earls of Derby and Warwick, who had acted as guarantors and ended up in a debtors' prison. A siege of Tournai failed to draw Philip into a battle and Edward's army dwindled rapidly through disease and desertion. On 25 September, the king agreed to the Truce of Esplechin.

More than two years in the Low Countries had seen just one victory, which was of little consequence in the overall picture. Edward's campaign in a marginal theatre of war had been to the detriment of other concerns, resulting in significant losses in Aquitaine and Scotland, which by 1341 was secure enough for Bruce loyalists to bring David II home. The king was massively in debt, and had to escape ignominiously from Ghent, where he had become a virtual prisoner of his creditors, in November 1340. Yet nothing better awaited him back across the Channel, where the English treasury was bankrupt and his English subjects mutinous. There was widespread resentment at his long absence, during which he had failed to attend to matters of justice and governance, and at the relentless financial demands and attempted manipulation of the wool trade over that period. The 'usually mighty English fiscal machine' had collapsed.[13] Blind to reality, Edward blamed his officials, above all Archbishop John Stratford of Canterbury, who had resigned the chancellorship earlier in 1340 (to his brother, Bishop Robert of Chichester) but was still the head of the regency administration.

The king set sail from Sluys, across the sea and up the Thames, where he arrived without warning at the water gate of the Tower of London around midnight on 30 November/1 December 1340. He ordered his ministers to appear before him and sacked them. It was a purge; the chancellor and treasurer (both bishops) were dismissed, the chief justice of common pleas and his four junior justices were all arrested, as were several others. Over the following weeks, Edward replaced a significant number of local officials. As a response to the fiscal emergency, this was a gross overreaction in which Edward ignored his own considerable responsibility, cost himself the supporters he would need when parliament next met, and prepared the ground for the crisis of 1341.

Archbishop Stratford remained Edward's primary target, and the king tried to attack him through his brother. However, the Bishop of Chichester claimed immunity from the king's courts as a cleric. Furiously, Edward appointed laymen as chancellor and treasurer to ensure they would be accountable to his justice should anything go wrong; it was until that point almost unheard of for these two posts not to be held by a bishop or senior clergyman. (After Edward's ire cooled, the treasurership returned to clerical hands later in 1341, and the chancellorship in 1345.) John Stratford had taken refuge in his cathedral, and the king now began a public campaign against the archbishop. This was a clash of formidable and stubborn personalities. Stratford was a powerful enemy who, in late December 1340, responded by hurling all manner of charges against the king, including comparisons with the evil rule of Edward II. In January 1341, the king summoned the archbishop before his council. Rather than following his brother in claiming benefit of clergy, Stratford based his refusal on the right of peers only to answer charges when brought before their fellow peers in parliament. Unlike his grandfather, Edward had notably avoided calling parliament to receive and address complaints about corruption and misgovernment while he was overseas, possibly afraid that members would rally to Stratford's cause.

Yet Edward needed money and could not postpone parliament any longer, so he summoned an assembly to meet at Westminster on 23 April 1341. Reconstructing the exact sequence of events is tricky, because of some major discrepancies between the official parliament roll, which sought to downplay the crisis which occurred, and various chroniclers, who sought to magnify and sometimes exaggerate it. The king's henchmen shut Archbishop Stratford out of the session and told him he could not enter until he answered an exchequer charge of non-payment of taxes. Stratford installed himself outside the Painted Chamber of the Palace of Westminster, meeting place of the Lords, on 28 April and declined to move until he was admitted. Meanwhile, royal courtiers who were not peers were inside the chamber, leading to an outraged protest from the Earl of Surrey and a request for Stratford's admission from the Earl of Arundel (in some sources, also supported by the Earls of Northampton and Salisbury, who would ordinarily be considered staunch loyalists). Edward had to yield and admit Stratford, then promptly had thirty-two charges read against him.

The king kept up the pressure for a week, but frantic compromise efforts were taking place behind the scenes. On 3 May, reconciliation was effected and an open conflict between the two men averted. Distrust remained, but Edward had totally misread the situation and allowed Stratford to win the sympathy of his peers. That the king realised he had acted arbitrarily and overreached himself is shown by the concessions made at the end of parliament, which included a statement by the king that peers (including royal ministers) would only be judged by their peers in parliament. While nineteenth- and twentieth-century historians may have overstated the nature of the constitutional crisis, it had indeed been a crisis. After the drama of Stratford, the king's relationship with his realm returned to stability. Despite the arguments over taxation, the 1341 parliament conceded the single largest tax of the thirteenth, fourteenth and fifteenth centuries. William de la Pole was impeached for the dodgy 1337 wool scheme. By the middle of 1341, money was pouring in and the royal finances had been remarkably transformed.

1341 had 'exposed some of the worst aspects of the king's character: his unreasonableness, his bullying, and his infuriating refusal to accept realities that did not suit him'. However, it also revealed much about his ability, through sheer force of personality, to turn imminent disaster into survival and recovery'.[14] As gradually became clear, Edward had learned his lesson, something his father had been manifestly incapable of doing. Over the next thirty years, he worked together with the nobility and the community of the realm with a common purpose, and these were years of domestic peace in which the king was largely successful. He listened to his subjects in parliament, providing the justice and forum for consent that had been lacking in the late 1330s. The understandable exception of Roger Mortimer aside, the king was not vindictive and worked to heal the wounds of the past. The nobility were treated as friends and were carefully involved in governance and military plans by the king. Where his father had alienated his nobility through his favouritism, and his grandfather had caused friction with his nobility through trying to dominate and impose his will, Edward III after 1340 enjoyed a harmonious, constructive relationship with his nobility which had little equal in medieval England. While he was still active and had his faculties, he faced no further serious criticism or problems from his subjects. This achievement should not be downplayed, and it was largely thanks to the king's extrovert, affable character, outgoing nature and skilful people management.

Of course, Edward could not resist the opportunity to return to action in France when it arose, not least as a way of restoring his fractured relations with the nobility. Several tournaments were held through 1341 as the king and his council made plans for a new invasion. However, the British Isles also needed Edward's attention. David II, back in Scotland, was now 17 and leading raids into northern England, necessitating a campaign during the winter of 1341–42. Edward marched to Newcastle in November, then into the Scottish Lowlands in early December. No Scots appeared to fight, so the English spent the Christmas period at Melrose and Roxburgh, enjoying jousts, before returning south in January 1342.

The situation in France was not favourable to Edward. Louis IV settled with the French and withdrew Edward's title as imperial vicar general in June 1341. Worse, in 1342, one of Philip VI's councillors was elected as Pope Clement VI. The Duke of Brittany had died without issue in April 1341, and the French ensured the selection of their candidate, Charles of Blois, by imprisoning the alternative – the deceased duke's half-brother, John de Montfort – in the Louvre. John's wife sought English aid, and Edward responded with alacrity. It took him until April 1342 before he could send the first troops, who returned with grim reports about the situation. Nevertheless, the king himself went to Brittany in October. While the English made some key gains, notably Brest, the campaign was another military failure, in which Edward and Philip VI replayed their game plans from 1339–40: Edward unsuccessfully besieged two key towns (Nantes and Vannes), Philip refused battle and waited for Edward's coffers to empty. The Truce of Malestroit was signed in January 1343.

With the king back in England from the start of March, English soldiers looted, pillaged and extorted their way across Brittany to maintain the pressure on Charles of Blois. When parliament met in April and May, the king created his eldest son Prince of Wales. Edward showed little desire to resume hostilities on the Scottish front, with a three-year truce agreed in June 1343. Indeed, after his return from Brittany he spent time relaxing, on pilgrimage and holding tournaments. Despite plans being made, there was no military activity by the king during 1343–44, and discussion about an Anglo-French truce continued. Royal finances continued to improve thanks to the willingness of parliament to grant taxes and good yields from customs duties. The defection or death of several allies in the Low Countries and Germany considerably reduced Edward's financial obligations in that sphere, and most had not proved useful militarily in any case. John de Montfort escaped to England in March 1345 and swore homage to Edward as King of France at Lambeth Palace in May. Encouraged by other French exiles at court, Edward planned an ambitious triple attack in 1345. The Earl of Derby landed at Bordeaux and undertook a campaign in Gascony. That was the only successful part of the plan. The Earl of Northampton headed for Brittany with John de Montfort, only for that campaign to end abruptly when John fell ill and died. Meanwhile the king never even made it to Normandy with his troops. Problems in Flanders forced him to divert there, but his presence changed nothing and he returned to England.

In summer 1346, Edward finally sailed for Normandy with a sizeable force. The delay had allowed him to craft a more realistic plan, and it brought together the English nobility in the service of their king. Here Edward's genial, inclusive kingship paid dividends. Where Edward I and Edward II had faced outright opposition to service overseas, Edward III had proved an adept manager of his lords since the crisis of 1341, and they responded by accompanying him willingly to France in 1346. Royal finances were in much healthier shape, thanks to parliament being prepared to grant generous taxes, the wool trade booming, and the adept financial management of the treasurer since 1344, Bishop William Edington of Winchester. In July 1346, Edward and his force made the shortest possible Channel crossing, leaving Portsmouth and landing on the undefended beaches of the Cotentin Peninsula, at Saint-Vaast-la-Hougue. Here the king knighted his eldest son, the Black Prince, who was now 16.

Edward's aim in this campaign was to draw Philip into battle, provoking him by a damaging march through his lands. The English moved rapidly and violently through the Cotentin, destroying countryside and sacking villages. Caen was then seized on 26 July, the troops indulging in a spree of rape and plunder. This caused Philip to head out with an army to meet the English, only to turn back again when he heard that the Flemish had invaded. Edward marched to Lisieux and onwards towards Paris, the French avoiding battle but breaking the bridges over the Seine to trap him on the south side of the river. Considerable damage was caused to wealthy Normandy by the army. The English king reached Poissy, less than fifteen miles from the French capital, where on 14 August a makeshift bridge over the Seine was constructed. The English progressed north to Beauvais and towards the River Somme, from where Edward intended to sail for home, his army now tired with supplies running low. Philip, with public opinion deriding his failure to act, had to abandon his non-engagement strategy.

Edward's fleet had not arrived, cutting off an immediate escape across the Channel and necessitating a move towards Flanders. Philip blocked the Somme crossings, but Edward managed to fight his way across at the ford at Blanchetaque and headed into the cover of the forest. On 26 August 1346, the French caught up with Edward near the village of Crécy, in Picardy. The French army outnumbered the English by around two to one. However, the English longbows proved superior to the French crossbows, having greater range and being much quicker to reload. This was also the first time the English are recorded to have used cannons in a pitched battle, although they had previously featured in sieges. Fighting was fierce, the Prince of Wales in the thick of it, but by the end of the day the field was strewn with the bodies of French soldiers, including the Duke of Lorraine and several counts, and the English had won one of their most famous victories of the Middle Ages.

Worse still for Philip, Edward's financial position was now such that he could afford to stay in France and capitalise on the triumph. Edward had made maximum propaganda use of his victory through envoys back home, and a brief parliament in September granted him two taxes plus a customary aid for the knighting of his eldest son. The English decided to besiege Calais, hoping to secure an entry point for future invasion and reduce the threat to the Channel. The citizens of Calais were not amenable and resisted fiercely, helped by a strongly fortified town and large garrison. Philip tried to distract Edward by persuading the Scots to invade northern England, but Edward resolved to ride out the threat and let the Scots do their worst as he entrenched himself outside Calais. Scottish troops rampaged through the countryside of the northern counties, but then the plan went badly wrong. On 17 October 1346, the Scots encountered an English army near Durham and were obliterated in the Battle of Neville's Cross. The Scottish chamberlain, chancellor, constable and marshal were all killed, while David II was captured (along with three earls and a large number of other lords and knights) and sent to the Tower of London as a prisoner. The English had scored major victories against both partners of the Auld Alliance within two months, and with the Scottish diversion having failed spectacularly, Philip now had to relieve Calais. The tables had turned. Now it was the French king who was short of money and whose men had little appetite for continuing the fight. Edward settled in, and not until nine months later was Philip able to march to the relief of Calais.

By the time he arrived at Sangatte, overlooking Calais, at the end of July 1347, the English position was overwhelmingly strong. Philip and the French tried to work out a plan, but the hesitation was too much for the exhausted defenders. Calais surrendered on 3 August and the relieving army slunk away without providing any relief. According to the chronicler Jean Froissart, Edward agreed to spare the citizens if six men presented themselves on behalf of the town. Half a dozen men (the 'six burghers') duly came in shirts, nooses round their necks, to the platform on which sat King Edward III and Queen Philippa. They threw themselves to the floor and begged for mercy, but after an exhausting siege of almost a year, Edward's patience had been exhausted and he ordered them beheaded, the symbolic price of him granting the town terms. Only the intercession of his wife made him bad-temperedly change his mind. Thanks to Auguste Rodin's famous sculpture, competed in 1889 and now outside the town hall in Calais, the episode of the burghers remains well known, either a reminder that even Edward III's affability had limits, or an example of his mastery of the theatrical.

Calais would remain in English hands until the reign of Mary I, two centuries later. His goal achieved, Edward agreed a truce with the French in September 1347 and sailed home as a victorious hero. He had the King of Scotland, the constable of France and several other high-ranking officials as his prisoners, and he celebrated his triumph ostentatiously and lavishly. Edward had always liked spectacle and splendour, and been a keen participant in tournaments throughout his personal rule. In the summer of 1348, this all came together in the foundation of the Order of the Garter.

Many European monarchs would create orders of chivalry during the fourteenth and fifteenth centuries, but the Garter is the only one to survive into modern times in more or less its original form. As fire later destroyed the earliest records, there are several mysterious questions about the order. The name and insignia is one. Garters were then male attire and it seems to have been one of the emblems of the Crécy campaign, although the fact that they later became known as female undergarments may account for the legends which subsequently arose to account for the name. The most famous, much later and certainly untrue, is that at a ball in Calais, the Countess of Salisbury's garter slipped from her leg during dancing. Edward III dealt with the sniggering courtiers by returning the garter (or in some versions, putting it on himself) with the words '*honi soit qui mal y pense*' ('shame on him who thinks evil of it'; the court language was still predominantly French). That is indeed the motto of the Order of the Garter, but it is much more likely to refer to Edward's claim to the French throne, which may also explain the order's colour being blue, the colour of the background on the French royal arms, rather than the traditional red of the English royal arms. The order's patron was St George, who from this point becomes clearly associated with England as her patron saint, and the membership was highly exclusive: the king, the Prince of Wales, and twenty-four knights personally chosen by the sovereign. Of the original twenty-six, all but two are known to have been on the Crécy campaign or served with the Earl of Derby in the parallel campaign in Aquitaine. Unlike Edward I, who had squandered his successes by not investing his nobility in the triumph afterwards, Edward III rewarded and invested his lords in his victory through including them in his new order in 1348.

In the same year, Edward founded St Stephen's college at Westminster, but it was the simultaneous foundation of a college at Windsor which was to be more famous.[15] Both were religious foundations, staffed by a dean, canons and vicars.

Construction of both chapels had been begun by Henry III: St Stephen's chapel was within the Palace of Westminster, while St Edward the Confessor's was within Windsor Castle. Edward III rededicated Windsor to the Blessed Virgin Mary and St George in addition to the Confessor, but it was not long before it became known simply as St George's, partly because it also served as the chapel for the Order of the Garter. Edward undertook significant reconstruction work at Windsor, his birthplace. While the chapel as seen today largely dates from the Yorkist and Tudor period, with subsequent alterations and restorations, Edward III is responsible for its significant association with the English/British monarchy. Here was a king undertaking his religious duties, combining military triumph with pious foundations. There were also other endowments of religious houses, he showed visible interest in major religious festivals, and he almost certainly continued touching for scrofula. Edward was England's feted king, victorious warrior and Christian sovereign.

Yet the exultant mood of summer 1348 was rapidly extinguished by the arrival of the Black Death. From the southern ports in the early summer, the plague spread rapidly and had reached London by the autumn. By 1349, all England was in its grip; as one chronicler famously and evocatively put it, 'the living were hardly able to bury the dead'.[16] The elite were not spared. Archbishop Stratford had died in August 1348, just before the Black Death arrived, but his appointed successor at Canterbury, John Offord, died of plague in May 1349 before he could be installed, and his successor, Thomas Bradwardine, managed just three months as archbishop before plague claimed him in August 1349. After the Covid pandemic of 2020, we can today better understand the terror this disease brought with it, and the reaction in the fourteenth century was in some ways strikingly similar. The medieval version of lockdowns and travel bans were imposed, towns closing their gates to outsiders, but it made no difference. Bubonic plague, spread by fleas carried by rats, caused gruesome symptoms. Because it was a new or especially virulent strain, there was no resistance in populations, resulting in an astronomical mortality rate. There is considerable debate over exactly how many died, estimates ranging from a quarter to almost two thirds of the English population, which on the most common calculations as much as halved from around five or six million to three million or less. In deaths, this was a catastrophe of infinitely greater magnitude than Covid. At the time, it was seen as a terrible judgement from God for moral failings.

Parliament did not meet for three years, the law courts were suspended and much normal business simply stopped. However, English government functioned remarkably effectively during the Black Death, in contrast to other countries such as France, and the king himself emerged with considerable credit: 'It was in his government's decisive and creating responses to the onset and aftermath of the Black Death that Edward III revealed the expansiveness and vision of his regime, and his own equally remarkably capacity for political leadership'.[17] In complete contrast to the late 1330s, the king instinctively trusted his ministers, who guided the country through the crisis. Especially significant were the chancellor, John Thoresby (1349–56) and the treasurer, William Edington (1344–56, then chancellor

1356–63), both bishops and men of administrative ability. Certain policies were to have long-lasting social and political consequences. With such high mortality, there was a major labour shortage, which had an impact on what workers could demand in wages. The response from the government was the 1349 Ordinance of Labourers, of which the most significant provisions fixed wages at pre-plague levels, ordered everyone under 60 to work, and imposed price controls on food. When parliament met again in 1351, it attempted to reinforce these provisions with the Statute of Labourers. Exactly how successful these measures were is debated, but these attempts to protect the landed elite at the expense of workers was one of the long-term causes of resentment behind the Peasants' Revolt in 1381. A massive reduction in population had fundamentally changed the labour market.[18]

As with Covid, plague did not simply disappear, but life returned to normal. There would be a recurrence of plague in the early 1360s and further outbreaks for centuries afterwards. None, however, had the devastating impact of the initial Black Death, and once the first couple of years of panic and high mortality had passed, people and government gradually resumed their pre-plague lives, albeit in a dramatically altered country. While warfare can easily dominate the narrative of the 1350s, considerable attention was given to domestic affairs during the decade. Between 1344 and 1354, the Earls of Gloucester, Huntingdon, Lancaster, Salisbury and Surrey all died, and Edward had to restock the peerage. His courtier, Ralph Stafford, was made Earl of Stafford, Henry of Grosmont was created Duke of Lancaster, and Roger Mortimer (grandson of the man the king had toppled in 1330) was restored as Earl of March.

This last was an act of conciliation which showed how different were the 1350s from the factionalism of the 1320s, when Edward had come to the throne. John Maltravers – who had been sentenced to death for his role in the Earl of Kent's death in 1330, but had escaped and been living in exile ever since – was pardoned, and once back in England was summoned to parliament as a peer in 1352. In that assembly, Maltravers petitioned for a confirmation of his pardon. Perhaps facing uncomfortable memories of the 1320s, when treason was a vaguely defined charge used as a tool of vengeance, or possibly aware of the outrage John II had caused in France by the treatment of some of his nobles, in the same parliament Edward III agreed to the Statute of Treasons. Treason was a sensitive issue for the nobility, as it carried the death penalty as well as risking confiscation of estates and the disinheriting of descendants. The 1352 statute clearly and narrowly defined the offences which counted as treason. In combination with the Ordinance and Statute of Labourers, this demonstrated Edward's support for the landed nobility. Moreover, it showed a king willing to apply the rule of law and place restraints on arbitrary royal action, a sign of the trust between king and nobility. No one in the 1350s was worried about Edward's commitment to justice and the rule of law, but there were concerns about a less scrupulous future king; the final years of his successor would show these to be fully justified. (Edward's relationships with some of his bishops was considerably more fractious, the feud with Thomas Lisle of Ely the most egregious case.[19]) The king continued to assert Crown rights, but he had found a way of working with his nobility which was subtler and more inclusive than the divisive regimes of his predecessors: the 'real secret of Edward III's success with the nobility in the 1350s' was 'the king's unusual ability to persuade even those less favoured by his regime that they remained valued members of it'.[20]

Edward also made efforts to win over the lower orders. He enforced laws on purveyance and introduced new parliamentary restrictions on feudal aids and military service. He played on strong anti-papal sentiment among the Commons; between 1309 and 1376, the papal Curia was based at Avignon in the south of France and saw a succession of French pontiffs under the influence of the French Crown, which made the English deeply suspicious. Edward allowed the passage of two anti-papal statutes: Provisors (1351) and Praemunire (1353). The first essentially banned papal provisions (the Pope appointing his choices to clerical benefices in England), the second prohibited appeals to the papal Curia. Despite the French war, the English government and the papacy were not on bad terms at this stage, which strongly suggests this was a populist move by the king, with the added benefit of asserting his authority over the Church in England. On the other hand, Edward was quite willing to face down opposition over some of his policies, such as sending the court of king's bench on tour to deal with legal delays, enforce legislation and tackle corruption. Justice was a major concern of Edward's in these years, and in marked contrast to the 1330s, he made sure to receive plenty of petitions from his subjects. Government finance was reformed and the wool trade properly regulated. Much of the minutiae was, of course, the work of Edward's ministers, but like his ancestor Henry II, Edward appointed and trusted able officials, and created a culture which resulted in a competent, efficient government.

Naturally, the king never lost sight of his overseas ambitions. Although there were skirmishes and all manner of political developments, including a plot to betray Calais which the king himself foiled in January 1350 (a secret operation reminiscent of his Nottingham coup twenty years earlier), the French war was largely suspended through the plague years. It meant Edward could not capitalise more fully on Crécy, although it is debatable how much he would have been able to do so even had the Black Death not intervened. He had won a notable battle and captured Calais (which cost a huge amount to maintain, leading to vociferous complaints in the 1350s), but beyond large expanses of blackened French countryside and a handful of important prisoners, he had little tangible to show from his French campaign.

The Scots seemed to have little interest in having their king back. A significant swathe of territory had been recaptured by the English, but the Scots refused to pay a ransom for David II. Edward had first met David in person after his return from Calais in 1347, and the two kings became friends, albeit one a prisoner of the other. In France, Philip VI died in 1350 and was succeeded by John II. John was a very different man to his father. Faced with the opposition of both Edward and Charles II (the Bad), King of Navarre and Count of Évreux, he was persuaded to make concessions. Charles was bought off in February 1354, while in April, the Treaty of Guînes agreed to give Edward Aquitaine within its 1216 borders, plus Anjou, Maine, Touraine and other concessions. This was far too much for the French council, which refused to ratify the draft treaty. A splendid diplomatic peace conference, held under papal auspices at Avignon in 1354–55, achieved nothing. The English began to intrigue with Charles the Bad, who was to prove as unreliable as previous expensive allies whom Edward had trusted too much.

With Charles' pledged support and a healthy financial situation, the king resolved on a new campaign in 1355. The precise plan and aims are unclear, but Charles predictably betrayed the English. Edward threw himself into the fray, crossing to Calais and launching a *chevauchée* (a lightning campaign to damage and plunder enemy territory) in Picardy in early November. This was sufficient to dissuade John from sending his troops to fight the Black Prince, who had been dispatched to Gascony in September, but a Scottish invasion forced Edward to return swiftly to England. With Berwick-upon-Tweed captured, the king made full speed to spend Christmas 1355 at Newcastle. In January 1356, Berwick was recaptured by the English, and in revenge Edward's force laid waste to southern Scotland in a brutal revenge campaign. At Roxburgh on 20 January, Edward Bruce was persuaded to renounce his title as King of Scots in return for having his debts paid and a generous annuity, which cleared the way for negotiations with the Scottish regency government of Robert Stewart. Edward returned south to positive news from France. Between September and December 1355, the Black Prince had led a massive *chevauchée* from the Atlantic to the Mediterranean, Bordeaux to Narbonne, and back, wasting the countryside, destroying walled towns and accumulating vast amounts of plunder.

Edward saw the opportunity to capitalise on this success. As preparations advanced, the French were involved in internecine disputes. Faced with rumours of a plot involving Charles the Bad, in April 1356 John II marched armed into a banquet hosted in Rouen by his heir, the dauphin, and arrested the Navarrese king. (The dauphin, another Charles, was the first French heir to bear this title, derived from the dolphin on the coat of arms of the hereditary ruler of the Dauphiné of Viennois, an inheritance sold to Philip VI in 1349 on condition that the heir to the throne use the title 'dauphin'.) The French king laid siege to fortresses held by Charles' allies, while Charles' brother, Philip, immediately joined himself to the English cause. With this civil war in France proving opportune, the Duke of Lancaster was sent to Normandy in June. After initial successes, the idea was that he would join the Black Prince in the Loire Valley, where they could combine against John.

The Black Prince began marching north in August and reached Tours, but the French had all the Loire crossings under their control, so the two English armies were unable to unite. Lancaster returned to Normandy, while in September King John set out to chase the Black Prince, who (faced with an army twice the size of his own) turned back towards Bordeaux. The French managed to overtake the English and cut off their route south, leaving the prince with little option but to fight. Despite the numerical inferiority, the Battle of Poitiers on 19 September 1356 was another English triumph. John and one of his sons were captured, along with a large number of his captains and men-at-arms. News reached England in early October, but the Black Prince did not return from Bordeaux with his prisoners and spoils until the spring of 1357, entering London in triumph on 24 May. John was placed under comfortable house arrest at the Duke of Lancaster's Savoy Palace, on the Strand. Edward III now had the Kings of both France and Scotland as his prisoners, and in a banquet in the Palace of Westminster, he symbolically sat with one captive king on each side. God really did seem to be smiling on the English; one chronicler recorded a popular quip of the time:

> Now is the pope a Frenchman born, and Christ an Englishman,
> And the world shall see what the pope can do, more than his
> Saviour can.[21]

The French seemed no more interested in having their king back than the Scots. A council established to rule in the king's absence was dominated by his enemies. Oblivious to the chaos across the Channel, in the autumn of 1357 Edward began negotiating terms with John and his imprisoned officials. Recognising the agreement with John would be trickier and more significant, the English finally agreed a ransom of 100,000 marks (£66,667) for David II in the Treaty of Berwick (October 1357), which required no territorial concessions but reserved Edward's claim to overlordship of Scotland. Attention turned back to France and the draft of the first Treaty of London was ready by early 1358. Under its terms, the French would pay an enormous ransom (four million *écus*, £666,667) and give Edward an expanded duchy of Aquitaine.

Meanwhile, France was on the verge of descending into anarchy. The Parisian mob stormed the royal palace in March 1358 and brutally murdered the dauphin's ministers. He had to flee and leave the city to a bloodthirsty regime under Charles the Bad, who had escaped from prison. That summer, northern France was gripped by the *Jacquerie*, a violent peasants' revolt. Not until the autumn did the dauphin regain control of Paris, but he was unable and unwilling to enforce the Treaty of London on his troubled realm. An irate Edward tore up the treaty in November 1358 and announced a new invasion of France for the following year. Afraid that Edward would join forces with Charles the Bad, John and his fellow prisoners agreed to even more humiliating terms in the second Treaty of London in March 1359. The provisions kept the ransom the same, but essentially gave Edward III a revived version of Henry II's Angevin 'empire'. The French brusquely refused to ratify the treaty. Whether such outrageous terms were a bargaining chip or an excuse for war on Edward's part is unclear, but they exposed the massive chasm that had opened between the French king and the dauphin. John was dispatched to the remote Somerton Castle in Lincolnshire as the English prepared for another campaign.

At the end of October 1359, the English crossed from Sandwich to Calais and set off on their invasion in three parts, led by the king, the Black Prince and the Duke of Lancaster. Edward headed for Reims, where the cathedral was the traditional coronation place of French kings. As a terrible, endlessly wet winter set in, the English army experienced hardship on the march to Champagne, arriving in Reims in early December. The city was heavily garrisoned and fully stocked with provisions, and Edward's siege lasted only five weeks before he abandoned it in January 1360. The campaign degenerated into an aimless exercise in destruction and pillage, which took Edward south around Troyes and as far as Guillon, then by April had the English burning the suburbs of Paris. Having failed to tempt the French to fight, they headed towards Chartres, where a tremendous thunderstorm meant the abandoning of equipment and supplies in the mud. As starvation and disease took hold, Lancaster informed the king that enough was enough. He had no hope of making good his claim to the French throne and risked becoming entangled in an endless conflict.

Diplomats negotiated at Brétigny, a hamlet near Chartres. As Edward had abandoned the ludicrously unrealistic claims of the second (1359) Treaty of London, terms were reached in a matter of days. The Treaty of Brétigny was agreed on 8 May 1360, essentially reinstating the provisions of the first (1358) Treaty of London. Edward would renounce his claim to the French throne, in return for an expanded Aquitaine, Calais and some northern territory, and a ransom of three million *écus* (£500,000) to be paid over six years. John II was to be set free while the instalments were paid, in return for twenty-five hostages, including his three younger sons. For Edward, the Treaty of Brétigny was a great success, given the weakness of his military position. He took ship for England from Honfleur on 19 May. John went to Calais with Edward in October, where at a formal ceremony the first ransom payment was made and the French king released. However, mistrusting the French, Edward refused to renounce his claim to their throne until after the territorial concessions had been made, so the French insisted on retaining nominal sovereignty in the ceded areas until the renunciation had been made. These issues were removed from the treaty and put in a separate document, providing that both would happen together before November 1361. In the long term, this amendment was to prove a fatal mistake.

Edward was at the height of his fame and renown. His court was the recognised centre of European chivalry, the cults of St George and King Arthur carefully promoted in an encouragement of Englishness. Envoys flocked to him from across Europe and beyond. (Despite the development of Middle English literature, not least *Sir Gawain and the Green Knight* and the works of Geoffrey Chaucer, in this period the court remained primarily French-speaking, government documents continued to be written in Latin or French, and Edward was not a patron of English writers.) Notable rebuilding and renovation works were undertaken at Windsor, Leeds Castle (Kent) and Sheen. The harmony Edward enjoyed with his nobility and his subjects was a source of envy to less fortunate rulers. Brétigny was the culmination of thirty years of determined war and diplomatic endeavour which had given the king an exalted reputation. Edward turned 50 in November 1362. He had been on the throne thirty-five years, as long as his two most illustrious post-Conquest predecessors, Henry II and Edward I. Had he died at this point, he would almost certainly have been mourned as one of the greatest of English kings, bequeathing a magnificent legacy to the ages. Yet as it transpired, he still had another fifteen years of life in him. These were to be the sad years, a period of gradual decay into feeble old age as his achievements collapsed around him and left him with a tarnished, much more complicated reputation. Part of the problem was that the glamorous edifice was built on illusory foundations. Ransom payments and war booty were allowing the king to live far beyond his normal means.

Domestically, the 1360s were years of harmony and success. The Black Death returned in 1361 and 1368, while a terrible hurricane (St Maurus' Wind) caused widespread damage in 1362, but the government responded well. To address concerns about law and order, in 1368 the government switched permanently to local commissions of the peace, where in each county a group of justices of the peace comprised lords, gentry and local lawyers, with a quorum made up of experts from the national courts who could assist with trying serious crimes. While not entirely new, JPs became an integral part of the English judicial system at this point thanks to Edward's policies.

The king and queen's marriage was notably happy. After the ambitious 'she-wolf' Isabella, Philippa was a quiet and gentle presence; the usually xenophobic English chroniclers could find little bad to say about her. By 1362, Edward and Philippa had five living sons (two more had died in infancy), although four of their five daughters had died. The king had a genuinely warm relationship with his family and remained on good terms with his heir and all his children, in part because he trusted his sons and involved them in his rule. (The king was not impressed with the Black Prince's clandestine marriage to the prince's widowed cousin, Joan of Kent, in 1361, but he accepted it and moved on.) Edward raised Aquitaine to the status of a principality and awarded it to the Black Prince, who had also been Duke of Cornwall since 1337. His second son, Lionel, was created Duke of Clarence, and the third, John of Gaunt, was elevated to Duke of Lancaster (the title free as the king's stalwart commander Henry of Grosmont had died without issue in 1361). The fourth son, Edmund of Langley, became Earl of Cambridge (and would become Duke of York in the following reign). The oldest two also had important roles. The Black Prince set sail to run Aquitaine, where he would spend the rest of the decade. Clarence had been governing Ireland since the previous year, sent there in response to a worrying degree of lawlessness and rebellion, although his efforts at ruling the Irish were not especially successful and he returned to England in 1366.

Apart from Clarence, who died in 1368, these newly elevated sons would become necessary as military commanders as the Brétigny settlement unravelled through the 1360s. It was a decade of tangled diplomacy on multiple fronts. The deadline for the renunciation of Edward's claim to the French throne and the French claim to the ceded territories passed, in part because of Edward's deep suspicion of the French. His construction of significant fortresses at Queenborough on the Isle of Sheppey and Hadleigh in Essex testify to this suspicion. John II's ransom rapidly fell into arrears, the French government being practically bankrupt. One of John's imprisoned sons, Louis of Anjou, escaped from Calais, so in January 1364 the honourable French king came to London in his stead. However, negotiations were ended by John's death in London on 8 April. He was succeeded by the dauphin as Charles V (the Wise). The new king was far less honourable but far more politically adept than his father. Over the next few years, he rebuilt French financial security and returned France to a significant power. While negotiating with England, his intention was always to undo Brétigny and destroy the English in France.

The Black Prince, so fine a soldier and military commander, was proving singularly inept as a politician and governor. He was interfering tactlessly and recklessly in all manner of quarrels beyond Aquitaine. The duchy was expensive to administer and garrison as it was, but the Black Prince wanted to be a noted figure on the European stage, which meant a large household and retinue, requiring even heavier taxation. In 1366–67, the prince interfered in a civil war in Castile, which cost a huge amount and destroyed his health. The tax he introduced to pay the debts of this campaign was wildly unpopular, and some key lords appealed to the *parlement* of Paris, France's highest court. Here, the agreement which had removed the renunciation question from the Treaty of Brétigny was revealed to have been a colossal mistake, even though it could not have been anticipated at the time. As sovereignty over Aquitaine had not been formally renounced, Charles V accepted the appeal and treated the Black Prince as a French vassal, and summoned him to appear before the *parlement*. A furious prince refused, and in May 1369 was declared a contumacious vassal, leading to the confiscation of Aquitaine. In retaliation, Edward III resumed calling himself King of France.

Edward's fortunes in France, however, were no longer militarily in his own hands. After his return from Calais at the end of 1360, he never returned to the Continent; several plans were aborted and the one expedition which actually progressed beyond planning, in autumn 1372, was thwarted by the weather. The last sixteen years of his reign were spent almost exclusively in the South East of England, Marlborough and Corfe about as far as he strayed out of this zone. Edward had once been as itinerant as his grandfather, Edward I, but as the years passed he preferred the gentler, more geographically limited horizons of his great grandfather, Henry III. Edward III was an ageing man, medicines and doctors accounting for ever greater sums in his accounts, who now enjoyed the comforts of manors such as Eltham, Havering and Sheen, with occasional visits to Westminster and Windsor. Queen Philippa died at Windsor on 15 August 1369. It was a blow which led Edward to become increasingly secluded, a hidden, private man rather than the extrovert, friendly public figure of the 1340s and 1350s. He had outlived his own generation: by 1370 not only was his wife dead, so too were all six of the companions he had created earls in 1337.

As Edward withdrew and others died, so government entered into the hands of a new generation who were less able and far more venal than their predecessors. Lonely, the king allowed his mistress to emerge into the public eye. His only known affair, with Alice Perrers, had begun in the early 1360s and produced three illegitimate children. (If there were other mistresses, they are not reliably recorded, and there are certainly no rumours of any previous bastards.) After Philippa died, the avaricious Alice would play a lead role at court as she stripped money from the royal coffers, making her unpopular.[22] She reflected badly on the king, and his own popularity began to suffer as a result. Edward's final years were sad, a slow decline poisoned by the corruption and greed of his mistress and his ministers.

It was left to his surviving adult sons to lead the fight against the French. Charles V's resurgent France was a very different foe to the divided realm of John II. Two of Charles' brothers, the Dukes of Anjou and Berry, made significant inroads into Aquitaine. The illness the Black Prince had picked up in Castile was debilitating and he would never recover. In August 1370, he began his final campaign, for which he had to be carried in a litter. His eldest son, 5-year-old Edward of Angoulême, died in September. At the start of 1371, a broken Black Prince returned to an England that was very different to the country he had left eight years earlier. The windfalls from the ransoms and war plunder had long since been spent, and the king was short of money. Parliament no longer granted taxes with the willingness it once had. With Edward's own generation dead, only his sons had any real investment in continuing the war against a resurgent France; as the French were not threatening England, few Englishmen saw the war as their concern. The Scottish border was peaceful; when the first Stewart king, Robert II, succeeded his uncle David II in February 1371, he continued to make the payments for David's ransom. There was some raiding in the borderlands by Scots in the mid-1370s, but it never amounted to a serious threat to English security. Feeling secure in England, Englishmen saw no need to pay for wars, especially against a backdrop of new plague outbreaks and a fall in wool prices.

Edward made one last effort against France in 1372, as the French placed ever greater pressure on the English in Aquitaine. Yet strategic thinking was still stuck in the 1350s and the hope was that a similar double-pronged assault would work, with the Earl of Pembroke going to Gascony and Edward to Brittany. The failure was abject. Pembroke (and his chests of silver) was captured off La Rochelle. Edward did not take ship until late August, months after originally planned. Adverse winds kept his fleet from making the crossing for weeks, and the king made it only as far as Winchelsea. Meanwhile, the French had overrun Poitou and the campaign was abandoned with Edward sulking in his cabin on the *Grace Dieu*.

In October, the Black Prince resigned Aquitaine back to his father. King and heir now stood back almost completely from government, which passed into the hands of John of Gaunt and others, who lacked the stature of the two Edwards. Gaunt's intervention in Aquitaine was disastrous. He had married Constance of Castile, daughter of King Peter the Cruel, who had been killed in the Castilian civil war in 1369. John claimed the throne of Castile in his wife's name, and sought to use the English cause in Aquitaine to make good that claim in 1373. He returned home, hugely unpopular, in 1374, and England largely abandoned help for Aquitaine. By the time the Truce of Bruges was agreed in June 1375, England's position in France had largely reverted to the Gascony Edward had inherited, plus Calais.

This was just one reason that the government and court had become enormously unpopular by the mid-1370s. Parliament was not happy at the financial demands being made and required significant concessions in return for taxation. One of these, in March 1371, was that the king would only appoint laymen to the chief positions of state, which meant Edward had to replace his chancellor, treasurer and keeper of the privy seal, all three of whom were bishops. That August, the king was taken ill in Wiltshire. Despite his attempt to lead a campaign to France the following year, Edward's almost complete withdrawal from government began with this illness. With the Black Prince also ailing, John of Gaunt became leader of the government by default. That government narrowed, involving far fewer of the nobility than it had in Edward's active years, and objections to the favouritism towards an ambitious few began to be heard.

As Edward's modern biographer observes, 'the medieval constitution, which adapted relatively easily to the problem of minority, had no real solution to that ultimate anomaly: the adult king who, through infirmity of body or mind, could not exercise the personal will from which all grace and good governance was believed to flow'.[23] With the king now a little-seen ceremonial figurehead, his ministers and courtiers were busy enriching themselves. Particularly vociferous complaints were raised about Alice Perrers, William Latimer (steward and then chamberlain of the king's household) and John Neville (Latimer's successor as steward), who were viewed as the most outrageously corrupt of the inner circle. However, there were plenty of others around them who were helping themselves to patronage. Further outbreaks of Black Death in 1368 and 1375 stalled demographic recovery and kept labour in short supply, while there were widespread concerns at the management of the economy. Resentment at the incompetence, naked avarice and corruption came to a head in 1376. The lengthy parliament which met between April and July was dubbed the Good Parliament by contemporaries for the way it tackled the state of government. Taxation was requested, but the Commons were deeply reluctant. A Herefordshire MP, Peter de la Mare, was elected their spokesman, essentially the first Speaker of the House of Commons. He and others began negotiations with John of Gaunt and the Lords. The Commons pushed hard for reform. William Latimer was impeached (the first time parliament is recorded as taking this step) and the king's ministers replaced with ones chosen by parliament. Alice Perrers was exiled. A long and ambitious list of common petitions was submitted in the cause of reform.

Edward was now 63, certainly venerable by the standards of the time, but at the same age his grandfather had still been marching angrily into war against the Scots. Edward's health had not held up nearly so well and he was an old, sick man. The Black Prince died at Kennington on 8 June, leaving his 9-year-old son, Richard of Bordeaux, as heir to a throne he looked likely to inherit very soon. John of Gaunt, who was arguably responsible for a large part of the problem anyway, was left to face the parliamentary onslaught alone. He would spend the following months working to reverse its actions. Peter de La Mare was arrested and imprisoned without charge in Nottingham Castle in November 1376. Gaunt attacked the privileges of the Londoners (who would take their revenge on his Savoy Palace during the Peasants' Revolt in 1381). Bishop William Wykeham of Winchester was punished for supporting the Commons in the Good Parliament, which infuriated the bishops, as did Gaunt having the radical and unorthodox John Wycliff preach around London that winter. At the cost of considerable unpopularity, Gaunt achieved his aim of undermining the reformers at the next parliament between January and March 1377: the Bad Parliament undid the Good Parliament.

Edward was now a spectator to his own reign. From August 1376 until February 1377 he was resident at Havering in Essex, after which he was taken by barge to Sheen. Just as a visibly frail Elizabeth II made strenuous efforts to appear at some of her Platinum Jubilee celebrations in June 2022, three months before her death, so Edward III made one last, painful effort to attend St George's Day and the Garter celebrations of his Golden Jubilee year at Windsor, which included knighting his grandson and heir, Richard. It was his last public performance. He returned to Sheen, where he died from a stroke on 21 June 1377. One chronicler relates that he died attended by a single priest, everyone else having fled in his dying hours, Alice Perrers heartlessly stripping the rings from the king's fingers as she did so. As the chronicler concerned, Thomas Walsingham, wrote in this passage of Perrers as an 'unspeakable whore' and 'shameless hussy', the story might say more about the monk's desire to demonise her than about actual events.[24] Regardless, it is hard to deny the sadness of Edward's end, even if Jean Froissart's more plausible account suggests plenty of family mourners were at the administration of the last rites and death.

From Sheen, a torchlit procession bore Edward's body to Wandsworth, then Southwark and over London Bridge to St Paul's Cathedral, thence to Westminster Abbey where his funeral took place on 5 July. A wooden mannequin was part of the obsequies, with a plaster face created from a death mask; this still survives in the abbey collections, the face bearing clear signs of the stroke(s) which killed him. He was buried next to his wife, in Edward the Confessor's Chapel. A tomb chest of Purbeck marble was erected over his remains, topped by a gilded effigy. His successor, Richard II, had the laudatory inscription cited at the start of this chapter placed around the tomb. Escaping the ghoulish thirst of eighteenth-century antiquarians for exhuming kings, Edward has lain in peace there, beside Philippa, ever since. His effigy has had more adventure, dispatched to the crypt of the Chapter House for protection during the First World War, then to the safety of the countryside during the Second World War. It suffered no harm, and rests tranquilly once more above the 'glory of the English'.

Edward through the Centuries

His government may have been unpopular by 1377, but the death of the only king most Englishmen had ever known brought genuine grief. Hainault-born Jean Froissart claimed that Edward 'departed this life, to the deep distress of the whole realm of England, for he had been a good king for them'.[25] Laudatory eulogies poured forth from the chroniclers. For the Augustinian Canon of Leicester, Henry Knighton, Edward was 'the flower of this world's knighthood, for whom to do battle was to reign', yet 'whilst he was terrible among his enemies', he 'was most mild and gracious to his subjects, excelling almost all his predecessors in goodness and mercy'.[26] At St Albans, Thomas Walsingham couldn't help a last dig at Alice Perrers, claiming that the king's 'excessive, wanton sexual couplings' were what 'ended his life the sooner'. Nevertheless, 'among all the world's kings and princes he had been a glorious king, benevolent, merciful and magnificent', a man who was 'big-hearted', 'friendly, unassuming and gentle to all men', 'a man of God', 'softly spoken and courteous', 'not puffed up or proud, but always courteous'. There was 'no kingdom under heaven which had brought forth such a noble, eminent and fortunate king', even if 'as he moved towards old age and went down the sky to his sunset, the happy events were gradually driven out by his sins and grew fewer'.[27]

For the English, Edward III's death brought uncertainty and fear: 'For fifty years, Edward had provided a focus of unity and a sense of permanence in a fast-changing world'.[28] As the minority governments of Richard II's early years unravelled and found themselves confronting the Peasants' Revolt, an atmosphere captured in the works of Geoffrey Chaucer and William Langland, so Edward's reign almost immediately came to seem like a golden age. The English had endured military defeats during Edward's reign, but the king had never been defeated in any campaign he had led personally, which allowed the creation of the myth of a king who in 'all his battles, by land and sea [...] always won the day and triumphed gloriously'.[29] This established Edward's reputation as a great and successful warrior. When Henry V resurrected the French war, his propaganda carefully traced a line of victories from Sluys to Crécy to Poitiers to Agincourt. Even after final English defeat in the Hundred Years' War, England retained a tangible sign of Edward's success in the form of Calais, while the abortive attempts of Edward IV and Henry VIII to reopen the Anglo-French conflict relied heavily on Edward III's tactics. He was the military king *par excellence.*

Yet nostalgia also developed from the fifteenth century for the non-military aspects of Edward's reign. The 1429 parliament recalled 'the time of King Edward and King Richard, in whose reigns much fortune and privilege was common in the households of this realm'.[30] Popular late fourteenth- and fifteenth-century stories, including some of the Robin Hood tales, celebrated Edward's reputation for justice and mercy. An envious Henry VIII, so desperate for sons of his own, celebrated Edward's blessings in this regard by including the arms of six of Edward's sons on the new gatehouse of Trinity College, Cambridge. As the years passed, people forgot the years of decay and created the legend of an ideal king, the victor of war and peace.

For the Tudors, Edward could be adopted as an honorary forbearer of the Church of England. Although recognised as a pious and conventional (Roman Catholic) sovereign in his own lifetime, whose only real clash with the Church was the dispute with Archbishop Stratford in 1341, the anti-papal legislation of the reign and the employment (by John of Gaunt) of John Wycliff demonstrated to post-Reformation Anglicans that Edward III was really a good Protestant. Although an example of Tudor wishful thinking which projected the realities of the sixteenth century onto the fourteenth, it showed how easily Edward's reign could be made a golden age of all manner of causes. The Stuarts were taken by the memory of consensus in the reign, so very different from the factionalism and discord of their own time. Under Charles I, there was an emphasis on the reign's statutes and their importance for liberty. The 1352 Statute of Treasons came to have a particular resonance as the realm slid towards civil war, notably cited in the defence of the Earl of Strafford.[31]

Stuart historians poured praise on Edward. Under James I, Samuel Daniel judged him 'a prince who knew his work, and did it', whose 'nature agreed with his office as only made for it'. Interestingly, he also believed that 'this king and his grandfather Edward the first, the best of our kings, had the two best wives'.[32] As the reign of James II was coming to its turbulent end in 1688, the first biography of Edward III was published. Joshua Barnes wrote an epic work running to more than 900 pages, and while it contains much research and scholarship, the approach is betrayed in the shortened version of the eye-wateringly long title, *The History of That Most Victorious Monarch Edward III*. The conclusion is gushing: 'He had the most virtues and fewest vices of any prince, that ever I read of; he was valiant, just, merciful, temperate, and wise; the best king, the best captain, the best lawgiver, the best friend, the best father, and the best husband in his days'.[33] This adulation was reflected in the following eras in the artistic choices of the Georgian and Victorian courts. When the new Houses of Parliament were completed in the 1840s, a fresco of Edward III awarding the Black Prince the Order of the Garter was commissioned for the House of Lords. In a famous Buckingham Palace ball of 1842, Queen Victoria and Prince Albert dressed as Philippa and Edward, a scene captured on canvas by Edwin Landseer.

Yet if this reflected Edward's reputation in court circles, a shift in attitudes had begun among historians. In the 1820s, John Lingard portrayed a king of great ambition and poor judgement, whose foreign wars unintentionally helped the English people gain control over the monarchy.[34] After the better part of five centuries in which he had been feted, Edward III was knocked from his pedestal. In 1868, William Longman dismissed the 'purposeless character of much of his war with France', criticising Edward's undoubted courage for being combined 'with no small amount of chivalrous rashness'. 'That he was unscrupulously despotic is clear enough', opines Longman, in contrast to previous centuries which had included precisely the opposite. Although 'possessed of qualities particularly qualified to excite the admiration of unthinking hero-worshippers', Edward has 'but little claim to commendation of the wise and thoughtful'.[35] It is a damning verdict, in which Edward and the Black Prince are condemned for their brutality and for neglecting their subjects' interests in pursuit of military glory. Six years later, another biographer echoed this condemnation, claiming that the reign's 'gigantic military efforts [...] only wasted the resources of the country, and, even when crowned with almost miraculous success, produced absolutely no abiding results'.[36] Suddenly, Edward III had become a brutal warrior who plundered his country to support pointless foreign wars, neglecting the governance of his realm, a similar charge to that levelled (with far more justice) against Richard I.

William Stubbs explicitly made this comparison in a highly critical verdict on Edward. The moralistic bishop saw the king as 'ambitious, unscrupulous, selfish, extravagant, and ostentatious', whose 'obligations as a king sat very lightly on him'; 'without foreign ambitions he might have risen to the dignity of a tyrant or sunk to the level of a voluptuary'. Indeed, Stubbs consciously sought to divorce Edward from the good that resulted from his time on the throne: 'whilst England knows no gratitude to the king for patriotism, sagacity, or industry, she owes very much to the reign'.[37] For the better part of three-quarters of a century thereafter, Edward III was viewed in these negative terms as a warrior who pursued pointless wars on the Continent at great expense and did nothing to further the constitution. The greatest indignity Edward suffered was at the hands of another Oxford don, Charles Oman, who dismissed Edward's military achievements, judging him 'a very competent tactician but a very unskilful strategist.'[38] He was even blamed by some for having too many sons, which led to 'the factions of York and Lancaster' and the Wars of the Roses a century later.[39] (That contemporaries saw this fertility as a divine blessing, and that large numbers of sons were wise in an age of high infant mortality, as the case of Edward I shows, seems to have escaped this bizarre line of thinking.[40]) Most damaging of all was the view of another Oxford academic, Charles Plummer, that Edward's reign saw the Crown concede too much to the nobility, which created the 'over-mighty subject' and damaged the Crown's authority for the rest of the Middle Ages, with devastating consequences in the fifteenth century. This made Edward responsible for what Plummer termed 'bastard feudalism', a dubious concept hotly debated ever since. What was not much debated for the first half of the twentieth century was Edward III's dreadful stock among historians.[41] Indeed, aside from some derivative popular works, biographers were dissuaded for the rest of the century, two twentieth-century academics, John Le Patourel and A. R. Myers, failing to complete the volume in the English Monarchs series before it was finally published by Mark Ormrod in 2010.[42]

Into mid-century, the negative approach to Edward was largely accepted and repeated. It was May McKisack who challenged what was, by the 1950s, received wisdom, observing that the criticisms of Stubbs and the Victorians 'would have astonished Edward's own contemporaries'. She pointed out that 'Edward III succeeded, where nearly all his predecessors had failed, in winning and holding the loyalty of his people and the affection of his magnates'. Listing his achievements, McKisack notes that his subjects 'saw him as the pattern of chivalry and the maker of England's fame, and when he lay upon his death-bed they mourned the passing of a great English king', wryly musing that it 'is not altogether easy to share Stubbs' confidence that they were wrong'. Despite having 'carried eulogy to the point of absurdity', Joshua Barnes' biography from 1688 was, incredibly, 'still, on balance, the best we have'. The king's 'achievement remains impressive', in spite of his failings, not least that he 'retrieved the dignity of the monarchy without forfeiting the affections of his people, who had to thank him for over thirty years of internal peace, for the restoration of their self-respect and for the winning of a military reputation in Europe which has seldom been equalled and seldom (if ever) surpassed'.

The rehabilitation had limits – 'Nobody today would describe Edward III as the greatest of English kings; but the historians have judged him too harshly' – yet with McKisack came the first indications that Edward's reputation had passed its nadir.[43] Most important was the attempt she and subsequent historians made to judge Edward by the standards of fourteenth-century Englishmen rather than Victorian bishops and academics. Also crucial was the work of K. B. McFarlane and his students in challenging Stubbs and Victorian ideas about bastard feudalism and the weakness of the Crown; while this has been more extensively pursued in relation to the fifteenth century,[44] it also allowed historians of the fourteenth to look at Edward's reign in different terms. Rather than anachronistic constitutional theories and generic overmighty subjects, scholars started to look at individuals and situations, how nobles (and kings) might have been motivated by something other than the selfish greed Victorian historians had ascribed to them by default. Looked at in this light, the co-operation and harmony between Edward III and his subjects over such a long period was remarkable.

Edward was still not a popular subject of study. Several biographies and works marked the 600th anniversary of the Black Prince's death in 1976, none that of his father the following year. Two popular biographies did appear in 1973 and 1983, both reflecting a definite change from the hostile approach of earlier in the century. The emphasis now was on the long domestic peace, the man who 'maintained the consensus of the realm over many decades, through war and natural disaster and unprecedented social change, allowing its institutions to grow and its sense of unity to mature'. It was noted that 'Henry V could not have become an English hero had he not had the precedent of Edward III to act upon'.[45] When Michael Prestwich published his study of the first three Edwards in 1980, he restored the military reputation of the third, 'a good leader of men [...] who could be rash, but he cannot be accused of foolhardiness'. Prestwich moreover dismissed the idea of a king with no domestic merit: the 'achievement of the government at home during the years of triumph abroad was considerable, if not spectacular'. In contrast to the received view from the previous century, 'Edward III was far more than a mere chivalric adventurer: he was a skilful ruler as well as a chivalric hero'.[46] A decade later, another scholar highlighted the 'extraordinary fulfilment of the potential of the medieval state, founded on cooperation and trust between the king, the landed elite, and the church', a trust which allowed Edward 'to extract more from his subjects than any other medieval king'. Essentially, 'Edward III had shown a remarkable talent for uniting the diverse elements of the English realm into a single cause'.[47]

A transformation of the understanding of Edward's reign came with the work of Mark Ormrod, whose D.Phil. thesis examined the king's government in England between 1346 and 1356. An extended version of this, published in 1990, was a study of the whole reign which focussed on the king's domestic rule, a contrast to many studies which neglected this element at the expense of the dramatic narrative of war; it was a study which 'argued that, beyond the trumpets and drums, there is another and still more fascinating history of this reign'. Ormrod emphasised that under Edward, 'most of the important changes in the structure of politics were carried through by co-operation and consensus'. To consider Edward's domestic success augmented rather than diminished the king's military success: 'When Edward III's achievements in domestic politics are finally and fully evaluated alongside his accomplishments in war, he may yet be permitted to re-enter the august and select band of great medieval rulers'. Over the next two decades, Ormrod published a large number of articles on various aspects of the reign, culminating in the most comprehensive scholarly biography of Edward in 2010. Detailed and judicious, this is the standard life of the reign, as the quotations scattered throughout this chapter demonstrate. While acknowledging Edward's flaws and failures, Ormrod showed that the successes of the reign were achieved because of, not in spite of, the king and his approach: 'a frank acknowledgment of Edward's limitations does comparatively little, however, to detract from the fact that his character and ambitions remained absolutely at the heart of English royal policy for at least forty years'. He was a king who had an 'undeniable and compelling ability to engage the hearts and minds of so many of his subjects, combatant and non-combatant alike, in the major military enterprises of the English king'. His great success and legacy was the way in which he built a harmonious, consensual polity: 'Edward III had demonstrated, in a manner all too often lost on other medieval kings, that the security and prosperity of the realm ultimately lay in the affective relationship established between ruler and people'.[48]

From the late 1980s, Edward became a more popular subject of study, and historians followed Prestwich and Ormrod in analysing him in much more positive terms. Richard W. Kaeuper praised a king whose generosity and widespread patronage avoided the problems of his grandfather and father, and who 'showed his willingness to yield gracefully on most matters other than the all-important matter of the war'. His acceptance of justices of the peace as part of the permanent mechanism of justice was a result of his 'prudent assessment of the support he needed to fight the war in France'.[49] A conference held in York in 1999 produced a volume of essays on various aspects of the reign, united by their acceptance that 'Edward's style of kingship [...] was successful kingship, and that the man himself, whatever quibbles or reservations might be allowed in relation to specific policies or actions, deserves the praise which, for the most part, his contemporaries heaped upon him'.[50]

One contributor to that volume, J. S. Bothwell, shortly afterwards produced a monograph about Edward's relations with the nobility. This vindicated McFarlane's argument that Edward had not, as the Victorians believed, been wasteful in his grants and weakened the power of the Crown, but had rather asserted royal control and linked patronage carefully to loyalty and service to the Crown.[51] Clifford J. Rogers examined the king as warrior and military strategist, dismissing the disdain of the Victorians and first half of the twentieth century to conclude that not only 'did the king guide the war effort intelligently, he inspired those who helped him fight it with some of his own spirit of confidence, chivalric boldness combined with pragmatic realism'.[52] A study of Edward's household knights judged that 'their central but ever-changing place in his reign was the result of a reactive king who had a firm grasp on what he wanted, what was expected of him, and who was willing to evolve to achieve both'.[53]

The new consensus on Edward was summarised in the best biography to appear between Joshua Barnes in 1688 and Mark Ormrod in 2010, by Ian Mortimer in 2006. While at times a little overdramatised, the volume brings a life and excitement to the reign that had long been sorely lacking among the king's biographers. For Mortimer, Edward was 'loyal, faithful, religious, unintellectual, romantic, adventurous, controlling, encouraging of sexual indulgence, straightforward, logical, fair and merciful', a list with contradictory elements that bears tribute to a complex human being. The faults and vices – 'overbearing pride, selfishness, conceit, occasional outbursts of uncontrollable anger, impetuousness, impatience' – are acknowledged too, but 'to pretend he was simply a warmonger, a religious cynic and a brutal thug, and that all the cultural achievements of the reign should be interpreted as the side-effects of his passion for women, power and war – as so many historians have done and continue to do – is simply wrong'. Edward was a great king who 'helped make the English nation what it is'.[54]

Jonathan Sumption's more recent, shorter biography is primarily a military one focussing on Edward's wars, and much of the domestic side of things is overlooked, which unbalances the picture. For Sumption, Edward was first and foremost a warrior who lacked key administrative abilities: 'Finance was always Edward III's weak point. He had little understanding of the problems of taxation or credit and was bored of administration'. Warfare, especially the French war, dominates the volume, at the expense of the domestic sphere which might show Edward's non-military achievements in a more positive light. As a soldier, Edward is rated highly, although Sumption attributes 'to accident or fortune' military decisions which others 'are inclined to attribute to foresight'. In the end, he views Edward as a 'heroic failure', one who 'outlived his own mental and physical powers'. Edward's ambitions were 'frustrated by their own contradictions'. And while he 'healed the bitter divisions he inherited from his father', he then 'bequeathed others to his successor, Richard II, which would one day contribute to his destruction'. In many ways, in its overwhelming focus on war and silence on so much domestic policy, the volume rather ignores the modern consensus to take a step back towards a more critical view of the king.[55]

In this respect, Sumption is an outlier. Having served his century as an unfashionable, heavily maligned king, Edward has been restored by other historians to the hero found in accounts from the fourteenth to the nineteenth centuries. There is more nuance, there are acknowledgments of his limitations and failings, but in the twenty-first century Edward III has once more been recognised as largely embodying the ideals of medieval English kingship.

Edward in Popular Culture

Edward III had the longest reign of any king in this volume, yet despite the romance and legends attached to his reign, he has made almost no impression on novelists, playwrights or screenwriters. May McKisack observed that although Edward III reigned fifty years, 'for many of his fellow-countrymen he remains a pasteboard figure'. As she shrewdly observed, his father and his grandson 'have stirred the imagination of poets and dramatists', but Edward himself never has, for he 'conformed to his age as he found it and accepted its standards' so 'has merged into the vanished age of chivalry and now partakes of its unreality'.[56] Edward was too normal, too successful at being a king in his own time, to excite those who want the unconventionality that allows them to misappropriate a king for later eras.

A play from the 1590s, *The Raigne of King Edward the Third* (usually known as *Edward III*) has been accepted by most scholars since the 1990s as at least part-authored by William Shakespeare, and in 1998 an edition was published in the *New Cambridge Shakespeare* series. Exactly what proportion of the play came from Shakespeare's pen is debated, although the editor of the *New Cambridge* edition suggests that it may have been excised from the Shakespearean canon because of its pronounced anti-Scottish nature.[57] It had been performed in the earlier twentieth century as an Elizabethan play, including BBC radio adaptions, and since the link to Shakespeare there have been Royal Shakespeare Company versions and several productions in the United States. However, discovering the Bard's involvement has not made it any more popular.

The rare subsequent occasions Edward has been a subject for dramatists are deservedly forgotten. William Blake wrote a piece entitled 'King Edward the Third' which was included in his *Poetic Sketches*. The volume published in 1783 was a limited edition, for circulation to Blake's friends and never intended for public distribution. Based around the French war, this unfinished fragment evokes considerable academic debate over whether it is intently jingoistic or purposefully ironic. However, is not likely to appeal to modern, general readers with its florid style. Gaetano Donizetti's *The Siege of Calais* (*L'assedio di Calais*) premiered in Naples in 1836, but was not performed after the 1830s until revived in Bergamo in 1988. It does not seem to have had a professional production in the UK until that of the English Touring Opera in 2013. On the same theme, George Bernard Shaw's single-act play, *The Six of Calais* (1934) was inspired by Rodin's sculpture. While described as a historical comedy, it is today amusing only to aficionados of Shaw.

Edward's appearances on screen are very rare and fleeting. In 1911, the American actor Charles Kent played the king in a short, silent film entitled *The Death of*

King Edward III. Blake Ritson played the king in *World Without End*, the 2012 TV adaption of Ken Follett's novel. Otherwise, Edward has been a side character in films about others. Michael Hordern took the part in *The Dark Avenger* (1955), a glorification of the Black Prince. Edward has a minor role as a boy in adaptions of Marlowe's *Edward II*, including that of Derek Jarman in 1991. Perhaps his most significant screen roles have been, ironically, on French TV, where Jean-Louis Broust (1972) and Aurélien Wilk (2005) played Edward in versions of Maurice Druon's *Accursed Kings* (*Les rois maudits*) novels. This meagre list is in sharp contrast to the memorable screen portrayals of Henry V.

When May McKisack wrote of Edward in 1960 that 'so far as I am able to discover, nobody since the eighteenth century has made him the subject of a play, a poem or even a novel', it was with understandable surprise.[58] There had in fact been some nineteenth- and early twentieth-century novels, mainly heroic works of jingoism aimed at boys, but none that would have seemed remotely worth reading to a distinguished professor. Since McKisack wrote, most of Edward's very infrequent novel appearances have been as a background character to other action. The later books of Maurice Druon's *Accursed Kings* series (1955–77), Bernard Cornwell's four-book *Grail Quest* series (2000–12) and Ken Follett's *World Without End* (2007) are good examples. He features in various novels about the Hundred Years' War, but none really shine any light on Edward or provide any unusual approach of interest. Edward as a main character is very rare, and often weird, as is the case with Evelyn Eaton's *The King is a Witch* (1965; the title says it all and is all that needs to be read). More recently, historical novelists have shown an interest in the Alice Perrers affair, examples including *The King's Mistress* by Emma Campion (a pen name of Candace Robb) and *The King's Concubine* by Anne O'Brien. Yet it is Perrers who is the protagonist and main interest of these stories.

It is strange that a king who reigned half a century, who oversaw some of the most spectacular military victories in the English national myth, was king during one of the most famous pandemics in history, and presided over a time of remarkable domestic transformation and harmony, has so little captured the popular mind. Perhaps it just shows that failures make better stories, that the dramatist cannot work so easily with a king who got along with his family (and everyone else) and was primarily a conspicuous success.

Verdict

It is perhaps a mundane fact that best sums up the success of Edward III. Where his predecessor and successor contrived to have themselves deposed and murdered after around twenty years each on the throne, Edward died naturally in his bed after half a century as king. If the final years were ones of decay and sadness, Edward III was genuinely mourned on his death and his subjects realised that his passing was a significant moment. For various reasons, few of his medieval successors would meet such a dignified end. Not until Elizabeth I would a monarch again live to such an age, while no sovereign would reign as long until George III.

Yet Edward is something of a forgotten figure in the history of the monarchy. His reign was full of action and drama, but few remember much about the king at the heart of it all. The Black Prince has attracted the romantic legends, while his father always seems to be in the shadows in the background. Maybe this made it easier for the historians of the nineteenth and early twentieth centuries to launch their assault on his memory, dismissing him as a thug who plundered the country to support a pointless war, forced to weaken his crown to do so. For all the praise of the previous centuries, there was no deeply embedded, popular heroic myth to challenge. Edward therefore made an easy target for the anachronistic judgements of the moralisers and constitutionalists, from which it has taken the more judicious historians of the late twentieth and twenty-first centuries to rescue him.

Judged against the standards of his own time, and indeed against other medieval wearers of the English crown, Edward emerges as a conspicuous success. He was a pious Christian king who was successful in war and very obviously took the counsel of his leading subjects, distributing patronage widely and generously. After the disastrous reign of his father, and the equally lamentable regime of Isabella and Mortimer, Edward restored trust in the monarchy and revived its prestige. His was a splendid court of chivalry to which European envoys flocked, the Order of the Garter and Windsor the most tangible signs of this. The humiliation of Edward II's dismal failures against the Scots were reversed, Bannockburn undone by Halidon Hill and Neville's Cross. Crécy and Poitiers, improbable victories achieved against sizeable numerical odds, restored pride in the English and showed the king, in contemporary terms, to have the blessing of God. Having the wisdom to select and trust able officials, Edward ensured that his government navigated surely through the tricky period of the Black Death, and gave the English Crown much greater financial stability. Above all, in a realm which had descended into a retributive bloodbath in the 1320s, Edward reasserted the rule of law. In following due process against Mortimer in 1330, Edward demonstratively halted the circus of show trials and mob executions which had defined the previous two regimes. In clearly defining treason in 1352, he reaffirmed this commitment to legal process and just rule. He may not have been a legal innovator or reformer on the scale of Henry II or Edward I, but we should not underestimate how significant was Edward III's achievement in this regard, especially given the ruthless predecessors he followed.

Of course, Edward was no saint or beacon of perfection. Behind all the ceremony and propaganda and glory of the late 1340s and 1350s, it is fair to question exactly what he was hoping to achieve, and the euphoria rather concealed the lack of defined, achievable purpose. He was a medieval king, and like all medieval kings he could be cruel and capricious. He was a Plantagenet, with a correspondingly hot temper. The clash with Stratford (himself no placid saint) and the treatment of his ministers in 1340–41 showed Edward at his very worst: angry, vengeful, spiteful and totally in denial about reality. Yet a key characteristic of Edward III, one very few medieval English monarchs shared, was his ability to learn from his mistakes and move on. He lacked his father's ability to bear a grudge and his grandfather's inherent stubbornness. With some limited exceptions, Edward did not vindictively pursue opponents down the years as Edward II had done and Richard II would do. In 1341, he gave in (albeit hardly with good grace) rather than try to ride out the opposition as Edward I had done in 1297–98. It was this wisdom and pragmatism at the heart of his kingship which, more than anything, convinced his subjects that the bad times were indeed over, that they could once more trust and work with their king.

Edward III's tragedy was that he outlived himself. The sad, lonely figure of 1377 was the palest shadow of the triumphant king who had secured the Treaty of Brétigny seventeen years earlier. Had his reign ended around 1364, he would have been remembered mainly for his great achievements and his services to English national pride. Like Henry V, who emulated Edward but did die at an opportune moment at the height of his success, it would have been his successor and his lieutenants who took the blame for the collapse of the essentially unworkable reality those achievements produced. Instead, Edward followed Henry II in surviving too long for the next generation, living to witness the undoing of a previously successful reign.

With the benefit of hindsight, it is possible to see that the superficial victory over France would never have been durable in the long term. Beyond all the nationalistic rhetoric around Crécy and Poitiers, the settlement of 1360 was unrealistic. Yet Edward had fostered the first real sense of 'Englishness', skilfully persuading his subjects of the value of investing in his plan. If the aims were unclear and unrealistic, the belief and assurance of Englishmen in 1360 was a stark contrast to the resignation and despair of Edward II's reign. Part of the problem, too, was that his immediate descendants lacked Edward's own abilities. Edward learned Henry II's lesson and gave his sons considerable responsibilities, but while the remarkable family harmony was a sharp contrast to the twelfth-century 'Devil's brood', Edward's family were not very much more competent than Henry's. The Black Prince was a fine warrior but a terrible administrator who failed to emulate his father's policies of consensus in a turbulent rule over Aquitaine. John of Gaunt would become a stabilising father figure in the 1390s, but while Edward was alive he was rash and often foolish, bearing heavy responsibility for the unpopularity of the court in the king's final years. Edward's heir, Richard II, showed some echoes of his grandfather in the courage with which he handled the Peasants' Revolt at the tender age of 14, but he had no interest in the French war and eventually destroyed himself through choosing arbitrary rule and fear over consensus. If some of the problems of the later fourteenth century had their origins in Edward's reign and policies, it is unfair to hold him accountable for the failings of those who came after him and were simply unable to play the game of kingship as skilfully.

Overall, Edward did indeed play that game remarkably well. Of all the medieval kings of England, only Stephen might rival Edward III in conviviality. Despite the many instances of temper and occasional flashes of brutality, it is this conviviality which most defines Edward. After the formidably grumpy, aloof Edward I and the petty, lazy Edward II, to have a king who was both friendly and competent must have been a welcome change for the English. He was an extrovert who enjoyed life but did his duty, a man who revelled in tournaments and garter balls but learned to make himself available to his people and administer justice. Edward used this humanity and warmth to his advantage. Apart from 1341, which was a petulant stand-off more than anything, he never faced domestic rebellion or revolt. He built a remarkable consensus among his nobility that allowed them to share in his glory and his success, ensuring that they were invested in helping him achieve his aims. The politics of consensus and the friendly, inclusive manner which ensured even the less favoured felt part of his endeavours meant that for much of his reign, the king was held in high esteem and great respect. He ascended a tarnished throne in a bitterly divided and defeated realm, and restored both the lustre of that throne and the harmony and glory of that realm. It was an achievement for which Edward deserves to take a place among the greatest of kings.

Chapter 5

Henry V: An Ideal King?

> In 1413 'began the short reign of a king who achieved – in scholarship as well as in the popular mind – an unparalleled reputation as the exemplar of successful medieval kingship'.[1]

> Henry V's truest and most lasting monument [...] is that antipathy and distrust which, sadly, all too many Frenchmen feel for those who speak English as their first language.[2]

Henry V's success was far greater than being an exemplar of medieval kingship. In a way true of no other monarch, his carefully cultivated self-image has captured the historical narrative ever since, making him the subject of fawning adulation even for many sober, modern academics. In the popular mind, his reputation is secured by the Battle of Agincourt. Thanks to Shakespeare's version, this has become a story of a small, plucky English force triumphing over an enormous French army, a proto-Churchillian standing alone and triumphing against the odds, which feeds perfectly into English Francophobia and rather ignores reality, not least the fact that Henry was the invader and aggressor. This is irrelevant in the popular mythology of one of those English victories torn from wider context to foster the national myth of determined heroism and triumph of the underdog. Henry's reign lasted only nine years, yet he is among the most famous and celebrated of English kings.

So lofty was the pedestal Henry occupied for nearly five centuries, that it was perhaps inevitable that some historians of the twentieth and twenty-first centuries would try to topple him from it. The modern era has seen not just challenges to the traditional view, but attempts to overturn it completely, to expose a war-crazed aggressor and zealous religious bigot. In turn, Henry's defenders have entrenched the traditional view more firmly. There is no doubt that Henry V's reign was a remarkable one, bringing him within a heartbeat of the throne of France, but was this an obsession that doomed his successor to destruction? Was Henry V really, as one twentieth-century historian enthused, the greatest man to rule England?

Henry's Life and Reign

Henry was born in Monmouth Castle on (probably) 16 September 1386, the eldest child of Earl Henry of Derby (Henry Bolingbroke) and Mary de Bohun. Derby was the eldest son of John of Gaunt, Duke of Lancaster and third son of Edward III. This made the new child heir to the immense Lancastrian inheritance and a future nobleman of great rank, but although a great-grandson of a king, no one could have imagined in 1386 that he would one day wear the crown himself, hence the uncertainty over his date of birth. His early years are not well recorded. Much of his time was spent in the Lancastrian heartland, at the likes of Kenilworth, Leicester and Tutbury. He had a fairly thorough academic education, and would know English, French and Latin as an adult. His father was a patron of Chaucer and other writers, an interest reflected in the culture in which Henry was raised, and which he would also patronise. For the most part, however, his education was conventional for a boy of his status.

Henry grew up in the troubled atmosphere of Richard II's reign. His mother died in 1394. The elder Henry was absent from his son's life for significant periods in the 1390s, including the crusade he undertook in Prussia and the Baltic. Nevertheless, as a junior member of the royal family, Henry of Monmouth was involved in major state events. Aged 10 in November 1396, he attended the wedding of his uncle, Richard II, to his second wife in Calais. He was also present at parliament in September 1397, when his father was created Duke of Hereford. However, Hereford's feud with another new duke, Thomas Mowbray of Norfolk, saw both of them dramatically banished by the king in October 1398. Hereford was sentenced to absence for a decade, and the following February his father, John of Gaunt, died. Richard refused to allow Hereford to enter his inheritance as Duke of Lancaster, although the king did grant the 12-year-old Henry an annuity.

In May 1399, Richard took Henry with him on an expedition to Ireland. Over the previous two years, the king had ruled arbitrarily and capriciously, making himself deeply unpopular with key members of the nobility. He still had no children, and the succession was far from certain. It is likely that Richard took the boy as a hostage, to prevent Henry Bolingbroke taking advantage of his absence in Ireland. Nevertheless, Richard seems to have treated Henry kindly; after taking the throne, Henry V would have Richard II solemnly reburied in Westminster Abbey, which suggests the boy had felt affection for the old king. (He had probably spent far more quality time with Richard than with his frequently absent father.) However, the use of young Henry as a deterrent failed spectacularly. Bolingbroke landed in Yorkshire at the end of June and Richard's regime collapsed in weeks, the king's return across the Irish Sea failing to save him. By mid-August, Richard was his cousin's prisoner. At Westminster at the end of September 1399, the king was deposed and replaced by Bolingbroke.

With the coronation of his father as King Henry IV on 13 October 1399, Henry of Monmouth's life changed markedly. At 13, he was no longer just a member of a cadet branch of the royal family, but heir to the throne. As Richard had hurried back to Wales, he had ordered Henry to remain in Ireland, imprisoned in imposing Trim Castle, but Henry was back in England in time to be knighted by his father the day before the coronation. At the service he carried the sword of justice, the first heir since the Norman Conquest to be old enough to participate in his father's coronation. On 15 October 1399, Henry was awarded the now traditional titles of the heir to the throne: Prince of Wales, Duke of Cornwall and Earl of Chester. Parliament acknowledged him as Henry IV's rightful successor before he took his seat in the House of Lords. This was the first time a Prince of Wales had been formally invested in parliament, an indication of the usurping king's need to secure the dynasty. Before the year was out, the prince had also been created Duke of Aquitaine and Lancaster. He was now a major landed magnate, second only to the king.

The insecurity of the new regime was shown at the very start of 1400, with a plot against the king by allies of Richard II. After the swift crushing of this rebellion, Richard was murdered in Pontefract Castle to prevent any others succumbing to the temptation to attempt his restoration (although rumours of his survival would persist). In August 1400, Henry was left as keeper of the realm when his father invaded Scotland. The following month, the Glyndŵr Revolt began. Owain Glyndŵr's dispute with his neighbour, Lord Reginald Grey of Ruthin, had developed into a Welsh independence movement. On 16 September 1400, Glyndŵr proclaimed himself Prince of Wales. His supporters attacked the major English settlements of Denbigh, Flint, Rhuddlan and Ruthin, also causing considerable damage to Oswestry and Welshpool. Henry IV was at Northampton on his way home from a mediocre Scottish campaign, in which he had failed to bring Robert III to battle or enforce his submission, and was forced to divert to Shrewsbury with his army. Arriving on 26 September, he launched a rapid campaign into North Wales, which included securing the key castles at Beaumaris, Caernarfon, Conwy, Criccieth, Denbigh and Harlech. By 15 October, the king was back at Shrewsbury.

The boy whose title Glyndŵr claimed was sent to Chester and the protection of the justiciar of North Wales and Chester, Sir Henry Percy ('Harry Hotspur'). Cheshire was the prince's earldom, but it had been the heartland of Richard II and the new dynasty was not popular there. Glyndŵr and major allies remained at large, but by the end of the year the English believed the revolt to have been suppressed. The parliament of January–March 1401 indulged widespread anti-Welsh sentiments with a spree of hostile measures. On Good Friday (1 April) 1401, two brothers, Rhys and Gwilym ap Tudur, led a daring assault which captured Conwy Castle. Though an isolated attack rather than a resumption of the general rising, it was an embarrassment for the English government. Henry Percy had to lead the siege, and Prince Henry was present with him for at least part of it. Conwy was handed back to the English around the end of May, and Rhys and Gwilym (but not all their accomplices) were pardoned. At Chester on 14 June, the Prince of Wales' council issued ordinances which took a hard line against any signs of dissent.

The flames of revolt were not so readily extinguished. Both king and prince took part in campaigning, but little tangible was achieved. As the conflict ground on, Earl Thomas Percy of Worcester was appointed lieutenant of South Wales in spring 1402, with his nephew Henry given the corresponding role in North Wales. Yet as the war continued fruitlessly through the summer, cracks began to appear in the relationship between the king and the Percy family. The Percys were the dominant noble family of the Scottish border. Earl Henry Percy of Northumberland (elder brother of Thomas and father of Hotspur) had provided critical support to Henry IV during his invasion of 1399. With the family often busy in the military defence of the Scottish March in 1402, and the lack of success in Wales, the king appointed others to the key roles further south, with Prince Henry being named lieutenant of the whole of Wales in April 1403. It made little difference to a war that was draining finances with no discernible gain. More seriously, it was a major factor in pushing the Percys into rebellion.

In early July 1403, Henry IV learned that Worcester and Hotspur had raised the standard of revolt. They were probably in treasonous correspondence with the Welsh rebels, so the king forced a fight before they or the Earl of Northumberland could send support. The two Percys had dashed to Shrewsbury to try to capture the prince, and it was there the showdown took place on 21 July 1403. By all accounts the prince fought courageously and the larger royal army emerged victorious. Hotspur was killed, Worcester captured and publicly executed on 23 July. Archers played a major part in the battle and Prince Henry was wounded by an arrow in the face. (Afterwards, he underwent surgery at Kenilworth Castle to remove the arrowhead, although later descriptions by contemporaries tactfully fail to mention the resulting scar, and the severity of the wound was until recently not noted by historians.[3]) The prince had acquitted himself commendably in his first battle.

The threat from the Percys had been neutralised, but that from the Welsh remained stubbornly unresolved. In the summer of 1403, as the king and his son were dealing with the Percys, Glyndŵr and the Welsh made striking gains, which included the southern castles of Carmarthen, Dryslwyn and Newcastle Emlyn. The loss of Carmarthen in particular was a humiliation which required the king to lead another campaign in September, lasting less than a fortnight. As winter arrived, Aberystwyth, Beaumaris, Caernarfon, Cardiff, Harlech and Kidwelly Castles were all besieged. As 1404 began, Caernarfon and Harlech – two of Edward I's mighty showpieces – were in real trouble. Prince Henry was once again appointed to oversee the war. From June, the prince initially based himself in Worcester, with Hereford and Leominster then his favoured bases for much of the rest of the year. The war was costly and Henry was struggling to raise the necessary sums. Owain Glyndŵr opened discussions with the French, held his own parliaments, and attracted notable defectors such as Bishops John Trefor of St Asaph and Lewis Byford of Bangor. By the end of the year, Aberystwyth and Harlech Castles had fallen to the Welsh, and English authority in Wales dangled by the slenderest of threads.

Early 1405 saw a modest reversal of fortunes, at least in South Wales. Prince Henry wrote to his father in March to report a victory at Grosmont, while at Usk in May, Gruffudd, Glyndŵr's eldest son, was captured. However, Wales was not the only concern of king and prince. Various plots against them continued to be foiled. Most serious was that of Henry Percy, Earl of Northumberland. He had been pardoned after the rebellion of his brother and son, and by early 1405 he was plotting against Henry IV. While making an ostentatious show of loyalty, Northumberland planned to capitalise on the king campaigning in Wales. By late May 1405, he had garrisoned his strongholds and taken refuge in Berwick, while parts of Yorkshire rose in revolt. In the city of York, one of the rebel leaders was Archbishop Richard Scrope, who inflamed the citizens with a sermon in York Minster. With his fellow leader, Thomas Mowbray, Earl of Norfolk and Earl Marshal, Scrope and an army of citizens and clergy camped out on Shipton Moor, just north of York.

There, on 29 May, they confronted an army led by Henry IV's third son, Prince John, and the Earl of Westmorland. Battle was avoided, but Scrope and Mowbray were arrested and taken to Pontefract. When the king arrived at Pontefract on 3 June, he ignored Scrope and ordered the city of York to be seized, continuing there himself. Fearing the consequences of Henry's anger, Archbishop Thomas Arundel of Canterbury rode rapidly north to plead for his fellow archbishop, arriving in York on 6 June. Whatever Henry promised Arundel, which was enough to convince the archbishop to go and rest, a trial took place that very morning, although according to one account the chief justice of the king's bench refused to be involved. Scrope and Mowbray were condemned and taken to the very place outside York where they had assembled their citizen army. There, they were beheaded. Execution of a bishop, never mind an archbishop, by a king after a trial in a secular court was unprecedented. When Henry IV's health later collapsed, contemporaries viewed this as divine retribution for his treatment of Scrope. In 1405, however, Henry crushed the opposition, taking Northumberland's seat of Alnwick and forcing him into Scottish exile. Prince Henry was involved in subduing the rebellion, although in exactly what ways is unclear; he was certainly at Newcastle-upon-Tyne in late June, and probably took part in the siege of Berwick. The fraught relationship with Scotland turned in England's favour in early 1406, when Prince James, heir to the Scottish throne, was captured on the way to France by English pirates and handed over to Henry IV. Just a fortnight later, Robert III died and his son became King James I. The English now had the King of Scotland as their prisoner, and he would stay in captivity for eighteen years.

The tide of fortune in Wales began to turn in favour of the English during 1406. The prince was granted substantial sums to prosecute the war and moderate military success followed. In the end, the Glyndŵr Revolt was defeated by attrition; the English had more resources and Prince Henry was willing to proceed patiently. There were setbacks, such as Glyndŵr's relieving the siege of Aberystwyth in 1407. However, the English retook the castle the following year, and Harlech was reclaimed in early 1409. Glyndŵr's family fell into English hands and his cause fizzled out. Owain himself evaded capture, but his last military action seems to have been a border raid in Shropshire in 1410. Thereafter, Glyndŵr largely vanishes from history. In mid-July 1415, preparing to embark for France, Henry V offered him a pardon, but Glyndŵr could not be found. It is likely that he died that autumn, but his date of death and burial place are unknown. A rebel who had set Wales ablaze and caused the English years of problems simply faded into obscurity. For the future Henry V, however, suppressing the revolt had provided an important education in military tactics and strategy, the realities and problems of war finance, and the value of competent, loyal lieutenants.

In the later years of the revolt, Henry was needed personally in Wales far less frequently. By December 1406, aged 20, the prince was a member of Henry IV's council. He became one of its most regular attendees from 1407, and with Archbishop Arundel he exercised significant influence. More than three decades separated the men in age. The essential tension was between a prince who felt himself lacking sufficient funds for the Welsh war and an archbishop who wanted to restrain spending. Parliament was also concerned to curb expenditure, although it did continue to grant both direct and indirect taxes. The collapse of Henry IV's health gave the council an unusual degree of responsibility. Prince Henry was now exercising considerable power in government. As friction with Arundel grew, the prince began to promote the interests of the Beauforts: Earl John of Somerset, Bishop Henry of Winchester, and Thomas. These three were the king's half-brothers, sons of John of Gaunt's third wife, Katherine Swynford. Katherine had first been Gaunt's mistress and the boys had been born while he was still married to Constance of Castile. In February 1407, the king legitimised them, but they were barred from the succession to the Crown. A Beaufort cousin, Thomas Chaucer (son of the famous Geoffrey and Philippa Roet, Katherine Swynford's sister) was chosen as Speaker of the Commons in the last three parliaments of Henry IV's reign, in 1407, 1410 and 1411. Prince Henry was making use of family ties to extend his influence.

This bore fruit in December 1409, when Archbishop Arundel was removed as chancellor. The prime mover was probably the prince, resentful at the lack of cash for his Welsh campaigns, but he must have had the backing of his father, annoyed at the limitations Arundel had placed on his expenditure. In January 1410, it was Thomas Beaufort who was named as the new chancellor. Yet the parliament which met that month was as concerned as Arundel that the king control his spending. The members were especially concerned about the royal household, and although they granted taxation, the sum was inadequate. Common petitions suggest a concern about law and order, and the management of the Scottish and Welsh borders. Prince Henry remained at the head of the royal council, largely responsible for the governance of England at this stage.

Bringing the king's finances under control was the most pressing issue they faced, but in 1411 relations with France became a problem which would divide the king and his son. In recent years, the French kingdom under Charles VI (Charles the Mad, 1380–1422) had descended into violent factionalism. Charles had suffered his first episode of madness in 1392, and for the rest of his life sanity would alternate with psychotic episodes. Philip the Bold, Duke of Burgundy, took over effective running of the country and held the peace until his death in 1404. Power was seized by Charles VI's brother, Louis, Duke of Orléans. In November 1407, the new Duke of Burgundy, John the Fearless, had Louis murdered in Paris. By 1411, two main groups were vying for control of France. One was the Burgundians, under Duke John. The other consisted of the new Duke of Orléans, Louis' son Charles, plus the Dukes of Alençon, Berry and Bourbon. This second group was known as the Armagnacs, since the father of Duke Charles' second wife was the Count of Armagnac. Both Burgundians and Armagnacs sought English support.

The main concern of the English was French compliance with the 1360 Treaty of Brétigny. Prince Henry favoured the Burgundians and the possibility of a marriage to one of John's daughters. In September 1411, a force led by the Earl of Arundel (closely tied to the prince) crossed the Channel and helped the Burgundians in a successful defence of Paris against the Armagnacs.[4] Whatever he felt about the merits of the competing French bids for support, Henry IV was threatened by his eldest son and the challenge he posed to his authority. There are even suggestions that some in the prince's circle tried to persuade the king to abdicate, which for Henry IV had uncomfortable and inconceivable echoes of his own supplanting of Richard II. In parliament on 30 November 1411, the king dismissed his council, including the prince. Archbishop Arundel was soon brought back as chancellor, and the prince and his associates would be excluded from power for the remainder of Henry IV's reign.

1412 was thus a year of strained relations between king and heir. King Henry agreed the Treaty of Bourges with the Armagnacs in May, although in the autumn the French factions managed to patch up their differences enough to repudiate all English alliances and interference. The king seemed to favour his second son, Thomas, created Duke of Clarence in July. Parliament had essentially accused Thomas of laziness in 1410, unimpressed that the lieutenant of Ireland spent remarkably little time in Ireland, so this must have been galling for his older brother. If it never came close to outright conflict, the two Henrys were publicly at odds. According to one account, the prince came to London with a large retinue in the summer, and when the king finally agreed to see his son, the younger man offered a dagger to the older so that he could kill him if he was no longer of use. Suspect, late and embellished though this story may be, it captures the hostility between the two.

The new council tried to charge the prince with embezzlement, but he was cleared in October. There were rumours of assassination plots against him. While there is no evidence Henry was the kind of playboy prince Shakespeare created in the Prince Hal of his *Henry IV*, we can discern enough discordant notes in the chronicles to indicate that he was a fun-loving young man, especially at this stage of his life when he had nothing else to occupy him. His work on the council and in Wales had shown that he had the interest and application necessary for governing, but his insecure father had taken away the opportunity. It is possible that there is some grain of truth in Shakespeare's overblown portrayal, for in 1412 Henry was a young man deprived of a meaningful role, impatient to wear the crown.

As it was, he did not have long to wait. His father was a sick man and his health finally gave out. Henry IV died in the Jerusalem Chamber of Westminster Abbey on 20 March 1413, aged only 45. His final years had seen a prematurely old, sick man at loggerheads with his heir, although reconciliation seems to have been effected by the time he died. Henry V was crowned in Westminster Abbey, in the middle of a snowstorm, on 9 April. For one contemporary chronicler, Thomas Walsingham, 'as soon as he was invested with the emblems of royalty, he suddenly became a different man'.[5] That the throne passed smoothly to Henry V, less than fourteen years since the usurpation, is a mark of Henry IV's success in establishing the Lancastrian dynasty.

The new king was 26, above average height and athletic. His most prominent features were his brown eyes and long neck; if the famous portrait in the Royal Collection, with the striking 'bowl' haircut, is based on the king's real appearance, he had a lean, angular face. Walsingham was not the only chronicler to see that Henry's accession changed him. Henry IV is unique in medieval England for having a single, undisputed heir throughout his entire reign. Henry V had been waiting for the crown with growing frustration. Now he had it, he demonstrated a 'strong personal concept of kingship': 'Throughout his reign, he took the responsibilities of kingship seriously, even obsessively'.[6] Whatever else might be said of Henry V as king, no one could accuse him of being frivolous, never mind much fun.

The most obvious mark of his transformation was Henry's conversion into one of the most pious of England's medieval kings. He took seriously his calling as an anointed sovereign, believing himself and his actions inspired by God's will. Although the title was not given by the papacy to the English king until Henry VIII's reign, a century later, Henry V viewed himself as defender of the (Roman Catholic) faith, with a duty to eradicate heresy. His confessors were Carmelite friars, a notably strict and orthodox order. Such confessors were perpetually kept available, along with a veritable host of preachers for the masses the king attended daily. In the early months of his reign he was a frequent visitor to Westminster Abbey. He owned devotional books more appropriate to a churchman than a military leader. Most surprisingly of all, he seems to have forsworn sex between his accession in 1413 and his marriage in 1420, demonstrating a commitment to celibacy that was more in keeping with the calling of a priest than the sexual appetites and promiscuity of many medieval (and post-medieval) monarchs. Only Edward the Confessor and Henry III can be considered in the same category of piety as Henry V.

In choosing his ministers, Henry was careful. Unsurprisingly, Archbishop Arundel was ousted as chancellor, replaced by Bishop Henry Beaufort of Winchester. At the start of the reign, Henry did not undertake a purge of his father's ministers, keeping those he considered competent and who commanded his trust. Likewise, the unsuitable friends from his days as prince were unceremoniously dropped, only the suitable associates selected for government. One of the latter, Earl Thomas Fitzalan of Arundel, became treasurer. New or better bishoprics were found for ecclesiastical members of the council, most notably Henry Chichele, who was translated from St Davids to Canterbury after Archbishop Arundel's death in

February 1414. Henry's emphasis in his government was on integrity, competence and loyalty. That he chose well is shown by the low ministerial turnover during the reign.

In general, the king was parsimonious with patronage, except with his immediate family. Thomas, the king's oldest brother, was replaced as Captain of Calais in early 1414, but relations between the two improved. His younger two brothers, John and Humphrey, were created Dukes of Bedford and Gloucester respectively. However, mindful of the financial problems of his father's reign, the titles were not accompanied by generous endowments. Keeping his household expenditure low and showing serious intent to avoid excessive costs was a priority of Henry's, which earned him the gratitude of his first parliament in May 1413. The king also sought to heal past wounds. Within weeks of his accession, he announced that Richard II's body would be moved from Kings Langley to Westminster Abbey, in which the former king had invested considerable resources and had intended as his burial place. In a splendid and carefully choreographed ceremony, the reburial took place in December 1413. It is likely, as Richard's biographer says, that Henry's motivation was 'his desire to atone for his father's usurpation and his need to silence the rumours that Richard was still alive'.[7] However, Richard had treated the young Henry well in Ireland and the boy seems to have been genuinely fond of him. The past was laid to rest and Henry's own legitimacy made manifest.

One of Henry's concerns, as his mind turned towards a campaign in France, was the reestablishment of law and order. Although this was a perennial concern of the Commons, one matter which had alarmed the ecclesiastical authorities was the growth of Lollardy. Grounded in the ideas of John Wycliff, the Lollards considered themselves a Church reform movement, while the Roman Catholic authorities viewed them as heretics. The main appeal was to intellectuals (Oxford, Wycliff's base, became the key centre for training preachers) and gentry, and it is unlikely that Lollards were especially numerous. Nevertheless, the prelates were alarmed, and in 1401 Henry IV's parliament passed a statute, *De Heretico Comburendo* ('Concerning the Burning of Heretics'), which provided strict measures for those found in possession of Lollard literature, with burning at the stake the penalty for those who refused to recant their views. Archbishop Arundel was an especially zealous persecutor, and in 1413 this brought him into conflict with a member of Henry V's circle, Sir John Oldcastle.

Oldcastle was a member of the Herefordshire gentry who, in Henry IV's reign, had served in Wales, and been both a Member of Parliament for, and sheriff of, the county. An advantageous marriage to an heiress saw him summoned to the House of Lords as Lord Cobham from 1409. However, the taint of a heretical circle of friends meant he was actively in Arundel's sights, although for some time protected by Henry as both prince and king. In August 1413, Henry V allowed Arundel to act against him. The resulting heresy trial condemned him to death on 25 September, but Henry gave him forty days in the Tower of London to recant. On 19 October, associates helped Oldcastle to escape. Rumours began to circulate of a plot with Oldcastle at its heart, and on 5 January 1414 two conspirators revealed the details: the plan was to kidnap the king and his brothers at Eltham Palace during the Twelfth Night celebrations. The mayor of London arrested further conspirators, and Oldcastle fled. From those arrested, it was learned that Lollard rebels were set to muster at St Giles' Fields on 9/10 January. Pre-empting them, and acting against the counsel of advisors who feared thousands of rebels (the true number turned out to be around 300), on the evening of 9 January Henry had the gates of London barred. The king then intercepted these rebels near St John's Priory in Clerkenwell. More than eighty were captured, of whom over half were tried and executed within a matter of days.

Trials and mopping up operations took place in London and the localities over the following months, and once the ringleaders had been executed lesser figures were often allowed to buy their pardon. The cost was high, and some men died in notoriously unsanitary Newgate Prison. However, Oldcastle was one of those who escaped, and one of Henry's main concerns was tracking him down. When parliament met at Leicester in May 1414, new provisions were enacted in the Statute of Lollards, requiring royal officials to swear to act vigorously against heresy, with new penalties for heretics devised. (Henry also used this parliament as an opportunity to deal with the major problems with law and order the country faced, especially violent feuds in the Midlands and North.[8]) Extra powers were given to assist the search for Oldcastle, but he remained at large throughout 1414 and 1415. He appears to have been in the Midlands, with reports that he tried to excite another rebellion in Worcestershire in December 1415. He was sighted in Oxfordshire in October 1416, and was in Northamptonshire in summer 1417. At the start of that year, the king had offered a generous reward for his capture. He was eventually arrested near Welshpool in November 1417. Taken to parliament at Westminster, he was condemned in the Lords on 14 December and executed immediately.

The Oldcastle Revolt changed Henry V's approach to heresy and orthodoxy. As his initial reluctance to let Arundel loose on Oldcastle demonstrates, he may have been a pious Christian king from the start, but he was not an especially zealous heresy hunter. After Oldcastle, in the later stages of the reign, he was much more vigorous in this regard, a zeal which won the approval of the Church but makes him a less attractive character today. While the revolt had been no real threat, it had exposed Lollardy in Henry's circle and the king probably felt the need to emphasise his orthodoxy. In 1415, perhaps mindful of the disdain Lollards had for monasticism, Henry founded a Carthusian house at Sheen, and a Bridgettine house at Isleworth, later moved and renamed Syon (after Mount Zion). The Bridgettines were a Swedish order, and highly unusually for post-Anglo-Saxon England, it was a double house, for men and women. Here was the orthodox, pious king committed to peace.

Paradoxically, however, the king of peace wanted a war to secure his kind of peace. By 1414, Henry's sights were on France. With Armagnacs and Burgundians united, albeit fragilely, Henry had focussed initially on renewing truces with the French. When civil war erupted again in France in early 1414, Henry saw promising opportunities. Charles VI and Duke John of Burgundy were both wooing him with marriage alliances. Henry seriously explored marriage with Catherine, Charles' 13-year-old daughter, at the start of 1414, but by late spring the Burgundians were trying to tempt him with counterproposals. In the autumn, Henry sent an embassy to Paris, offering to renounce his claim to the French throne in return for the outstanding balance of John II's ransom (from nearly six decades earlier) and full implementation of the terms of the Treaty of Brétigny, plus additional territory. It is unclear whether or not Henry was making demands so outrageous that he could justify war when the French rejected them, as they duly did. When parliament met in November 1414, the chancellor's opening speech outlined Henry's plan to wage war against the French, for which the Commons and the convocation of Canterbury both enthusiastically voted generous taxes. The nobility were more cautious and persuaded Henry to send a new embassy to France in early 1415, with considerably less provocative terms.

In February 1415, Burgundian and Armagnac factions once again made peace, and the English demands were again rejected. The French saw Henry as young and inexperienced, not a threat to be taken seriously, and the scene immortalised in Shakespeare where the dauphin sent him tennis balls to play with is very likely true. The sources disagree on the date, but the 'tone fits better with Henry's stance in 1415 than 1414', and 'reflects Henry's poor international reputation in the early stages of his reign'.[9] Faced with this insult, Henry had little option but war, although that was probably his preference anyway. The French sent an embassy to the English king at Winchester in June 1415, although with no real intention of it achieving anything; they wanted Henry to appear to be the aggressor. Henry responded with propaganda entreaties of his own to Sigismund of Luxembourg, King of the Germans since 1410 and later Holy Roman Emperor (1433–37).

The king had some difficulty raising both troops and funds for his campaign, even having to pawn some of the royal jewels to captains serving on the expedition. Before he left England in the summer of 1415, he faced the most serious internal challenge of his reign in what became known as the Southampton Plot, led by Earl Richard of Cambridge (the king's cousin), Sir Thomas Grey from Northumberland, and Henry, Lord Scrope of Masham. Such a challenge was totally unexpected, and contemporary writers blamed the devil and French bribes. Although the official version of events was written down on the parliament roll, outlining the conspirators' intention to kill Henry and his three brothers and replace the king with Edmund Mortimer, Earl of March, much about the plot remains murky. When March informed the king, Henry acted swiftly and had Cambridge, Grey and Scrope arrested at Portchester. They were tried on 5 August and immediately executed, the king showing no mercy to friends who had betrayed him. By this stage, 'his obsession with invading France, which he saw as his God-given mission, overruled all other sentiments'.[10] Anything which threatened this mission, such as the Southampton Plot, was dealt with ruthlessly. This achieved, Henry set sail for France on 11 August 1415.

It was more than half a century since an English king had led a campaign in France, Edward III's expedition of 1359–60 beyond living memory for most. In 1415, Henry took with him a larger army than had his great-grandfather on that occasion, something of a contrast to the idea popularised by Shakespeare of a small force, the 'happy few'. Considerable efforts had been invested in the preparations, not least the acquisition of some 1500 ships. He intended to conquer and occupy rather than copy Edward's destructive *chevauchées*, hiring troops for twelve months and taking siege teams with him. Conquest would place Henry in a strong negotiating position, while securing ports in Normandy would help to protect the southern coast and make the Channel safer for English shipping, which would go down well with merchants at home. Piracy had been a major problem in the reign of Henry IV, while the French had used the Channel ports to send troops to support both Glyndŵr and the Scots. Arriving in France, he set to work besieging Harfleur. At the mouth of the Seine, the river on which lay Rouen and Paris, Harfleur was 'the most important port of Normandy, the key to the capture of the duchy'.[11] This made it an obvious first target in retrospect, but it was far less obvious to the French at the time, so Harfleur was not fully prepared.

The siege lasted five weeks, longer than Henry anticipated. Dysentery afflicted the troops, one victim being Henry's friend Richard Courtenay, Bishop of Norwich. The king's brother, Thomas of Clarence, was also sent home sick, as was another friend, the Earl of Arundel, who died in October. Disease plagued the citizens inside the walls. Frustrated, Henry began citing the Bible, quoting Deuteronomy 20:10–14 ('if [a town] does not submit to you peacefully [...] you shall besiege it; and when the LORD your God gives it into your hand, you shall put all the males to the sword') as a threat. Today, it makes him seem like a cruel zealot, but for Henry it was an expression of what he saw as his divine mission. Realising that no help was coming from their king or his heir, the citizens of Harfleur surrendered on 22 September. In a show of theatrical piety, Henry received the surrender in majesty, then entered the town barefoot and attended prayers at the Church of Saint-Martin. Given the serious damage caused to Harfleur's defences, and the risk of a French recovery attempt, Henry left Earl Thomas of Dorset in charge with an enormous garrison, perhaps 2000 troops. The port held a crucial place in Henry's plans for the future colonisation of Normandy.

As much as a third of his army was now out of action, brought low by disease or needed to defend Harfleur. Henry opted to make for English-held Calais. Provocatively, and in full expectation of not receiving an answer, he also challenged the dauphin to single combat. He took the quickest route to Calais to avoid encountering the French. For all the preparations, the aim of the expedition had possibly never been more ambitious than establishing another secure entry point.[12] On 12 October, Henry discovered that the French held the ford over the Somme at Blanchetaque, and that a French army was waiting for him on the northern bank. He therefore moved rapidly along the river, to a poorly guarded place beyond Péronne (more than sixty miles inland) where he could take his men across the Somme on 19 October. The following day, French messengers informed Henry that they intended to do battle before he reached Calais. The two forces encountered one another near Azincourt, around thirty-five miles south-south-east of Calais, on 24 October.

When battle was joined, on 25 October 1415, the odds were in favour of the French. The English had marched some 250 miles in the previous seventeen days. The French army was larger (perhaps 12,000 versus 8,500), and Henry's force had a disproportionately high number of archers. In their favour, the English had had chance to serve together for two months, and were led by their king, who was proving an effective leader, and whose personal courage was noted (during the battle he would protect his wounded brother, Duke Humphrey of Gloucester). Henry heard three Masses on the morning of the battle. The French had assembled haphazardly, and neither Charles VI nor the dauphin was present, leaving the army under the command of the inexperienced Duke Charles of Orléans. There had been disagreement among the French about joining battle, the cautious opposition of experienced commanders overruled by the younger, more impetuous royal dukes. To counter the cavalry, Henry had the archers drive sharpened, six-foot stakes into the ground in front of them. In the end, it was the way Henry used his archers to devastating effect that made the difference, causing disarray in the ranks of French cavalry and leading the foot soldiers to become so packed together that many drowned in mud or suffocated rather than succumbing to arrows or weapons. Troops in the rear fled rather than charging into this carnage. In addition to many captured, several leading French noblemen were killed. The English suffered far fewer casualties, the leading victims being the king's cousin, Duke Edward of York (elder brother of the Earl of Cambridge executed after the Southampton Plot), and the Earl of Suffolk.

Considering the battle won, Henry had prisoners rounded up, while his men began to remove their helmets and leave their positions. Then the Duke of Brabant arrived, very late. Knowing he could not respond to a new attack, Henry ordered the prisoners killed. Several were in a house to which the English set fire, others were slain with weapons. None of the sources criticise this action, whatever feelings it might arouse in the twenty-first century, and it was fully in keeping with contemporary standards of warfare. Henry would not be cheated of his victory. The extent of this 'massacre' has been exaggerated; probably only around half of some 2000 captives were killed, at most, as Henry brought many back to England, and the killing stopped when it was realised that the French posed no threat. Nevertheless, the act has been controversial and 'the only "black mark" against the king which has had any real chance of sticking'.[13] Today it seems brutal and would probably count as a war crime, but in the fifteenth century it was considered perfectly acceptable, as keeping the prisoners alive could have endangered his men while they faced a new attack. That said, to kill unarmed men in cold blood was against Christian teaching of the time, so however justified by contemporary military conventions, it was highly questionable from a man who made so much of his Christian piety.

The mythical status of the battle is demonstrated by the way the name was rapidly anglicised, Azincourt becoming Agincourt. It stands with Hastings and Bosworth as the most famous of medieval English battles, and the amount written about those two is dwarfed by the avalanche of literature on Agincourt. It is Henry's greatest achievement, the one thing most people are likely to remember, and is deeply ingrained into English national consciousness. At the time, it did not really achieve much, at least in the short term. It certainly did not have the decisive impact of the Battle of Poitiers (1356), where the capture of the French king and several nobles severely weakened the French position, although had the French won, none of Henry's future successes would have been possible. The main success of Agincourt was to allow Henry to exploit the campaign for full propaganda effect at home, which was done shamelessly by the chancellor when parliament opened (with Henry still in France) on 4 November. Parliament lasted only nine days and happily granted him more taxes. On 23 November, having met Archbishop Chichele at Canterbury and attended a thanksgiving service in the cathedral on the way, Henry made a triumphant entrance into London, accompanied by extravagant pageantry. He made considerable capital out of what he portrayed as the divine favour Agincourt represented.

God did not seem to be smiling on the English remaining in France in the early months of 1416. The French were making concerted efforts to retake Harfleur, which by April included a naval blockade which reduced the English captain, the Earl of Dorset, to despair. As an English enclave, Harfleur was hugely vulnerable to French pressure, not least because of the problem of supplies. Henry had stated his intention of returning to France, but in May he received Sigismund of Luxembourg in England. The King of the Germans hoped to bring England and France to peace in order to improve the chances of ending the papal schism. Prior to England, he had visited Paris, although with mixed success, and Henry ensured he received a welcome from suitable magnates at key points along his route to London. Sigismund was joined at the end of the month by Count William of Holland, Zealand and Hainault, but their suggestion that Harfleur be handed over to the German king as guardian was unacceptable to both England and France. Instead, Sigismund agreed an alliance with Henry at Canterbury on 15 August. Agincourt had considerably improved Henry's international standing, although Sigismund's four-month visit was extremely expensive for the English exchequer.

The alliance was also problematic for Sigismund. In 1414, he had successfully convened the Council of Constance, intending to succeed where the 1409 Council of Pisa had failed in ending the Great Schism, begun in 1378 with the election of two Popes, based in Rome and Avignon. Each time one of these rivals died, a successor was elected by that camp. The Council of Pisa deposed Gregory XII and Benedict XIII, and elected Alexander V. Gregory and Benedict refused to accept this, and when Alexander died in 1410 he was replaced by a man who took the name John XXIII. When Sigismund convened the Council of Constance, he did so to resolve the problem that there were now three simultaneous Popes. Henry V duly sent a suitably learned delegation to represent England, which had generally backed the Roman Pope (Avignon being in France and its antipope seen as a French puppet). Sigismund's visit to France and England in 1416 aimed to focus French and English attention on this resolution. The alliance with England naturally created problems with the French delegation. Nevertheless, by 1417 the Council had managed to remove all three Popes. While Sigismund wanted reform before a papal election, Henry saw the dangers in a long delay and risked his alliance (which never produced many tangible benefits in any case) by supporting the case for an election. Martin V, an Italian acceptable to all sides, was duly elected in November. While attention in 1414–17 tends to focus on Henry's exploits in France, it is important to remember that he was closely involved in the process at Constance, choosing episcopal ambassadors from the start, staying informed, and issuing instructions to the English delegation to break the deadlock in the summer of 1417. It is easy to forget that Henry took England's place in the universal Church seriously, even while vigorously maintaining the rights of the Crown over appointments, and this was a significant part of his religious outlook.

On the same day as the Treaty of Canterbury was sealed, 15 August 1416, the king's brother John, Duke of Bedford won an emphatic naval victory in the Battle of the Seine. The crushing English victory in the mouth of the river saved Harfleur and ended French hopes of recapturing the town. Henry wanted to launch a new campaign in France, but first he crossed to Calais, where Sigismund brokered an agreement between the English king and Duke John of Burgundy. Once Henry was back across the Channel, Chancellor Henry Beaufort successfully persuaded the parliament of October–November 1416 to endorse the next French mission, the Commons granting another subsidy. The convocations of both Canterbury and York were equally generous with clerical grants. There were strong anti-French sentiments, with parliament confirming the alliance with Sigismund. However, there were some concerns about the debts from previous campaigns and the king had to make strategic concessions. At the end of the session Thomas Beaufort, who had undertaken the defence of Harfleur so energetically as its captain, was elevated from Earl of Dorset to Duke of Exeter.

Not everyone was as ready to pay for the king's wars. Cheshire, a county palatine with special governance arrangements and not represented in parliament, saw a degree of unrest in late 1416, with considerable resistance to the tax burden agreed at a special meeting on behalf of the county.[14] The king embarked on a public relations exercise to encourage support, making particular use of his portrayal of Agincourt as a God-given victory. From the very start, at Henry's instigation, the memory of the battle was turned into both a religious and national triumph, the myth being consciously created from the beginning by the victor himself. The feast of Saints Crispin and Crispinian was linked to the battle in the prayers for 25 October, a connection immortalised by Shakespeare. Further religious overtones came when Henry timed his 1417 crossing, with a slightly smaller force of 10,000, to land in Normandy (at the mouth of the River Touques) on 1 August. This was the feast of St Peter *ad Vincula* (in Chains), commemorating the Biblical passage in Acts 12 where an angel frees Peter from King Herod's prison. Henry's message was that like God's angel, he was coming to free the Normans (Peter) from the captivity of the French (Herod). No other king of England ever presented himself in such messianic terms, yet it was language and symbolism like this which lay at the heart of Henry's kingship. For him, this was almost a holy war, a belief that God had made him his agent to vanquish the French.

In practical terms, the 1417 campaign aimed to (re)capture the duchy of Normandy, lost by King John in 1204. Henry evoked the shared Anglo-Norman past of 1066–1204, playing on Norman mistrust of government from Paris. However, it is entirely possible that even at this early stage, his eyes were on a much greater prize: the French crown. After landing, he besieged Caen and captured it within two weeks, the citizens swiftly realising (after a heavy battering of the walls) that they would get no help from the French government. He began a march south, capturing places along the route, and impressing the parliament of November 1417 enough to grant him yet more taxes. That same month, if not earlier, Henry publicly began to call himself Duke of Normandy. Over the following months, he made good his title. After Falaise fell in February 1418, he felt confident enough to send his brothers, Clarence and Gloucester, in different directions with portions of the army, to speed up the conquest. Gloucester faced most trouble with his five-month siege of Cherbourg, which finally fell in September. Meanwhile, at the end of July 1418, Henry besieged Rouen.

The siege lasted six months. Henry was acutely aware of Rouen's importance; it would be the largest place to fall to a successful siege in the entire Hundred Years' War. Wishing to avoid destructive bombardment, the king opted to starve the city into submission, refusing to allow the women and children to leave. French efforts to organise a relief force were obstructed by renewed infighting. Rouen surrendered in January 1419, and Henry appeared formally as Duke of Normandy in the Norman capital; ever alert to religious symbolism, his appearance in ducal robes took place on the feast of Candlemas, 2 February. Except for Mont Saint-Michel, the rest of Normandy then fell easily into his hands.

The French now had to try to reach accommodation with Henry despite their divisions. After a period of uneasy peace between Armagnac and Burgundian factions, in May 1418 John the Fearless had seized Paris, taking control of the king and queen. Dauphin Charles had fled south. Wanting to keep the two sides divided, and avoid the risk a united France would pose, Henry negotiated with both the Burgundian government and the Armagnac opposition, and began doing so even before Rouen fell. He started with the Armagnacs, negotiations with the dauphin taking place at Alençon in October 1418. Henry aimed high, but emerged only with a truce. Discussions with the Burgundians followed at Pont-de-l'Arche in November. Negotiations stalled, but it is unlikely Henry expected anything else; he was toying with a divided enemy.

By the time negotiations resumed with the Burgundians at Meulan in May–June 1419, Henry was in an even stronger position, Normandy now his. This time, the French offered full enforcement of the Treaty of Brétigny, Normandy, and the hand of Charles VI's 18-year-old daughter, Catherine, with a dowry of a million écus. Catherine was at Meulan, the first time Henry set eyes on her, but marriage to her had been the thread running constantly through all his demands since 1413. King Charles and Queen Isabeau were also present. The negotiations at Meulan were undertaken in good faith, Catherine's presence suggesting that the French were serious about her engagement to Henry. However, the French suddenly cooled, and it turned out the dauphin and John the Fearless had been conducting parallel discussions, reaching an agreement at Pouilly-le-Fort on 11 July. Henry responded by resuming hostilities and making towards Paris. He took Pontoise and Gisors, and by mid-August was within sight of the capital. Whether he could have taken the city is highly doubtful, but the question soon became irrelevant.

John the Fearless and the dauphin had arranged a meeting on the bridge over the Seine at Montereau, fifty miles south-east of Paris, on 10 September 1419. When the duke walked onto the bridge, one of the dauphin's men assassinated him, vengeance for the duke's own assassination of the Duke of Orléans in 1407. Whether the 16-year-old dauphin was involved is unclear, but the murder of the Duke of Burgundy tore apart the fragile accord between Armagnacs and Burgundians. The bitter enmity between the two sides was exposed, and Henry no longer faced a united foe. The Burgundians were compelled to make an alliance with the English. It soon became clear that the events in Montereau had cleared the path for Henry V of England to become heir to the kingdom of France.

Philip the Good, the new Duke of Burgundy (1419-67), was in Lille. Charles VI and his wife were in Troyes, where Duke John had placed them. Most royal councillors were in Paris, and supported by the pro-Burgundian Parisians, they approached Henry to seek a truce. Henry's ambassadors asserted their king's right to the throne of France, in a carefully-worded statement to reassure the French that he would never subject the French Crown or kingdom to his English Crown. Marriage to Catherine remained a condition. The royal council responded that these demands were different to the ones made in July, but for Henry, the circumstances had changed significantly. He wanted to act quickly, and nuanced his plan so that Charles VI would remain king for the rest of his life, Henry then succeeding him as heir, disinheriting the dauphin. Diplomats shuttled between Philip in Lille, Charles in Troyes, and Paris.

For Philip, avenging his father's death and receiving English military support were paramount, so he agreed to the terms at Arras on 2 December. Henry sent envoys to persuade the French king and queen, and Philip went to Troyes in March 1420. The Earl of Warwick headed the final negotiation party for the English, and the Treaty of Troyes was agreed on 9 April. The terms were essentially those Henry had demanded, but with compromises. Charles would remain king until his death, being succeeded by Henry. The realms of England and France were to be kept separate. Normandy would remain Henry's until he became French king, then be reintegrated into France. Burgundian lands in Normandy were to be restored. Ever the master of the theatrical, Henry made his way, on 8 May, from Pontoise to Saint-Denis, the abbey north of Paris where the kings of France were buried. From there, he journeyed to Troyes. The Treaty of Troyes was sealed on 21 May 1420, with a ceremony in the cathedral in which Charles formally recognised Henry as his heir. The same day, Catherine and Henry were betrothed. They were married on 2 June in St John's Church in Troyes.

Henry also became regent of France. With his new wife, Duke Philip and King Charles, he went to Burgundy to besiege Sens, a city in the dauphin's hands.

It quickly fell, as (with more resistance) did Montereau, allowing the recovery of John the Fearless' hastily buried body, which was taken for formal burial in Dijon, Burgundy's capital. Melun was next, although it held out against a siege involving heavy use of cannon until November. The Treaty of Troyes had certainly not been universally accepted by Frenchmen, and the dauphin had escaped south. War continued, although it was a peculiar kind of civil war with Henry's new status. On 1 December 1420, Advent Sunday, Charles and Henry ceremonially entered Paris together, followed by Clarence and Bedford, Henry's brothers. A procession replete with symbolism and pageantry ended in Notre-Dame. The next day, Isabeau and Catherine entered Paris. The French Estates General ratified the Treaty of Troyes in Paris on 6 December. On 23 December, a session of the *parlement* of Paris (France's highest court) formally disinherited the dauphin. While Henry largely acted in Charles' name or alongside Charles, the French king's continuing mental health problems meant Henry did sometimes act alone. He was an active regent of France, who intervened fully in government and appointments.

With his two older brothers with him in France, Henry's youngest brother, Humphrey, Duke of Gloucester, had been left as keeper of the realm in England, and he was finding that the English were not responding to the Treaty of Troyes with unalloyed delight. Before his departures for France in 1415 and 1417, the king had justified his wars with a combination of quasi-crusading religious language and xenophobia. This played nicely to the xenophobic tendencies of the English, the Commons and clergy granting him notably generous taxes. Now, post-Troyes, the English were suddenly being asked to see the French as friends and share their king. They wanted, in reverse, exactly the same assurances that Henry had given the French – that England would never be subjected to a king of France or French rule, and that its independence and customs would be fully maintained. The Commons submitted this request to Gloucester among its petitions, and also asked the duke to 'request, encourage and persuade' the king and queen 'to return and come back to this kingdom within a very short space of time [...] for the comfort, relief and support of the aforesaid commons'.[15] Not only did they not want to share their king, they wanted him back home. The mood of the Commons meant that Gloucester made no attempt to have parliament ratify the Treaty of Troyes in the assembly, preferring to wait until Henry was back in person, and there was no request for taxation.

Aside from resentment that Henry had now been abroad for more than three years, there was also a general sense of weariness. Recruiting troops had proved increasingly difficult in 1419–20. Heavy taxation since 1415 had taken its toll, and in 1419 the king had resorted to the dubious and distinctly unchivalrous tactic of having his stepmother, Henry IV's widow Joan, charged with witchcraft so he could take her dowry and estates. As often happened when the king was overseas for a lengthy period, law and order started to break down. While the English administrative system was remarkably resilient and capable of functioning through royal absences, protracted absences caused resentment; England was starting to look like little more than a source of funding for Henry's ambitions in France.

Officials could not substitute for the impact of the king's personal presence, nor take his place as the fount of justice. It didn't help that Henry was a micromanager and insisted on most things being referred to him across the Channel, causing delays. Despite feeling he had much to which to attend in France, he knew he needed to return to England. Henry and Catherine arrived at Dover on 1 February 1421.

Catherine was crowned Queen of England in Westminster Abbey on 23 February, although her husband was absent on tour. He first travelled from St Albans to Bristol, Hereford and Shrewsbury. The newly-crowned Catherine joined him at Kenilworth Castle, one of his favourite places, in March. It is likely that this reunion saw the conception of their son, before king and queen went to Leicester, Coventry, back to Leicester for Easter, Nottingham and Pontefract, the castle where the Duke of Orléans was imprisoned. Henry then went on a mini pilgrimage by himself to the shrines at Beverley and Bridlington, before making his way via York, Newark, King's Lynn and Walsingham (another shrine) to Windsor. After a long absence, this was a chance to show himself, to hear petitions, to give alms and to raise money.

Henry's mind remained focussed on France and he continued his cross-Channel micromanagement in reverse. His brother, Thomas of Clarence, was killed in a skirmish in Anjou on 22 March 1421. Henry had lost a brother, while in his absence the English had lost in France for the first time since he began his campaigns; he would need and want to return soon. When parliament met in May, the Treaty of Troyes was finally ratified, although Henry avoided requesting a tax; even a king so notoriously successful at squeezing taxes from the Commons knew he had no chance of persuading them to agree to a peacetime tax with no threat to England. These formalities completed, he left England again after scarcely four months. As it turned out, he would return in a coffin. Before leaving Dover, he made his will. Landing at Calais on 10 June, he went to Paris, then campaigned down to Orléans, assisted the Duke of Burgundy's siege of Chartres, and turned his attention to Meaux. This town was strongly fortified and the siege lasted from October 1421 to May 1422. Such stubbornness unleashed Henry's rage, and after submission the defenders were executed or sent to English and Welsh prisons. Back in England, Catherine gave birth to a son, the future Henry VI, at Windsor on 6 December 1421. With an heir now making the succession a little more secure, and bringing several wavering French towns onside, the queen travelled to France in May 1422, where she joined her husband in Paris at the end of the month. Everything seemed perfect for the happy couple's future.

Yet there were murmurings of discontent in French sources at the lavishness of the English court and the way in which Henry was so obviously usurping Charles VI's authority. Things were not all rosy back in England, since Henry could not personally direct a law and order campaign, as he had in 1413–14. There were concerns at the efforts of Henry and his officials to extend the scope of treason beyond the bounds set down in Edward III's 1352 Statue of Treasons, resistance to which led to machinations to circumvent due process by the government.[16] While Henry had successfully managed 'parliaments and convocations to effect one of the most intense bouts of taxation experienced in England over the course of the Hundred Years War',[17] by 1422 parliament was very much of the mind that England should not be paying for the king's efforts to make good his French title. This was the position they maintained in the following reign.

When the joint English and French courts reached Senlis on 12 June, it was clear that Henry was not well. By early July, Henry was obviously and seriously ill, and the symptoms of his intestinal condition (possibly dysentery picked up in the unsanitary conditions of the siege at Meaux) grew worse over the following weeks. When he arrived at Vincennes Castle, just east of Paris, on 13 August, he was dying. On 26 August, he made a codicil to his will, entrusting his son and heir to his youngest brother, Duke Humphrey of Gloucester, although the infant's education was to be overseen by the loyal Duke of Exeter. Instructions were given to those around his deathbed, who included his other surviving brother, Duke John of Bedford. On 31 August 1422, at the age of 35, Henry V died at Vincennes. His entrails were removed and buried at Saint-Maur-des-Fossés, and his body taken in procession to Saint-Denis, Rouen and finally Calais. After crossing the Channel to land at Dover, the funeral procession made its way via Canterbury to Southwark, where it arrived on 5 November. The king's coffin was taken to London and St Paul's, then on 6 November to Westminster Abbey. On the 7th, the funeral took place ahead of Henry's burial near the shrine of Edward the Confessor. His chantry chapel was only built in the 1430s, and his effigy was far less successful than the king it represented. The silver on it was stolen in the sixteenth century, then at some stage its hands and head also vanished; those seen today are 1970s replicas.[18]

Henry's legacy was at best problematic, at worst disastrous. Charles VI outlived his son-in-law by less than two months, dying on 21 October 1422. Henry VI of England theoretically became King of France too. Bedford effectively ruled France until his death in 1435, making some progress until the siege of Orléans was lifted in 1429 by Joan of Arc. Charles VII, the dauphin whom Henry V had disinherited, began to conquer back territory and was crowned at Reims on 17 July 1429. In response, Henry VI was crowned King of England on 6 November, then King of France on 16 December 1431, but notably in Notre-Dame de Paris rather than the traditional coronation church, Reims Cathedral. Even once Joan of Arc had been burned at the stake for heresy in 1431 (123 of the 131 clerics who tried and condemned her were French), Charles' resurgence continued, and after Bedford's death the tide flowed resolutely against the English. By 1453, the Hundred Years' War was lost and the English retained only Calais. The defeat came amid a turbulent atmosphere in England, Henry VI having proved inept as king, and became a major cause of the Wars of the Roses.

There is one final comment to be made about Henry, which suggests at best he was a less perfect man than he desired people to believe, at worst that he was deeply egocentric showman. In the will he made at Dover, he endowed a chantry chapel where he intended three Masses a day to be said in perpetuity, as well as paying for an astonishing 20,000 requiem Masses for his soul; 'No one else in medieval England ever thought it necessary to invest so heavily in the purchase of paradise'.[19] Amidst this and all the provisions he made at Vincennes as he lay dying, and the elaborate plans for his own body and soul, he forgot his queen. Catherine, the woman he had been so desperate to marry, was not part of his future vision in this life or the next. She went on to marry Owen Tudor, through their son Edmund becoming grandmother to Henry VII. The Queen Mother died in 1437 and was not buried with her first husband, but instead in front of the Lady Chapel altar in Westminster Abbey. When the Lady Chapel was demolished to build her grandson's replacement, where he was to be buried, her corpse had to be moved. It was placed, or more accurately dumped, in her husband's chapel, in an entirely inadequate coffin of loose planks. This 'temporary' arrangement lasted nearly three centuries, and in a grotesque incident in 1669, Samuel Pepys records how he kissed the 232-year-old corpse. It was clearly something of a tourist attraction and a combination of decay, morbid souvenir hunting and vandalism meant that by the time the Dean of Westminster had it reburied in a recently renovated vault, Catherine's body was in a terrible state. Not until 1878 was what was left of her mortal remains interred beneath a new tomb altar in her husband's chapel. One senses Henry would have cared little for these posthumous tribulations of his queen. In his short reign, it had always been about his reputation and memory. Others were only accessories to that.

Henry through the Centuries

English views of Henry V were positive from the very beginning, not surprising for a 'master of the art of political propaganda' who from his accession 'embarked on a deliberate stratagem of image-creation'.[20] The large number of sources reflect the image Henry wanted to portray of himself, the pious Christian king serving as God's instrument. In this 'glorified one-dimensional image of the king',[21] they focus on his suppression of Lollardy and defence of religious orthodoxy, and the justice of his campaign in France as proved by its results. If there were no official historians of the reign, Henry had no need of them, for the chroniclers shamelessly told the story he desired they tell, with plenty of embellishments to make him seem even more heroic. Indeed, evidence from a collection of sermons preserved in the Bodleian Library has the preacher present Henry as a knightly Christ-like figure, saviour of both the Church and England.[22] That said, it is worth remembering John Matusiak's point that successful propaganda has to 'convince in order to be worthwhile', which is only possible if 'it accords, at least partially, with the preconceptions of those to whom it is addressed'.[23]

Arguably the most valuable source for the first half of the reign is the *Gesta Henrici Quinti* (*Deeds of Henry the Fifth*). While anonymous, it is clearly the work of a clerical member of the court, and it can be confidently dated to a period between November 1416 and July 1417. It opens with a sentence about the coronation of the 'most serene prince, the King of England and France and lord of Ireland'. The next sentence is adulatory.

> When, young in years but old in experience, he began his reign, like the true elect of God savouring the things that are above, he applied his mind with all devotion to encompass what could promote the honour of God, the extension of the Church, the deliverance of his country, and the peace and tranquillity of kingdoms.

The work ends looking forward to Henry's 1417 campaign, in a hope that 'the two swords, the sword of the French and the sword of England, may return to the rightful government of a single ruler', all set in the context of a lengthy prayer.[24] In between, Henry is a combination of saint and warrior, perfectly combined into the ideal of kingship. Even the St Albans monk, Thomas Walsingham, not averse to acerbic attacks on kings, was driven to adoring praise after Henry's death.

> He did not leave his like on earth among Christian princes [...] He had a pious mind and his words were few and well-judged. Far-sighted in his planning and shrewd in judgement, he showed modesty in his bearing and magnanimity. He worked unceasingly, frequently went on pilgrimage and was a generous alms-giver. He was a devout Christian and supported and honoured the ministers and servants of the church. He was also a distinguished and fortunate leader in war, who in all his battles always came off the victor. His construction of new buildings and his foundation of monasteries were on a magnificent scale. He was a munificent giver of presents, and in all matters he hunted down and fought against the enemies of faith and the church.[25]

It is unlikely Henry could have improved on this obituary had he written it himself. What is more extraordinary is that in a country where there was 'virtually no tradition of royal biography', beyond the pen portraits in the chronicles, Henry was 'honoured with such an abundance of literature'.[26] Notably, these all focussed on Henry as king; discussion of any troublesome period of youth would have detracted from the image of perfection. In addition to the *Gesta* and an obtuse verse work by Thomas Elmham, both written during Henry's lifetime, there was a further laudatory work by Tito Livio (or Titus Livius), the *Vita Henrici Quinti* (*Life of Henry the Fifth*). This was commissioned in the late 1430s by Duke Humphrey of Gloucester, Henry's lone surviving brother after the death of Bedford in 1435. Gloucester commissioned Livio to write the work after Henry VI had assumed control of government in 1437. The duke effectively led the opposition to his nephew, and Livio's piece (while also praising Gloucester's own courage and part in Henry V's successes) was intended as a reminder of the glory days of the 1410s and an encouragement to the king to emulate his father in resuming hostilities in France. The *Vita*, 'even more than earlier lives, does seem to have been an overtly propagandist work', heavily coloured by Gloucester's memories and motivations two decades after the events described.[27] While these works, and several other largely derivative ones from later in the century (although a recent argument suggests one work long believed derivative, the anonymous *Vita et Gesta Henrici Quinti*, was actually written slightly earlier than and was plagiarised by Livio[28]) were all in Latin, similar views of Henry can be found in works written in English, such as the Brut chronicle and the closely related London chronicles. The quasi-hagiographical approach was not restricted to clerical or court circles.

Naturally enough, French views of Henry during the fifteenth century were somewhat different. There was respect for his military valour and achievements, but also criticism and outright hostility.[29] Views range from the relatively favourable monk of Saint-Denis to the hostile, bitter account of Jean Juvénal des Ursins, a cleric in the service of Charles VII who was later Bishop of Beauvais and Archbishop of Reims. If nearly all respect his courage and abilities as a warrior, even the favourable comment on his ruthlessness. This is a reminder that the idea of Henry as some Christ-like saviour of France, so willingly parroted by the English sources, originated with the king himself and was not how the French saw matters.

The arrival of the Tudors saw Henry's English reputation undiminished. France remained the traditional and greatest foe, so Henry V's victory over the French was celebrated alongside his embodiment of English knightly virtue. This was especially true of the early reign of Henry VIII, who consciously modelled himself on his ancestor and even launched his own invasion of France in 1513. Tudor writing about Henry V drew heavily on the fifteenth-century texts, with the first life in English (completed in 1514) essentially a translation of Tito Livio. So entrenched was Henry's positive reputation that despite being the most orthodox Roman Catholic and ostentatiously pious of medieval kings, Protestant historians in the Reformation era made no serious attempt to remove him from his pedestal. The exception was John Foxe, who in the second edition of his *Book of Martyrs* (1570) was critical of Henry's suppression of Lollards and treatment of heretics, which he viewed (reversing the conventional medieval understanding) as an attack on the true Church. For Foxe, Henry's death at a young age and after a reign of only nine years, and from illness rather than heroically in battle, was divine punishment for this persecution. Yet this made little difference to Henry's popularity; that 'Henry's reputation could withstand these cultural and intellectual reversals is testament to the endurance of happy memories in the life of a nation'.[30]

Shakespeare was to have an enormous impact on subsequent historical writing as well as popular thought about Henry, and even today historians struggle to break free from his spell. There was little in the way of new approaches or ideas in the seventeenth century, as writers contentedly echoed the praise of the fifteenth and sixteenth centuries. The start of the eighteenth century brought the first work we might recognise as a biography of Henry in the modern sense. Thomas Goodwin opened by evoking the mood of England on Henry's accession, a people 'uncertain whether the young King would be a publick Blessing or Calamity to the Nation', drawing attention to the 'Violences of his Youth' and the 'wild Sallies and Disorders'.[31] Here was Shakespeare's wild Prince Harry metamorphosing into responsible King Henry. However, Goodwin's *History of the Reign of Henry the Fifth* (1704) made unusually wide use of both published and unpublished material, and for all the problems it may pose today, is justly considered a genuine attempt to write the history of the reign from research. If Henry still emerged as a hero, it was not because Goodwin uncritically repeated the work of others.[32]

If the overwhelming image of the king remained positive, so positive that few bothered to write about him except in broader works, discordant notes began to creep in. Whereas the prevailing view, formulated and promoted by Henry himself and repeated ever since, was that the king had been forced to wage war on France because they denied him his just rights, from the eighteenth century dissident voices began to question this narrative of altruism and justice. Perhaps unsurprisingly, the first of these was a Frenchman, the exiled Huguenot Paul de Rapin. In an account which praises the king highly, he nevertheless notes that the conquest of France was 'not so wonderful, as it appears, when abstracted from all its Circumstances'. The task was made much easier, Rapin argues, by the divisions among the French. For that reason, he rated Edward III's achievements more highly, since 'Edward had to deal with all France united against him, and the difficulties he encountered in his Conquests, were incomparably greater, and required an abler Head to surmount them, than those which opposed the Progress of Henry V'.[33] David Hume likewise observed that the 'civil disorders of France [...] opened a full career to his ambition'.[34] If no one challenged Henry's military genius (as it was frequently termed), there was a small but increasing tendency to temper it with this reminder of the fortunate circumstances upon which he capitalised. There was also a growing sense that Henry was an aggressor rather than the wronged party denied his rights. Similar approaches can be found through to the end of the nineteenth century, when J. R. Green argued that Edward III 'had been forced into the struggle against his will by the ceaseless attacks of France, and his claim of the crown was but an afterthought to secure the alliance of Flanders', whereas Henry V's war 'was in fact an aggression on the part of a nation tempted by the helplessness of its opponent and galled by the memory of former defeat'. Aggressor Henry may have been, but Green's summing up of the king was still lyrically positive.[35]

Any challenge to Henry's greatness was dismissed by Victorian constitutional historians, led by William Stubbs, who saw Henry as 'a king acting throughout his reign in the closest harmony with his parliament, putting himself forward as the first man of a nation fairly at one with itself on all political questions, a leader in heart and soul worthy of England, and crowning his leadership with ample signal successes'. Stubbs did address criticisms of Henry for 'a great war, which according to modern ideas was without justification in its origin and continuance, and which resulted in an exhaustion from which the nation did not revive for a century', but only to dismiss them as an anachronistic standard by which to judge a man the bishop viewed as 'one of the greatest and purest characters in English history, a figure not unworthy to be placed by the side of Edward I'.[36] Although entertaining some doubts about the legitimacy and cost of Henry's French claims,

Charles Kingsford's *Henry V: The Typical Medieval Hero* (1901) followed very much in this tradition of praise verging on hero-worship.

An exhaustive (and exhausting) survey of the reign was begun by James Hamilton Wylie, who had already produced a similarly overdetailed, meandering four volumes on Henry IV. Wylie died in 1914, while the second volume was in proof stage, and the third was published fifteen years later by William Templeton Waugh. Unfortunately, the two authors were not in accord when it came to their views of Henry's character. Insofar as it is possible to deduce Wylie's views from the voluminously tedious stream of little details, he was no fan of a king he judged deceitful and lucky. Waugh, by contrast, concluded that Henry was 'indisputably the greatest Englishman of his day' and when compared to Charles VI, King Sigismund, and Dukes John and Philip of Burgundy, 'he towers above them all – more forceful in arms, more discreet in council, more steadfast in purpose, and, with all his imperfections, more honourable in life'.[37]

While Henry V's popular reputation remained high through the twentieth century, there was some divergence in views and the first critical judgements emerged, more confidently after the Second World War. Since the end of the Napoleonic Wars, France had turned from archenemy into ally alongside whom the United Kingdom had fought in two world wars. The horror of those two conflicts made war seem anything but glorious and worthy of celebration. Henry, a man whose reputation was built on military aggression against France, was a much more complicated hero in an anti-war era where the French were friends. For insular English nationalists, this remained the source of his appeal, but as the nationalist terrors unleashed in the first half of the twentieth century made many Europeans far more suspicious of nationalism and related ideologies, so Henry ceased to be so universally revered. Religion too became increasingly problematic as the twentieth century wore on. While Henry's piety was no issue, his persecution of Lollards was uncomfortable in an age of religious tolerance, where such intolerant zeal was anathema. His quasi-messianic approach to his invasion of France was a definite source of unease in the post-Nazi Western Europe of the Iron Curtain era, which had grown deeply suspicious of nationalist, messianic figures cloaking their territorial ambitions in the language of just rights. Perhaps unsurprisingly, French historians were often among the most critical.

Yet Englishmen were becoming critical too. John Harvey's eccentric sketch presents Henry as 'a true child of his age, partaking in a full measure of the grotesque qualities that cast a wan and flickering light upon the scene'. Harvey explained that he 'dwelt upon the miseries of the fifteenth century and the crimes of Henry V because they point the moral that even the best of men and kings can be corrupted by the spirit of their age'. He looks beyond the 'dark and horrifying aspects of his character' to some of the achievements, but this language – 'crimes', 'dark and horrifying' – points towards a very different approach to Henry's war record in France.[38] The tension was between recognising that acts of violence and cruelty which would be twentieth century war crimes were an accepted part of medieval life, and avoiding celebrating those who perpetrated them in purely heroic terms.

In the thirty or so years after Harvey, academic historians were often ambivalent, recognising Henry's piety, leadership and military skill, but equally dubious about the justice and aims of his French war, and about his zeal and intolerance. Surprisingly, although Henry continued high in popular esteem, popular historians of the 1960s and 1970s were notably more negative than academic ones. Listing Henry's 'formidable catalogue of achievement', Harold F. Hutchison continued, 'it is legitimate to inquire whether all of this achievement was really worth while or even a success'. Noting that 'on his deathbed Henry never gave a thought to his queen', Hutchison argues that in 'every ceremonial occasion of his life, Henry remained cold and aloof [...] his character seems just as chilly as his face'. Referring to the legend developed through the Tudor century, the ultimate verdict is brutal but ambivalent: 'It is sad that history must also record the cold, priggish, ruthless efficiency of the father of that legend, the barrenness of his glory and the futility of his achievement, yet it cannot forbear tribute to an organizing genius who was a hero to his own day, an upholder of the hard logic of implacably justice, and a heroic myth for generations to come'.[39] Seeing him as 'the product of his times', Peter Earle is even more ambiguous: 'If he was a hypocrite he was a very successful one, for he has succeeded in fooling not only his contemporaries but also our greatest playwright and many modern historians'.[40]

Such ambiguity was less prevalent elsewhere. In a biography of John the Fearless, Richard Vaughan wrote of the 'perfidious Henry V', who with King Sigismund and John himself was one of 'the three champion double-crossers of the age'. In the subsequent biography of John's heir, Philip the Good, Vaughan saw Henry as 'ambitious and, above all, a ruthless soldier'.[41] By contrast, Sir Winston Churchill, in a chapter tellingly entitled 'The Empire of Henry V', saw a reign in which a 'gleam of splendour falls across the dark, troubled story of medieval England', with a man 'more deeply loved by his subjects of all classed than any King has been in England'.[42] (It is unclear on what Churchill based this assertion.) The influential historian K. B. McFarlane gave a famous, almost hagiographical verdict, but not before undergoing a Damascene conversion worthy of Shakespeare's Prince Hal. In 1936, McFarlane saw Henry as misguided and the begetter of a poisoned legacy: 'It is the tragedy of his reign that he gave a wrong direction to national aspirations which he did so much to stimulate, that he led his people in pursuit of the chimera of foreign conquest, an adventure from which they recoiled exhausted and embittered after more than thirty years of useless sacrifice'.[43] However, in a lecture delivered in 1954 (but not published until 1972), McFarlane hyperbolically proclaimed Henry 'the greatest man that ever ruled England'.[44] Intriguingly, at a similar time his fellow Oxford scholar, E. F. Jacob, shifted in the opposite direction. From a largely positive, admiring portrait in 1947, by the time he published his volume in the *Oxford History of England* in 1961, Jacob was much more ambiguous about Henry's merits, achievements and legacy, judging him 'an adventurer, not a statesman', one who 'bound his country to a settlement which quickly became out of date'.[45]

McFarlane's lectures were prepared posthumously for publication by another Oxford don, G. L. Harriss, who would have agreed wholeheartedly with the conclusion McFarlane ultimately reached. In 1985, Harriss edited and contributed several essays to a volume entitled *Henry V: The Practice of Kingship*. His own contributions leave little doubt that he considered Henry the greatest of medieval kings, the perfect embodiment of medieval kingship; there are saints' lives which are less positive about their subject. More cautious notes were sounded in the essays by Christopher Allmand and Maurice Keen. Allmand concluded equivocally about Henry's achievements that it 'would be left to future and far-distant generations to ask whether it had all been worthwhile'. Keen ended by observing that Henry had 'high ambitions and great gifts; it is not quite so clear that he was the kind of man who could think through to the end where these were leading him'. Two decades later, Harriss toned down the adulation, but he never lost his admiration for the king. Another contributor to the 1985 volume, Edward Powell, expanded his essay into a monograph about criminal justice under Henry V. Examining the subject in detail, it follows firmly in the tradition of praising the king: 'No king came closer to embodying the contemporary ideal of the just king than Henry V', whose 'success in the administration of justice must rank with his greatest achievements'.[46]

Others in the 1980s were far less appreciative of Henry. In a biography which, as the title (*Henry V as Warlord*) indicates, focuses on the king's military exploits, Desmond Seward was scathing. He opined that the 'horror unleashed by him was unforgivable, and also unforgettable', arguing that even in 'the midst of all his hero worship Shakespeare somehow discerns the sheer callous cruelty of the king'. In the end, 'for all his brilliance, Henry V's ambition ended by bankrupting and discrediting his son, and ruining his dynasty'. Seward's main charge is that it was Henry who 'dug a chasm between French and English, a chasm which has grown deeper down the centuries'.[47] Indeed, while much more complimentary of Henry's abilities, Charles VI's biographer observed that the core problem was that Henry was an Englishman who didn't understand how to be king in France.

> King Henry was king of England. A good king, admittedly. For the English. In France, he was a stranger. And despite the fine promises and his excellent administration, he did not treat the French as he should, 'in the way of France'.[48]

In a study focussed on the 1415 Southampton Plot, but which ranged considerably more widely, T. B. Pugh argued that the risks Henry 'took in the pursuit of his French ambitions were too great and the burdens involved for Englishmen were too heavy to be endured for long'. Pugh took aim at Henry's reputation for justice, noting the 'greed and rapacity' that caused him to mistreat his stepmother and other widows. 'It is', he wrote, 'indeniable [*sic*] that Henry V's personal character was cold and singularly lacking in generosity'. Ultimately, despite being 'more talented than any of his predecessors on the English throne since Henry II', 'Henry V was a man of limited vision and outlook'.[49]

1992 saw the standard academic life of the king published by Christopher Allmand in the English Monarchs series. Allmand had already authored a monograph on Lancastrian Normandy, and his main work was on Henry as warrior. While the first part of the volume is chronological, it does skip a little confusingly through Henry's years as Prince of Wales, and the thematic second half is only likely to appeal to scholars of the reign. A sober, considered biography, it is nevertheless approving. Considerable stress is laid in the idea that Henry was pursuing what he saw as his rights in France rather than personal ambitions, as Allmand tries to make the case that the motivations were too complex to be readily dismissed. He recognises the complexities, but in the end, Henry 'emerges as a ruler whose already high reputation is not only maintained but enhanced'.[50] On the other hand, Allmand distinguishes between Henry's domestic and overseas achievements, accepting that Henry VI was left an impossible inheritance in France, in part because Henry V failed to realise that the spirit of national consciousness he was fostering in England was also developing among the French. Altering the French succession was much easier in theory than to effect in practice.

Mark Ormrod noted that the 'modern adulation of Henry V rests almost completely on his ability to mobilise the existing administrative, fiscal and judicial systems and make them work more effectively', but 'remarkably few historians seem prepared to admit' that 'Henry's reluctance or inability to undertake far-reaching reforms of the fiscal and financial systems had a devastating impact on his successor's regime'. In fact, 'Henry V may indeed be said to have contributed directly, even decisively, to the bankruptcy of the Lancastrian regime'. (Ormrod did later concede Henry was more successful in this regard than he had allowed.[51]) A.J. Pollard observed that modern historians should not 'see Henry, as he wanted the world to see him, as the special beneficiary of divine providence', as he 'was a master of propaganda'. This was an important reminder, for historians have sometimes proved very susceptible to that propaganda more than half a millennium later. For Pollard, that 'Henry was able and successful is not to be denied'. But he challenged G.L. Harriss, asserting that Henry 'did not, as King of England, fulfil, "to near perfection, the traditional role"'. (Questioning McFarlane's verdict on Henry as 'the greatest man that ever ruled England', Pollard noted that this 'begs a question about the women'.) Henry is criticised for his 'high-handedness with the law, his purges of those whose loyalty he suspected, and the rapaciousness of his last years, as well as his 'intolerance of criticism or dissent'. His military ambitions 'ran out of control' and he 'was fortunate to die before his fame was tarnished'. As he put it more bluntly in a later, brief biography, Henry's 'ambition was, quite simply, too gigantic'.[52]

Keith Dockray's 2004 volume was a different kind of biography. The first third of the book was a valuable overview of Henry's reputation across the centuries, before rewinding to tell the story. Dockray views Henry V as 'a less stereotypically virtuous later medieval king' than many have claimed. While possessing 'real charisma and personal magnetism', 'he successfully sold himself, or an image of himself, to the English people'. This hid some of his less admirable traits: 'Very much the autocrat (as his letters demonstrate only too graphically), he could be domineering, inflexible, ruthless, vindictive and, on occasion, inhumane even by the not very exacting standards of the fifteenth century'. Dockray's work is balanced between his achievements and failures, looking at how his reputation was constructed and fed into English national consciousness, but the final verdict, as others have argued, is that 'Henry V probably was fortunate to die suddenly before his reputation became irrevocably tarnished', since his 'legacy, in the last analysis, was bleak'.[53] The same year, Malcolm Mercer – in a lavishly illustrated colour volume with photographs and translations of some key documents held in The National Archives – concluded more positively that 'Henry V restored English national pride and gave the English a hero to be proud of'.[54] More iconoclastic and striking was David Rundle's description of the 'second Lancastrian king, that intoxicating cocktail of testosterone and piety'.[55]

A 2013 volume of essays pointed towards new research and thinking about Henry V. Appropriately enough, in a tidy echo of Shakespeare, it had been preceded by two similar volumes about Henry IV. The tone was generally admiring, although far less glowingly so than the volume G. L. Harriss had edited in 1985, the emphasis more on detailed examination of underexplored themes. The legacy of Henry's role in the previous reign was fully linked to the king's own. Gwilym Dodd looked at how the origins of Henry's success 'lay in the circumstances of his father's reign', because 'a network of men who had proven their loyalty and their abilities to the Prince was already well established when he became king'. And there were notes of criticism, occasionally sharp. In one of the most lucid accounts of the Oldcastle Revolt, Maureen Jurkowski took issue with Henry V's reputation as a paragon of justice. She observed that 'Henry's propensity to lock up suspected Lollards without charge, denying them access to justice, showed a flagrant disrespect for the principles of the common law'. The conclusion is scathing: 'if Henry V displayed scant regard for the existing common law, bending it to his personal will, he had even less respect for his subjects; it is not what we would expect from an "exemplar of justice"'. Alison McHardy examined how Henry effectively used the chapel royal as part of his propaganda machine, suggesting that the author of the *Gesta Henrici Quinti* came from among Henry's clergy, and that 'to a great extent every succeeding generation has been under its spell'.[56]

John Matusiak's biography of the same year is carefully considered, containing one of the clearest accounts of Henry's childhood and youth, but ultimately follows in the tradition of admiration. Interestingly, and not entirely convincingly, he seems to argue that Henry's successes were his, whereas the failures were attributable to a less successful tangible context.

> The result was a reign of spectacular success or unbridled folly according to chosen perspective. Ultimately, in fact, there were

> elements of both as events unfolded. But if the success seems to have sprung in no small measure from the man himself, the folly belongs rather more, perhaps, to the age that produced him.

In the end, and perhaps as Henry would have wanted, for Matusiak it comes down to reputation, so 'Henry should be remembered not only for what he did – or failed to do – but also for what he came to epitomise, since he left behind an ideal as well as a testing situation'. It is 'this ideal – of good and wise governance, heroism and nationhood – that rightly left his subjects and subsequent generations in no doubt about his stature'.[57]

The run up to the six hundredth anniversary of Agincourt in 2015 brought a predictable avalanche of publications on the battle, of highly variable quality. Among the best of the popular works, if a little gushing at times, was Juliet Barker's volume, while Ian Mortimer took a more original approach to the year. Mortimer encapsulated the paradox of Henry, that 'deeply flawed individual', a 'wanton destroyer of lives' who shows that 'a man may be a hero and yet a monster'.[58] Anne Curry, an academic who has written widely on Henry and Agincourt, published a collection of the various sources and interpretations in 2000, a seminal new history of the battle in 2005, and in the anniversary year was one of the editors of a richly illustrated volume which brought together contributions from scholars with the latest thinking. The same year, Curry published a short biography of Henry V in the Penguin Monarchs series. Like many biographies, it was a little sketchy on his years as Prince of Wales, but a lively introduction to his reign, incorporating many recent lines of research. As in her earlier work, she follows in the tradition of most recent academics in being an admirer of the king, dismissing those who question his achievements, although her extensive guide to further reading was scrupulous in including works by more critical historians.[59]

A welcome corrective to the wider narrative came with the publication of Chris Given-Wilson's biography of Henry's father in 2016. The implicit story had always been that Henry V had inherited a troubled realm in 1413, hence his successes shine all the brighter. Given-Wilson gave a more positive portrayal of Henry IV, noting that the 'conspiracy of approval enveloping Henry V has been slow to recognize the solidity of his father's legacy, a historiographical distortion extended almost by default to the unwarranted assumption that the prince was responsible for most of the good things that happened during the later years of the reign'. Recognising Henry's constraints and failings, Given-Wilson nevertheless argues that 'on the scale of the possible for a usurper, Henry IV's achievement ranks high. Unlike his son, he is not remembered as a great king, but it is not impossible to imagine that, given different circumstances, he could have been'.[60] It is worth remembering that Henry IV successfully passed the throne on to an adult son who faced no challenge to his title, a rather different legacy to that left by Henry V.

Malcolm Vale's 2016 biography aimed to 'explore aspects of Henry V's character, personality and behaviour which are outside the traditional and stereotypical depiction of him as a soldier, a warrior-king par excellence'. Rather than the chronicles and narrative sources, which focus overwhelmingly on the military side of the king, Vale therefore prioritises other records to shape his picture of the king, based on his letters and documents to show his interest in the English language, and in his religious and artistic interests. The idea, curiously old-fashioned, is that 'to read what Henry V himself read, handle what he himself handled [...] may bring us as close as we will ever get to that remarkable individual'. Yet the result, as one reviewer observed, was that 'Henry V is presented here as a figure in isolation'. The main problem is that Vale is so obviously an admirer of Henry, hence the essential tone of the book is an effort to shield him from criticism by challenging the very validity of asking critical questions. At the start, the author asks whether we 'need to adopt what are often arbitrary, absolute criteria in our attempt to arrive at a better understanding of our human subject?' The conclusion is that 'historical writing ought not to be a form of advocacy in which denigration and the exposure of alleged inadequacies have a primary role to play'. However, it is arguable that Henry himself laid the ground for such an approach by so careful a management of his image, and Vale seems much more inclined to accept the positive than allow for the negative. It is surely valid to ask whether Henry met the ideal of himself he so boldly promoted, and to deny the validity of that exercise risks turning history into hero worship. As the same reviewer noted, while Vale successfully captures much of the positive about the king, he ignores or suppresses the inconvenient additional truth, that Henry was 'also a charmless martinet'.[61]

From a king almost universally admired at his death (at least in English sources), Henry V has become divisive in the twenty-first century. He created a heroic, quasi-saintly image of himself that held for a long time, and still does hold to a remarkable extent. Yet changing standards and contexts have brought questions and sharp criticisms. After the catastrophic, genocidal wars of the twentieth century and the aggressive actions of nuclear superpowers, a king primarily remembered as a soldier who launched an aggressive war of conquest has become a much more complicated figure. How far these debates have permeated into popular thought is open to question, because the genius of a sixteenth-century playwright has firmly fixed one particular version of the king in the English mind.

Henry in Popular Culture

When considering popular approaches to Henry V, all roads lead to William Shakespeare. Only in the case of Richard III have perceptions of a king been so obviously and effectively shaped by one of the Bard's plays, and his role in Henry's afterlife is even more dominant as it has never attracted the same ire as his portrayal of Richard later provoked among that king's defenders. Shakespeare's work is superficially the epitome of Henry's own propaganda, drawing on the adulatory lives of the fifteenth and sixteenth centuries which stemmed from the story of his life Henry wanted to be the official version. In setting this version down in dramatic form, Shakespeare ensured that Henry's legend endured in the popular mind in his preferred form into the next millennium, where the biographies from which he drew the heroic mythology would have lived on only in the work of dedicated scholars. Shakespeare was Henry V's most effective PR man, even if that was never his intention and his motivations were more complex.

Henry V is part of the cycle of plays which covers the period from Richard II to Henry VII's triumph at Bosworth, but it is also the third part of a trilogy within that cycle. The two parts of *Henry IV* are largely about the younger Henry's transition from playboy Prince Harry to mature, responsible King Henry (Henry IV scarcely appears in the second of the plays named after him), with *Henry V* the culmination of that dramatic story. Although not the only play about Henry V staged in the 1590s (Henry provided an obvious model of English victory in pride in the tense aftermath of the Spanish Armada), Shakespeare's has been by far the most famous and durable. Interestingly, in its avowedly English context, Shakespeare branched out into linguistic diversity. Prior to *Henry V*, everyone in Shakespeare's plays had spoken English, irrespective of what language the conversation might have employed in a historical setting. The notable portions of French dialogue in Henry V strongly suggest that The Bard had found a translator, rather than that he had suddenly learnt French. To those subjected to the play at school, these are amongst the most tedious parts; Act 3 Scene 4 is entirely about Katherine [*sic* in Shakespeare] being taught the (stereotypically French accented) English names for body parts, while in Act 5 Scene 2, Henry switches between English and French in talking to Katherine, even though he is a French speaker conversing with a woman who has no English.

Beyond the patriotic front, *Henry V* is not a very satisfying play, largely because its protagonist was not a very interesting man. The genius of *Richard II* and *Richard III* derives from the way Shakespeare plays with the psychology of two flawed but fascinating characters, but Henry was a rather dull man obsessed with Masses and war. This is satirised in a 2017 episode of the BBC satirical comedy *Upstart Crow*, in which Shakespeare (played by David Mitchell) is reluctant to make Henry V the subject of a new play, despite the urgings of his landlady's daughter.

> Kate: 'You should do Henry V. Such a heroic figure.'
>
> Shakespeare: 'Henry V was an utter bore and everyone knows it. A pious, humourless killjoy who attended three masses a day, foreswore the company of women, and marched round France killing people because apparently it's what God really, really wanted.'[62]

There are indeed hints in the real play that Shakespeare had problems with Henry as a lead character. He does his best with this, plotting the transition of the riotous prince in the two parts of *Henry IV* to the serious king of *Henry V*. The last play is full of stirring rhetoric and rousing speeches, including some of the most famous and quoted of Shakespeare's lines ('once more unto the breach'). Yet beneath this is what can be read as a reflection on the cost of war. Henry's brutality is laid bare in the scene before the gates of Harfleur. There are definite indications that The Bard was troubled by the destructiveness and human cost of war, which leads to a tension in the play, a question of whether it is glorification or warning.

This tension is evident in the two famous film adaptions of the twentieth century, by Laurence Olivier in 1944 and Kenneth Branagh in 1989. Both give the two main soliloquies in a dramatic, inspirational fashion, but there are some key differences. Olivier's film was made as propaganda on Winston Churchill's orders, an effort to boost British morale as the Second World War drew to a close, and the government provided some of the funding. It is meant to show a heroic Henry, and some of his more brutal acts Shakespeare included are deliberately excised by Olivier, not least the threats against Harfleur and the killing of prisoners at Agincourt, a battle which takes place on a sunny field. By contrast, Branagh's Agincourt takes place in the rain in the mud, and his film portrays an altogether more gory, brutal side to war. If Henry is no less heroic, it reflects more of Shakespeare's apparent ambiguity about warfare.

Henry V has been frequently performed on stage since the nineteenth century. In more recent times, famous actors like Richard Burton, Christopher Plummer, Ian Holm, Timothy Dalton, Kenneth Branagh and Jude Law have taken the lead role in theatre versions, although perhaps the most unlikely Henry was *Star Trek*'s future Captain Kirk, William Shatner, who gave a single performance as Plummer's understudy at the Stratford Shakespeare Festival in Ontario, Canada in 1956 (his main role was the Duke of Gloucester). Periodically, the BBC have also produced adaptions of the fifteenth century plays for television. In 1960, as part of *An Age of Kings* (a version of the whole set of plays from *Richard II* to *Richard III*), Robert Hardy played Henry; he became so interested in medieval warfare as a result that he presented a documentary on Agincourt in 1963 and later wrote two books on the longbow. David Gwillim took the title role in 1979 (part of the ambitious BBC Shakespeare Series), Michael Pennington in 1989 (as part of *The Wars of the Roses* performed by the English Shakespeare Company and screened on the BBC), and Tom Hiddleston in 2012 (in *The Hollow Crown*).

Versions of Shakespeare's play have dominated portrayals of Henry V onscreen. Dan O'Herlihy played Prince Hal in *The Black Shield of Falworth*, a film starring Tony Curtis in a plot against Henry IV which was never going to be a classic. Otherwise, Shakespeare remains the basis for screenplays even when it is not the actual play being shown. In 1965, Orson Welles produced what was effectively a vanity project which liberally mixed together parts of different Shakespeare plays. *Chimes at Midnight* (*Campanadas a Medianoche*, as it was a joint Spanish, French and Swiss production, but known in most countries as *Falstaff*) was made because Welles felt an affiliation with the character of Falstaff and wanted to play him. (Falstaff has been the subject of a number of TV movies over the years, although mainly based on his role in *The Merry Wives of Windsor*.) A 2019 Netflix film, *The King*, was a modernised version of the Shakespearean story starring Timothée Chalamet as Henry. This took considerable liberties with both Shakespeare and history, not least the scene in which Henry IV informs his eldest son, Henry, that he is making his second son, Thomas, heir to the crown, which has no basis in fact or possibility, or Henry killing Hotspur in single combat. Pedants also got very exercised about the precise types of armour and weaponry employed, and French critics were scathing about its strongly anti-French sentiments, but the film does echo Shakespeare in capturing something of the violence and brutality of war.

Literature has struggled to break free from Shakespeare's shadow. In the eighteenth century, William Kenrick wrote a sequel to *Henry IV, Part 2*, entitled *Falstaff's Wedding*. The 1760 version has a serious storyline (a plot to assassinate Henry V), while an entirely different 1766 version is written as a farce. Since then, however, Henry V has not been a major character elsewhere in literature. Modern novelists have found Queen Catherine a much more interesting character around whom to base novels. Joanna Hickson's *The Agincourt Queen* (2013) is told from the perspective of Catherine's wet nurse turned close servant, and follows her from childhood, Henry V only making a brief (and not entirely flattering) appearance at the end. *The Forbidden Queen* (2013) by Anne O'Brien also starts in childhood, although goes into the story beyond Henry's death. *The Queen's Secret* (1989) by Jean Plaidy covers her time with Owen Tudor after Henry's death. (Plaidy also wrote *The Star of Lancaster* (1981), which covers the reigns of Henry IV and Henry V, although the second half feels much more rushed and less satisfactory.) Some suspension of historical belief is required in many of the novels about Catherine, but her life story is more interesting and much easier to fictionalise.

Most of the novels about Henry V have not stood the test of time, if they were even worth reading on publication. A. M. Morgan's *Harry of Monmouth* (1956) is a little dated in style, but remains a good read. *A Bloody Field by Shrewsbury*, by Edith Pargeter (best known as the author of the Cadfael series under the name Ellis Peters) covers the years from Richard II to the Battle of Shrewsbury. Notably, this captures something of the young Henry of Monmouth's affection for Richard II. *Good King Harry* (1984) takes the form of the king's memoirs, although the life of the author Diana Giardina – who ran as an independent candidate for governor of West Virginia in 2000 – is arguably more interesting than her novel.

More satisfying than most efforts is the fifth volume in Mercedes Rochelle's *The Plantagenet Legacy* series, *The Agincourt King* (2024). Covering the period from Oldcastle's Revolt in 1414 to Bedford's victory at the Battle of the Seine in 1416, a large chunk of the novel is told through the eyes of Humphrey of Gloucester. It is largely true to the known facts and is a decent fictionalisation of these years, including incidents like the citing of Deuteronomy at Harfleur. Notably, it gives Henry the Plantagenet temper, which emerges occasionally to frighten those around him and make him a more rounded character. An equally interesting Henry is found in Bernard Cornwell's *Azincourt*. It tells the story of Nicholas Hook, a fictional archer who serves in the Agincourt campaign after being saved from execution for his crimes. Henry appears occasionally in person, and his character is explained as the result of his surviving the Battle of Shrewsbury.

> 'See that scar on his face? Took an arrow there, smack in the cheek and it didn't kill him! And ever since he's been convicted that God is his best friend and now he's set on burning God's enemies.'

This manifests itself in ways which are very uncomfortable for us, as in the scene where Henry watches Lollards burned at the stake.

> The flames reached the second man and he screamed. Henry, the fifth King of England to carry that name, calmly watched the Lollard's soul go to hell.

Henry's religion is taken seriously and his conviction that he was called by God is repeatedly discussed by characters throughout the novel. Yet one of the most penetrating analyses is put into the mouth of a priest speaking to Hook, as they pause after crossing the Somme.

> 'Our gracious king', the priest said, 'is so mad that he might just be hoping the French will catch us.'
>
> 'Mad? Like the French king?'
>
> 'The French king is really mad', Father Christopher said, 'no, our king is just convinced of God's favour.'
>
> 'Is that madness?'
>
> […]
>
> 'I hope to God we have escaped', Hook said.
>
> 'And our king half hopes that', Father Christopher said, 'and half hoped that he can prove God's favour.'
>
> 'And that's his madness?'
>
> 'Beware of certainty. There are men in the French army, Hook, who are as convinced as Henry that God is on their side. They're good men too. They pray, they give alms, they confess their sins and they vow never to sin again. They are very good men. Can they be wrong in their conviction?'[63]

The idea that in his way, Henry was consumed by madness as much as Charles VI, albeit of a different form, is an intriguing one. Cornwell reminds the reader, as historians tend not to do, that the French were as convinced of divine blessing as the English. After all, the French ultimately won the war.

Verdict

Few (if any) medieval kings of England enjoy the acclaim afforded Henry V. No other king has so successfully controlled his image in his lifetime and beyond. He wanted to be seen as a pious warrior, claiming his just rights and enhancing the glory of England, and that is just how he has been portrayed for most of the six centuries since his death. It is as if Agincourt makes him untouchable, the triumph of the battle obscuring its complicated aftermath. Victory on that October day in 1415 continues to resonate with the nationalisms of a country that often prefers living in the fleeting glory days of the past to facing the insignificance of the present. Nor is it only popular Francophobia which lauds Henry; it is amazing how many scholars who would criticise other kings leap touchily to Henry's defence at the merest hint of a threat to his reputation. Henry V is a rare king indeed to find hero-worshippers inside academia as well as in popular thought.

In many ways, of course, his life and reign can be portrayed as a tremendous success. As prince, his commitment to the protracted struggle was what eventually defeated the Glyndŵr Revolt. As king, in just nine short years, he reopened the Hundred Years' War and restored English military pride, making England a country once more to be reckoned with, at the same time as reestablishing the authority of the Crown in England. Faced with the Oldcastle rebellion and the Southampton plotters, Henry acted resolutely and easily saw off the threat. There can be no questioning his courage, his military achievements, and his commitment in warfare, both at home as prince and overseas as king. From Harfleur to Agincourt to the conquests and sieges which eventually led to Troyes, he was resolute in his search for victory. He took risks, but calculated ones, and he generally played his hand well. Before 1420, he largely carried parliament and popular opinion with him, and was incredibly successful at squeezing money from laity and clergy alike to fund his ambitions.

Such dedication and zeal, however, hides another side to Henry. The adulation and hero-worship often serves to conceal the fact that as king, he seems to have been quite dull. His insistence on micromanagement, never quite trusting his officials, was detrimental to speedy, efficient government on both sides of the Channel. He was obsessed with two things: war and religion. In the fifteenth century, his piety was commended, at least by the orthodox clerics who wrote the story of the reign. Harsh action against (perceived) heresy was one of the ways the Church judged a fifteenth-century king, so it would be anachronistic to criticise Henry for conforming to those expectations. However, it did lead him to subvert due process when it came to religious dissenters, a serious challenge to his reputation as a model of justice.

Moreover, Henry's religiosity increasingly gave way to a troublingly messianic zeal. His language around the invasion of France took on the guise of a holy war, Henry the Christ-like saviour claiming his God-given rights in France and liberating the French from their evil rulers. It was extraordinarily bold, revealing a personal arrogance that is often glossed over. Worse, this messianic belief in his own vocation led to some of the brutalities which are most often cited against him. Citing Old Testament texts about God punishing those who resisted him, or pitilessly punishing besieged French citizens who thought rather differently about God's plan than did the King of England, brought a new and disturbing element into the Hundred Years' War. Historians have tended to be generous to Henry in accepting he believed this, but in light of the naked aggression of the invasion and the fact we lack access to the king's private thoughts, we must remain agnostic on whether he was genuine or a brilliantly cynical showman. His piety was commendable to contemporaries and unproblematic to us, but the extraordinary way in which it manifested itself was novel then and is problematic for us. The tension between self-belief and its consequences might be compared to a more modern example. When Tony Blair declared about the Iraq War, in a speech in his Sedgefield constituency shortly before he stood down as prime minister in 2007, that 'hand on heart, I did what I thought was right', there were many who asked whether his belief in it being right made it so. Henry V and Tony Blair rarely appear in the same sentence, but in both cases we might ask whether a sincere but flawed personal conviction is sufficient justification for war.

It is no accident that most accounts of the reign end up focussing heavily on the military story, for it was Henry's overriding passion. Given that, it is interesting to compare the treatment of Henry V with an earlier warrior king, Richard I. As recounted in Chapter 2, since Victorian times there has been an influential school of thought which is heavily critical of the Lionheart for his neglect of a kingdom from which he was almost permanently absent, using England as a bank to fund his reckless overseas campaigns. Yet while it is frequently noted that Richard spent a mere six months of a ten-year reign in England, it is far less frequently observed that Henry was out of the kingdom for more than half of his reign. He spent only four months of the five years between July 1417 and his death in August 1422 in England, and was the first English king to die outside the realm since Richard in 1199. Unlike Richard, Henry was extremely fortunate to have three loyal brothers and two loyal uncles dutifully helping him to achieve his aims. While there does not seem to have been a strong emotional connection between the brothers, such reliable siblings were a luxury indeed for a medieval king. This support provided by Clarence, Bedford and Gloucester is too rarely acknowledged, for in other reigns the king's absences from England would have seen a brother stirring up trouble, as indeed did Richard's brother John.

While his Crusade to the Holy Land can attract valid criticism of neglecting his core duties as ruler, Richard's time on the Continent is easier to justify – he was raised in France, culturally French, and ruled sizeable territories in France alongside England. Henry's background was very different, entirely English, and his naked wars of conquest very different to Richard's defensive campaigns in France. If Henry never extracted quite such enormous sums as Richard, whose ransom was a severe drain on English finances, he still drew large amounts from the English taxpayer in order to finance his wars in France. At times, Henry as much as Richard treated England like a bank to underwrite his French ambitions. An unconscious, nationalistic bias has crept into the historiography here, for Richard can be portrayed as a Frenchman abusing England, whereas Henry was an Englishman who taught the French a lesson. The uncomfortable similarities are overlooked by those who want to celebrate an English hero.

They were not quite so overlooked at the time. By late 1420, after Henry had been confirmed as heir to the French throne, the voices in England calling for his return grew more insistent. The king had been away for more than three years and for all its sophistication, late medieval English government still revolved around the person of the monarch. There is a definite sense, in the growing unease of the Commons, that Henry was now embarking on something more than they wanted, which is why they were keen that he guarantee the separateness of the two kingdoms. While Henry is often portrayed as the model of Englishness, there were real concerns that England would suffer when her king took another crown, and he does not seem to have fully appreciated that his personal ambitions did not reflect the desires or aims of his English subjects. Likewise, he appears to have had little understanding of how he appeared to many of the French like an unwelcome foreign conqueror. This would have created serious problems had he not died young.

Had he lived longer, it seems very unlikely that he would have been able to maintain the degree of unity and support in England that he enjoyed before the Treaty of Troyes. He may have been heir to the French crown, but a large swathe of France remained loyal to the dauphin. Some of the sieges of 1421–22 were protracted and grim, and Henry would probably have faced far more of them in the following years. It is hard to know whether his military abilities and reputation would have made any difference, but it is improbable. Very possibly, events would not have transpired so very differently had Henry V been crowned King of France and lived another decade or two. England would not have been any happier to fund a French war to support the king's vanity project than it was for Henry VI's minority regime. Much of France would have been equally unprepared to accept an Englishman as their king, especially after the divisions on which Henry had capitalised were patched up. Making good the King of England's claim to the crown of France was always going to be expensive and gruelling, and was quite possibly always doomed. In dying when he did, Henry avoided that reckoning and left his successors to confront defeat and take the blame for his ambitions and messianic aggression. Henry VI was a manifestly hopeless king when he grew up, but many of the seeds of his destruction were sown by his father in his unyielding obsession for conquest and glory. Henry V was fortunate to die young and be hailed a hero, before he had to deal with the consequences of his actions.

That he was hailed a hero regardless is testament to his ability to control the narrative. Henry V was one of the propaganda geniuses of English history. He projected an image which was seized upon by clerical contemporaries eager to celebrate his victories over their enemies (the French and the Lollards), given popular appeal by Shakespeare, and has been widely accepted ever since. Having achieved fame and enjoyed the success of Agincourt and Troyes, Henry then died at the perfect moment to secure his reputation, before he faced the difficult, perhaps impossible task of consolidating these successes and making good his claim to the French throne while not alienating his English subjects. The failures of Henry VI's reign, in other circumstances, may well have been those of Henry V's. In nine years on the throne, he had time to make spectacular early progress, but was spared the consequences of his choices. It is hard to argue that this makes him a great king. At best, the jury is out on a monarch who bequeathed the most problematic of legacies to his infant son.

Conclusion

In medieval terms where a king's end might reflect divine judgement on his rule, none of the five discussed in this volume would seem to have been in God's favour when they died. Henry II was hounded to death by his son, who as Richard I himself fell to a painful end at the hands of an opportunistic crossbowman. Edward I succumbed to age and exhaustion. Edward III faded into a sad, lonely senility, while Henry V was cut down by disease. None had a heroic death in battle, nor met a dignified end. Nevertheless, posterity – less concerned about any links between divine favour and manner of death – has tended to look positively on them all, at least before the different approaches of the nineteenth and twentieth centuries began to challenge some of the heroic narratives.

That is not to say that verdicts have been constantly or universally positive. If Richard I and Henry V were ostentatiously lamented on their deaths, and Edward I genuinely mourned, there was more ambiguity at the time about Edward III and (especially) Henry II. In all cases, it was what followed their demise that elevated their reputations; it is notable that only Richard I immediately followed another successful king, and his own success is contested. The unpredictability of mortality played its part. Henry II and Edward III lived too long. Neither were old by modern standards, Henry 56 and Edward 64, but they seemed old and past it by the standards of the time. Had they both died earlier, Henry in around 1182 and Edward in about 1364, their reputations would be even higher and untarnished by the failures of their last years. Richard I and Henry V, in contrast, died young and at the perfect time for their reputations. Had either lived longer, there was a strong likelihood that they would have faced major problems and been judged far less positively.

For that reason, it is hard to number Richard I and Henry V among the best medieval monarchs. Both actively courted fame and sought to control how they would be remembered, Henry the most adept self-propagandist of any medieval king, and the aura surrounding their military reputations tends to obscure everything else. There is no doubt that both were brave men, if we understand by bravery the demonstration of courage in battle, and excellent soldiers, with striking military victories to their names. Both were clearly leaders who had the ability to inspire their troops. We cannot doubt that the Church approved of Richard's crusade and Henry's persecution of Lollards, however unpalatable we find both today. Additionally, Henry was a competent ruler who (until 1420) worked well with parliament, made serious efforts to address problems with law and order, and was remarkably successful in presenting his ambitions as an exercise in national pride and divine mission, so that people were willing to back him and fund those ambitions.

Yet in both cases, death handily saved them from the serious problems they created. Richard and Henry were soldiers above all else, and military action came to dominate their lives and be that for which they lived and reigned. For all their personal achievements and military prowess, for all they won dramatic battles, the wars they began were ultimately lost. The sheen of chivalry obscures the darkness in two men who could be brutal and cruel. Both Richard and Henry extracted enormous sums from England to fund their personal schemes. While being bankrolled by English silver, both kings neglected the kingdom and their subjects to pursue personal vanity projects, in Richard's case a crusade, in Henry's the invasion of France. Their ambitions were too enormous, and both failed, although Henry left his brothers and son to be held responsible for those failures. Too often, the hero worship of Henry V glosses over the extent to which some of the major problems of Henry VI's reign were the direct consequence of his father's unrealistic ambitions and messianic beliefs. While the problems of Richard's successor, John, were largely of his own making, it is entirely plausible that things would have fallen apart in a different way had the older brother lived longer. Richard I and Henry V were not great kings, nor among the best of medieval monarchs, which is the reason both have so polarised modern historians between ardent defenders and iconoclastic critics. The two were ambitious showmen who were lucky to die at the perfect moment to secure unmerited reputations for greatness.

In contrast, Henry II, Edward I and Edward III do number among the greatest of England's (and Europe's) medieval kings. None, of course, was perfect, and their failings must be acknowledged. Henry II's reputation will always be marred by the murder of Becket, even if the archbishop was insufferable, and his failure to control his family led to an undeservedly sad ending of failure. Edward I, in a category in which there is stiff competition, was one of the most irascible bullies to rule England. He provoked more than one clash by an inability to compromise, and through inflexibility failed to secure final victory in his Scottish ambitions. Edward III's hounding of Stratford and the consequent crisis was the result of a king who was unable to accept responsibility for his own shortcomings. Yet Henry survived Becket, Edward I survived 1297–98, and Edward III survived 1340–41, because the quality of their kingship was generally recognised. Unlike Richard I and Henry V, these three were tested in long reigns and passed the test.

Henry II and the two Edwards were rounded rulers, warriors for whom military victory was not the only objective. Henry and Edward I understood the value of their personal presence in lands they ruled and claimed to rule, hence their itineraries were often punishing. All three were good and largely successful soldiers and commanders. If Henry's military record is less famous as he fought no pitched battles, his victory against all odds in 1173–74 is proof of his abilities. No account of Edward I can omit his conquest of Wales or war against Scotland, nor can the story of Edward III be told without Crécy and the start of the Hundred Years' War. However, the stories of these three reigns contain far more than tales of battles, sieges and conquests. In their different ways, each fundamentally changed the nature of kingship and the country over which they ruled.

Key to this was the way in which they used the skills of others. Henry II reigned before parliament, but he was prepared to listen to counsel. While Edward I sometimes had an adversarial relationship with parliament, in his early years he used the assembly constructively for the most sustained legislative output of the Middle Ages. Both he and Henry II were adept at choosing competent ministers who could run their administrations. Edward III forged a common purpose with his nobility, making a virtue of friendship in monarchy, and learned to engage skilfully and productively with parliament. All (unlike the micromanaging Henry V) knew how and when to delegate to achieve the best results. We might quibble over their direct responsibility for key policies and achievements, but they chose the people and created the culture in which they were possible.

More significantly, each of the three reestablished the authority of the Crown following a tumultuous previous reign. Henry II rapidly and effectively restored order and royal control following the civil war which tore apart Stephen's reign; Edward brought stability to a monarchy weakened after the civil wars provoked by Henry III's inadequacies and favouritism; while Edward III brought back harmony to the realm and dignity to a Crown badly tarnished by the violence and conflict of Edward II's disastrous reign. The last case is especially important, for after the bloodletting and revenge killings of the 1310s and 1320s, Edward played a crucial role in reasserting due process and the rule of law. Yet as well as bringing back stability and royal authority, these three kings actively sought to make changes to improve the law in line with their role as the fount of justice. Henry II increased and sped up access to justice, laying the foundations for what we know as the common law. Edward I's early years saw a considerable volume of legislation which aimed to reform and codify the legal system. In the 1352 Statute of Treasons, Edward III consciously allowed limits to be placed on arbitrary and capricious royal action. Reestablishing the power of and respect for the crown at the start of their reigns was a prelude to more substantive and lasting later reform.

The difference between these three on the one hand, and Richard I and Henry V on the other, is that their vision and legacy went beyond the personal. That is not to say that they were not also motivated by personal interest and selfishness, but that there was something enduring to what they achieved. Richard and Henry V left heroic tales and grand narratives, but bequeathed nothing of substance to posterity. In contrast, we can still see something of Henry II and Edward I's legal innovations, of Edward I's imposing castles (controversial though it might be in Wales to see them as an achievement), of Edward III's Windsor and the Order of the Garter. Their kingship blended acquiesce to tradition with innovation, which transformed the English monarchy, leaving lasting results. England in 1189, 1307 and 1377 was very different to the country the kings inherited in 1154, 1272 and 1327, and while there were plenty of other factors involved, the way these three reestablished royal authority and shaped the monarchy were significant considerations. Henry II, Edward I and Edward III were only human beings, often deeply flawed ones, but as kings they were indeed the best of England's medieval monarchs.

Notes

Preface

1. Denis Judd, *George VI* (revised edition: 2012), p. 263.
2. Sarah Bradford, *George VI* (revised edition: 2011), p. 611.
3. Phil Bradford, *The Worst Medieval Monarchs* (2023), pp. vii–xi.
4. Timothy Bolton, *Cnut the Great* (2017); Ryan Lavelle, *Cnut: The North Sea King* (2017), p. 88.
5. David Bates, *William the Conqueror* (2016), p. 512.

Introduction

1. W. L. Warren, *The Governance of Norman and Angevin England, 1086–1272* (1987), p. 17.
2. Bradford, *Worst Medieval Monarchs*, pp. xi–xxvi.

Chapter 1 – Henry II: A Just King?

1. Richard Barber, *Henry Plantagenet: A Biography* (1964), p. 204.
2. *Radulfi de Diceto Decani Lundoniensis Opera Historica*, ed. William Stubbs, 2 vols (1876), II, p. 351.
3. Emilie Amt, *The Accession of Henry II in England: Royal Government Restored 1149–1159* (1993), p. 47.
4. W. L. Warren, *Henry II* (Yale edition: 2000), p. 630.
5. Amt, *Accession of Henry II*, pp. 79–81.
6. *Chronica Magistri Rogeri de Houdene*, ed. William Stubbs, 4 vols (1878–81), I, p. 218.
7. A. L. Poole, *From Domesday Book to Magna Carta* (2nd edition: 1955), p. 198.
8. Foliot's bitter and lengthy letter of 1166 is one of the strongest attacks on Becket's conduct by a contemporary: *The Correspondence of Thomas Becket, Archbishop of Canterbury 1162–1170*, ed. and trans. Anne Duggan, 2 vols (2000), II, pp. 498–537.

9. Warren, *Henry II*, p. 193.
10. R. R. Davies, *The Age of Conquest: Wales 1063–1415* (2000), p. 53.
11. Paul Brand, 'Henry II and the Creation of the English Common Law', in *Henry II: New Interpretations*, eds. Christopher Harper-Bill and Nicholas Vincent (2007), p. 224.
12. Robert Bartlett, *Trial by Fire and Water: The Medieval Judicial Ordeal* (1986); Robert Bartlett, *England under the Norman and Angevin Kings* (2000), pp. 180–81.
13. Nicholas Vincent, 'The Court of Henry II', in *Henry II*, eds. Harper-Bill and Vincent, p. 332.
14. *Gesta Regis Henrici Secundi et Ricardi Primi*, ed. William Stubbs, 2 vols (1867), I, p. 4.
15. Richard Barber, *The Devil's Crown: A History of Henry II and His Sons* (1978), p. 52.
16. Nick Barratt, *The Restless Kings: Henry II, His Sons and the Wars for the Plantagenet Crown* (2018), p. 167.
17. *The History of William Marshal*, trans. Nigel Bryant (2016), p. 119.
18. David Carpenter, *Henry III: The Rise to Power and Personal Rule, 1207–1258* (2020), pp. 601–602.
19. Daniel Prigent, *Fontevraud: L'Abbaye Royale* (4th edition, 2023), pp. 28–31. The movement of the effigies in modern times can be seen in photos in history books, which reflect the changing positioning and configurations.
20. *History of William Marshal*, p. 122.
21. The quotes in the following paragraphs are from the translations of William of Newburgh, Gerald of Wales and Walter Map found in *English Historical Documents Volume II: 1042–1189*, eds. David C. Douglas and George W. Greenaway (2nd edition: 1981), pp. 348–404, 406–20.
22. Antonia Gransden, *Historical Writing in England I* (1974), p. 219.
23. Michael Staunton, *The Historians of Angevin England* (2017), pp. 153–64.
24. John Gillingham, 'Roger of Howden's Documents: Kings and Taxation in England in the Later Twelfth Century', in *English Medieval Government and Administration: Essays in Honour of J. R. Maddicott*, eds. Nigel Saul and Nicholas Vincent (2023), pp. 65–85.
25. *The Lives of Thomas Becket*, ed. and trans. Michael Staunton (2001), p. 238.
26. G. W. Bernard, *The King's Reformation: Henry VIII and the Remaking of the English Church* (2005), p. 489.
27. Aude De Mézerac-Zanetti, 'Liturgical Changes to the Cult of Saints Under Henry VIII', *Studies in Church History* 47 (2011), p. 186.
28. Samuel Daniel, *The Collection of the History of England* (5th edition: 1685), p. 111.
29. James Tyrrell, *The General History of England*, 5 vols (1700–4), II, p. 455.
30. David Hume, *The History of England from Julius Caesar to the Revolution in 1688*, 6 vols (1879 edition), I, p. 435.
31. George Lyttelton, *The History of the Life of King Henry the Second and of the Age in which He Lived*, 6 vols (3rd edition: 1788), VI, p. 358.
32. Anne Duggan, *Thomas Becket* (2004), pp. 245–52.
33. Augustine Thierry, *Histoire de la Conquête de l'Angleterre par les Normands*, 3 vols (1825), II, p. 364.
34. William Stubbs, *The Constitutional History of England in its Origin and Development*, 3 vols (1874–78), I, pp. 483, 484, 530.
35. L. F. Salzmann, *Henry II* (1914), pp. 234–35.
36. John Harvey, *The Plantagenets* (1948), p. 57.
37. Poole, *Domesday Book to Magna Carta*, pp. 318, 321.

38. Winston S. Churchill, *History of the English-Speaking Peoples*, 4 vols (1956–58), I, pp. 146, 156.
39. J. E. A. Jolliffe, *Angevin Kingship* (2nd edition, 1955).
40. John T. Appleby, *Henry II: The Vanquished King* (1962), pp. vii, 342.
41. Richard Barber, *Henry Plantagenet: A Biography* (1964), p. 364.
42. Warren, *Henry II*, pp. 79, 514, 630, 633.
43. Frank Barlow, *Thomas Becket* (1986); John Guy, *Thomas Becket. Warrior, Priest, Rebel, Victim: A 900-Year-Old Story Retold* (2012).
44. Duggan, *Thomas Becket*; *Correspondence of Thomas Becket*; *Lives of Thomas Becket*.
45. Jean Flori, *Eleanor of Aquitaine: Queen and Rebel* (2007); Ralph V. Turner, *Eleanor of Aquitaine: Queen of France, Queen of England* (2009).
46. Matthew Strickland, *Henry the Young King, 1155-–1183* (2016).
47. *The Letters and Charters of Henry II, King of England 1154–1189*, ed. Nicholas Vincent, 7 vols (2020–23).
48. Amt, *Accession of Henry II*, pp. 28–29, 80, 126–27, 181.
49. Graeme J. White, *Restoration and Reform 1153–1165: Recovery from Civil War in England* (2000), p. 215.
50. John D. Hosler, *Henry II: A Medieval Soldier at War, 1147–1189* (2007), pp. 230–31.
51. John Gillingham, *The Angevin Empire* (2nd edition: 2001); Martin Aurell, *The Plantagenet Empire, 1154–1224* (2007); Jean Favier, *Les Plantagenêts: Origines et Destin d'un Empire* (2004); Amaury Chauou, *Les Plantagenêts et leur Cour, 1154–1216* (2019); Martin Aurell *et al.*, *Les Plantagenêts dans les Pays de la Loire* (2021); Martin Aurell *et al.*, *Les Plantagenêts et le Maine* (2022).
52. Christian Thevenot, *Henri II Plantagenêt* (2003), p. 175.
53. Claudia Gold, *King of the North Wind: The Life of Henry II in Five Acts* (2018), p. xxxi.
54. Claudia Gold, 'King Henry II? The Muslim Monarch of Medieval England?', *BBC History Magazine* (February 2020).
55. Matthew Lewis, *Henry II and Eleanor of Aquitaine: Founding an Empire* (2021), pp. 324, 325.
56. Sharon Penman, *Devil's Brood* (2008), pp. 721–22.
57. The quotes in the following paragraphs are from Ariana Franklin, *The Death Maze* (2008), pp. 35, 36, 37, 133, 402, 406, 423; *Relics of the Dead* (2009), p. 380; and *The Assassin's Prayer* (2010), p. 45.
58. E. M. Rose, *The Murder of William of Norwich: The Origins of the Blood Libel in Medieval Europe* (2015).
59. US Senate Hearing 115–99, online at <https://www.congress.gov/event/115th-congress/senate-event/LC50143/text> [last accessed 22 February 2025].

Chapter 2 – Richard I: A Wild King?

1. Walter Carruthers Sellars and Robert Julian Yeatman, *1066 and All That* (1930), p. 23.
2. Jim Bradbury, *Philip Augustus: King of France 1180–1223* (1998), p. 333.
3. *Christians and Jews in Angevin England: The York Massacre of 1190, Narratives and Contexts*, eds. Sarah Rees Jones and Sethina Watson (2013).
4. Ralph V. Turner and Richard R. Heiser, *The Reign of Richard Lionheart: Ruler of the Angevin Empire, 1189–1199* (2000), p. 89.
5. *The Chronicle of Richard of Devizes*, ed. and trans. John T. Appleby (1963), p. 9.

6. Ralph V. Turner, 'Richard Lionheart and English Episcopal Elections', *Albion* 29 (1997), pp. 1–13.
7. Thomas Asbridge, *Richard I: The Crusader King* (2018), p. 43; John Gillingham, *Richard I* (1999), pp. 145, 153.
8. Gillingham, *Richard I*, pp. 224–25.
9. Jean Flori, *Richard the Lionheart: King and Knight* (1999), p. 124.
10. Asbridge, *Richard I*, p. 64.
11. *Chronica Magistri Rogeri de Houdene*, III, pp. 216–17.
12. Flori, *Richard the Lionheart*, p. 187.
13. John Gillingham, *The Life and Times of Richard I* (1973), pp. 212–13.
14. John Gillingham, 'The Unromantic Death of Richard I', in *Richard Coeur de Lion: Kingship and War in the Twelfth Century* (1994), p. 178.
15. Frank Barlow, *William Rufus* (Yale edition: 2000), p. 437.
16. Cited by Poole, *Domesday Book to Magna Carta*, p. 349.
17. *Feet of Fines of the Ninth Year of the Reign of King Richard I, A.D. 1197 to A.D. 1198*, Pipe Roll Society 23 (1898), p. 79.
18. Gillingham, *Richard I*, p. 122.
19. *Thomas Wright's Political Songs from the Reign of John to that of Edward II*, ed. Peter Coss (1996), pp. 58, 128.
20. *Vita Edwardi Secundi*, ed. and trans. Wendy R. Childs (2005), p. 69.
21. W. Mark Ormrod, *Edward III* (2011), p. 15.
22. *Polychronicon Ranulphi Higden Monachi Cestrensis*, 9 vols (1865-86), V, p. 336.
23. Daniel, *History of England*, p. 126.
24. Edward Gibbon, *The History of the Decline and Fall of the Roman Empire*, 8 vols (Folio Society edition: 1989), pp. 334–35.
25. Hume, *History of England*, I, pp. 465–66.
26. Stubbs, *Constitutional History*, I, pp. 550–51.
27. Ted Widmer, *Martin Van Buren* (2005), p. 35.
28. Harvey, *Plantagenets*, p. 75.
29. John Gillingham, 'Some Legends of Richard the Lionheart: Their Development and Influence', in Gillingham, *Richard Coeur de Lion*, p. 189, n. 46.
30. Harvey, *Plantagenets*, pp. 65–66.
31. *Radulfi de Diceto*, I, p. 399.
32. Doris Kearns Goodwin, *Team of Rivals: The Political Genius of Abraham Lincoln* (2005), p. 58.
33. James A. Brundage, *Richard Lionheart: A Biography* (2005), p. 275; John Gillingham, 'Richard I and Berengaria of Navarre', in Gillingham, *Richard Coeur de Lion*, p. 135; Flori, *Richard the Lionheart*, p. 81.
34. Poole, *Domesday Book to Magna Carta*, pp. 349–50.
35. Churchill, *History of the English-Speaking Peoples*, I, p. 168.
36. John T. Appleby, *England without Richard, 1189–1199* (1965), pp. 233–34.
37. John Julius Norwich, *The Normans in Sicily* (1992), p. 725.
38. Brundage, *Richard Lionheart*, pp. 258, 260–61, 263.
39. Gillingham, *Life and Times of Richard I*; John Gillingham, *Richard the Lionheart* (1978); Gillingham, *Richard I*; Gillingham, *Richard Coeur de Lion*; Gillingham, *Angevin Empire*.
40. Bradbury, *Philip Augustus*, p. 333.
41. Flori, *Richard the Lionheart*, p. 412.

42. Janet L. Nelson, 'Preface', in *Richard Coeur de Lion in History and Myth*, ed. Janet L. Nelson (1992), p. xi.
43. Michael Markowski, 'Richard Lionheart: Bad King, Bad Crusader?', *Journal of Medieval History* 23 (1997), pp. 361, 364, 365.
44. Turner and Heiser, *Reign of Richard Lionheart*, pp. 241, 242–3, 244, 248.
45. Asbridge, *Richard I*, pp. 5, 28–30, 49, 56, 79, 94.
46. Douglas Boyd, *Lionheart* (2014), p. 11.
47. W. B. Bartlett, *Richard the Lionheart: The Crusader King of England* (2018), p. 371.
48. J. O. Prestwich, 'Richard Coeur de Lion: *Rex Bellicosus*', in *Richard Coeur de Lion*, ed. Nelson, pp. 3–4.
49. *Tales of a Minstrel of Reims in the Thirteenth Century*, trans. Samuel N. Rosenberg (2022).
50. *Richard Coer de Lyon*, ed. Peter Larkin (2015).
51. Martin H. Jones and David Hook in *Richard Coeur de Lion*, ed. Nelson, pp. 70–140; Bradford B. Broughton, *The Legends of King Richard I Coeur de Lion* (1966).
52. *The Viking Opera Guide*, ed. Amanda Holden (1993), p. 405.
53. *The Times* (10 June 1853).
54. Mike Horswell, *The Rise and Fall of British Crusader Medievalism, c.1825–1945* (2018).
55. *Punch* (19 December 1917).
56. Eitan Bar-Yosef, 'The Last Crusade? British Propaganda and the Palestine Campaign, 1917–18', *Journal of Contemporary History* 36 (2001), pp. 87–88.
57. Thomas Asbridge, *The Crusades* (2010), p. 681.
58. James White, *The Adventures of King Richard Cœur-de-Lion*, 3 vols (1791), I, p. 2.
59. Franklin, *Assassin's Prayer*, p. 139.
60. Neil Price, *The Children of Ash and Elm* (2020), p. 25.

Chapter 3 – Edward I: A Strong King?

1. *Thomas Wright's Political Songs*, p. 93.
2. Marc Morris, *A Great and Terrible King: Edward I and the Forging of Britain* (2008).
3. There is some debate over this number. For a list of those children for whom there is clear evidence, see Michael Prestwich, *Edward I* (Yale edition: 1997), p. 126.
4. Morris, *Great and Terrible King*, p. 42.
5. Andy King, *Edward I: A New King Arthur?* (2016), p. 15.
6. Oliver de Laborderie, J. R. Maddicott and D. A. Carpenter, 'The Last Hours of Simon de Montfort: A New Account', *English Historical Review* 115 (2000), p. 412.
7. Cited in King, *Edward I*, p. 24.
8. Paul Doherty, *The Great Crown Jewels Robbery of 1303* (2005), pp. 19–20.
9. Carpenter, *Henry III: Rise to Power*, pp. 168, 175.
10. David Carpenter, *Henry III: Reform, Rebellion, Civil War, Settlement, 1258–1272* (2023), p. xi.
11. Margaret Howell, *Eleanor of Provence: Queenship in Thirteenth-Century England* (1998), p. 300.
12. Morris, *Great and Terrible King*, p. 171.
13. King, *Edward I*, p. 30.
14. *Early Common Petitions in the English Parliament, c.1290–c.1420*, eds. W. Mark Ormrod, Helen Killick and Phil Bradford (2017), pp. 74–75, 81–82.

15. King, *Edward I*, p. 33.
16. Robin R. Mundill, *England's Jewish Solution: Experiment and Expulsion, 1262–1290* (1998), p. 277.
17. Morris, *Great and Terrible King*, p. 228.
18. Doherty, *Crown Jewels Robbery*, p. 17.
19. Richard Oram, *The Kings and Queens of Scotland* (2001), p. 116.
20. Jean Favier, *Philippe le Bel* (1978), p. 210.
21. Stubbs, *Constitutional History*, II, p. 133.
22. *The Chronicle of Lanercost*, trans. Herbert Maxwell (1913), pp. 162–63; J. H. Denton, *Robert Winchelsey and the Crown, 1294–1313: A Study in the Defence of Ecclesiastical Liberty* (1980), p. 126.
23. *The Chronicle of Walter of Guisborough*, ed. Harry Rothwell (1957), pp. 289–90, but see the comments in Andy King, 'Crisis? What Crisis? 1297 and the Civil War that Never Was', in *Edward I: New Interpretations*, eds. Andy King and Andrew M. Spencer (2020), pp. 167–68.
24. *Flores Historiarum*, ed. Henry Richards Luard, 3 vols (1890), III, p. 296.
25. King, 'Crisis? What Crisis?', p. 182.
26. *Willelmi Rishanger, quondam Monachi S. Albani, et quorundam Anonymorum, Chronica et Annales, Regnantibus Henrico Tertio et Edwardo Primo*, ed. Henry Thomas Riley (1865), p. 405.
27. Morris, *Great and Terrible King*, p. 344.
28. Matthew Strickland, 'Treason, Feud and the Growth of State Violence: Edward I and the "War of the Earl of Carrick", 1306–7', in *War, Government and Aristocracy in the British Isles, c.1150–1500: Essays in Honour of Michael Prestwich*, eds. Chris Given-Wilson, Ann Kettle and Len Scales (2008), p. 86.
29. *Proctors for Parliament: Clergy, Community and Politics c.1248–1539*, eds. Phil Bradford and Alison K. McHardy, 2 vols (2017–18), I, pp. 223–32.
30. *English Historical Documents Volume III: 1189–1327*, ed. Harry Rothwell (1975), pp. 264–65.
31. John Barbour, *The Bruce*, ed. and trans. A. A. M. Duncan (1997), p. 166.
32. *John of Fordun's Chronicle of the Scottish Nation*, trans. Felix J. H. Skene (1872), p. 336.
33. This period is summarised in G. Templeman, 'Edward I and the Historians', *Cambridge Historical Journal* 10 (1950), pp. 16–35.
34. Stubbs, *Constitutional History*, II, pp. 105, 106, 153.
35. T. F. Tout, *Edward the First* (1893), pp. 7, 193, 229.
36. Edward Jenks, *Edward Plantagenet (Edward I): The English Justinian, or, The Making of the Common Law* (1902), p. iii.
37. T. F. Tout, *Chapters in the Administrative History of Mediaeval England*, 6 vols (1920–33), II, pp. 10, 190.
38. F. M. Powicke, *King Henry III and the Lord Edward: The Community of the Realm in the Thirteenth Century*, 2 vols (1947), II, pp.724–25.
39. Maurice Powicke, *The Thirteenth Century, 1216–1307* (2nd edition: 1962), pp. 228, 230.
40. T. F. T. Plucknett, *Legislation of Edward I* (1949), p. 1.
41. Harvey, *Plantagenets*, pp. 110, 122.
42. Churchill, *History of the English-Speaking Peoples*, I, pp. 209, 218, 226, 227.
43. L. F. Salzman, *Edward I* (1968), p. 197.
44. K. B. McFarlane, *The Nobility of Later Medieval England* (1973), p. 121; 'Had Edward I a "Policy" towards the Earls?', *History* 50 (1965), pp. 58, 159.

45. J. Beverley Smith, *Llywelyn ap Gruffudd, Tywysog Cymru* (1986), translated as *Llywelyn ap Gruffudd: Prince of Wales* (1998).
46. Fiona Watson, *Under the Hammer: Edward I and Scotland, 1286–1307* (1998), p. 213; Andrew Fisher, *William Wallace* (2nd edition: 2002), p. 242; G. W. S. Barrow, *Robert Bruce and the Community of the Realm of Scotland* (3rd edition: 1988), p. 137.
47. Michael Prestwich, *War, Politics and Finance under Edward I* (1972), p. 290; *The Three Edwards: War and State in England, 1272–1377* (1980), p. 41; *Edward I*, pp. 296, 297, 511, 567; *Plantagenet England 1225–1360* (2005), p. 177.
48. Robin Frame, *The Political Development of the British Isles 1100–1400* (1990), p. 143.
49. R. R. Davies, *The First English Empire: Power and Identities in the British Isles 1093–1343* (2000), p. 27.
50. Anthony Seldon, *Major: A Political Life* (1997), p. 664.
51. John Carmi Parsons, *Eleanor of Castile: Queen and Society in Thirteenth-Century England* (1995); Howell, *Eleanor of Provence*; J. R. Maddicott, *Simon de Montfort* (1994).
52. Sandra Raban, *England under Edward I and Edward II, 1259–1327* (2000), p. 141.
53. Morris, *Great and Terrible King*, pp. 370, 371, 372, 375, 377.
54. Caroline Burt, *Edward I and the Governance of England, 1272–1307* (2013), p. 241.
55. Andrew M. Spencer, *Nobility and Kingship in Medieval England: The Earls and Edward I, 1272–1307* (2014), p. 265.
56. King, *Edward I*, pp. 48, 75, 81, 90, 93–4, 98, 101.
57. Powicke, *Thirteenth* Century, p. 227.
58. The quotes which follow are from Paul Doherty, *Satan in St Mary's* (1986), p. 18; *Crown in Darkness* (1988), pp. 170, 176; *Spy in Chancery* (1988), pp. 16, 164.
59. Prestwich, *Edward I*, p. 435.

Chapter 4 – Edward III: A Romantic King?

1. *The Brut, or the Chronicles of England*, ed. Friedrich W. D. Brie (1906), p. 334.
2. Translation of the Latin inscription on Edward's tomb in Westminster Abbey.
3. Jonathan Sumption, *Edward III: A Heroic Failure* (2016), p. 103.
4. This is covered in greater detail in Bradford, *Worst Medieval Monarchs*, pp. 70–86.
5. Sumption, *Edward III*, p. 18.
6. Caroline Shenton, 'Edward III and the Coup of 1330', in *The Age of Edward III*, ed. J. S. Bothwell (2001), p. 15.
7. Phil Bradford, 'A Silent Presence: The English King in Parliament in the Fourteenth Century', *Historical Research* 84 (2011), p. 208.
8. Ormrod, *Edward III*, p. 92.
9. James Bothwell, 'An Emotional Pragmatism: Edward III and Death', in *Monarchy, State and Culture in Late Medieval England*, eds. Gwilym Dodd and Craig Taylor (2020), pp. 39–70.
10. W. M. Ormrod, 'Competing Capitals? York and London in the Fourteenth Century', in *Courts and Regions in Medieval Europe*, eds. Sarah Rees Jones, Richard Marks and A. J. Minnis (2000); Sarah Rees Jones, *York: The Making of a City 1068–1350* (2013), pp. 126–27.
11. Sumption, *Edward III*, p. 40.
12. Ormrod, *Edward III*, p. 196.

13. Ibid., p. 228.
14. Ibid., p. 245.
15. *St George's Chapel Windsor in the Fourteenth Century*, ed. Nigel Saul (2005); Elizabeth Biggs, *St Stephen's College, Westminster: A Royal Chapel and English Kingship, 1348–1548* (2020).
16. 'The Anonimalle Chronicle', in *The Black Death*, ed. and trans. Rosemary Horrox (1994), p. 62.
17. Ormrod, *Edward III*, p. 356.
18. L. R. Poos, 'The Social Context of Statute of Labourers Enforcement', *Law and History Review* 1 (1983), pp. 27–52; Christopher Dyer, *Everyday Life in Medieval England* (1994), pp. 167–219.
19. John Aberth, *Criminal Churchmen in the Age of Edward III: The Case of Bishop Thomas de Lisle* (1996).
20. Ormrod, *Edward III*, p. 367.
21. *Knighton's Chronicle, 1337–1396*, ed. and trans. G. H. Martin (1995), p. 151.
22. Laura Tompkins, '"Edward III's Gold-Digging Mistress": Alice Perrers, Gender, and Financial Power at the English Royal Court, 1360–1377', in *Women and Economic Power in Premodern Royal Courts*, ed. Cathleen Sarti (2020), pp. 59–71.
23. Ormrod, *Edward III*, p. 549.
24. *The Chronica Maiora of Thomas Walsingham (1376–1422)*, trans. David Preest (2005), p. 32.
25. Jean Froissart, *Chronicles*, ed. and trans. Geoffrey Brereton (1968), p. 195.
26. *Knighton's Chronicle*, p. 197.
27. *Chronica Maiora*, pp. 32–33.
28. Ormrod, *Edward III*, p. 584.
29. *Chronica Maiora*, p. 32.
30. *The Parliament Rolls of Medieval England*, eds. Chris Given-Wilson *et al.* (2005), X, p. 430.
31. John Adamson, *The Noble Revolt: The Overthrow of Charles I* (2007), p. 205.
32. Daniel, *History of England*, pp. 261, 262.
33. Joshua Barnes, *The History of That Most Victorious Monarch Edward III* (1688), p. 911.
34. John Lingard, *The History of England*, 10 vols (1883 edition), III, pp. 206–7.
35. William Longman, *The History of the Life and Times of Edward the Third*, 2 vols (1869), II, pp. 296, 297, 298.
36. W. Warburton, *Edward III* (4th edition: 1887), p. 252.
37. Stubbs, *Constitutional History*, II, pp. 393–94.
38. Charles Oman, *A History of the Art of War* (1898), p. 591.
39. T. F. Tout, *The History of England from the Accession of Henry III to the Death of Edward III* (1905), p. 431.
40. W. M. Ormrod, 'Edward III and His Family', *Journal of British Studies* 26 (1987), pp. 398–422.
41. John Fortescue, *The Governance of England*, ed. Charles Plummer (1885), pp. 15–16.
42. Ormrod, *Edward III*, pp. xi–xii.
43. May McKisack, *The Fourteenth Century, 1307–1399* (1959), pp. 270-71; May McKisack, 'Edward III and the Historians', *History* 45 (1960), pp. 2, 14, 15.
44. John Watts, *Henry VI and the Politics of Kingship* (1996).

45. Paul Johnson, *The Life and Times of Edward III* (1973), p. 217; Michael Packe, *King Edward III* (1983), p. 300.
46. Prestwich, *Three Edwards*, pp. 189, 244.
47. Scott L. Waugh, *England in the Reign of Edward III* (1991), pp. 4, 236.
48. W. M. Ormrod, *The Reign of Edward III: Crown and Society in England 1327–1377* (1990), pp. 201, 203; Ormrod, *Edward III*, pp. 599, 602, 603.
49. Richard W. Kaeuper, *War, Justice and Public Order: England and France in the Later Middle Ages* (1988), pp. 32, 81.
50. Chris Given-Wilson and Michael Prestwich, 'Introduction', in *Age of Edward III*, ed. Bothwell, p. 1.
51. J. S. Bothwell, *Edward III and the English Peerage* (2004).
52. Clifford J. Rogers, *War Cruel and Sharp: English Strategy Under Edward III, 1327–1360* (2000), p. 422.
53. Matthew Hefferman, *The Household Knights of Edward III* (2021), p. 265.
54. Ian Mortimer, *The Perfect King: The Life of Edward III, Father of the English Nation* (2006), pp. 401–2.
55. Sumption, *Edward III*, pp. 39, 103, 104, 107.
56. McKisack, 'Edward III', pp. 269–70.
57. *King Edward III*, ed. Giorgio Melchiori (1998), pp. 12–13.
58. McKisack, 'Edward III', p. 1.

Chapter 5 – Henry V: An Ideal King?

1. *Henry V: New Interpretations*, ed. Gwilym Dodd (2013), p. ix.
2. Desmond Seward, *Henry V as Warlord* (1987), p. 220.
3. Timothy D. Amer, 'The Disappearing Scar of Henry V: Triage, Trauma, and the Treatment of Henry's Wounding at the Battle of Shrewsbury', *Journal of Medieval and Early Modern Studies* 49 (2019), pp. 347–76.
4. Anthony Tuck, 'The Earl of Arundel's Expedition to France, 1411', in *The Reign of Henry IV: Rebellion and Survival, 1403–13*, eds. Gwilym Dodd and Douglas Biggs (2008), pp. 228–39.
5. *Chronica Maiora*, p. 389.
6. Anne Curry, *Henry V: Playboy Prince to Warrior King* (2015), p. 35.
7. Nigel Saul, *Richard II* (1997), p. 428.
8. Edward Powell, *Kingship, Law and Society: Criminal Justice in the Reign of Henry V* (1989), pp. 168–94.
9. Curry, *Henry V*, p. 55.
10. Ibid., p. 59.
11. Christopher Allmand, *Henry V* (Yale edition: 1997), p. 79.
12. Ibid., pp. 83–84.
13. Ibid., p. 93.
14. Michael Bennett, 'Henry V and the Cheshire Tax Revolt of 1416', in *Henry V*, ed. Dodd, pp. 171–86.
15. *Parliament Rolls of Medieval England*, IX, pp. 254, 258–9.
16. Powell, *Kingship, Law and Society*, pp. 131, 255–59.
17. W. Mark Ormrod, 'Henry V and the English Taxpayer', in *Henry V*, ed. Dodd, p. 187.

18. *The Funeral Achievements of Henry V at Westminster Abbey*, eds. Anne Curry and Susan Jenkins (2022).
19. Patrick Strong and Felicity Strong, 'The Last Will and Codicils of Henry V', *English Historical Review* 96 (1981), pp. 79–102; T. B. Pugh, *Henry V and the Southampton Plot* (1988), p. 144.
20. Keith Dockray, *Henry V* (2004), p. 13.
21. John Matusiak, *Henry V* (2013), p. 2.
22. Jennifer Depold, 'Christ as King and Kings as Christ', *Medieval Sermon Studies* 64 (2020), pp. 22–34.
23. Matusiak, *Henry V*, p. 11.
24. *Gesta Henrici Quinti: The Deeds of Henry the Fifth*, eds. and trans. Frank Taylor and John S. Roskell (1975), pp. 3, 181.
25. *Chronica Maiora of Thomas Walsingham*, p. 446.
26. Antonia Gransden, *Historical Writing in England II* (1982), p. 196.
27. Dockray, *Henry V*, p. 20.
28. David Rundle, 'The Unoriginality of Tito Livio Frulovisi's *Vita Henrici Quinti*', *English Historical Review* 123 (2008), pp. 1109–31.
29. The French sources are discussed in Dockray, *Henry V*, pp. 33–43, and Matusiak, *Henry V*, pp. 8–10.
30. Susan Royal, 'History, Heresy and Henry V', in *Memory and the English Reformation*, eds. Alexandra Walsham *et al.* (2020), p. 285.
31. Thomas Goodwin, *The History of the Reign of Henry the Fifth, King of England* (1704), p. 2.
32. Christopher Allmand, 'Writing History in the Eighteenth Century: Thomas Goodwin's *The History of the Reign of Henry the Fifth* (1704)', in *Henry V*, ed. Dodd, pp. 273–88.
33. Paul de Rapin, *History of England*, 13 vols (1727), I, p. 530.
34. Hume, *History*, III, p. 97.
35. John Richard Green, *A Short History of the English People*, pp. 540, 546–47.
36. Stubbs, *Constitutional History*, III, pp. 74, 75, 77.
37. James Hamilton Wylie and William Templeton Waugh, *The Reign of Henry the Fifth*, 3 vols (1914–29), III, p. 426.
38. Harvey, *Plantagenets*, pp. 171, 174.
39. Harold F. Hutchison, *Henry V* (1967), pp. 219, 223, 225.
40. Peter Earle, *The Life and Times of Henry V* (1972), p. 215.
41. Richard Vaughan, *John the Fearless* (2002 edition), pp. 205, 214; *Philip the Good* (2002 edition), p. 11.
42. Churchill, *History of the English-Speaking Peoples*, I, pp. 292, 300.
43. K. B. McFarlane in *The Cambridge Medieval History*, VIII (1936), pp. 384–85.
44. K. B. McFarlane, *Lancastrian Kings and Lollard Knights* (1972), p. 133.
45. E. F. Jacob, *Henry V and the Invasion of France* (1947); *The Fifteenth Century, 1399–1485* (1961), p. 202.
46. G. L. Harriss (ed.), *Henry V: The Practice of Kingship* (1985), pp. 135, 199; Gerald Harriss, *Shaping the Nation: England 1360–1461* (2005), pp. 588–94; Powell, *Kingship, Law and Society*, p. 275.
47. Seward, *Henry V*, pp. 216, 218, 220.
48. Françoise Autrand, *Charles VI: La Folie du Roi* (1986), p. 589.
49. Pugh, *Henry V*, pp. 138, 139, 145.
50. Allmand, *Henry V*, p. 443.

51. W. M. Ormrod, *Political Life in Medieval England, 1300–1450* (1995), pp. 136–37; Ormrod, 'Henry V and the English Taxpayer', pp. 215–16.
52. A. J. Pollard, *Late Medieval England 1399–1509* (2000), pp. 87–88, 91 n. 47; A. J. Pollard, *Henry V* (2014), p. 113.
53. Dockray, *Henry V*, pp. 213, 214, 242.
54. Malcolm Mercer, *Henry V: The Rebirth of Chivalry* (2004), p. 105.
55. Rundle, 'Unoriginality', p. 1110.
56. Gwilym Dodd, 'Henry V's Establishment: Service, Loyalty and Reward in 1413'; Maureen Jurkowski, 'Henry V's Suppression of the Oldcastle Revolt'; and Alison K. McHardy, 'Religion, Court Culture and Propaganda: The Chapel Royal in the Reign of Henry V', in *Henry V*, ed. Dodd, pp. 64, 127, 129, 156.
57. Matusiak, *Henry V*, pp. 19, 245.
58. Juliet Barker, *Agincourt: The King, the Campaign, the Battle* (2005); Ian Mortimer, *1415: Henry V's Year of Glory* (2009), pp. 4–5.
59. Anne Curry, *The Battle of Agincourt: Sources and Interpretations* (2000); Anne Curry, *Agincourt: A New History* (2005); *The Battle of Agincourt*, eds. Anne Curry and Malcolm Mercer (2015); Curry, *Henry V*.
60. Chris Given-Wilson, *Henry IV* (2016), p. 541.
61. Macolm Vale, *Henry V: The Conscience of a King* (2016), pp. xv, 4, 278, 279; review by A. K. McHardy in *English Historical Review* 133 (2018), pp. 694–96.
62. *Upstart Crow*, 'I Know Thee Not, Old Man' (Series 2, Episode 2, 2017).
63. Bernard Cornwell, *Azincourt* (2008), pp. 31, 37, 319–20.

Bibliography

Printed Primary Sources

Anglo-Scottish Relations 1174–1328: Some Selected Documents, ed. E. L. G. Stones (Nelson, London, 1965).

Barbour, John, *The Bruce*, ed. and trans. A. A. M. Duncan (Canongate, Edinburgh, 1997).

The Black Death, ed. and trans. Rosemary Horrox (Manchester University Press, Manchester, 1994).

The Brut, or the Chronicles of England, ed. Friedrich W. D. Brie (Early English Text Society, London, 1906).

Chronica Magistri Rogeri de Houdene, ed. William Stubbs, 4 vols (Rolls Series: London, 1878–81).

The Chronica Maiora of Thomas Walsingham (1376–1422), trans. David Preest (Boydell Press, Woodbridge, 2005).

The Chronicle of Lanercost, trans. Herbert Maxwell (facsimile reprint: Llanerch Press, Cribyn, 2001 [original edition 1913]).

The Chronicle of Richard of Devizes, ed. and trans. John T. Appleby (Thomas Nelson and Sons, London, 1963).

The Chronicle of Walter of Guisborough, ed. Harry Rothwell (Camden Society, London, 1957).

The Correspondence of Thomas Becket, Archbishop of Canterbury 1162–1170, ed. and trans. Anne Duggan, 2 vols (Oxford University Press, Oxford, 2000).

Dialogus de Scaccario: The Dialogue of the Exchequer; Constitutio Domus Regis: Disposition of the King's Household, eds. and trans. Emilie Amt and S. D. Church (Oxford University Press, Oxford, 2007).

Documents Illustrating the Crisis of 1297–98 in England, ed. Michael Prestwich, Camden Society, 4th Series 24 (Royal Historical Society, London, 1980).

Early Common Petitions in the English Parliament, c.1290–c.1420, eds. W. Mark Ormrod, Helen Killick and Phil Bradford (Cambridge University Press for the Royal Historical Society, Cambridge, 2017).

English Historical Documents Volume II: 1042–1189, eds. David C. Douglas and George W. Greenaway (2nd edition: Eyre Methuen, London, 1981).

English Historical Documents Volume III: 1189–1327, ed. Harry Rothwell (Eyre and Spottiswoode, London, 1975).

Feet of Fines of the Ninth Year of the Reign of King Richard I, A.D. 1197 to A.D. 1198, Pipe Roll Society 23 (1898).

Flores Historiarum, ed. Henry Richards Luard, 3 vols. (Rolls Series: London, 1890).

Fortescue, John, *The Governance of England*, ed. Charles Plummer (Clarendon Press, Oxford, 1885).

Froissart, Jean, *Chronicles*, ed. and trans. Geoffrey Brereton (Penguin, Harmondsworth, 1968).

Gerald of Wales, *De Principis Instructione: Instruction for a Ruler*, ed. and trans. Robert Bartlett (Oxford University Press, Oxford, 2018).

Gesta Henrici Quinti: The Deeds of Henry the Fifth, eds. and trans. Frank Taylor and John S. Roskell (Clarendon Press, Oxford, 1975).

Gesta Regis Henrici Secundi et Ricardi Primi, ed. William Stubbs, 2 vols (Rolls Series: London, 1867).

The History of William Marshal, trans. Nigel Bryant (Boydell Press, Woodbridge, 2016).

John of Fordun's Chronicle of the Scottish Nation, trans. Felix J. H. Skene (Edmonston and Douglas, Edinburgh, 1872).

Knighton's Chronicle, 1337–1396, ed. and trans. G. H. Martin (Oxford University Press, Oxford 1995).

The Letters and Charters of Henry II, King of England 1154–1189, ed. Nicholas Vincent, 7 vols (Oxford University Press, Oxford, 2020–23).

The Lives of Thomas Becket, ed. and trans. Michael Staunton (Manchester University Press, Manchester, 2001).

The Parliament Rolls of Medieval England, ed. Chris Given-Wilson *et al.* (Boydell Press, Woodbridge, 2005).

Polychronicon Ranulphi Higden Monachi Cestrensis, eds. Churchill Babbington and Joseph Rawson Lumby, 9 vols (Rolls Series: London, 1865–86).

Proctors for Parliament: Clergy, Community and Politics c.1248–1539 (The National Archives, Series SC 10), eds. Phil Bradford and Alison K. McHardy, 2 vols (Boydell Press for the Canterbury and York Society, Woodbridge, 2017–18).

Radulfi de Diceto Decani Lundoniensis Opera Historica, ed. William Stubbs, 2 vols (Rolls Series: London, 1876).

Richard Coer de Lyon, ed. Peter Larkin (Medieval Institute Publications, Kalamazoo, 2015).

Tales of a Minstrel of Reims in the Thirteenth Century, trans. Samuel N. Rosenberg (Washington D.C., Catholic University of America Press, 2022).

Thomas Wright's Political Songs from the Reign of John to that of Edward II, ed. Peter Coss (Cambridge University Press, Cambridge, 1996).

Vita Edwardi Secundi, ed. and trans. Wendy R. Childs (Oxford University Press, Oxford, 2005).

Walter Map, *De Nugis Curialium*, ed. and trans. C. N. L. Brooke and R. A. B. Mynors (Oxford University Press, Oxford, 1983).

Willelmi Rishanger, quondam Monachi S. Albani, et quorundam Anonymorum, Chronica et Annales, Regnantibus Henrico Tertio et Edwardo Primo, ed. Henry Thomas Riley (Rolls Series: London, 1865).

Secondary Sources

Aberth, John, *Criminal Churchmen in the Age of Edward III: The Case of Bishop Thomas de Lisle* (Pennsylvania State University Press, University Park, 1996).

Adamson, John, *The Noble Revolt: The Overthrow of Charles I* (Weidenfeld and Nicolson, London, 2007).

Allmand, Christopher, *Henry V* (Yale edition: Yale University Press, New Haven and London, 1997 [original edition 1992]).

Allmand, C. T., 'Henry V the Soldier, and the War in France', in *Henry V*, ed. Harriss, pp. 117–35.

Allmand, Christopher, *The Hundred Years War: England and France at War, c.1300–c.1450* (Cambridge University Press, Cambridge, 1989).

Allmand, C. T., *Lancastrian Normandy: The History of an Occupation* (Clarendon Press, Oxford, 1983).

Allmand, Christopher, 'Writing History in the Eighteenth Century: Thomas Goodwin's *The History of the Reign of Henry the Fifth* (1704)', in *Henry V*, ed. Dodd, pp. 273–88.

Allmand, Christopher (ed.), *War, Government and Power in Medieval France* (Liverpool University Press, Liverpool, 2000).

Ambler, S. T., 'Magna Carta: Its Confirmation at Simon de Montfort's Parliament of 1265', *English Historical Review* 130 (2015), pp. 801–30.

Ambler, Sophie Thérèse, *The Song of Simon de Montfort: England's First Revolutionary and the Death of Chivalry* (Picador, London 2019).

Ambler, Sophie, 'The Surrender of Gloucester Castle in June 1265', in *English Medieval Government and Administration*, eds. Saul and Vincent, pp. 257–77.

Amer, Timothy D., 'The Disappearing Scar of Henry V: Triage, Trauma, and the Treatment of Henry's Wounding at the Battle of Shrewsbury', *Journal of Medieval and Early Modern Studies* 49 (2019), pp. 347–76.

Amt, Emilie, *The Accession of Henry II in England: Royal Government Restored 1149–1159* (Boydell Press, Woodbridge, 1993).

Appleby, John T., *England without Richard, 1189–1199* (G. Bell and Sons, London, 1965).

Appleby, John T., *Henry II: The Vanquished King* (G. Bell and Sons, London, 1962).

Asbridge, Thomas, *The Crusades: The War for the Holy Land* (Pocket Books, London, 2010).

Asbridge, Thomas, *Richard I: The Crusader King* (Penguin, London, 2018).

Aurell, Martin, *The Plantagenet Empire, 1154–1224* (Routledge, Abingdon, 2007).

Aurell, Martin, 'Political Culture and Medieval Historiography: The Revolt against King Henry II, 1173–1174', *History* 102 (2017), pp. 752–71.

Aurell, Martin, *et al.* (eds.), *Les Plantagenêts dans les Pays de la Loire* (Région Pays de la Loire, Nantes, 2021).

Aurell, Martin, *et al.* (eds.), *Les Plantagenêts et le Maine* (Presse Universitaires de Rennes, Rennes, 2022).

Autrand, Françoise, *Charles VI: La Folie du Roi* (Fayard, Paris, 1986).

Bachrach, David S., 'The Ecclesia Anglicana Goes to War: Prayers, Propaganda, and Conquest during the Reign of Edward I of England, 1272–1307', *Albion* 36 (2004), pp. 393–406.

Baldwin, John, 'La Décennie Décisive: Les Années 1190–1203 dans le Règne de Philippe Auguste', *Revue Historique* 266 (1981), pp. 311–337.

Bar-Yosef, Eitan, 'The Last Crusade? British Propaganda and the Palestine Campaign, 1917–18', *Journal of Contemporary History* 36 (2001), pp. 87–109.

Barber, Richard, *Henry Plantagenet: A Biography* (Barrie and Rockliff, London, 1964).

Barber, Richard, *Henry II: A Prince among Princes* (Penguin, London, 2015).

Barber, Richard, *The Devil's Crown: A History of Henry II and His Sons* (BBC Publications, London, 1978).

Barker, Juliet, *Agincourt: The King, the Campaign, the Battle* (Little, Brown, London, 2005).

Barlow, Frank, *Thomas Becket* (Weidenfeld and Nicolson, London, 1986).

Barlow, Frank, *William Rufus* (Yale edition: Yale University Press, London and New Haven, 2000).

Barnes, Joshua, *The History of That Most Victorious Monarch Edward III* (John Hayes, Cambridge, 1688).

Barratt, Nick, 'Finance and the Economy in the Reign of Henry II', in *Henry II: New Interpretations*, ed. Harper-Bill and Vincent, pp. 242–56.

Barratt, Nick, *The Restless Kings: Henry II, His Sons and the Wars for the Plantagenet Crown* (Faber and Faber, London, 2018).

Barrow, G. W. S., *Robert Bruce and the Community of the Realm of Scotland* (3rd edition: Edinburgh University Press, Edinburgh, 1988 [original edition 1965]).

Bartlett, Robert, *Blood Royal: Dynastic Politics in Medieval Europe* (Cambridge University Press, Cambridge, 2020).

Bartlett, Robert, *England under the Norman and Angevin Kings* (Clarendon Press, Oxford, 2000).

Bartlett, Robert, *Trial by Fire and Water: The Medieval Judicial Ordeal* (Clarendon Press, Oxford, 1986).

Bartlett, W. B., *Richard the Lionheart: The Crusader King of England* (Amberley, Stroud, 2018).

Bates, David, *William the Conqueror* (Yale University Press, New Haven and London, 2016).

Bautier, Robert-Henri, '"Empire Plantagenêt" ou "Espace Plantagenêt". Y-eut-il une Civilisation du Monde Plantagenêt?', *Cahiers de Civilisation Médiévale* 29 (1986), pp. 139–47.

Bennett, Michael, 'Henry V and the Cheshire Tax Revolt of 1416', in *Henry V*, ed. Dodd, pp. 171–86.

Berard, Christopher Michael, *Arthurianism in Early Plantagenet England: From Henry II to Edward I* (Boydell Press, Woodbridge, 2019).

Bernard, G. W., *The King's Reformation: Henry VIII and the Remaking of the English Church* (Yale University Press, New Haven and London, 2005).

Bienvenu, Jean-Marc, 'Aliénor d'Aquitaine et Fontevraud', *Cahiers de Civilisation Médiévale* 29 (1986), pp. 15–27.

Bienvenu, Jean-Marc, 'Henri II Plantegenêt et Fontevraud', *Cahiers de Civilisation Médiévale* 37 (1994), pp. 25–32.

Biggs, Elizabeth, *St Stephen's College, Westminster: A Royal Chapel and English Kingship, 1348–1548* (Boydell Press, Woodbridge, 2020).

Billaud, Rod, 'The Lord Edward and the Administration of Justice across his Apanage, 1254–72', in *Edward I*, ed. King and Spencer, pp. 9–23.

Bolton, J. L., *The Medieval English Economy 1150–1500* (J. M. Dent and Sons, London, 1980).

Bolton, Timothy, *Cnut the Great* (Yale University Press, New Haven and London, 2017).

Bothwell, J. S., 'Edward III, the English Peerage and the 1337 Earls: Estate Redistribution in Fourteenth-Century England', in *Age of Edward III*, ed. Bothwell, pp. 35–52.

Bothwell, J. S., *Edward III and the English Peerage: Royal Patronage, Social Mobility and Political Control in Fourteenth-Century England* (Boydell Press, Woodbridge, 2004).

Bothwell, James, 'An Emotional Pragmatism: Edward III and Death', in *Monarchy, State and Culture in Late Medieval England: Essays in Honour of W. Mark Ormrod*, eds. Gwilym Dodd and Craig Taylor (York Medieval Press, York, 2020), pp. 39–70.

Bothwell, J. S. (ed.), *The Age of Edward III* (York Medieval Press, York, 2001).

Boyd, Douglas, *Lionheart: The True Story of England's Crusader King* (The History Press, Stroud, 2014).

Bradbury, Jim *Philip Augustus: King of France 1180–1223* (Longman, Harlow, 1998).

Bradford, Phil, 'A Silent Presence: The English King in Parliament in the Fourteenth Century', *Historical Research* 84 (2011), pp. 189–211.

Bradford, Phil, *The Worst Medieval Monarchs: Incompetent, Evil and Tyrannous Kings* (Pen and Sword, Barnsley, 2023).

Bradford, Sarah, *George VI* (revised edition: Penguin, London, 2011 [original edition 1989]).

Brand, Paul, 'Henry II and the Creation of the English Common Law', in *Henry II: New Interpretations*, eds. Harper-Bill and Vincent, pp. 215–41.

Brand, Paul, 'Petitions and Parliament in the Reign of Edward I', in *Parchment and People: Parliament in the Middle Ages*, ed. Linda Clark (Edinburgh University Press, Edinburgh, 2004), pp. 14–38.

Brand, Paul, 'Understanding Early Petitions: An Analysis of the Content of Petitions to Parliament in the Reign of Edward I', in *Medieval Petitions*, eds. Ormrod, Dodd and Musson, pp. 99–119.

Brodie, Hugh, 'Punching above Gwynedd's Weight: Llywelyn ap Gruffudd's Diplomatic Communication and the Road to War in 1277', *Studia Celtica* 53 (2019), pp. 21–47.

Broughton, Bradford B., *The Legends of King Richard I Coeur de Lion: A Study of Sources and Variations to the Year 1600* (Mouton and Co., The Hague, 1966).

Brown, Michael, 'Aristocratic Politics and the Crisis of Scottish Kingship, 1286–96', *Scottish Historical Review* 90 (2011), pp. 1–16.

Brown, Michael, 'Hearts and Bodies: Edward I and the Scottish Magnates, 1296–1307', in *Edward I*, eds. King and Spencer, pp. 105–24.

Brundage, James A., *Richard Lionheart: A Biography* (Charles Scribner's Sons, New York, 1974).

Burgess, Clive, 'St George's College, Windsor: Context and Consequence', in *St George's Chapel Windsor*, ed. Saul, pp. 63–96.

Burt, Caroline, *Edward I and the Governance of England, 1272–1307* (Cambridge University Press, Cambridge, 2013).

Burt, Caroline, 'Law and Order in the Reign of Edward I: Some New Thoughts', in *Edward I*, eds. King and Spencer, pp. 44–65.

Cam, Helen M., *The Hundred and the Hundred Rolls: An Outline of Medieval Government in Medieval England* (Methuen and Co., London, 1930).

Carpenter, David, *Henry III: The Rise to Power and Personal Rule, 1207–1258* (Yale University Press, New Haven and London, 2020).

Carpenter, David, *Henry III: Reform, Rebellion, Civil War, Settlement, 1258–1272* (Yale University Press, New Haven and London, 2023).

Cassidy, Richard, 'Simon de Montfort's Sheriffs, 1264–5', *Historical Research* 91 (2018), pp. 3–21.

Chauou, Amaury, *Les Plantagenêts et leur Cour, 1154–1216* (Presses Universitaires de France, Paris, 2019).

Church, Stephen, *Henry III: A Simple and God-Fearing King* (Allen Lane, London, 2017).

Churchill, Winston S., *History of the English-Speaking Peoples*, 4 vols (Cassell, London, 1956–58).

Crouch, David, *William Marshal* (3rd edition: Routledge, Abingdon, 2016).

Curry, Anne, *Agincourt: A New History* (Tempus, Stroud, 2005).

Curry, Anne, *The Battle of Agincourt: Sources and Interpretations* (Boydell Press, Woodbridge, 2000).
Curry, Anne, *Henry V: Playboy Prince to Warrior King* (Allen Lane, London, 2015).
Curry, Anne, *The Hundred Years War* (Basingstoke, Macmillan, 1993).
Curry, Anne, 'The Making of a Prince: The Finances of "the Young Lord Henry"', in *Henry V*, ed. Dodd, pp. 11–33.
Curry, Anne, 'Two Kingdoms, One King: The Treaty of Troyes (1420) and the Creation of a Double Monarchy of England and France', in *'The Contending Kingdoms': France and England 1320–1700*, ed. Glenn Richardson (Aldershot, Ashgate, 2008), pp. 23–41.
Curry, Anne and Jenkins, Susan (eds.), *The Funeral Achievements of Henry V at Westminster Abbey: The Arms and Armour of Death* (Boydell Press, Woodbridge, 2022).
Curry, Anne and Mercer, Malcom (eds.), *The Battle of Agincourt* (Yale University Press with Royal Armouries, New Haven and London, 2015).
Daniel, Samuel, *The Collection of the History of England* (5th edition: London, 1685).
Davies, R. R., *The Age of Conquest: Wales 1063–1415* (Oxford University Press, Oxford, 2000).
Davies, R. R., *The First English Empire: Power and Identities in the British Isles 1093–1343* (Oxford University Press, Oxford, 2000).
De Laborderie, Oliver; Maddicott, J. R.; and Carpenter, D. A., 'The Last Hours of Simon de Montfort: A New Account', *English Historical Review* 115 (2000), pp. 378–412.
Denton, J. H., *Robert Winchelsey and the Crown, 1294–1313: A Study in the Defence of Ecclesiastical Liberty* (Cambridge University Press, Cambridge, 1980).
Depold, Jennifer, 'Christ as King and Kings as Christ', *Medieval Sermon Studies* 64 (2020), pp. 22–34.
Devaux, Jean, 'From the Court of Hainault to the Court of England: The Example of John Froissart', in *War, Government and Power*, ed. Allmand, pp. 1–20.
Dockray, Keith, *Henry V* (Tempus, Stroud, 2004).
Dodd, Gwilym, 'Henry V's Establishment: Service, Loyalty and Reward in 1413', in *Henry V*, ed. Dodd, pp. 35–76.
Dodd, Gwilym, *Justice and Grace: Private Petitioning and the English Parliament in the Late Middle Ages* (Oxford University Press, Oxford, 2007).
Dodd, Gwilym (ed.), *Henry V: New Interpretations* (York Medieval Press, York, 2013).
Dodd, Gwilym and Biggs, Douglas (eds.), *Henry IV: The Establishment of the Regime, 1399–1406* (York Medieval Press, York, 2003).
Dodd, Gwilym and Biggs, Douglas (eds.), *The Reign of Henry IV: Rebellion and Survival, 1403–13* (York Medieval Press, York, 2008).
Dodson, Adrian, *The Royal Tombs of Great Britain: An Illustrated History* (Duckworth, London, 2004).
Doherty, Paul, *The Great Crown Jewels Robbery of 1303* (Constable, London, 2005).
Duffy, Seán, 'Henry II and England's Insular Neighbours', in *Henry II: New Interpretations*, eds. Harper-Bill and Vincent, pp. 129–53.
Duggan, Anne, 'Henry II, the English Church and the Papacy, 1154–76', in *Henry II: New Interpretations*, eds. Harper-Bill and Vincent, pp. 154–83.
Duggan, Anne, *Thomas Becket* (Arnold, London, 2004).
Dunbabin, Jean, 'Henry II and Louis VII', in *Henry II: New Interpretations*, eds. Harper-Bill and Vincent, pp. 47–62.
Duncan, Archie, 'Revisiting Norham, May–June 1291', in *War, Government and Aristocracy in the British Isles*, ed. Given-Wilson *et al.*, pp. 69–83.

Dyer, Christopher, *Everyday Life in Medieval England* (Hambledon and London, London, 1994).

Dyer, Christopher, *Standards of Living in the Middle Ages: Social Change in England, c.1200–1500* (2nd edition: Cambridge University Press, Cambridge, 1998).

Earle, Peter, *The Life and Times of Henry V* (Weidenfeld and Nicolson, London, 1972).

Everard, J. A., *Brittany and the Angevins: Province and Empire, 1158–1203* (Cambridge University Press, Cambridge, 2000).

Favier, Jean, *Philippe le Bel* (Fayard, Paris, 1978).

Favier, Jean, *Les Plantagenêts: Origines et Destin d'un Empire* (Fayard, Paris, 2004).

Fisher, Andrew, *William Wallace* (2nd edition: John Donald, Edinburgh, 2002 [original edition 1986]).

Flori, Jean, *Eleanor of Aquitaine: Queen and Rebel* (Edinburgh University Press, Edinburgh, 2007).

Flori, Jean, *Richard the Lionheart: King and Knight* (Edinburgh University Press, Edinburgh, 1999).

Frame, Robin, *The Political Development of the British Isles 1100–1400* (Oxford University Press, Oxford, 1990).

Harper-Bill, Christopher and Vincent, Nicholas (eds.), *Henry II: New Interpretations* (Boydell Press, Woodbridge, 2007).

Holden, Amanda (ed.), *The Viking Opera Guide* (Viking, London, 1993).

Gibbon, Edward, *The History of the Decline and Fall of the Roman Empire*, 8 vols (Folio Society edition: The Folio Society, London, 1989).

Gillingham, John, *The Angevin Empire* (2nd edition: London, Arnold, 2001).

Gillingham, John, 'Doing Homage to the King of France', in *Henry II: New Interpretations*, eds. Harper-Bill and Vincent, pp. 63–84.

Gillingham, John, *The Life and Times of Richard I* (Weidenfeld and Nicolson, London, 1973).

Gillingham, John, *Richard I* (Yale University Press, New Haven and London, 1999).

Gillingham, John, 'Richard I and Berengaria of Navarre', *Bulletin of the Institute of Historical Research* 53 (1981), pp. 157–73; reprinted in Gillingham, *Richard Coeur de Lion*, pp. 119–39.

Gillingham, John, *Richard Coeur de Lion: Kingship, Chivalry and War in the Twelfth Century* (Hambledon Press, London, 1994).

Gillingham, John, *Richard the Lionheart* (Weidenfeld and Nicolson, London, 1978).

Gillingham, John, 'Roger of Howden's Documents: Kings and Taxation in England in the Later Twelfth Century', in *English Medieval Government and Administration*, eds. Saul and Vincent, pp. 65–85.

Gillingham, John, 'Some Legends of Richard the Lionheart: Their Development and Influence', in Gillingham, *Richard Coeur de Lion*, pp. 181–92.

Gillingham, John, 'The Unromantic Death of Richard I', *Speculum* 54 (1979), pp. 18–41; reprinted in Gillingham, *Richard Coeur de Lion*, pp. 155–80.

Given-Wilson, Chris, *Henry IV* (Yale University Press, New Haven and London, 2016).

Given-Wilson, Chris; Kettle, Ann; and Scales, Len, *War, Government and Aristocracy in the British Isles, c.1150–1500: Essays in Honour of Michael Prestwich* (Boydell Press, Woodbridge, 2008).

Gold, Claudia, 'King Henry II? The Muslim Monarch of Medieval England?', *BBC History Magazine* (February 2020).

Gold, Claudia, *King of the North Wind: The Life of Henry II in Five Acts* (William Collins, London, 2018).

Goodwin, Doris Kearns, *Team of Rivals: The Political Genius of Abraham Lincoln* (Penguin, London, 2005).

Goodwin, Thomas, *The History of the Reign of Henry the Fifth, King of England, etc., in Nine Books* (London, 1704).

Gransden, Antonia, *Historical Writing in England I: c.550–c.1307* (Routledge, London, 1974).

Gransden, Antonia, *Historical Writing in England II: c.1307 to the Early Sixteenth Century* (Routledge, London, 1982).

Grant, Alexander, 'The Death of John Comyn: What Was Going On?', *Scottish Historical Review* 86 (2007), pp. 176–224.

Green, John Richard, *A Short History of the English People* (Macmillan, London, 1882).

Guenée, Bernard, *La Folie de Charles VI: Roi Bien-Aimé* (Perrin, Paris, 2004).

Guy, John, *Thomas Becket. Warrior, Priest, Rebel, Victim: A 900-Year-Old Story Retold* (Viking, London, 2012).

Harris, Simon J., 'Taking Your Chances: Petitioning in the Last Years of Edward II and the First Years of Edward III', in *Medieval Petitions*, eds. Ormrod, Dodd and Musson, pp. 173–92.

Harriss, Gerald, *Shaping the Nation: England 1360–1461* (Clarendon Press, Oxford, 2005).

Harriss, G. L. (ed.), *Henry V: The Practice of Kingship* (Oxford University Press, Oxford, 1985).

Harvey, John, *The Plantagenets* (Batsford, London, 1948).

Hefferan, Matthew, 'Edward III's Household Knights and the Crécy Campaign of 1346', *Historical Research* 92 (2019), pp. 24–49.

Hefferan, Matthew, *The Household Knights of Edward III: Warfare, Politics and Kingship in Fourteenth-Century England* (Boydell Press, Woodbridge, 2021).

Hook, David, 'The Figure of Richard I in Medieval Spanish Literature', in *Richard Coeur de Lion in History and Myth*, ed. Nelson, pp. 117–40.

Horswell, Mike, *The Rise and Fall of British Crusader Medievalism, c.1825–1945* (Routledge, Abingdon, 2018).

Hosler, John D., 'The "Golden Age of Historiography": Records and Writers in the Reign of Henry II', *History Compass* 12 (2014), pp. 398–411.

Hosler, John D., *Henry II: A Medieval Soldier at War, 1147–1189* (Brill, Leiden, 2007).

Howell, Margaret, *Eleanor of Provence: Queenship in Thirteenth-Century England* (Blackwell, Oxford, 1998).

Hume, David, *The History of England from Julius Caesar to the Revolution in 1688*, 6 vols (Harper and Bros., New York, 1879 edition).

Huscroft, Richard, *Expulsion: England's Jewish Solution* (Tempus, Stroud, 2006).

Huscroft, Richard, 'A Tale of Two Ministers: Robert Burnell, Walter Langton and the Government of Edward I', in *Edward I*, eds. King and Spencer, pp. 24–43.

Hutchison, Harold F., *Henry V: A Biography* (Eyre and Spottiswoode, London, 1967).

Jacob, E. F., *The Fifteenth Century, 1399–1485* (Clarendon Press, Oxford, 1961).

Jacob, E. F., *Henry V and the Invasion of France* (English Universities Press, London, 1947).

Jenks, Edward, *Edward Plantagenet (Edward I): The English Justinian, or, The Making of the Common Law* (G. P. Putnam and Sons, New York, 1902).

Johnson, Paul, *The Life and Times of Edward III* (Weidenfeld and Nicolson, London, 1973).

Jolliffe, J. E. A., *Angevin Kingship* (2nd edition: Adam and Charles Black, London, 1963).

Jones, Martin H., 'Richard the Lionheart in German Literature of the Middle Ages', in *Richard Coeur de Lion in History and Myth*, ed. Nelson, pp. 70–116.

Judd, Denis, *George VI* (revised edition: I. B. Tauris, London, 2012 [original edition 1982]).
Jurkowski, Maureen, 'Henry V's Suppression of the Oldcastle Revolt', in *Henry V*, ed. Dodd, pp. 103–29.
Jurkowski, M., Smith, C. L. and Crook, D., *Lay Taxes in England and Wales, 1188–1688* (PRO Publications, Kew, 1998).
Kaeuper, Richard W., *Bankers to the Crown: The Riccardi of Lucca and Edward I* (Princeton University Press, Princeton, 1973).
Kaeuper, Richard W., *War, Justice and Public Order: England and France in the Later Middle Ages* (Clarendon Press, Oxford, 1988).
Keen, Maurice, 'Diplomacy', in *Henry V*, ed. Harriss, pp. 181–99.
King, Andy, 'Crisis? What Crisis? 1297 and the Civil War that Never Was', in *Edward I*, eds. King and Spencer, pp. 163–84.
King, Andy, *Edward I: A New King Arthur?* (Allen Lane, London, 2016).
King, Andy and Spencer, Andrew M. (eds.), *Edward I: New Interpretations* (York Medieval Press, York, 2020).
Kingsford, C. L., 'The Early Biographies of Henry V', *English Historical Review* 25 (1910), pp. 58–92.
Kingsford, Charles L., *Henry V: The Typical Medieval Hero* (G. P. Putnam's Sons, New York, 1901).
Lavelle, Ryan, *Cnut: The North Sea King* (Allen Lane, London, 2017).
Lewis, Matthew, *Henry II and Eleanor of Aquitaine: Founding an Empire* (Amberley, Stroud, 2021).
Lingard, John, *The History of England from the First Invasion by the Romans to the Accession of William and Mary in 1688*, 10 vols (J. C. Nimmo and Bain, London, 1883 edition [original edition 1819–49]).
Longman, William, *The History of the Life and Times of Edward the Third*, 2 vols (Longman, Green and Co., London, 1869).
Lunt, William E., *Financial Relations of the Papacy with England to 1327* (Medieval Academy of America, Cambridge, MA, 1939).
Lyttelton, George, *The History of the Life of King Henry the Second and of the Age in which He Lived*, 6 vols (3rd edition: London, 1788).
McCallum, Robin, 'The Crown's Ecclesiastical Creditors: Loans from the English Church to Edward II and Edward III, 1307–1377', *English Historical Review* 136 (2021), pp. 1385–1418.
McCallum, Robin, 'Loans from English Provincial Towns to the Crown during the Reigns of Edward II and Edward III', *Historical Research* 91 (2018), 60527.
Maddicott, J. R., *The Origins of the English Parliament, 924–1327* (Oxford University Press, Oxford, 2010).
Maddicott, J. R., *Simon de Montfort* (Cambridge University Press, Cambridge, 1994).
Maddicott, John, 'Who was Simon de Montfort, Earl of Leicester?', *Transactions of the Royal Historical Society*, 6th Series, 26 (2016), pp. 43–58.
Markowski, Michael, 'Richard Lionheart: Bad King, Bad Crusader?', *Journal of Medieval History* 23 (1997), pp. 351–65.
Matusiak, John, *Henry V* (Routledge, Abingdon, 2013).
McFarlane, K. B., 'England: The Lancastrian Kings, 1399–1461', in *The Cambridge Medieval History*, vol. VIII (Cambridge University Press, Cambridge, 1936).
McFarlane, K. B., 'Had Edward I A "Policy" towards the Earls?', *History* 50 (1965), pp. 145–59.

McFarlane, K. B., *Lancastrian Kings and Lollard Knights* (Oxford University Press, Oxford, 1972).

McFarlane, K. B., *The Nobility of Later Medieval England: The Ford Lectures for 1953 and Related Studies* (Oxford University Press, Oxford, 1973).

McKisack, May, 'Edward III and the Historians', *History* 45 (1960), pp. 1–15.

McKisack, May, *The Fourteenth Century, 1307–1399* (Oxford University Press, Oxford, 1959).

McHardy, Alison K., 'Religion, Court Culture and Propaganda: The Chapel Royal in the Reign of Henry V', in *Henry V*, ed. Dodd, pp. 131–56.

McHardy, A. K., 'Review of *Henry V: The Conscience of a King* by Malcolm Vale', *English Historical Review* 133 (2018), pp. 694–96.

McHardy, A. K., 'Some Reflections on Edward III's Use of Propaganda', in *Age of Edward III*, ed. Bothwell, pp. 171–92.

Mercer, Malcolm, *Henry V: The Rebirth of Chivalry* (The National Archives, Kew, 2004).

Morey, Adrian and Brooke, C. N. L., *Gilbert Foliot and His Letters* (Cambridge University Press, Cambridge, 1965).

Morgan, D. A. L., 'The Banner-bearer of Christ and Our Lady's Knight: How God became an Englishman Revisited', in *St George's Chapel Windsor*, ed. Saul, pp. 51–61.

Morgan, D. A. L., 'The Political After-Life of Edward III: The Apotheosis of a Warmonger', *English Historical Review* 112 (1997), pp. 856–81.

Morris, J. E., *The Welsh Wars of Edward I* (reprint edition: Sutton Publishing, Stroud, 1998 [original edition 1901]).

Morris, Marc, *A Great and Terrible King: Edward I and the Forging of Britain* (Hutchinson, London, 2008).

Mortimer, Ian, *1415: Henry V's Year of Glory* (Bodley Head, London, 2009).

Mortimer, Ian, *The Perfect King: The Life of Edward III, Father of the English Nation* (Jonathan Cape, London, 2006).

Mortimer, Richard, *Angevin England* (Blackwell, Oxford, 1994).

Mundill, Robin R., *England's Jewish Solution: Experiment and Expulsion, 1262–1290* (Cambridge University Press, Cambridge, 1998).

Musson, Anthony, 'Second "English Justinian" or Pragmatic Opportunist? A Re-Examination of the Legal Legislation of Edward III's Reign', in *Age of Edward III*, ed. Bothwell, pp. 69–88.

Nelson, Janet L. (ed.), *Richard Coeur de Lion in History and Myth* (King's College London, London, 1992).

Nicholson, Ranald, *Edward III and the Scots: The Formative Years of a Military Career, 1327 to 1335* (Oxford University Press, Oxford, 1965).

Norgate, Kate, *Richard the Lionheart* (Macmillan and Co., London, 1924).

Norwich, John Julius, *The Normans in Sicily* (omnibus edition: Penguin, London, 1992).

Oman, Charles, *A History of the Art of War: The Middle Ages, from the Fourth to the Fourteenth Century* (Methuen and Co., London, 1898).

Oram, Richard, *The Kings and Queens of Scotland* (Tempus, Stroud, 2001).

Ormrod, W. M., 'Competing Capitals? York and London in the Fourteenth Century', in *Courts and Regions in Medieval Europe*, eds. Sarah Rees Jones, Richard Marks and A. J. Minnis (York Medieval Press, York, 2000), pp. 75–98.

Ormrod, W. Mark, *Edward III* (Yale University Press, New Haven and London, 2011).

Ormrod, W. M., 'Edward III and His Family', *Journal of British Studies* 26 (1987), pp. 398–422.

Ormrod, W. M., 'For Arthur and St George: Edward III, Windsor Castle and the Order of the Garter', in *St George's Chapel Windsor*, ed. Saul, pp. 13–34.

Ormrod, W. Mark, 'The Foundation and Early Development of the Order of the Garter in England, 1348–1399', *Frühmittelalterliche Studien, 50*, pp. 361–392.

Ormrod, W. Mark, 'Henry V and the English Taxpayer', in *Henry V*, ed. Dodd, pp. 187–216.

Ormrod, W. Mark, 'Murmur, Clamour and Noise: Voicing Complaint and Remedy in Petitions to the English Crown, *c.*1300–*c.*1460', in *Medieval Petitions*, eds. Ormrod, Dodd and Musson, pp. 135–55.

Ormrod, W. M., 'The Personal Religion of Edward III', *Speculum* 64 (1989), pp. 849–77.

Ormrod, W. M., *Political Life in Medieval England, 1300–1450* (Macmillan, Basingstoke, 1995).

Ormrod, W. M., 'A Problem of Precedence: Edward III, the Double Monarchy, and the Royal Style', in *Age of Edward III*, ed. Bothwell, pp. 133–53.

Ormrod, W. M., *The Reign of Edward III: Crown and Society in England 1327–1377* (Yale University Press, New Haven and London, 1990).

Ormrod, W. Mark; Dodd, Gwilym; and Musson, Anthony (eds.), *Medieval Petitions: Grace and Grievance* (York Medieval Press, York, 2009).

Packe, Michael, *King Edward III* (Routledge and Kegan Paul, London, 1983).

Parsons, John Carmi, *Eleanor of Castile: Queen and Society in Thirteenth-Century England* (St Martin's Press, New York, 1995).

Penman, Michael, 'The Bruce Dynasty, Becket and Scottish Pilgrimage to Canterbury, *c.*1178–*c.*1404', *Journal of Medieval History* 32 (2006), pp. 346–70.

Penman, Michael, *David II, 1329–71* (Tuckwell Press, East Linton, 2004).

Penman, Michael, *Robert the Bruce: King of the Scots* (Yale University Press, New Haven and London, 2014).

Pépin, Guilhem, 'Petitions from Gascony: Testimonies of a Special Relationship', in *Medieval Petitions*, ed. Ormrod, Dodd and Musson, pp. 120–34.

Plucknett, T. F. T., *Legislation of Edward I* (Clarendon Press, Oxford, 1949).

Pollard, A. J., *Henry V* (The History Press, Stroud, 2014).

Pollard, A. J., *Late Medieval England 1399–1509* (Pearson, Harlow, 2000).

Pons, Nicole, 'Intellectual Patterns and Affective Reactions in Defence of the Dauphin Charles, 1419–1422', in *War, Government and Power*, ed. Allmand, pp. 54–69.

Poole, A. L., *From Domesday Book to Magna Carta* (2nd edition: Clarendon Press, Oxford, 1955).

Poos, L. R., 'The Social Context of Statute of Labourers Enforcement', *Law and History Review* 1 (1983), pp. 27–52.

Powell, Edward, *Kingship, Law and Society: Criminal Justice in the Reign of Henry V* (Clarendon Press, Oxford, 1989).

Powell, Edward, 'The Restoration of Law and Order', in *Henry V*, ed. Harriss, pp. 53–74.

Power, Daniel, 'Henry, Duke of the Normans (1149/50–1189), in *Henry II: New Interpretations*, eds. Harper-Bill and Vincent, pp. 85–128.

Power, Daniel, *The Norman Frontier in the Twelfth and Thirteenth Centuries* (Cambridge University Press, Cambridge, 2004).

Powicke, F. M., *King Henry III and the Lord Edward: The Community of the Realm in the Thirteenth Century*, 2 vols (Clarendon Press, Oxford, 1947).

Powicke, Maurice, *The Thirteenth Century, 1216–1307* (2nd edition: Clarendon Press, Oxford, 1962 [original edition 1953]).

Prestwich, J. O., 'Richard Coeur de Lion: *Rex Bellicosus*', in *Richard Coeur de Lion in History and Myth*, ed. Nelson, pp. 1–16.

Prestwich, Michael, *Armies and Warfare in the Middle Ages: The English Experience* (Yale University Press, New Haven and London, 1996).

Prestwich, Michael, *Edward I* (Yale edition: Yale University Press, New Haven and London, 1997 [original edition 1988]).

Prestwich, Michael, 'Edward I and the Maid of Norway', *Scottish Historical Review* 69 (1990), pp. 157–74.

Prestwich, Michael, 'Edward I's Armies', *Journal of Medieval History* 37 (2011), pp. 233–44.

Prestwich, Michael, *Plantagenet England 1225–1360* (Clarendon Press, Oxford, 2005).

Prestwich, Michael, *The Three Edwards: War and State in England, 1272–1377* (2nd edition: Routledge, London, 2003 [original edition 1980]).

Prestwich, Michael, *War, Politics and Finance under Edward I* (Faber and Faber, London, 1972).

Price, Neil, *The Children of Ash and Elm: A History of the Vikings* (Allen Lane, London, 2020).

Prigent, Daniel, *Fontevraud: L'Abbaye Royale* (4th edition: Fontevraud-L'Abbaye, 2023).

Pugh, T. B., *Henry V and the Southampton Plot* (Alan Sutton, Gloucester, 1988).

Pysiak, Jerzy, 'Philippe Auguste. Un Roi de la Fin des Temps?', *Annales* 57 (2002), pp. 1165–90.

Raban, Sandra, *A Second Domesday? The Hundred Rolls of 1279–80* (Oxford University Press, Oxford, 2004).

Raban, Sandra, *England under Edward I and Edward II, 1259–1327* (Blackwell, Oxford, 2000).

Rapin, Paul de, *History of England*, trans. Nicholas Tindal, 13 vols (London, 1727).

Raven, Matt, 'The Earldom Endowments of 1337: Political Thought and the Practice of Kingship in Late Medieval England', *English Historical Review* 136 (2021), pp. 498–529.

Raven, Matt, 'The Earls of Edward III and the Polity: the Earls of Arundel and Northampton in the Localities, 1330–60', *Historical Research* 92 (2019), pp. 681–704.

Rees Jones, Sarah, *York: The Making of a City 1068–1350* (Oxford University Press, Oxford, 2013).

Rees Jones, Sarah and Watson, Sethina (eds.), *Christians and Jews in Angevin England: The York Massacre of 1190, Narratives and Contexts* (York Medieval Press, York, 2013).

Reid, Norman H., *Alexander III, 1249–1286: First Among Equals* (John Donald, Edinburgh, 2019).

Rogers, Clifford J., 'The Anglo-French Peace Negotiations of 1354–1360 Reconsidered', in *Age of Edward III*, ed. Bothwell, pp. 193–213.

Rogers, Clifford J., *War Cruel and Sharp: English Strategy Under Edward III, 1327–1360* (Boydell Press, Woodbridge, 2000).

Rose, E. M., *The Murder of William of Norwich: The Origins of the Blood Libel in Medieval Europe* (Oxford University Press, Oxford, 2015).

Royal, Susan, 'History, Heresy and Henry V', in *Memory and the English Reformation*, ed. Alexandra Walsham, Bronwyn Wallace, Ceri Law and Brian Cummings (Cambridge University Press, Cambridge, 2020).

Rundle, David, 'The Unoriginality of Tito Livio Frulovisi's *Vita Henrici Quinti*', *English Historical Review* 123 (2008), pp. 1109–31.

Salzman, L. F., *Edward I* (Constable, London, 1968).

Salzmann, L. F., *Henry II* (Houghton Mifflin Company, Boston and New York, 1914).

Saul, Nigel, *Richard II* (Yale University Press, New Haven and London, 1997).

Saul, Nigel, 'Servants of God and Crown: The Canons of St George's Chapel, 1348–1420', in *St George's Chapel Windsor*, ed. Saul, pp. 97–115.

Saul, Nigel (ed.), *St George's Chapel Windsor in the Fourteenth Century* (Boydell Press, Woodbridge, 2005).

Saul, Nigel and Vincent, Nicholas (eds.), *English Medieval Government and Administration: Essays in Honour of J. R. Maddicott*, Pipe Roll Society, New Series 65 (Boydell Press, Woodbridge, 2023).

Seldon, Anthony, *Major: A Political Life* (Weidenfeld and Nicolson, London, 1997).

Seward, Desmond, *Henry V as Warlord* (Sidgwick and Jackson, London, 1987).

Shenton, Caroline, 'Edward III and the Coup of 1330', in *Age of Edward III*, ed. Bothwell, pp. 13–34.

Simpson, Grant G., 'The Claim of Florence, Count of Holland, to the Scottish Throne, 1291–2', *Scottish Historical Review* 36 (1957), pp. 111–24.

Smith, Brendan (ed.), *The Cambridge History of Ireland, Volume I: 600–1500* (Cambridge University Press, Cambridge, 2018).

Smith, J. Beverley, *Llywelyn ap Gruffudd: Prince of Wales* (2nd edition: University of Wales Press, Cardiff, 2014 [original Welsh edition 1986, original English edition 1998]).

Spencer, Andrew, 'The Comital Military Retinue in the Reign of Edward I', *Historical Research* 83 (2010), pp. 46–59.

Spencer, Andrew M., *Nobility and Kingship in Medieval England: The Earls and Edward I, 1272–1307* (Cambridge University Press, Cambridge, 2014).

Spencer, Andrew M., 'Royal Patronage and the Earls in the Reign of Edward I', *History* 93 (2008), pp. 20–46.

Staunton, Michael, *The Historians of Angevin England* (Oxford University Press, Oxford, 2017).

Strickland, Matthew, *Henry the Young King, 1155–1183* (Yale University Press, New Haven and London, 2016).

Strickland, Matthew, 'Treason, Feud and the Growth of State Violence: Edward I and the "War of the Earl of Carrick", 1306–7', in *War, Government and Aristocracy in the British Isles*, eds. Given-Wilson *et al.*, pp. 84–113.

Strickland, Matthew, 'On the Instruction of a Prince: The Upbringing of Henry, the Young King', in *Henry II: New Interpretations*, eds. Harper-Bill and Vincent, pp. 184–214.

Strong, Patrick and Strong, Felicity, 'The Last Will and Codicils of Henry V', *English Historical Review* 96 (1981), pp. 79–102.

Stubbs, William, *The Constitutional History of England in its Origin and Development*, 3 vols (Clarendon Press, Oxford, 1874–78).

Sumption, Jonathan, *Edward III: A Heroic Failure* (Allen Lane, London, 2016).

Taylor, Craig, 'Edward III and the Plantagenet Claim to the French Throne', in *Age of Edward III*, ed. Bothwell, pp. 155–69.

Taylor, Craig, 'Henry V, Flower of Chivalry', in *Henry V*, ed. Dodd, pp. 217–47.

Taylor, Craig, 'War, Propaganda and Diplomacy in Fifteenth-Century France', in *War, Government and Power*, ed. Allmand, pp. 70–91.

Templeman, G., 'Edward I and the Historians', *Cambridge Historical Journal* 10 (1950), pp. 16–35.

Thevenot, Christian, *Henri II Plantagenêt* (Editions Alan Sutton, Saint-Cyr-sur-Loire, 2003).

Thierry, Augustine, *Histoire de la Conquête de l'Angleterre par les Normands*, 3 vols (Paris, 1825).

Tompkins, Laura, 'Alice Perrers and the Goldsmiths' Mistery: New Evidence Concerning the Identity of the Mistress of Edward III', *English Historical Review* 130 (2015), pp. 1361–91.

Tompkins, Laura, '"Edward III's Gold-Digging Mistress": Alice Perrers, Gender, and Financial Power at the English Royal Court, 1360–1377', in *Women and Economic Power in Premodern Royal Courts*, ed. Cathleen Sarti (Arc Humanities Press, Leeds, 2020), pp. 59–71.

Tompkins, Laura, '"Said the Mistress to the Bishop": Alice Perrers, William Wykeham and Court Networks in Fourteenth-Century England', in *Ruling Fourteenth-Century England: Essays in Honour of Christopher Given-Wilson*, eds. Rémy Ambühl, James Bothwell and Laura Tompkins (Boydell Press, Woodbridge, 2019), pp. 205–25.

Tout, T. F., *Chapters in the Administrative History of Mediaeval England*, 6 vols (Manchester University Press, Manchester, 1920–33).

Tout, T. F., *Edward the First* (Macmillan and Co., London, 1893).

Tout, T. F., *The History of England from the Accession of Henry III to the Death of Edward III (1216–1377)* (Longmans, Green and Co., London, 1905).

Tuck, Anthony, *Crown and Nobility: England 1272–1461* (2nd edition: Blackwell, Oxford 1999 [original edition 1985]).

Tuck, Anthony, 'The Earl of Arundel's Expedition to France, 1411', in *The Reign of Henry IV*, eds. Dodd and Biggs, pp. 228–39.

Turner, Ralph V., *Eleanor of Aquitaine: Queen of France, Queen of England* (Yale University Press, New Haven and London, 2009).

Turner, Ralph V., 'Richard Lionheart and English Episcopal Elections', *Albion* 29 (1997), pp. 1–13.

Turner, Ralph V. and Heiser, Richard R., *The Reign of Richard Lionheart: Ruler of the Angevin Empire, 1189–1199* (Longman, Harlow, 2000).

Tyrrell, James, *The General History of England*, 5 vols (London, 1700–4).

Vale, Juliet, 'Image and Identity in the Prehistory of the Order of the Garter', in *St George's Chapel Windsor*, ed. Saul, pp. 35–50.

Vale, Malcolm, *Henry V: The Conscience of a King* (Yale University Press, New Haven and London, 2016).

Vaughan, Richard, *John the Fearless* (Reprint edition: Boydell Press, Woodbridge, 2002 [original edition 1966]).

Vaughan, Richard, *Philip the Good* (Reprint edition: Boydell Press, Woodbridge, 2002 [original edition 1970]).

Veach, Colin, 'Conquest and Conquerors', in *Cambridge History of Ireland I*, ed. Smith, pp. 157–81.

Verduyn, Anthony, 'The Politics of Law and Order during the Early Years of Edward III', *English Historical Review* 108 (1993), pp. 842–67.

Vincent, Nicholas, 'Angevin Ireland', in *Cambridge History of Ireland I*, ed. Smith, pp. 185–221.

Vincent, Nicholas, 'Introduction: Henry II and the Historians', in *Henry II: New Interpretations*, eds. Harper-Bill and Vincent, pp. 1–23.

Vincent, Nicholas, 'The Court of Henry II', in *Henry II: New Interpretations*, eds. Harper-Bill and Vincent, pp. 278–334.

Warburton, W., *Edward III* (4th edition: Longmans, Green and Co., 1887 [original edition 1875]).

Warren, W. L., *The Governance of Norman and Angevin England, 1086–1272* (Edward Arnold, London, 1987).

Warren, W. L., *Henry II* (Yale edition: Yale University Press, New Haven and London, 2000 [original edition 1973]).

Watson, Fiona, *Under the Hammer: Edward I and Scotland, 1286–1307* (Tuckwell Press, East Linton, 1998).

Watts, John, *Henry VI and the Politics of Kingship* (Cambridge University Press, Cambridge, 1996).

Waugh, Scott L., *England in the Reign of Edward III* (Cambridge University Press, Cambridge, 1991).

Weiler, Björn, 'The *Commendatio Lamentabilis* for Edward I and Plantagenet Kingship', in *War, Government and Aristocracy in the British Isles*, eds. Given-Wilson *et al.*, pp. 114–30.

White, Graeme J., *Restoration and Reform 1153–1165: Recovery from Civil War in England* (Cambridge University Press, Cambridge, 2000).

Widmer, Ted, *Martin Van Buren* (Times Books, New York, 2005).

Williams, Diane M. and Kenyon, John R. (eds), *The Impact of the Edwardian Castles in Wales* (Oxbow Books, Oxford, 2010).

Wilkinson, B., 'The Protest of the Earls of Arundel and Surrey in the Crisis of 1341', *English Historical Review* 46 (1931), pp. 177–93.

Wilkinson, Louise J., '"Is Still Not the Blood of the Blessed Martyr Thomas Fully Avenged?" Thomas Becket's Cult at Canterbury under Henry III and Edward I', *History* 105 (2020), pp. 673–90.

Wilkinson, Louise J., 'Royal Daughters and Diplomacy at the Court of Edward I', in *Edward I*, eds. King and Spencer, pp. 84–104.

Wylie, James Hamilton and Waugh, William Templeton, *The Reign of Henry the Fifth*, 3 vols (Cambridge University Press, Cambridge, 1914–29).

Young, Charles R., *The Royal Forests of Medieval England* (University of Pennsylvania Press, Philadelphia, 1979).

Index